A SOCIALIST DEFECTOR

A SOCIALIST DEFECTOR

From Harvard to Karl-Marx-Allee

by Victor Grossman (Stephen Wechsler)

MONTHLY REVIEW PRESS

New York

Library of Congress Cataloging-in-Publication Data

Names: Grossman, Victor, 1928– author.
Title: A socialist defector : from Harvard to Karl-Marx-Allee / by Victor
  Grossman (Stephen Wechsler).
Description: New York : Monthly Review Press, [2019] | Includes index.
Identifiers: LCCN 2018058321 (print) | LCCN 2018058697 (ebook) | ISBN
  9781583677407 (trade) | ISBN 9781583677414 (institutional) | ISBN
  9781583677384 (pbk.) | ISBN 9781583677391 (hardcover)
Subjects: LCSH: Grossman, Victor, 1928– | Defectors—Germany
  (East)—Biography. | Defectors—United States—Biography. |
  Journalists—Germany (East)—Biography. | Americans—Germany
  (East)—Biography. | Harvard University—Alumni and alumnae—Biography. |
  Communists—United States—Biography. | Germany (East)—Description and
  travel. | Cold War.
Classification: LCC DD287.7.G75 (ebook) | LCC DD287.7.G75 A3 2019 (print) |
  DDC 943/.4087092 [B] —dc23
LC record available at https://lccn.loc.gov/2018058321

Typeset in Bulmer Monotype and Bliss

MONTHLY REVIEW PRESS, NEW YORK
monthlyreview.org

5 4 3 2 1

CONTENTS

A Socialist Defector | 7

Index | 335

1—Wrong Way?

I was ten years old in the summer of 1938 when a jolly, somewhat nutty airplane mechanic named Corrigan, instead of flying back from New York to California in his air jalopy as officially authorized, flew it solo, secretly and illegally, across the Atlantic to Ireland. On his return he got a hilarious confetti welcome—and the term "wrong-way Corrigan" went into the language of the day.

Fourteen years later I did something maybe even nuttier. The water barrier I crossed was far narrower, about 400 or 500 yards across the Danube River. But I didn't fly, I fled, and not in a plane but swimming. At that time the river divided the U.S. Zone from the USSR Zone in Austria, so I was piercing the Iron Curtain—but also in the wrong direction. I certainly did not expect any confetti welcome. Nor did I get any.

That cold water immersion obviously didn't kill me. But didn't it at least cure me? And didn't it ruin my life, making me a traitor to everything decent in the world, starting with the United States? What in the name of God or the devil made me commit such an amazing blunder? How soon did I begin to regret it? This book will try to answer those questions, while raising many new ones, for me and possibly some readers as well.

My immediate motivation was clear. Drafted into the U.S. Army in 1951 in the icy days later known as the McCarthy era, and in great fear

of the new McCarran Act with its threat of unlimited years in prison as
a "foreign agent" (or in concentration camps authorized by the same
law), I signed the paper required of all Korean War draftees that I had
never been a member of the 120 listed organizations, many long gone,
all "taboo" and nearly all leftist. I had indeed been in about a dozen,
not only the Joint Anti-Fascist Refugee Appeal (for Spanish Civil War
victims) and the Southern Negro Youth Congress (out of sympathy
and support) but also, as a student opposed to atom bombs, anti-union
laws, and racism—and believing in socialism—in the most ostracized of
them all, the Communist Party. I was not a card-carrying member only
because the Party no longer gave out membership cards.

My hope was that if I kept my nose clean and my mouth shut then
the two years of army service might come and go without a check on
my past delinquency. At first, I was very lucky, I was sent not to Korea
but to Germany. Then luck turned sharply against me: they did check
up—and discovered my perjury. Ordered to report to a military judge, I
read the threatened punishment for my crime—up to $10,000 and five
years in prison. Five years behind bars, in Leavenworth? With no one
to consult or advise me I simply panicked. The threat of prison is what
made me wade in and swim across the swift but not at all blue Danube.

What has that got to do with this book? Everything. Upon arrival, the
Soviet authorities, without consulting my possible preferences, held me
briefly in confinement and then released me into a town of East Germany,
the still very young German Democratic Republic, or GDR.

Thus, after twenty-four years growing up in New York and New
Jersey, after nine schools, public and private (two years each at posh
Dalton and Fieldston Schools), a B.A. at Harvard, unskilled factory
work in Buffalo, and a long hitchhike trip from one U.S. coast to the
other and back, I now became an inside witness to the growth, development, and demise of the GDR and of what has happened since. As a
worker again and once more as a student, when I became the one and
only person in the world with a diploma from both Harvard and the
Karl Marx University of Leipzig (and since the latter has dropped the
name, I will undoubtedly retain this distinction) I became finally a freelance journalist and lecturer and got to visit nearly every town and city

and many a village. I saw, heard, and took part in almost every phase of GDR life, while my base and main vantage point was my apartment near downtown East Berlin, less than a mile from its famous, or infamous, Wall.

I think I can hear two reactions: one sympathetic: "My God, you poor guy! How in blazes did you survive such a long ordeal in that hellhole?"

Or unsympathetic: "Thirty-eight years locked up in there? Serves you damned right for your treacherous act!"

To the second reaction I would mildly absolve myself by noting that the man who framed the law that frightened me from the start, Senator Pat McCarran of Nevada, turned out to be the rottenest, most vicious anti-Semite in Washington, DC. That paper, which my fear made me sign when I was drafted, thus totally altering my life, was later ruled unconstitutional by the Supreme Court. And I can add that in 1994 the U.S. Army mercifully decided to discharge me, with no punishment at all, after forty-two years. But to both reactions I would reply that life in general, politics in particular, and most specifically the GDR story, are just not that simple.

My first twenty-four years were spent in the world's leading land of free enterprise. By strange circumstance, in 1952, I landed in a country with a "planned economy," variously referred to as communist, "real socialist," "command economy," or some far saltier appellations. In 1990, after thirty-eight years, this time with no swimming involved, I was again back in a free market system.

Even at my ripe old age, I make no claim to be wiser or more correct than anyone else. But we live in a time when many good people are hunting for answers to severe problems facing our world, often fearlessly exploring a wide range of possible solutions. My life journey taught me lessons and led to conclusions that might be of interest, even value. I offer no ready-to-bake recipes but only some ideas, if only because, more than most Americans, I had an unusual opportunity to make comparisons.

"What? Opportunity? Comparisons?" some voices will retort. "Are you stupid? Or simply stubborn? Need anyone even consider contradictions between good and evil, justice and injustice, freedom and totalitarian dictatorship? Don't you know the words of that great freedom-fighter Winston Churchill: 'Democracy is the worst form of government, except for all the others'? Can there really be any doubts about that corpse of a misbegotten regime daring to call itself the German Democratic Republic?"

Was it my ancestral background, my schooling, or my checkered past that imbued me with a firm rule to look at things "on the one hand"—but then, too, "on the other hand"? Life and politics are hardly drawn in one or even two dimensions. This does not always apply, it is true, and not everywhere. But, rightly or wrongly, this habit forced its way into my thinking about the GDR and East Berlin both before and after the "fall of the Wall" in 1989–90. However, before I reflect about capitalism, socialism, communism, freedom, and democracy or any other isms or solutions for the world's troubles, I want to describe some of what I experienced.

2—Future Dreams in an Ancient Town

After many hours, and finding no sign of the Red Army, I was finally picked up by the Austrian police, barefoot and bedraggled from my fateful Danubian swim, and escorted, as I demanded, to the Soviet Kommandantur (because, very wisely, I did not trust the cops). I was briefly questioned, then driven the next day to Soviet HQ in Baden near Vienna, and politely but unceremoniously locked up in a small, very primitive cell, under armed guard, for a period of two weeks. After some initial skepticism about the long day I had spent hunting for the Soviet armed forces I had expected to find patrolling this stretch of the Iron Curtain, the guards became friendly. I had fascinating discussions on literature and cinema with the armed soldier outside my cell; using my ten, at most twenty Russian words, mostly from names of books. I would say "Anna Karenina?" He would gradually understand me despite my false pronunciation and then say with a big smile: "*Da, da, chital, khorosho!*"—"Yes, yes. I've read it. Good!" Since I had also seen a number of Soviet films, like *Gulliver* and *Lenin in October*, these exchanges and evaluations lasted a while, to our mutual satisfaction, and I learned new vocabulary. Most essential was *"ubornaya"* for "toilet."

After twice reading the three available books in English, one a history of Scotland, and getting a complete new outfit of clothes and accessories ("And for you a red tie!"), I was driven to an unknown destination, which turned out to be the GDR, and was placed in an isolated room in a building in Potsdam, near Berlin. I had a one-hour daily walk in the garden behind the guarded house and about once a week got a visit from a friendly fellow called "George," with only a slight Russian accent, who asked me about myself, chatted about politics, showed me match tricks, and asked if I was interested in moving to Western Europe. I definitely wasn't and that was dropped.

I suggested assuming a new name to protect my family from difficulties, so he told me to choose one. Try as I could, I could think of no new moniker. When a decision became necessary he asked if Victor Grossman was okay. I didn't like it at all but, having failed in my own search, accepted it, also in the knowledge that unlike, say, Murphy or Johnson, it retained some of my Jewish identity (though it was seen by some as German, until I corrected them).

After two months, and another set of clothes from the Soviets plus one now from the GDR authorities, I landed in Bautzen, a town of 45,000 inhabitants in a corner of East Germany near the Czech and Polish borders. What I found was certainly not the communist-type Utopia I may have been dreaming of. The war, less than eight years earlier, had not spared the town, long a battle-point: a few remaining ruins, cleared lots, and a cemetery of Soviet soldiers attested to that. But I saw no signs of the hunger or rags that press reports might have led me to expect; life seemed to move along fairly normally. The few vehicles were old, sometimes unusual: delivery trucks with two wheels in back but one in front, or cars with wood ovens mounted in back as motors. In 1952 the shops offered basic groceries and textiles and were quite spartan; I recall long hunts for handkerchiefs and a new washrag. For a few weeks razor blades were short, which meant lining up to get old ones resharpened. Toilet paper was unavailable, so newspapers or pulpy magazines (but no Sears and Roebucks catalogues) were torn into neat squares.

It seems that the Soviet authorities had chosen Bautzen to settle deserters from Western armies because it was as far as possible from West Berlin and West German borders but not directly on a crossing point to Poland or Czechoslovakia. Also, it was large enough to provide jobs but not too large to lose track of us in a big city atmosphere. Our numbers changed, since there were new arrivals every month or so but a similar number would abscond westward again. About fifteen to twenty were Americans, about ten were British, and five to ten were French with a similar number from North African French colonies who deserted so as not to be sent to fight in Indochina. There were a few from the Netherlands, a Spaniard, an Irishman, a Mexican, and a Nigerian. Many were not there for political reasons; some had fled because of various conflicts, often connected with drinking, a few because their relationships with German women were prohibited; of these one such was too "Red East German," a few were African Americans with white women friends. Some of the British had rejected service in Korea. It was a strange bunch. New arrivals were put up in a hotel, then rooms were found or apartments for families. In general, those who found female partners or wives tended to integrate quite well while single GIs, with no trade and almost no German, and no TV as yet, gathered at various dives or the all-night bar at the train station, thus often missing shifts at their usually low-level jobs, or getting into trouble. One interesting exception was a black American, a trained baker and a boxer, who became a favorite athlete until his age caught up with him. Since he worked regularly and neither smoked nor drank, he had a pleasant apartment on the central square of town, and because he was perhaps the first person of color ever seen in this out-of-the-way town, he often attracted and enjoyed a bunch of happy kids, like the Pied Piper. Though he traveled to matches, the rest of us had only one restriction—not to leave the county without permission. It was a very big county, and since we had as yet little reason to travel this hardly worried us.

After a week or so a job was found for me. I received about 250 marks a month in wages, always paid in cash. Rent for my furnished room was 25 marks a month. Like every working person in the GDR I received a hot lunch, which was the main meal of the day in Germany, for one mark or less, and since I had been given enough clothing, shopping problems bothered me less than those of a sanitary nature. Typically for prewar housing, there was no flush toilet but an indoor privy a half-flight down from my room; the pail of water to flush it had to be constantly refilled. So did the pitcher with basin in my room for washing and shaving. Baths were at a bathhouse. And almost every day power was cut off, always unexpectedly; matches and candles had to be kept handy. Like nearly all homes in those days, my room was heated by a big ceramic oven. That required making a fire every day, a technique with newspaper, kindling, and black coal briquettes, which had to be carried up from the cellar after bringing down the ashes from the day before. The coal had to burn thoroughly, for about an hour, before the oven could be safely screwed shut. I soon gave up and lived for one icy winter in a room heated only on Sundays by my merciful but slightly scornful landlady, who also invited me to join the family for Sunday dinners.

Of course, even for a New Yorker whose family seldom had it easy and almost never lived in a comfortable, roomy apartment, one free of roaches and bugs, life was rather primitive. But I rarely complained or even grumbled about it; I had chosen this path myself and could blame no one, except those distant politicians who passed the McCarran Act.

Then too, at twenty-four, I was very much a devoted young communist. I had not chosen the GDR but I was now here. The aim of the government and ruling party, declared four months before my arrival and proclaimed constantly ever since, was to "build socialism." That was my aim, too, making me willing to endure growing pains, if that's what they were, and generally take the bad with the good.

Was there really any good?

My start in this workers' paradise was helping to tote heavy oak and beech planks at a large factory. This required a long, early walk to work—there were no buses yet—and an equally long, far more tired walk back after work. In those early years there was still a half-day's work on Saturday. I soon learned to balance one end of a plank on one shoulder while the man in front of me carried his end on the other. It was hard work; I hope they eventually modernized it after I left. In our "brigade" of five men, Jakob, the "brigadier," received the assignments—how many oak or beech planks were needed—and did the required paper work. Jakob, as a member of the German minority, had been forced to leave his Hungarian home at war's end. Although I could speak German pretty fluently by then, his accent was at first hard for me to understand. He was an easygoing fellow, however, and we got along well from the start.

There were certainly differences from the two factories I had worked in in Buffalo. There we had to bring our own lunch or run to a diner we called the "Greasy Spoon." In the factory in Bautzen there was both a breakfast room for the mid-morning break, called "second breakfast," with as much free ersatz coffee as you wanted; the canteen, run by the union, served the not fancy but quite adequate hot lunch, which always included potatoes with meat or fish and vegetables.

Unlike at the Buffalo factory, in the Bautzen factory there was visible propagandizing, with slogans urging socialism and improved labor effectivity, always in white letters on red cloth, but few paid any attention to them (except me, at first). In general, there and in many factories I visited in later years, I found a rather relaxed atmosphere, perhaps in part because, with every hand needed, no one feared losing their job. In fact, whenever the workload permitted, it was possible to visit a doctor, a dentist, a hairdresser, and even a little cooperative grocery, where now and again some goods were on sale that were not easy to find, if at all, in shops outside the factory. That meant that if the factory grocery offered imported lemons or raisins or fresh, early tomatoes, strawberries, or cherries, a considerable line quickly formed. Work could wait! And that explained what had at first puzzled me: why people came to work not with a lunchbox but with a worn but capacious briefcase.

I think everyone was automatically in the union, but I can hardly recall the union meetings—perhaps my language handicap induced me to skip them. I think everyone, or almost everyone, also felt obliged to pay a few pfennigs in dues as a member of the German-Soviet

Friendship Society—even me. I had been moved when the victory of Stalingrad over the Nazi Wehrmacht ten years earlier was marked by a special ceremony in the center of town—in Germany!—but now I think that many of my fellow workers saw the occasion largely as a chance to get home a little earlier than usual with no loss of pay.

A memory note: A workmate, pointing to a big furnace, said, "When Friedrich Flick owned this plant during the war that's where they threw corpses of foreign workers or prisoners of war. Too many hours, too heavy work and too little to eat."

A very different but also moving note for me: Seeing a train pull into the station, still using an old steam locomotive, and reading, painted on it in big white letters, "Free the Rosenbergs!"—the Jewish couple facing death in Sing-Sing prison.

My factory job lasted only five months. At that time, before my second winter, I had the greatest luck. I found and fell for my Renate. Coming from a village too far to commute daily, she also had a rented room, nicer than mine. And it was, like her, warm and cozy in the evening.

I SOON DISCOVERED customs that were neither good nor bad, just unusual, even comical. Like the constant handshaking at any and every occasion, such as with every single member of my work team each morning, then all over again at quitting time. Or little girls' curtseys and boys' forelock-tossing bows of the head when introduced. Also, the "Guten Tag" and "Auf Wiedersehen" greetings on entering and leaving every grocery or bakery, whether or not anyone was listening. Or the reluctance of young fathers to push a baby carriage and, if there were no escaping it, to do so with one sidewise outstretched hand while looking away, as if the child belonged to someone else. Completely taboo for males in those days was carrying a bouquet of flowers, even if concealed under paper. Later, these taboos disappeared.

Then there were the language problems: the (impossible) need to know whether a noun is masculine, feminine, or neuter and treat it accordingly, which Mark Twain happily satirized by noting that a red beet is a "she" but a pretty girl an "it." One witty Turkish woman I know of, having the usual trouble with such rulings, asked her teacher why the word for "table" was masculine—"*der Tisch*." Looking under one she said, "I don't see anything masculine about it!" I found that *Gift* means poison, *Mist* means manure, a glove is a *Handschuh* or, almost a desecration, a nipple is a *Brustwarze*—a "breast wart." Some words caused visiting Americans fewer blushes than laughs: "*Schmuck*" meaning jewelry, and the polite wish to patrons driving away after a restaurant meal to have a good trip: "*gute Fahrt*."

While improving my German and adjusting to customs, I soon noticed the political tensions in the air, reflecting different directions and varying types of people. Some, most to my liking, were warm-hearted people who rejected everything from the Nazi past and were dedicated to creating a fair socialist society. I also found narrow-minded dogmatists, who spouted clichés, surely believing them, but could hardly grasp basic humane concepts and were all too quick to browbeat those with doubts or "wrong ideas." I had already met some such people in various political parties in the United States, including my own. Often disarmingly similar were the careerists who could parrot the correct vocabulary but were primarily devoted to advancing personal interests. As everywhere, I guess, there were also slow thinkers and downright idiots. And then there were those who, rarely uttering their views out loud, hated the GDR and any idea of socialism, pined for the rule of West German Chancellor Adenauer, dreamed of retaking provinces they had been forced to leave or had learned little or nothing from the defeat of fascism. But humans are complicated creatures who waver, learn, even alter their views. There was a wide range of mixtures and borderline cases; it was neither simple nor really wise to paste people into one or another pigeon hole.

A key factor in my positive outlook was, of course, finding Renate, then a stenographer-typist in a construction company. Not only did I no longer freeze evenings in my lonely room, hunting and pecking at my newly bought typewriter until my fingers were too cold to function, but now, as spring came upon us, we could enjoy wonderful strolls through shabby but oh-so-romantic cobblestone alleyways in the Old Town, baroque squares, and pathways around the sturdy city walls of this beautiful, thousand-year-old town, perched on cliffs above a swift little river. Together we enjoyed good plays and concerts (a new experience for my village-bred girlfriend) in the fine theater and a memorable candle-lit performance of Bach's *Christmas Oratorio* in the magnificent cathedral, one of only three church buildings in all Germany which was half Lutheran, half Roman Catholic, and quite amicably divided by a little fence right down the middle.

3—Hot Times in Germany

Germany, too, was divided, though by no means amicably and not nearly down the middle. In this larger edifice the Federal Republic (FRG) occupied far, far more pews and almost exclusively the better ones. The main sermon preached in its pulpit, aside from demanding the return of lost territories, was about German unity: brothers and sisters in the two states must no longer be separated. But the commandment often evoked, unlike the ten from Mount Sinai, was not carved in stone from the start. The unity problem trod dramatically onto the world stage in June 1948 when Britain, France, and the United States suddenly introduced a new monetary currency in their West German occupation zones and, even more divisively, into the populous political island of West Berlin in the middle of the Soviet Zone. There was no Wall or other barrier then. Anyone could shop in the East or West, so the switch to a new currency immediately threatened to flood the East with old currency, suddenly useless in the West, and thus swiftly wreck the entire Eastern economy. Inevitable countermeasures triggered the Airlift to supply West Berlin with food and fuel.

The belligerent politician and later secretary of state John Foster Dulles revealed, but not very publicly, that it was always possible to cool the situation by agreeing on the currency question, but then explained that, firstly, "The deadlock is of great advantage to the United States for propaganda purposes, secondly, the danger of settling the Berlin dispute resides in the fact that it would then be impossible to avoid facing the problem of a German peace treaty. The United States would

then be faced with a Soviet proposal for the withdrawal of all occu-
pation troops and the establishment of a central German government.
Frankly I do not know what we would say to that." (Overseas Writers
Association, January 10, 1949, quoted in Democratic German Report,
DGR, February 2, 1962, 32.)

He was right. The Berlin Airlift proved immensely advantageous for
Cold War political acoustics and a dissonant propaganda disaster for
the USSR. It also split Berlin and Germany for over forty years.

This had occurred while I was a student at Harvard and resulted
in harsh repercussions for the Progressive Party candidate, Henry
Wallace, a campaign in which I was actively engaged. Four years later,
in 1952, I arrived in divided Germany as a simple Private 1st Class.
But while the U.S. Army was sifting through my political past, present,
and possible future, Germany's past, present, and future were being
surveyed by far more important figures, President Harry Truman and
Joseph Stalin. On March 10, 1952, Stalin made an unexpected offer to
remove Soviet troops and control from East Germany, to support free
all-German elections, and to permit unification and full German sovereignty. The offer came with one condition, a result of the Nazis' near
total destruction and virtual genocide in the Soviet Union a decade
earlier: Germany must be "free, neutral, and demilitarized" and, like
Finland or Austria, in no pacts, Eastern or Western.

The response was a resounding "No!" U.S. policy had long aimed
at pumping up West Germany. Its powerful, rebuilt industrial base,
strategic location, and top-drawer generals with "Eastern" experience
were major chess pieces in the worsening Cold War, or someday in a
hot one (which a few firebrands were demanding). As the German-
born banker and former Roosevelt adviser, James Warburg, vainly told
the Senate Foreign Relations Committee on March 28: the Soviet proposal might be a bluff, but it seemed "that our government is afraid to
call the bluff for fear that it may not be a bluff at all" and lead to unity.
(Senate Committee on Foreign Relations, March 28, 1952.)

To this "No" a loud "Nein!" was added. Chancellor Adenauer also
feared such unity, preferring an expanding Western ambience with
his two-thirds of Germany bound up in it. Only a few West Germans

had the courage to blame him for rebuffing this chance at unification. Instead, in Paris, he signed onto a "European Defense Community" with a large German military component, a plan ditched by the French people two years later. All East German proposals to heal the split were ignored; thus, by 1952, the chips were down. One result was the GDR leaders' call to move on and build socialism in their corner of the country. That smaller corner where, a few months later, I was to land.

As a foreign newcomer who still read no newspapers and heard no radio, I could hardly comprehend such fateful events. But as 1953 moved along. I could see that something was not okay. Earlier rapid improvements in life were slowing down with signs of going into reverse. Even a breakfast staple of mine, ersatz honey, defied past trends—its price went up, not down.

With hopes of unification giving way to increasing fears of Western annexation attempts, the decision to "build socialism," a lifelong goal of most East German leaders, now required the rapid buildup of an industry to produce coke, iron, and steel, basics increasingly hard to get from traditional West German sources. It was also seen necessary to counter Western rearmament with GDR armed forces. Both endeavors consumed billions of marks. To pay for them and "clear the decks" politically, a stringent, tough policy was adopted, rough on private businesses and wealthier farmers but also on workers, whose wages were to be tied to stricter norms, or quotas, aimed at increasing productivity without putting too many more inflationary 10- or 20-mark bills into pay envelopes. During my first winter and spring I could sense the growing unhappiness at all of this.

In March 1953, Stalin died. What would that mean for the world, for the USSR, for us in the GDR? We could not peer through the distant thick Kremlin walls and perceive that the new ruling team in Moscow, noting that the economic strategy in the young GDR was not going well at all, had concluded that urgent changes were needed if menacing dangers were to be prevented. They pushed the GDR rulers into a sudden, quick reversal.

On June 11, the New Course was announced, annulling all unpleasant restrictions, cuts, pressures, and many jail sentences, with one important exception. The tighter production norms would remain unchanged. This exception neglected the main cause of anger for the working people who were always hailed as the foundation of the new republic, and so the entire turnaround proved to be too little and too late. On June 16 and 17, first in East Berlin, then in many towns and cities around the GDR, there were demonstrations, stoppages, as well as violence by workers and those who jumped on board with them, including young toughs from West Berlin. A few local official buildings were seized, a Berlin department store was set ablaze, and prisoners were freed, allegedly including virulent Nazi war criminals.

Workers in a railroad coach factory in nearby Görlitz also went on strike for a day or two. In its sister plant in Bautzen, where I had been working seven weeks earlier, little work was done on June 17, but there was no strike. A tiny riot by young men in Bautzen attracted only a handful of workers and ended quickly when a truckload of Soviet soldiers arrived and fired some shots into the air.

There were some casualties elsewhere, but Soviet military involvement, also involving tanks (with orders not to shoot), soon ended the uprising. Historians still argue about whether it was based solely on the resistance of downtrodden workers, as claimed and celebrated to this day, or was fostered by Western propaganda and provocateurs, as GDR media asserted. In my view it was both. Genuinely angry protests reflecting disappointment and frustration were quickly utilized from without, especially in the twisted divided city of Berlin. A key factor was the CIA-financed radio station RIAS (Radio in the American Sector) in West Berlin. Egon Bahr, then RIAS director and later a leading Social Democrat, admitted—or boasted—that though RIAS had not planned or directed it, its broadcasts had acted "as the catalyst of the uprising . . . without RIAS the uprising would never have taken place in this form." (Interview with Nana Brink, Deutschlandfunk Kultur, January 9, 2006). Indeed, RIAS broadcast the call for a general strike. The basic goal, it seems clear, was what is now called "regime change," an early version of the Maidan Square "uprising" in Kiev in 2014 (and many other countries). Most GDR citizens did not take part, but few had been happy in the preceding months.

As for me, since I had left the factory and taken a job as cultural director of a new clubhouse for the thirty or forty Western army deserters
then settled in Bautzen, responsible for chess, billiards, and ping-pong
tournaments, for outings, dances, films, and such, these events had
little effect on me, although I was happy when the price of my artificial honey and other items was reduced and those power stoppages for
homes, requiring candles and matches, were finally eliminated.

After six months I quit as cultural director and joined the other
deserters in a special one-year apprenticeship in any one of four handicraft skills. Since few had ever learned a non-military trade I found this
a clever, wise, and humane idea, with all receiving a generous monthly
stipend, more for those with dependents. And to my amazement, I
learned how to work a lathe machine.

Before I could test my new skill, however, and perhaps luckily not
just for me but for the economy, I got a very different opportunity—
to take a four-year course in journalism at Karl Marx University in
Leipzig. Although I was already twenty-six, I was only too happy to
move from a small town to the GDR's second-largest city, with a half-
million inhabitants and a famous old culture, Johann Sebastian Bach
being its main gem, along with Goethe, Schumann, Mendelssohn-
Bartholdy, and an annual book fair nearly as old as printed books. Plus,
there was a monstrous monument from 1913 celebrating the defeat of
Napoleon there in 1813. I had no problem getting accustomed to city
life, nor did Renate, now my fiancée, who had found herself a job and a
room in Leipzig even before I arrived.

4—Leipzig and Karl Marx University

A year later, we got married. We were assigned a room-and-a-quarter in
the apartment of an elderly, by no means welcoming couple. An interest-
free 2,000-mark credit for all Bautzen ex-soldiers allowed us to set up a
household centered around a big bed and a big desk. Though Renate's
job as stenographer-typist was not well paid, students received schol-
arships, 180 or 240 marks a month, with possible bonuses, and a small

but growing number of foreign students, including me, got 300. After buying our main furniture, no other major purchases were possible, yet we were able to get along quite well without financial worries. My hot meal of the day, as in the Bautzen factory and like Renate's in her publicly owned wholesale firm, cost a pittance. The New Course in June 1953 ended reparation payments to the USSR and meant a steady increase in the amount and assortment of consumer goods. Once again people looked forward to May Day and the "Day of the Republic" on October 7 when the press had page-long lists of price cuts on food, clothing, and other goods. We bought our groceries in consumer cooperatives or private retail shops, where our ration coupons enabled us to buy meat, milk, butter, and sugar at very low prices. Since rations varied according to one's job and profession (lowest for non-working seniors), jealousy and not a little bitterness were often involved, but pregnant or nursing mothers received higher rations, and this category soon included Renate! When monthly ration coupons were used up, people could buy all they wanted (and could afford) at the well-stocked but highly priced nationally owned shops called HO (an abbreviation for Retail Organization). Nationally owned restaurants (*Gaststätten*) added a letter, forming the interesting abbreviation over the entrance: HOG.

When our son was born, we were assigned two rooms and a small kitchen, again within a larger apartment but with a friendlier widow. Everyone had to be housed, no one could be homeless, but since the huge apartment construction projects did not start up for another decade, many, like it or not, had to share their larger apartments.

After our first joy at our unplanned but dearly loved baby we faced the unhappy necessity, first due to Renate's short illness, then because of our work, of placing him in a weekly nursery for student mothers, fetching him only for weekends. This cost almost nothing but often meant tears on Monday morning. Otherwise we led an untroubled life, always with enough for our Sunday schnitzel, potatoes, mushrooms, and vegetable, plus a self-made plum cake which, lacking an oven, we gave to a bakery on Saturday and fetched fresh and warm on Sunday. We had enough for the movies, the theater, and occasionally the opera. Regular medical and dental care and medicines, a special gymnastics course for expectant mothers, the ambulance and virtually private delivery of little Thomas were all covered by national low-cost insurance, with six weeks paid leave before and eight weeks afterward, which were later greatly increased. Breast-feeding was also rewarded, and homemakers, almost always women, got one free paid "household day" every month. Life was markedly improving, though at uneven rates for different groups and never without a variety of shortages. Disposable diapers and prepared baby food did not arrive until we had our second son, Timothy, six years later, which meant that I did a lot of helping with diaper-washing and squeezing of carrot juice, mashing potatoes, or other baby needs.

Despite all improvements, the conflicting, often hostile, standpoints I had noticed in Bautzen were still quite evident in Leipzig. One flight above us, the widow and daughter of a man executed by the Nazis for his communist underground activity were fully devoted to the GDR. So were a young couple, puppeteers, who lived a flight below us. A young pastor and his wife were clearly if mildly opposed to "this system"; relations between the GDR leadership and the Lutheran Church were at one of their periodic low points. A man on the ground floor, expelled from now Polish Silesia, was violently anti-GDR and often traveled to West Berlin to join in angry rallies, sanctioned by the Western occupation authorities and the West German government, to demand the return of the "lost provinces." The GDR, in sharp contrast, recognized the new borders and signed friendship treaties with the Communist-led governments of Poland and Czechoslovakia, while its media played down or omitted references to Silesia, East Prussia, Sudetenland, and the other lost areas. Every effort was made to integrate their former inhabitants, never referred to as "refugees" as in the West but as "re-settlers." Many who rejected such integration moved westward.

The atmosphere at the Journalism School was free of such conflicts. Some students had also been forced to leave "lost homelands," but I heard no complaints on this issue, certainly not from my roommate, who came, as an orphan, from East Prussia. Nearly all those who chose journalism—and were accepted as students—were pro-GDR; our department wasn't called the Roter Kloster (Red Cloister) for nothing. It was very different from, say, the Medical School, with its many offspring of doctors, relatively prosperous yet often far from satisfied with socialist medical policies.

From the start, we were apportioned into "seminar groups" of about twenty-five students each, all of whom had the same classes in the first two years and kept together for political meetings, cultural evenings, trips to the movies or a concert, and occasional trips to help clear the last of Leipzig's rubble, help in the potato or sugar beet harvest, or, in one case, tamp in rail tracks in an open-pit lignite mine (for a week with pay). Of our group, over the four years, two disappeared and moved to the West, a relatively low average in those days.

We in the Red Cloister also noted some variations, beginning with the professors. Two were dyed-in-the-wool dogmatists. The one who taught basic communist theory, "Historical Materialism," defended every party and government policy up until the very day it was altered— and then defended the new policy just as uncompromisingly. The other, of Romanian-Jewish background, had been a daring left-wing fighter during the First World War and in the Hungarian Revolution of 1919. Forced to flee to the USSR, he had tried to reeducate fascist Romanian, Hungarian, and German prisoners of war during the Second World War. I wondered how successful his efforts had been, for he was no teacher and the students laughed at his weak endeavors. Perhaps he was given the job out of respect for his past.

But our dean, Hermann Budzislavski, who taught German Press History with a stress on progressive journalists, gave dynamic lectures, with constant pacing back and forth and changing of eyeglasses. He was popular with everyone. While a wartime exile in the United States, as a Jewish leftist, he had been an assistant of the famous journalist Dorothy Thompson, the wife of author Sinclair Lewis.

Wieland Herzfelde, who had also found refuge in the United States (and was also Jewish), taught World Literature, with a stress on the classics. He himself was part of German history, having built up and managed the legendary Malik publishing house until 1933. With his famous brother John Heartfield and the great artist Georg Grosz, he had led the German section of the Dada art movement and developed political photomontage, with witty, biting attacks on the Nazis, from whom they escaped in 1933 by the skin of their teeth. The brothers, on arrival in the GDR from Britain and the United States, had been treated with shocking distrust at first; those were the shameful Stalin-motivated years of mistrust of "Western emigrants," often Jewish. But then Stalin was dead, and so was that evil period, and they soon came to deserved honors. As professor, Herzfelde made high demands, assigning lots and lots of great books to read, but was therefore not so popular with some students.

Most popular was Hedwig Voegt from Hamburg, imprisoned three times for fighting the Nazis, who came to the GDR after the war to study and became an expert on German literature. Her moving lectures inspired admiration and love for many great writers, for me largely unknown till then.

Many professors and administrators had been active anti-fascists. University rector Georg Mayer retained, to my amazement, the ancient title "His Magnificence" and wore the traditional golden chain at ceremonies. But he also joked that as a young fraternity student the titles "Bottle-Mayer," "Duel Mayer," and "Bordello-Mayer" had all applied to him. Later I learned that the Nazis had thrown him out of academia for his courageous opposition.

Sadly, two famous anti-fascist professors in other departments proved too independent for GDR leaders. The philosopher Ernst Bloch was dropped from his position in 1957 and left the GDR in 1961; literature scholar Hans Meyer left in 1963. Neither, I believe, ever abandoned his belief in a socialist future.

Those were turbulent times for socialists or communists, with many ups and downs. The uprising of June 17, 1953, caused very unpleasant shake-ups for some near the top but brought not only more consumer goods and an end to rising prices, taxes, and power blackouts but a loosening of many strictures on political discussion. All this thanks in great measure to the new man in Moscow, Nikita Khrushchev, whose "secret speech" in February 1956 detailed immense crimes committed during the Stalin years. (http://www.fordham.edu/halsall/

mod/1956khrushchev-secret1.html) Countless prisoners in the Soviet
Union were freed, pressures were reduced, and books written that,
in translated editions in the GDR, broke many political taboos. Ilya
Ehrenburg's *The Thaw* gave the era its name. One unexpected result
of this thaw was a brief uprising in Poznan in Poland and a new leadership there under the once-imprisoned and far less dogmatic Wladislaw
Gomulka. The always hostile BBC, in its broadcast for the GDR, aired
an acerbic joke: A young prisoner asks his older cellmate, "What are
you in for?"—"I denounced Gomulka. And you?"—"That's odd. I'm
in for praising him." Just then a third man is locked into the cell. And
why? "I'm Gomulka!"

My marriage after my first college year meant living "off campus,"
so I was not so closely involved in "private-level" exchanges. But I
couldn't fail to notice the increase in discussion, often reflecting hopes,
like my own, for a far more elastic, realistic approach to our "unbending
principles." This was reflected in our first printed student newspaper.
One article reviewed the East Berlin political cabaret *Der Distel* (The
Thistle), which satirized attempts to ignore events in nearby Poland.
Another urged that the Leipzig press should also print the critical letters to the editor. My article called for more balanced, less simplistic
media reports about the United States. Other articles were also mildly
critical; none were "oppositional."

But the Polish upsets were followed by an uprising in Hungary,
with angry workers waging a brief civil war, enthusiastically encouraged by the Catholic Church and Voice of America. Party employees
and government employees, including security service agents, were
hanged or otherwise killed, and when Soviet tanks moved in there
were deaths on all sides. These tragic events caused a crisis in the
world's left-wing movements and also frightened GDR leaders politically and perhaps personally, although, as I heard it, moving their
homes out of Berlin to an inaccessible enclave to the north was due
less to their fears than to the worries of their security officers. But it was
certainly their fears that led to another tightening of screws generally.
A second issue of our student newspaper was long in coming—and
then tame as a lapdog. Political "deviations" by students, or in one

case by a teacher, were harshly castigated. The teacher lost his job, but rather than "proving himself" at some temporary industrial job, as demanded, he too took the option, still open before the Wall, and went west.

And me? I received the U.S.-Communist newspaper *Daily Worker*, which, after Khrushchev's speech, had opened its "Letters" pages to an amazingly critical debate. The hot arguments and hot words and my American background made finding my way especially complicated. I wondered whether the constraints on free discussion and one-sidedness in the GDR press were too similar to what I had experienced in the United States. Was this a mirror image of McCarthyism? Could I approve of it?

There was a semi-official rebuttal to such doubts. The pressures in the GDR were actually the opposite of those used by McCarthyites, who aimed at suffocating all efforts at progress for workers and unions, for blacks and women in their fights for equality, and squelching all opposition to the Cold War, or a hot one with atomic weapons. GDR pressures, it was averred, were the opposite—to strengthen a society where working-class youngsters got a free college education, no one was jobless, and everyone was medically insured.

I could not dismiss such a justification out of hand. In the United States, I had experienced the merciless offensive of the powers-that-be against all opposition, most dramatically at Peekskill in 1949, when state troopers supported the goon mobs that threw rocks at us at a concert with Pete Seeger and the great singer and actor Paul Robeson. All the windows in my bus had been shattered, along with any possible illusions. Every dirty, even bloody method was used to silence us. Could I get distressed at countermeasures aimed at stymieing such elements here in this most sensitive spot in the world, where nose cones of opposing atomic missiles faced each other? But were such countermeasures really the most effective method? And what about morality? I had plenty to chew on.

Again, ups followed downs. The atmosphere improved with the flight of Sputnik on October 4, 1957, and recurrent Soviet space successes that followed. Today many are unaware of the alarm in the

United States over the triumph in the Eastern bloc. The GDR press was delirious with each new achievement: the Sputnik starting things off; the first animal in space—the dog Laika, who unfortunately could not return; the first human, Yuri Gagarin, who could. Then the first two men together, then three men, the circling, filming, and hitting the moon (but not landing), the first woman in space in June 1963. For the GDR media each new feat was proof of the superiority of socialism. An American sour-grapes comment on this one-upmanship was that "before we send a woman into space the Russians will have sent up the Leningrad Symphony Orchestra." (Meg Waite Clayton, "Female Astronauts: Breaking the Glass Atmosphere," *Los Angeles Times*, June 15, 2013.) Some years later the tables were turned—but very quietly in the GDR.

There was good news closer to home for the GDR. In May 1958 rationing was finally dropped. Instead of a dual price system with cheap ration card staples and all you wanted at higher prices there was now a single-price system, uniform in the whole country, for goods like bakery, butcher, and dairy products. Amazingly—some said unwisely— these new prices stayed firmly frozen for over thirty years, until the end of the GDR.

In September 1958 my four college years came to an end. Some dogmatic aspects had been troubling, but on the whole I had found a friendly, often quite jolly atmosphere among most students, now full of curiosity and expectation as to their future careers. I celebrated with a spaghetti Bolognese feast for the twenty-odd members of my group and directed that the males do the main work, shaping little meatballs, slicing onions and mushrooms. That was totally new for most of them, but a big success. And now I had a second diploma. It was not an M.A., but that never bothered me.

After a happy two-week vacation with Renate and our two-year-old Thomas on the cliffs of "Saxon Switzerland" along the Elbe River, where I had first seen the GDR six years earlier, I landed in Berlin, at first in a rented room on the city outskirts and commuting every week-end to Leipzig.

5—Life in Doubled Berlin

What a different world I found! Though not like the picture of East Berlin so often conjured up with nothing but military parades, cloak-and-dagger Stasi men snooping everywhere and long lines of angry customers, it was nevertheless a highly unusual town, with countless complexities.

This was before the Berlin Wall; people moved back and forth between East and West through that strange open door in the Iron Curtain. And did they ever move back and forth! Bonn and Washington, with sights set on impressing and winning people in East Berlin and the GDR, used West Berlin as a magic magnet, pouring in billions to repair war damage, renovate older buildings, build new ones and, by slashing taxes, attract lots of industry and fine shops with quantities of fancy goods. One symbol was the KaDeWe (Kaufhaus des Westens) department store with a legendary assortment of delicacies. Closing times for nightclubs, bars, and dance-halls were eliminated, and well-subsidized cultural events were offered for every taste, with the desired effect on large numbers of Easterners. U.S. culture, from bebop and theater of the absurd to Disney and dungarees, all of it attractive, swamped West Germany and, just as intended, spilled over eastward in great quantity, if not always quality.

The existence of two currencies had strange effects unknown to the Western world. Many East Berliners commuted to West Berlin, happily undercutting wage levels there. Measly 200 West-marks were magi-cally transformed by the many Western money-changing offices into 800 or more GDR marks—the rate changed daily. An untrained East Berliner, perhaps a cleaning woman, could return eastward on payday with more in her purse than a highly trained GDR engineer. Many such commuters bought butter, a large sausage, or a dozen eggs at low East Berlin prices, sneaked them across in the subway or el under their coats and sold them to West Berliners at well under the going price. Translating this into GDR marks meant a nice additional source of income. A woeful story about hard times in the East might also get a sympathetic gift from an employer, maybe a pack or two of Luckies or Camels that could be sold for a stiff price back in East Berlin. With 50,000 to 80,000 commuters it certainly worsened a perpetual East Berlin lack of labor power.

For many, smuggling was part of everyday life. At the last station before crossing into West Berlin, two GDR customs men walked through the el or subway cars and collared some who were all too conspicuous, perhaps a middle-aged or elderly woman looking strangely pregnant. They could hardly control such butter-eggs-sausage smuggling; their trained eyes were keener to catch professional smugglers of valuable GDR products like cameras, children's goods, or Meissen (that is, Dresden) chinaware.

The two currencies caused endless problems. The largely artificial 4:1 or 5:1 exchange rate led many West Berliners to cross over for themselves and buy groceries in East Berlin at dirt-cheap prices, thus helping to empty the not so heavily laden East Berlin shelves. This was then prevented; a show of ID was demanded (which all Germans possessed) to prove GDR identity for every purchase, even an ice-cream cone or a bockwurst (a hot dog equivalent). Though an awful bother, most East Berliners agreed with this and wished that ID also be required for services like beauty parlors and physical therapists. It wasn't, and those businesses near the sector borders were full of cross-over West Berlin customers using West-marks or West cigarettes as bribes to avoid waiting and get the best treatment at a very low price.

Along the west side of the zigzag border, glittering movie theaters lured East Berlin kids to Hollywood cowboy or gangster films with special low ticket prices to overcome the currency disadvantage. Superman-type comic books were sold to them at cut-rate prices. East Berlin adults crossed over to see Hollywood and West German films, good and not so good; one hit was Kazan's *On the Waterfront*. Highbrow crossovers went to West Berlin theaters to see dramas then popular in the Western world. I soon realized that most East Berliners did cross over, whether commuting to a West Berlin job then spending a Saturday night dancing or at a show, or purchasing items, modern, fashionable, or simply in short supply in the GDR. East Berlin, despite constant improvement and a better assortment of goods than elsewhere in the GDR, could never keep pace with the enticing offerings of a Marshall Plan—subsidized, booming capitalist economy just a few streets away.

As I mentioned, this migration was not entirely one-sided. Excluded from ID requirements in East Berlin besides hairdressers and physical therapists were books, records, and theater tickets, already extremely inexpensive. Even opera tickets cost only 15 East-marks. Thanks to the exchange rate, this meant that West Berliners, for the best seats in the East, paid little more than they would for a serving of coffee and cake, making it harder for us East Berliners to get good seats, or sometimes any at all. But it was well worth the effort, as I will soon describe.

Berlin, already split before the Wall, had its amusing features. At one corner in downtown East Berlin you could look north and read the GDR version of the evening news in rotating electric letters at Friedrichstrasse Station. If you turned your head 90 degrees westward you could read a very contrary CIA version rotating from a tall RIAS radio tower in West Berlin.

A few subway lines moved from one West Berlin borough to another, crossing through a part of East Berlin and stopping at stations there. So for some stretches passengers were mixed. I enjoyed seeing one passenger reading about evil drugs and joblessness in the West while another, sitting peacefully next to him, read about the hunger and oppression in the Soviet Zone he was passing through.

I watched West Berlin loudspeaker trucks drive right up to the unguarded borderline, loudly blaring anti-GDR messages. As soon as possible, a sound truck arrived on the Eastern side and, almost bumper to bumper, blasted loud music to drown it out until it drove off to the next location.

As for me, fearful of somehow being recognized or simply asked to identify myself, if only as witness to some accident, I never risked putting one toe across a border marked only by the famous signposts "You are now leaving the American (or British or French) Sector." I was also a bit nervous since the street where, after a year, we got a new little apartment that was separated from the U.S. sector only by unlighted gardens. I was doubly glad when, after a lucky swap, we got a centrally

heated apartment in the very safe Stalin Allee, which, happily, five
months after we moved there, was renamed Karl-Marx-Allee.

6—Berlin's Cultural Scene

Renate and I were not greatly tempted by the goodies across the dividing line (and we did get a few goodies from my parents). The stage and
the opera, which we had greatly enjoyed in Bautzen and Leipzig, meant
more to us. Despite fantastically low prices, the quality in East Berlin
was superb.

The first play after the war, in September 1945 in East Berlin, had
been Gottfried Lessing's 1779 classic *Nathan the Wise*, a call for tolerance between religions, a vigorous rejection of anti-Semitism and
fully taboo in the Nazi years. Those first audiences, huddled in the
unheated auditorium of the famous Deutsches Theater, often physi-
cally hungry, were also hungry for cultural fresh air. Its producer,
Gustav von Wangenheim, a communist theater man, had fled from the
Nazis to the USSR and during the war called on German soldiers at
the front to lay down their arms. Then he taught German POWs at the
"anti-fascist schools." The Nazis had sentenced him to death in absentia. His response was *Nathan the Wise*, four months after their defeat.
His second production was Thornton Wilder's *Our Town*, its Berlin
premiere and first introduction to recent American drama.

Similar sentiments motivated many people of stage, screen, and the
arts who came out of hiding, literally or figuratively, or returned from
exile in a dozen countries. Von Wangenheim was followed by Wolfgang
Langhoff, arrested by the Nazis the night of the Reichstag fire in 1933,
tortured and sent to toil as one of the "peat bog soldiers," prisoners made famous by their song, which, after his release and flight to
Switzerland, he had edited and publicized. His first great success was
Goethe's *Faust* and even more an adaptation of Aristophanes' ancient
comedy *Peace* by the brilliant writer Peter Hacks, newly arrived from
West Germany. At the premiere the ovation lasted three-quarters of an
hour, the stage "iron curtain" had to be raised fifteen times!

The manager of the wrecked and rebuilt Volksbühne (People's Stage) was Fritz Wisten, also a leftist, and Jewish, arrested and mistreated by the Nazis but saved from deportation and death because his actress wife was Aryan. They were even able to conceal and rescue a few colleagues from the Jewish Cultural Association that he had once headed. At the Volksbühne, we enjoyed jolly but still hard-hitting plays by old Molière from seventeenth-century France.

Most of all I loved the Brecht theater. The great Bertolt Brecht arrived in Berlin in 1948 with his wife, Helene Weigel, forced to flee his exile home in California by the House Un-American Activities Committee. Neither Switzerland nor Austria offered him a chance to produce his plays, but then East Berlin gave his new Berliner Ensemble the same beautiful, baroque theater where his *Three-Penny Opera* had triumphed in 1928. The first production was his play *Mother Courage*, about a woman who sells goods to soldiers during the Thirty Years War (1618–1648) and, despite one tragic loss after another, never comprehends that war is never good for "little people" like her. The role, wonderfully played by his wife, was an early source of controversy. Mother Courage was far from the "socialist hero" type often sought in those years. It was really hard to identify with her. Brecht did not want audiences to "identify," however, but to reflect and draw their own conclusions; most in the audience had also been forced to learn that war brought nothing but misery and ruins. Mother Courage's run-down little wagon circling at center stage became a legend.

Co-starring with Weigel, and even more legendary, was the actor and singer Ernst Busch. The Spanish Civil War songs he recorded during the fascist bombing of Barcelona in 1938, based on the international song book he compiled, are still loved in many countries. After Spain's defeat, he was turned over to the Gestapo and narrowly escaped death when the penitentiary was bombed. Now, defying partial facial laming, he triumphed again and again, once again with the song "Mackie Messer" ("Mack the Knife") from *The Three-Penny Opera* and above all in the title role in *The Life of Galileo*. Every production in the Brecht theater was noteworthy, unique—and a treat.

And then there was opera, far more popular here than in the United States. The State Opera House on Unter den Linden boulevard, built for King Frederick II (Frederick the Great), whose classical lines made it my favorite building, was managed by Max Burkhardt, who had spent six years behind bars, partly in solitary confinement, and also survived only because his wife, thanks to false documents, was an Aryan. I recall Shostakovich's *The Nose*, not only its music and absurdly funny plot, but because our balcony seats were five meters from the loge where Party head Walter Ulbricht was also enjoying the premiere. Also, in *Tosca,* otherwise done beautifully, I recall how the heroic tenor Cavaradossi's can of paint defied stage directions by fall-ing from its scaffold position and rolling slowly downward, with all eyes on it except those of the oblivious hero, till it fell into the orches-tra. Best of all was the jolly *Barber of Seville*, a production so appealing with its ironic charm that it is still being offered.

Good as the State Opera House was, the rival Komische Oper (Comic Opera), headed by the great Austrian Walter Felsenstein, was even better. It featured no world-famous singers, just very good ones who could also act. Felsenstein and his team rehearsed even the smallest roles for months till they attained, for us, perfection. Every performance was a true delight, from the eerie cellar and riotous court in Offenbach's *Barbe-Bleue* or *Bluebeard* to the overwhelming gale and heart-rending ending in Verdi's *Otello,* to Janáček's *Cunning Little Vixen*, which even delighted Renate's parents, no opera-goers, with its jolly barnyard full of chickens, its forest with wonderful birds and ani-mals played by children, and the melancholy arias of love and aging in a Slovak tavern. They were all unforgettable.

For those who liked operettas or an occasional musical there was the Metropol Theater, and for revues, chorus lines, and big circus shows the Friedrichstadt Palast. I come later to political cabaret.

Indeed, East Berlin had oodles to offer in the cultural field. In 1959 West Berlin Mayor Willy Brandt, a Social Democrat, speaking to an American TV interviewer about the GDR, said that "to live under communism would be worse than an atomic war." And yet, as one living "under communism" in this so horrible land, I found that its theater and opera, which matched any in Europe, offered at least a few compensations of which Willy Brandt was perhaps unaware.

7—Filmmakers and Other Anti-Fascists

Renate and I saw more movies than plays and operas, of course, and both Eastern and Western films were always a frequent subject of discussion, critical or admiring. The GDR's one film company, DEFA, was often the center of debate.

East Germany was well ahead in reviving postwar movie-making, aided by Soviet advisers like Lt. Col. Alexander Dymschitz, an expert on German culture who supported many first steps in a new cultural life. In November 1945, a group of writers and filmmakers, former emigrants and some who had remained but had never been Nazis, discussed possible plans. As Paul Wandel, the head of the group, recalled: "When we first met in the wrecked Hotel Adlon to discuss the future of German film, most of those present doubted whether there was any point to it at all." (Stephen Brockman, *A Critical History of German Film*, Rochester: Camden House, 2010, 188–89). Conditions were abysmal; the first director once asked his assistant to find a little butter so he could stay on his feet. But, they concluded, "Film today must offer answers to our people's basic questions." And so DEFA was founded.

Its first task was tackling questions about fascism. Within a year, the first postwar German film, *The Murderers Are Amongst Us*, warned that men guilty of war crimes were already regaining wealth and influence. This film, which started the world career of the fine actress Hildegard Knef, was followed in 1947 by *Marriage in the Shadows*, a poignant yet hard-hitting tragedy about Hitler's genocide against Jews. Eleven million tickets were sold, mostly in East Germany; nearly every adult must have seen it, a factor of great importance in combating Nazi ideology. A year later *The Blum Affair* laid bare the roots of anti-Semitism before 1933. Such anti-fascist films, among DEFA's best, some real masterpieces, were almost completely ignored or boycotted west of the Elbe and abroad.

Instead, West Germany was inundated with two hundred Hollywood films a year plus dubious pre-1945 German revivals. When filming was finally begun, wartime rubble was occasionally shown, but, for years, almost nothing about the reasons for it. Romances on happy Alpine slopes and meadows were frequent, at times with the same directors who once produced rabid Nazi films.

In all cultural fields the prevailing atmosphere in East Berlin was unambiguously anti-fascist. The first head of the artists' association, Otto Nagel, had been thrown out of a leadership position by the Nazis in 1933, imprisoned in Sachsenhausen, then released with a strict ban on painting even at home. His successor was Leah Grundig, arrested by the Nazis but able to emigrate to Palestine (there was no Israel then). Her husband, Hans, also a noted artist, was first imprisoned, then sent on suicide missions into battle on the Eastern Front, where he deserted. The writers' association was headed first by a writer who had fought the fascists in Spain, then by Anna Seghers, an exile in France, Cuba, and then Mexico, whose anti-Nazi novel *The Seventh Cross* was filmed with Spencer Tracy in Hollywood.

The composers elected a president who had not been an anti-fascist but was no Nazi, just a good composer, and the composers' secretary-general at his side had been active in the Dutch underground resistance. The dean of East Berlin's musical conservatory, Eberhard Rebling, after an amazing escape from a Nazi police van, had also been active in the underground in Amsterdam.

The leading cultural organization, the Academy of Arts, was similar. Its first chosen chair was Heinrich Mann, Thomas Mann's brother, whose novel, filmed as *The Blue Angel*, had made Marlene Dietrich a star, died just before leaving his California exile. The equally famous novelist Arnold Zweig came from exile in Palestine to replace him, followed by the exiled poet Johannes R. Becher, author Willi Bredel, a veteran of Nazi prisons and front action in the Spanish Civil War, and Konrad Wolf, who had been a young lieutenant in the Red Army and later a master film director—in my eyes one of the very greatest. His father was a world-famous writer, Friedrich Wolf, his brother was the master spy chief Markus Wolf, the East German–Jewish counterpart to Bonn's ex-Nazi general, Reinhard Gehlen.

8—Democratic German Report

After four months working at Seven Seas Books, which published books in English by leftists whose views hampered or prevented sales in their home countries, I became an assistant at *Democratic German Report*, a biweekly bulletin financed by the GDR. Its masterful English editor, John Peet, twice wounded in Spain, had been Reuters correspondent in Vienna, Warsaw, and West Berlin until, at a sensational press conference in 1951, he accused Reuters and the British press of distorting news from the east and moved to the GDR.

The bulletin reported positively on the GDR but not in the simplistic tones so common in Eastern Bloc publications. He loved wit and irony and liked to quote insipid reports by "daring" Western journalists, who, the minute they risked stepping into East Berlin, found that the sun stopped shining and everyone looked glum. Some incidents were far from glum. One of our readers, an English shop steward touring Eastern Europe by bike, had faced a dilemma at the West-East German border. Western citizens could drive the 120 kilometers through GDR territory to West Berlin, but only on the Autobahn, where bicycling was forbidden. Everyone looked worried until a bright driver put the bike on his truck and told the jolly Englishman, with ragged shorts and a big handlebar mustache, to hop in. In West Berlin he set up his pup tent near the Reichstag. When the police chased him away at dawn, he came to us for help. John Peet called the international office of the GDR labor federation: "We have a British union official here. Can you arrange accommodations?" With high political expectations, they reserved their fanciest guest suite. I must give credit where it is due: the official who came to fetch him with a big car hid any surprise at seeing our somewhat scruffy shop steward, and brought him and his bike to the suite without a word of disappointment.

Since Peet hated travel, I drove around and wrote reports on what I found. At the factory complex where the GDR's legendary little Trabant cars were made, looking for an interview with a worker, not an official, I picked at random a friendly-looking man making car seats (who turned out to be a rare Baptist church member). He agreed to talk to me and was given a twenty-minute (paid) break. Without a trace of tact, I asked him mercilessly about his earnings, his home, how many suits, coats, and shoes he and his wife owned, about summer vacation trips and the like, and reported it exactly in my article. (Allen Mann [pseudonym of Victor Grossman], "Meet Herr Mueller: GDR Car-Worker," *Democratic German Report* (hereinafter *DGR*), March 3, 1961, 37–39.)

Two months later we had another visitor from London, a young bus driver, his little daughter, and pregnant wife. After reading my report, they wanted to move to the GDR. The husband said, "I don't have three suits or two overcoats, just one each"; and the woman added, "When could we ever afford a vacation trip?" Their immigration attempt, certainly unwise and officially more than difficult (they spoke not a word of German), ended when the wife became ill and they had to return to London. The episode gave me new food for thought about comparisons—in all directions.

So did my trip to the huge Ernst Thälmann Works in Magdeburg, with its 30,000 employees. I was impressed by its kindergartens and bookshop, its clinic with a medical staff of ninety, and all outpatient facilities. Krupp, its pre-1945 owner, had offered a total of two nurses. I learned of the good contact between a work team I visited and the 9th-grade school class that joined them biweekly, in line with school curriculum, to gain simple skills and learn of factory life. Some Sundays they played soccer together. I noted a sign hanging from the ceiling in one work hall: "Our factory library has thousands of books. How many have you already read?" And in another hall, even bigger: "Our work team saw Bertolt Brecht's *Mother Courage* and enjoyed Gerhart Hauptmann's *The Beaver Coat*. When were you last at the theater? When are you going again?" With the GDR's demise this modern complex was split up and sold to five short-lived private firms. Little but empty ruins remain. (Allen Mann [VG], "A Krupp Factory Under Socialism," *DGR,* October 14, 1960, 166–67)

9—Nazis and Anti-Nazis

A major aim of *DGR* was to expose former Nazis still in leadership in West Germany, where the major parties eloquently praised democracy and free elections so long as all those taking part had basically similar goals. But one with very different goals, the Communist Party, was forbidden in 1956, its publications shut down and its leaders arrested. A second rule, quickly learned, was that entrée into the Western community of nations could be achieved by paying compensation to Jewish survivors (if in the West) and, after its birth, paying restitution to Israel and suppressing any and all criticism of its policies. Behind this libertarian "rebirth" and its "economic miracle," I found that the praise of West Germany for turning over a new leaf was based on well-packaged lies.

Many in the West hated fascism and wanted to create a better Germany. Some U.S. and British officers who themselves fought the Nazis were able to get some of the biggest and worst hanged or locked up, and General Dwight Eisenhower declared shortly after war's end that National Socialists were nowhere "indispensable." But many were mysteriously spirited away to South America or Washington, and before long U.S. and British policy was altered. By 1947, with the Soviets no longer seen as allies but as foes, German industrial know-how and military skills were very desirable. In what was called "de-Nazification," those investigated sought good buddies who testified, perhaps in expectation of return assistance, that they had simply been oh-so-unwilling cogs in all the repression and mass murder and had on one occasion actually helped some Jewish friend or family to get away, or at least expressed a desire to do so. Only a very few unlucky leopards with too many guilty spots, or too few buddies, lost jobs or spent a couple of easy years in prison before being amnestied, to resume their hunt for prey.

A great help in climbing back up was an addendum to Article 131, passed unanimously by the first Bundestag in 1951, which permitted, indeed required, government institutions to fill at least 20 percent of their staffs with people employed there before May 1945, no lower than in their former rank, and excluding only a few who were officially ruled guilty. Full pensions were guaranteed to retirees. For several hundred thousand that meant it was back again to their former elevated status. (Timothy Scott Brown, "West Germany and the Global Sixties: The Anti-Authoritarian Revolt, 1962–1978," in *Basic Law*. i.e. Grundgesetz, Cambridge: Cambridge University Press, 2013), 93.)

10—Diplomats

Our eight-page *Democratic German Report*, to help spoil their return, put facts from GDR research sources into good English and mailed them to all British Labour MPs and many journalists. In 1962 we had our biggest coup, headlined "THE PLAGUE." (*DGR,* January 19, 1962, 17–21; March 16, 1962, 20; April 13, 1962, 76; and May 11, 1962, 87.) On a world map we placed a swastika on every country where the West German ambassador had belonged to the Nazi Party. Over fifty were splattered from Santiago to Stockholm, from Washington to Wellington. We added membership numbers and a few details: in 1943 Dr. Ernst-Günther Mohr, then legation counselor, boasted to Berlin that "after 11 months the de-Judification of the Netherlands is almost three-quarters completed." In 1962 he was ambassador to Switzerland. Our story, often with the map, was picked up in twenty countries, but in West Germany not for two months. Then *Der Spiegel* finally risked a brief mention, and was promptly, angrily accused by the influential paper *Christ und Welt* of repeating propaganda from an "obscure and clumsy propaganda sheet." Peet noted maliciously that neither publication denied a single one of the facts and that the editor of *Christ und Welt* had himself been a leading Nazi propagandist and SS captain. Dr. Mohr was soon removed, then sent as ambassador to safely fascistic Argentina. ("Berlin Notebook," *DGR,* April 13, 1962, 76.)

The West German government tried to respond to jabs and attacks, mostly from Britain, often thanks to facts from our *Democratic German Report*. They insisted that there were no alternatives and that the GDR leadership was also loaded with Nazis. Bonn's media connections guaranteed this campaign no little success, above all in the United States, where many accepted West Germany's voluble regret for past sins and its assertions that East Germany had no regrets for them.

UNTIL THE MID-1970s, thanks to Bonn's pressure, the GDR was recognized by few countries outside the Eastern Bloc and thus needed few ambassadors. But who were they?

The first GDR ambassador to Poland, with the delicate task of breaking political ice and anti-German feelings, was the famous author and medical doctor Friedrich Wolf, whose taboo-breaking play and film *Zyankali* (Cyanide), a moving appeal for abortion rights, had shaken up pre-Hitler Germany. Wolf, a Jewish anti-Nazi, had to flee in 1933. His *Professor Mamlock*, perhaps the first major work about what was to become the Holocaust, premiered in 1934 at Warsaw's Yiddish Art Theater, then in Tel Aviv, New York, Moscow, and around the non-fascist world. It was filmed in the USSR in 1938 and again in 1961 in the GDR (directed by his son Konrad Wolf).

His successor in Warsaw was Stefan Heymann, who survived Dachau, Auschwitz, and Buchenwald. As the political situation in Poland grew stormier he was followed by Josef Hegen, known as a hard-liner, perhaps as a result of his past. After fleeing to the USSR and working as a machinist until the war, he parachuted behind Nazi lines, fought as a partisan in Poland till he was captured and sent to Mauthausen concentration camp.

An ambassador to North Vietnam was Eduard Claudius. A mason by trade and active union leader, later a writer, he fled the Nazis and was one of the first to volunteer in Spain. He was wounded, then interned in France and Switzerland where Hermann Hesse helped save him from deportation to Germany. When released, he joined the Garibaldi partisans fighting the Nazis in Italy and later became a popular author in the GDR and, briefly, a diplomat.

Almost all those first ambassadors had been Communists-in-exile, fought in Spain or the Resistance, or been imprisoned. One spent seven years in solitary confinement. Another was one of the "peat bog soldiers" made famous by the great song. One man was beaten so viciously by stormtroopers that he lost an eye. Most were of working-class origin; they had to learn on the job to be diplomats. Not one had been in the fascist Foreign Service. Adenauer once replied to criticism on his appointments: "One cannot build up a Foreign Ministry without giving leading positions to persons with past experience." The obvious question is: Okay, but what kind of experience? (Hennig Köhler, *Adenauer: Politische Biographie*, Berlin: Propyläen, 1994, 971–74.)

11—School Days

Schools were even more important than diplomats, and Hitler had paid great attention to them. Most teachers were in the Nazi Party. Renate shuddered at any thought of their brutally sadistic ways.

The French and British armies in West Germany showed relatively little interest in the matter. The Americans did; things were at first tough in the U.S. Zone: 11,310 Nazi-era teachers were dismissed. Then came the big anti-Soviet emphasis and resultant appeasement. In Bavaria, for example, 1,800 fired teachers had been pensioned off or had moved away or died. But 8,820 were back in their schoolrooms by 1951, using textbooks that often skirted any analysis or rejection of the Nazi era. The main labor union newspaper, examining West German schoolbooks in 1960, wrote: "There are even history books which deal with the persecution of the Jews in only one line. The average lies between 8 lines and 15 lines." (*Welt der Arbeit* No. 9, 1960, quoted in *DGR* Notebook, August 31, 1960, 148.)

Some West German schoolbooks offered sentences like these on racism: "Here is what you must know about Africa: European settlers and plantations opened up the continent. . . . European missionaries tamed the wild Negroes, brought them the great message of Christ's

Kingdom and taught them Christian neighborliness." (*Erdkunde*, vol. 2, Ansbach: Prägel Verlag, 1959, quoted in *DGR*, "White Supermen," December 21, 1962, 211.) Or: "For centuries the habits and customs of the inhabitants of the West African jungle have been preserved: they have only become somewhat milder with the passage of time. The cruelties that were once usual are today sternly punished if the white overseers learn of them." (Moritz Diesterweg, *Von Erdteil zu Erdteil*, Frankfurt am Main, 1959, August 31, 1962, 148, quoted in *DGR*, "White Supermen," December 21, 1962, 211.) And so on, ad nauseam, while corporal punishment was only outlawed slowly, state by state, and is still allowed in Bavaria.

IN EAST GERMANY 20,000 Nazi teachers, the overwhelming majority, were dismissed for good. The huge gap was gradually filled, usually after brief courses, by so-called "New Teachers." Two of my brothers-in-law were among them; one told me with a laugh how he had been signed on as sports teacher because he was an avid soccer player. Before long Geography, then Science, were piled on, with him hardly a week or two ahead of his pupils. Not ideal, but these "New Teachers," highly dedicated and strongly anti-fascist, remained a basic positive feature in GDR schools. And corporal punishment was strictly forbidden from the start.

In a later section, I will discuss various other aspects and some problems in the GDR schools.

12—Judges, Police, and Gehlen

Democratic German Report let it be widely known that 800 to 1,000 West German judges and prosecutors had once judged or prosecuted for the Nazis, often insisting on death sentences for listening to the BBC, casting doubt on final victory, or helping a fleeing Jew. In 1962, in one ironic episode, the government tried to outlaw the Victims of Nazi Persecution Association (VVN) as a Communist-front organization. The trial had hardly begun when the defense noted that all three presiding judges had been in the SS, the Nazi Party, the stormtroopers, or the Gestapo. The trial was quickly abandoned but led to the discovery that out of forty-nine judges in this third-highest West German court forty had similar backgrounds.

The *New Statesman* of London remarked, December 7, 1962: "Surely if Dr. Adenauer wants to punish the representatives of those who suffered in the concentration camps he can find somewhere in his Reich one single judge to try their guilt who has not himself been a Nazi."

Years later, *Der Spiegel* noted: "In 1953 at least 72% of all Federal Supreme Court judges, Germany's highest court for criminal and civil law, had had Nazi connections. By 1962, in the criminal division, it reached 80%. . . . Except for two military court martial chairmen . . . not a single judge in the Federal Republic has ever been convicted of perversion of justice."

It was as bad or worse with the police. *Der Spiegel* noted: "Hardly anyone in law enforcement was untainted by a Nazi past." The historian Jan Kiepe found that "especially the leadership of the postwar West German police consisted of men who had been active in the police system of the Third Reich and supported its criminal system." (Beste, Ralf, Bönisch et al., "The Role Ex-Nazis Played in Early West Germany," trans. Christopher Sultan, *Spiegel Online*, March 6, 2012.)

AND HOW WAS it on my side? In East German courtrooms, 80 or 90 percent of all judges, prosecutors and other officials had been Nazi Party members. In 1945, they lost their jobs. To fill the wide gap, schools for judges were set up by December 1945, with thirty to forty students in each province taking six- to eight-month courses, then by 1947 a year-long course. Most were blue- or white-collar workers; at the factory where I worked in 1953 I heard loudspeaker calls for anyone interested to apply for such a school. Becoming a judge was more complicated than becoming a teacher. The university law schools, still conservative, demanded that a proper law degree must remain a requirement, but the new leaders, with the Soviets, overruled them. A number of these young judges were too severe, not only toward Nazis but also toward opponents of the new system, especially in the early years. Close ties with the legal system of the Soviet occupation force led to some tragic results. But there was always a sharp contrast with West German courts, which were run by ex-Nazis who handed down sentences based on thought patterns and even laws of Hitler Germany.

It was similar with the police. Happily, I had little contact with cops except when I had to renew a police stamp on my foreigner's ID, and later get visas for travel outside the GDR. But, as I learned, police staff had also been cleansed of Nazis. On a lecture tour, I visited a school for police trainees and recall big mural portraits on the two dormitories, artistically amateurish but for me symbolic: the Russian poet Pushkin, partly of African descent, and the German-Jewish Heinrich Heine, whose books were banned by Hitler.

One interesting effect of the change was that, aside from severity in political matters, the number of convictions for felonies decreased from half a million in 1946 to 230,000 in 1950, in part due to settling down after the war, but this was also a sign that both "new cops" and "new judges" were somehow different.

REINHARD GEHLEN WAS a special case. As Hitler's head of German Arms East, the boss of military espionage against Soviet forces, he obeyed Wehrmacht orders: "All leniency or humanity toward prisoners of war is strictly condemned." He obtained much of his information by means of torture and hunger; up to three million or more Soviet prisoners of war died of planned starvation. Although a major war criminal, Gehlen used his mass of facts on the Red Army to buy his way free from punishment and was flown to Washington in May 1945 with his filmed notes and six of his Nazi staff to help a newly forming CIA build up an espionage force for a future conflict. Then this mystery man, who wore his dark glasses indoors and outdoors, set up his "Organisation Gehlen" in a walled complex near Munich. President Truman allegedly said: "I don't care if he screws goats. As long as he helps us we'll use him."

In 1956, his unit metamorphosed into the Bundesnachrichtendienst (BND, the Federal Intelligence Service), a kid sister of the CIA. Gehlen hired men from the Gestapo and Heinrich Himmler's security service, such as Konrad Fiebig, whose death squad murdered 11,000 Jews in Belarus. When word about good jobs got around, countless thugs of this type were hired but kept out of any spotlight. One British newspaper called them "the Gestapo boys," but most politicians agreed with Truman. As CIA official Harry Rositzke said about Gehlen: "It was absolutely necessary to use every son of a bitch. The main thing—he was an anti-Communist." Gehlen replied to any criticism of his hiring practices by pointing out that, in percentage terms, he employed fewer such men "than most cabinet ministries." His BND also spied (illegally) on "undesirable anti-militarists and leftists" inside Germany. (Joseph C. Goulden, *The Dictionary of Espionage: Spyspeak into English*, Mineola, NY: Dover, 89–90.)

13—Dr. Hans Globke

The man who secretly arranged for Gehlen's organization to become the BND was Dr. Hans Globke. A Roman Catholic, he did not join the Nazi Party but supported it even before it gained power, as in his official note to the police: "Efforts by Jews . . . to alter their names cannot be supported. The fact that they became Christians is no reason for a name change and the argument that this is because of anti-Semitic tendencies . . . cannot be accepted." An ambitious legal expert, when Hitler took over he climbed the career ladder to a top job in the Interior Ministry.

Globke co-authored the official legal commentary about degrees of "Jewishness," based on one's grandparents, later a question of life or death. In 1935, to "protect the racially homogenous German people from alien blood," he helped frame laws severely punishing sex or marriage between Jews and Aryans. In 1937, he detailed a law requiring a red "*J*" on the passports of Jews, hindering escape at Swiss or other borders. In 1939, he helped with a law requiring those with "un-Jewish" given names to add "Israel" or "Sara" as a middle name, visible on house doors, making it easier to find Jews when transports to the annihilation camps began. Globke helped extend these rules to Austria after German occupation, to Czech areas in 1938 and 1939, and in

1941 to Slovakia, a Nazi vassal state. Its Jews were soon on the freight trains to Auschwitz.

After the war, Globke, claiming earlier contacts with anti-Nazi Catholics, was soon cleared. Konrad Adenauer hired him, naming him state secretary (deputy minister) in 1953. During their garden strolls, Globke helped plan strategy, acted as contact man with Bundestag allies, decided who could meet the boss, and oversaw the Party treasury. Above all, he managed appointments of key men and watched over their loyalty. Globke, as the conservative *Die Welt* noted, "controls the complete personnel policy of the republic and . . . is in command of the secret service." This made him "the second most powerful man in the country." Only a few Social Democrats voiced mild disapproval. Maybe, like J. Edgar Hoover, he kept files on politicians' dirty pasts, especially their dirty Nazi pasts.

In July 1960, the GDR (and the *Democratic German Report*) offered incriminating facts about Globke to West German officials. These were mocked as "more Communist propaganda." But as more nasty facts seeped out, Adenauer feared they might hurt his fourth-term election chances in 1961 against West Berlin's Social Democratic mayor Willy Brandt. So Defense Minister Franz Josef Strauss attacked Brandt's anti-fascist emigration as a betrayal of German patriotic duties. Years later, their deal was revealed: no more attacks on Brandt as a "draft-dodging" traitor and no mention of Globke's past.

But then Franz Bauer, a former Jewish emigrant and uniquely anti-fascist prosecutor in Hesse, defied all attempts to hush up the whereabouts of major war criminal Adolf Eichmann in Argentina and tipped off Israel. After Eichmann's sensational streetside capture in May 1960, he was put on trial in Israel, not in mild West Germany. Would he spill any beans about his Nazi-era ties with Globke? CIA-boss Allen Dulles and Gehlen's BDN were able to edit Eichmann's memoirs in *Life* magazine and spent 50,000 marks to keep a book exposé off the market. The next job was to keep Globke's name out of both the trial and media. When the GDR's top legal expert, also a former Jewish emigrant, went to Israel as a co-plaintiff, Gehlen agents broke into his hotel room and stole the Eichmann-Globke documents, and when the Knesset quickly voted to rule out co-plaintiffs, the GDR lawyer was condemned to the sidelines. Once Eichmann did mention Globke; the men from Bonn raced madly to reach the nearest phone, but the media made sure this ripple went almost fully unnoticed. Israeli cooperation was rewarded; after the trial Adenauer okayed 240 million marks' worth of military weapons aid.

The GDR media was far from silent, however, and in 1963 there was a public fourteen-day trial of Globke in East Berlin. As our bulletin reported: "The court heard witnesses from all parts of Europe who testified on Globke's role in the liquidation of the Jews during the Second World War and in 'Germanization' measures in many occupied countries. The main evidence consisted of original Nazi documents. . . . On July 23 the GDR Supreme Court, trying Globke in absentia, found him guilty of crimes against humanity, war crimes and murder and sentenced him to life at hard labor."

This show trial was roundly condemned as communist propaganda, but the undeniable facts disturbed too many people, especially in Britain. Within three months, two weeks before Adenauer resigned, at age eighty-even, Globke did the same, at sixty-five. Although he was awarded a Distinguished Cross of Merit, his retirement plans in his Lake Geneva villa were dashed when Switzerland refused entry to the "second most important man in Bonn." (Globke material based on *Der Spiegel*, January 23, 1963; and *DGR*, esp. June 14, 1963, 91–93.)

14—The Top Ranks

Globke was no lone wolf. In an earlier East Berlin "absentia" trial, Minister Theodor Oberländer had been convicted, while a top-ranking officer in the conquered city of Lvov (Ukrainian L'viv, German Lemberg), for the brutal massacres of Jews and Poles. Bonn denied it all again, but the extreme anti-Semitism and racism of this far-right politician were hideous enough to upset Western media. Five days after the East Berlin trial, in April 1960, Oberländer also resigned. (*DGR*, April 29, 1960, 67; May 13, 1960, 74.)

Out of twenty-one ministers in the cabinet of Ludwig Erhard, Adenauer's successor, ten had been in the Nazi Party, eleven had been Wehrmacht officers, others were judges or prosecutors. The Foreign Minister had joined the Storm Troopers. Many still dreamed of claiming not only the GDR but other "lost territories" as well. Minister von Merkatz, once instructor at a Nazi espionage school, insisted, "Now we must win back what Bismarck and others won." Minister Hans-Christoph Seebohm said, "European culture can only be found where Germans live." He demanded a return of the Czech Sudetenland regions given Hitler at Munich in 1938. Defense Minister Franz-Josef Strauss stated, "We are living in a technical age in which the combined strength of our allies is sufficient to wipe the Soviet Union off the map"; he rejected appeals for a "nuclear-free" Central Europe, and urged that the Bundestag approve nuclear weapons so West Germany could keep up with its NATO allies. He said: "There must be a continuity of tradition between the German soldiers of World War II and the German soldiers of the future. The duties the future soldier will face will be the same as those faced by the older generation of soldiers."

The state secretaries (deputy ministers) were even worse. Thirteen of twenty held good posts before 1945. Ludger Westrick headed Germany's biggest aluminum company, crucial in making warplanes. Over 75 percent of his "employees" were POWs or forced laborers, including older women and children of thirteen. Nazi big-shot Hermann Goering made him a "War Economy Leader." Westrick became Globke's successor as head of the Chancellery.

Karl Friedrich Vialon had been in charge of registering the clothing, valuables, furniture, and other property of 120,000 Jews in the ghettos of Riga and Belorussia. Despite evidence sent by GDR authorities, nothing came of the trials on his complicity. In one he stated: "I deny emphatically that I had any knowledge about the extermination of Jews." I wondered how many of those killed in Riga were my relatives, less lucky than my grandparents who had escaped earlier pogroms and emigrated.

Challenged on such appointments, Adenauer made a famous, all too apt reply: "It's time we ended all this snooping around for Nazis; you can be sure that if we once get started nobody can tell where it will end." But I, for *Democratic German Report*, kept snooping around.

A dramatic episode involved Erhard's successor, Chancellor Kurt Georg Kiesinger. After joining the Nazi Party when Hitler took over, faithful to the end in the Radio Department of the Foreign Ministry and as liaison man with Goebbels's Propaganda Ministry, he was soon "de-Nazified" and reached the top in 1966 in a coalition with the Social Democrats of Vice-Chancellor Willy Brandt.

Beate Klarsfeld, as an au pair in Paris, married a Jewish Frenchman whose father was murdered during the Occupation. He told her things she had never heard about in her West German school. Together, they began exposing powerful ex-Nazis. Just before the thirtieth anniversary of the mass attacks on Jews that the Nazis called Kristallnacht, she used a journalist pass at a congress of the Christian Democratic Union, climbed onto the podium and gave Chancellor Kiesinger a resounding slap in the face, shouting "Nazi, Nazi!" and adding: "In the name of millions of victims who died in World War Two." She was sentenced to a year in prison but not jailed; the event was simply too embarrassing. A year later Kiesinger lost a tight race and stepped down.

SO WHAT DID the past of GDR government big shots look like?

Minister-President Otto Grotewohl, once a leading Social Democrat, was twice arrested by the Nazis and blacklisted from his profession. Construction Minister Ernst Scholz, forced to flee Germany in 1937, joined the International Brigade in Spain and, escaping from internment in France, became a machine-gunner with the Resistance as a member of "Free Germany in the West." This won him honorary citizenship in the town of d'Ivry-sur-Seine, which he helped liberate.

Grete Kuckhoff was a friend of Mildred Harnack, an American anti-Nazi in Berlin. The two women and their husbands became leaders of an underground group famous under its Gestapo nickname as "Rote Kapelle" (Red Orchestra). Caught by the Nazis in 1943, three were guillotined. She, too, was condemned to die, but the sentence was changed to ten years in prison. After liberation, she helped build a new financial system and became first president of the GDR state bank.

Hilde Benjamin, from a well-to-do family (an exception), had been a lawyer defending people victimized during the Depression years. She married a "poor people's doctor," a Jewish Communist who was killed in 1942 in Mauthausen concentration camp. (His brother, the famous philosopher and literary critic Walter Benjamin, took his life to escape the Nazis.) She was barred from her practice and her son was rejected by the university. In the GDR, she became a top jurist and in 1953 Minister of Justice. West German media attacked her relentlessly as a brutal hardliner, calling her "Bloody Hilde." Few if any mentioned her past travails and losses.

Most powerful in the GDR (if we postpone questions on the role of the USSR) was the Politburo, the highest body in the dominant Socialist Unity Party, or SED, often called the Communist Party out-side the GDR, thus oversimplifying the complex question of the 1946 fusion of East German Communists and Social Democrats. Its head, Walter Ulbricht, had organized Communist resistance to the Nazis from Prague, Paris, then Moscow. His successor, Erich Honecker, who pushed him out in 1971, had been imprisoned in a Nazi penitentiary from 1935 to 1945. Horst Sindermann spent twelve years behind bars. Hermann Axen, responsible for foreign affairs, barely survived Auschwitz and Buchenwald. Albert Norden, also Jewish (his father, a rabbi, was killed in Theresienstadt), co-authored a famous Brown Book in 1933 in Paris, exposing the Nazis during the Reichstag fire trial, and was active as an exile in the United States. Heinrich Rau, Alfred Neumann, and Kurt Hager were volunteers in Spain, as was Heinz Hoffmann, who became defense minister and commander of the army.

15—Men in Uniform

After the war, German armies were not supposed to exist ever again. But this clear decision by the victorious powers was soon muddied, then derailed by the Cold War, as each side blamed the other for steps largely planned behind tightly closed doors in Washington and Moscow.

Konrad Adenauer was more than eager to please U.S. Occupation Force boss John J. McCloy by rebuilding a strong military. The reward: a speedy grant of sovereignty to his gestating republic and the easing of sentences against Hitler's bloody generals. Their onetime buddies and most media demanded amnesty for all comrades-in-arms still imprisoned or due to be hanged for their mass murder sprees; otherwise they would refuse to cooperate. In most cases, they were successful.

By March 1949 Adenauer requested NATO membership for West Germany, and in October 1950 ten ex-officers met secretly to kick things off. Top dog was Adolf Heusinger. In 1923, he had called Hitler "the man sent by God to lead the Germans. . . ." As Operations Department chief in the Wehrmacht he helped plan strategy for nearly every war front, meeting with Hitler 600–700 times and so close, literally, that the bomb that almost killed Der Führer on July 20, 1944, also wounded him. Hitler's suspicions of nearly every top officer meant house arrest for Heusinger; he was freed after three months but this sufficed later as his anti-Nazi alibi. After working with the Organisation Gehlen until 1950, he became Adenauer's main military adviser.

Another secret planner with a similar alibi, Hans Speidel, had been chief of staff in Occupied France and signed orders to deport Communists and Jews to the death camps. A third man had been commander at the bloody battle of Monte Cassino, a fourth had commanded tank units in the invasions of Poland, Yugoslavia, and Russia, then become supreme commander in Italy. They soon agreed to form new armed forces, the Bundeswehr, and to join NATO.

The new commanders with golden epaulet stars and access to ever more murderous weapons were quite a bunch. The first Inspector General—top boss—was that same Adolf Heusinger who blessed Hitler's arrival on earth. He had coordinated the suppression of anti-Nazi partisans and sent out orders to all units on the Eastern Front: "Troops are entitled and obliged to use every method in the fight, including measures against women and children. Any form of reluctance would be a crime against the German people." Such methods, he admitted at the Nuremberg trials, provided an opportunity for the "systematic diminishing of the Slavic and Jewish populations."

But Bonn insisted: "General Heusinger has a stainless past and personality." Here, from Greece, is one out of many samples of his stainlessness: "Operation Kalavrita continued without contact with the enemy. As reprisal measure 9 villages were destroyed, 142 male inhabitants shot. (signed) Heusinger," December 1943. (Documents of American Prosecution for Nuremberg trial, Case 7, Vol. 8, 1948.)

After his term as Inspector General and after receiving the Grand Order of Merit with Star and Sash, Heusinger became chairman of NATO's Permanent Military Committee in Washington. His successor was Friedrich Foertsch, convicted in the USSR for destroying the ancient cities of Pskov, Pushkin, Novgorod, and parts of Leningrad but released to West Germany in 1955 at the request of Adenauer. Within a year he was a Major General, then Bundeswehr boss.

His follower, Heinz Trettner, had been in the Legion Condor sent to help overthrow Spain's elected government and was squadron captain of the unit that blasted the Basque town of Guernica, raining bombs on civilians for four hours in a rehearsal for the world war and inspiring Picasso's *Guernica*, one of the greatest antiwar paintings of all time.

The last Wehrmacht vet in this job, Ulrich de Maizière, had been too young to make it to general but, as a General Staff member in the Reich Chancellery, he was praised by Hitler, who "admired his precise manner of expression" in his reports. He did finally reach the top—in 1967.

All but one top Bundeswehr officer had been a wartime general, admiral, or colonel in the Nazis' Wehrmacht; three hundred had been officers in the Waffen-SS, condemned as a war criminal organization at the Nuremberg trials. When confronted with his re-polishing of pre-1945 brass, Adenauer responded tartly: "There has been no breach in the honor of the former German Wehrmacht. . . . No one may reproach the career soldiers on account of their earlier activities." And, he quipped, "NATO would not accept any 18-year-old generals." (Gunther Latsch und Klaus Wiegrefe,"Einsatz im Machtspiel," *Der Spiegel,* November 12, 2001.)

WHAT ABOUT THE GDR? After the Korean War began in 1950 and the West rejected Stalin's proposal of a united, democratic, and neutral

Germany in 1952, the GDR saw to building its own armed forces and set up a "barracked" police force (Kasernierte Volkspolizei), an early step in that direction. In May 1955, the Western Bundeswehr was established and the Federal Republic joined NATO; five days later the Warsaw Pact was formed in the Eastern Bloc, with the GDR as member, and eight months later the National People's Army (NVA) was founded in the East. Compulsory military service began in West Germany in July 1956; the GDR waited for that until 1961 when the building of the Berlin Wall hindered draft dodging.

In West Germany, four hundred top former officers took command. But where could the East's NVA find experienced officers? It, too, could not "accept 18-year-old generals." Those men, mostly Communists, who had fought in Spain, the resistance, or in an Allied army were usually in the ranks, firing a machine gun or driving a vehicle. About forty veterans of the International Brigades with higher levels of experience had already been scattered to build up a Nazi-free police force, transportation and border controls, and an "intelligence" structure, later known as the Stasi. The scarcity of experienced military men explains why the GDR resorted to using trained Wehrmacht officers.

Although it was a pity this was found necessary, it was hardly the same as in West Germany. Only nine former generals were taken on in the GDR armed forces; all nine, while prisoners in the Soviet Union, had rejected allegiance to Hitler, defying powerful peer pressure from fellow officers and repercussions against their families in Germany. They had joined the anti-fascist Association of German Officers, with about a hundred members, or the far larger National Committee for a Free Germany, founded near Moscow in July 1943 for all ranks, with an executive committee of twenty-eight POWs and ten exiled Communists, headed by a captured major, a lieutenant, and the popular poet Erich Weinert. It is never easy to see into people's souls and judge motivations and beliefs; many had been shaken in their faith in Hitler after he ordered their abandonment at Stalingrad or after the Wehrmacht's decisive defeat in the giant Battle of Kursk. Perhaps some simply hoped for earlier release. But all had taken the crucial step of rejecting the Nazis. If they agreed to help build up armed forces in the

GDR and had the experience so rare among anti-Nazi resistance survivors, they were accepted.

Three of the nine former Wehrmacht generals were briefly in the GDR's ruling command structure. One, after his capture, had actively engaged in teaching at an anti-fascist school to win over German prisoners of war. Another had become a Communist, taken part in fighting at the front, and was condemned to death in absentia by a Nazi court. The third had been a technician. Next to these three, commanding the new National People's Army, were six men who had not served as Wehrmacht officers. Top man and later defense minister Heinz Hoffmann had been active in the anti-Nazi underground and was wounded fighting Franco. Friedrich Dickel had also fought in Spain. Walter Verner, an admiral, was active in the Danish resistance. Heinz Kessler, sent as a soldier to the USSR, had immediately deserted and helped found the National Committee for a Free Germany. Kurt Wagner was arrested by the Nazis in 1935 and kept in prison till the end of the war.

Within a year it was decided that the former Wehrmacht generals were no longer needed and should be retired as soon as possible; the last was pensioned off in February 1957.

Aside from those nine generals, 400 to 500 mostly junior officers and noncoms were also taken on, recruited among POWs who had volunteered to attend anti-fascist schools. They too were eased out as soon as possible, but unfortunately their influence on training practices could not be eliminated. Even worse, two extremely bad decisions were made, intended, it was explained, to avoid any resemblance to either Soviet soldiers or American troops, but rather to harken back to older military traditions considered progressive, basically the fight to free Prussia from Napoleon's occupation. Thus a new uniform was designed that looked far too much like that worn by the Wehrmacht. Worse yet, a military tradition, allegedly far older than Hitler and used in many other countries' armies but horribly weighted in Germany, was also adopted, at least for ceremonial marches: the high-kicking goose-step. The inevitable result: constant attempts to label the People's Army as neo-Nazi, as opposed to the democratic nature of the Bundeswehr.

Blindly stupid as these two decisions were, a look in depth at the two armies showed weightier differences, not only in the 9-to-400 ratio and very brief careers of old Wehrmacht generals in the East but in a fateful concept, doggedly maintained in the West: "We soldiers simply served our nation patriotically, only the SS committed atrocities" or "Hitler was to blame, not us." General Heusinger's words to his officers were clear: "Let us stick to the old principles, the principles we used to have." Only in the past few years has this line been dropped, at least officially.

The difference was visible in the naming of army camps (*Kaserne*), which were, in West Germany, "reminders of valiant traditions." Here are some of the heroes they chose to honor:

- Maj. Gen. Eduard Dietl, one of the first officers to join the Nazi Party in 1921, stated (before a fatal plane crash), "We are engaged in a battle of destiny for the German people, while the Jews of the whole world have united to destroy Germany and Europe. . . . War is the relentless purifier of destiny. I declare solemnly: I believe in the Führer!" The *Kaserne* was named after him as late as 1964 and not renamed until 1995, and even then against the will of his war veteran admirers.
- Gen. Ludwig Kübler fought partisans in Yugoslavia and was condemned to death in absentia by a Yugoslav court for his atrocities. Quote: "Terror against terror . . . in war everything is proper and justified if it leads to success."
- Col. Helmut Lent shot down 110 planes and received the highest Nazi decoration. Air Force boss Hermann Goering called him "an enthusiastic soldier, a hard and tough fighter and shining hero . . . not only a soldier but a passionate supporter of our National Socialist worldview."
- Col. Werner Mölders fought for Franco as a Condor Legion pilot and, before dying in a crash, shot down more Allied planes than any other pilot. Bonn also named a fighter squadron after him.

About a quarter of the four hundred Bundeswehr camps were named for such "heroes" of the First or Second World War. Only eleven had opposed Hitler, usually in the plot of July 20, 1944. After years-long efforts by the Green Party's Petra Kelly, all Condor Legion names were finally dropped in 2005, despite bitter resistance from former Inspector General Trettner, who had helped command it. Many Nazi names were altered in 2012 and 2013, perhaps under pressure from new Eastern European allies. But some still stubbornly bear the names of military men who fought for Hitler to the end.

THE NAMES OF the 173 GDR army bases were completely different. Nine derived from the Peasants' War of 1525, sixty from anti-war activists before 1933, and 108 had been anti-fascist resistance fighters. Not one was a First or Second World War hero. Here is a sampling:

- Thomas Müntzer, the preacher who led poor peasants and early members of the working class against the feudal lords until he was defeated and beheaded in 1525.
- Robert Uhrig, an active Communist and anti-Nazi, led a large underground group in Berlin factories with ties to anti-fascist groups in Copenhagen, Prague, and Amsterdam. Arrested with two hundred others in 1942, he was sent to Sachsenhausen and beheaded in August 1944.
- Hugo Eberlein, a top Communist leader, worked in exile in France to unite Communists, Social Democrats, and other anti-fascists against Hitler. He was able to escape capture there and flee to the USSR, only to get caught up in the Stalin-era purges. Arrested and deported to a camp in the far north in 1939, he was executed in 1941. Taking his name, I think, was an honorable decision.
- Anton Saefkow, arrested in April 1933, was kept in Nazi prisons and camps until July 1939. After his release, he began organizing again and helped create the largest underground organization, with connections to the group planning Hitler's assassination. The Gestapo was able to break it up; it arrested Saefkow and beheaded him. He ended his last letter to his wife Änne with a sentiment which became basic for many people in the later GDR who tried to keep his memory alive—including his peace-activist and historian daughter:

In this final letter I want to thank you, my comrade, for all the great-
ness and beauty you gave me in our life together. . . . Not until today
did these lines and thoughts of you bring my first tears since the sen-
tencing. Until now my mind helped me withstand thoughts of the
pain which will tear me apart. As you know, I am of a fighting nature
and will die courageously. I wanted nothing but to achieve goodness
in the world.

Such names of GDR bases, many such names, were dropped in a
single day after unification in 1990.

16—A Journalistic Episode

Here is a rare example of justice finally prevailing in West Germany,
this time in the field of journalism.

An extremely popular Sunday TV program, similar to *Meet the
Press*, featured Werner Höfer and guest journalists. Viewed by millions, also in East Germany, many like me found it interesting, even
snappy, despite Höfer's smart-alec, supercilious tone. I did not like his
decidedly right-leaning views, but others evidently did; after seventeen
years Höfer got a Federal Cross of Merit and directorships of two West
German state-owned TV channels.

Few knew that in 1962 a GDR Politburo member, Albert Norden,
had raised questions about Höfer's past. Norden, once a refugee in
New York, whose father, a rabbi, had been killed at Theresienstadt,
was an expert on old Nazis. As usual, the Western media ignored all
"propaganda from East Berlin."

But an old classmate and friend of the victim never gave up his fight
to unmask Höfer, and his story was finally published by *Der Spiegel* in
1987. It seems that Höfer had written diligently for the worst of the Nazi
press. Of course, whole squads of leading West German journalists had
done the same. But a special tragedy was involved here. In September
1943 one of Germany's best young pianists, Karlrobert Kreiten, age
twenty-seven, had privately uttered his fears that Germany's war,

"already doomed to defeat, . . . would lead to the total downfall of Germany and its culture."

A visiting neighbor reported his remarks, the Gestapo cops were informed, he was sentenced, and, despite pleas by leading musicians, executed by hanging. Star columnist Werner Höfer then wrote an op-ed article not only justifying but praising the hanging of an artist "who sowed not faith but doubt, not confidence but libel, not morale but desperation," adding that "no one today can feel sympathy and, in the case of an artist who does wrong, call for more forgiveness than for any normal wrongdoer." His words were a clear threat to all other doubters.

In 1987, Höfer squirmed and lied, claiming the newspaper had altered his words. But there it was in black and white, and this top TV journalist finally had to quit in disgrace after seventeen self-righteous years. Two questions remained: Had he ever changed his views? And how many other top journalists, without such an episode or persevering accuser, remained on the job? (Christian Felchow, "Der Fall Werner Höfer," *Spiegel Online*, June 2, 2010.)

17—Powers Behind the Throne

One group has too frequently been ignored in discussions of postwar Germany. As early as the First World War it was Big Business that bore the main guilt for aggression, aggrandizement, "Big Bertha" artillery monsters, and poison gas. The November Revolution ended its war in 1918 and raised hopes for a peaceful, even socialist Germany, but it was soon able to smash such hopes and renew its interrupted drive to conquer Europe and regain its former colonies. A decade later, when millions of angry, often desperate, Great Depression victims threatened such plans, it turned to a brutal movement and a leader with a mesmerizing charisma, financing their upward climb, helping them win power, and joining in their monstrous war of conquest.

Herbert Quandt, the BMW boss, said: "Why did Hitler gain power? Because, I can say frankly, he declared war on Communism in Germany, over and over and in an impressive and robust manner." (C. H. Beck,

Der Aufstieg der Quandts: Eine deutsche Unternehmerdynastie,
Munich: Joachim Scholtyseck, 2011.)

The banker Baron Kurt von Schroeder made it even clearer in 1947
at the War Crimes Court in Nuremberg: "The business world . . .
wanted to see a strong Führer gain power in Germany, one who could
form a government that would stay in power a long time. . . . A common
interest of the economy lay in its fear of Bolshevism and the hope that
the National Socialists, once in power, would establish an enduring
political and economic foundation for Germany." (Eberhard Czichon,
Wer verhalf Hitler zur Macht?, Cologne: Pahl Rugenstein, 1967, 78.)

Maybe I should explain that the name National Socialism given
his movement by Hitler did not have the slightest connection with
the socialism anyone else meant. The word was simply stolen to lure
people who blamed war profiteers and other capitalists for the mass
murder of the First World War and wanted big changes. That word
national aimed, all too successfully, at twisting people's anger and
wounded national pride after military defeat and humiliation by the
victorious powers at Versailles, toward chauvinism and revenge. The
name was unofficially shortened to the abbreviated "Nazi."

Emblematic for the Nazi-Big Business alliance is the Krupp corporation. Founded in 1811, it got rich making wheel rims for the
U.S. railroad boom in the 1870s, and it also made weapons for every
German war since 1864. The Hitler regime rewarded Krupp's support: over 280,000 slave laborers toiled in its eighty-one factories;
70,000 died miserably. One Krupp plant was next to Auschwitz, saving
"transport" costs for those no longer able to toil. The minimum working age toward war's end was twelve years.

A major early Nazi supporter was the Thyssen family, steel producers, which, despite personal differences with Hitler, was heavily
laden with guilt from start to finish. On March 24, 1945, at its family
palace in Austria, daughter Margareta Thyssen held a party for Nazi
bigwigs. She ordered up 180 Hungarian Jews, too sick and exhausted
to continue digging defenses against the approaching Red Army, and
handed weapons to fifteen guests. "The Jews were forced to undress
completely and then try to flee from the drunken guests who, after

murdering them, returned to the palace for drinking and dancing till morning." The hostess fled to Switzerland, became a highly successful racehorse breeder, and was never tried. Two key witnesses were mysteriously murdered. (David R. L. Litchfield, "The Killer Countess," *Independent*, London, October 7, 2007.)

The giant I.G. Farben chemical trust (Industrial Company Dyes) produced poison gas for the First World War, became Europe's richest trust, divvied up world markets with DuPont and Standard Oil, was a major financier of Hitler, and built the Monowitz annex to Auschwitz to produce Zyklon Two for the gas chambers where all were sent who could no longer work.

At a U.S. Military trial in 1947–48, ten I. G. Farben bosses were acquitted; thirteen got brief sentences of one to eight years but were all free by 1952 and soon back on top of the pile. Heinrich Bütefish, a Nazi Party man and SS lieutenant-colonel, was awarded a War Merit Cross with Knight's Cross by Hitler for managing fuel production at Auschwitz-Monowitz. After a brief jail term, he climbed so high that President Heinrich Lübke awarded him a Distinguished Service Cross of Merit in 1964. But a West Berlin researcher and a top GDR expert uncovered his Auschwitz past, which the authorities "had not known about," forcing President Heinrich Lübke, who himself helped build barracks for slave laborers at the V-1 and V-2 rocket base, to ask Bütefisch to please return the fancy cross.

His former colleague, Fritz ter Meer, head of the Auschwitz chemicals department, stated in his trial that "no particular harm was done to the prisoners because they would have been killed anyway." Amnestied in 1950, he was soon chairman of the board at the aspirin company Bayer, one of I. G. Farben's giant daughters. Fritz ter Meer too was offered the Merit Cross but was smart enough to bow out before yet another scandal could occur. Bayer reached third place worldwide in chemical sales, with another I. G. Farben daughter, BASF, in first place. After merging with Monsanto, Bayer will probably overtake BASF.

Most blatant was the coal and steel empire of Friedrich Flick, a major donor to the Nazis, who made 3 billion marks by using 40,000 to 60,000 forced laborers and camp inmates, often toiling half-naked in icy snow, working with chemical poisons without gloves, goggles, or proper gear for little food, no beds, and many beatings. Over 10,000 died. Sentenced to seven years in a high-comfort prison but pardoned in 1950, Flick soon controlled a hundred companies worth 8 billion marks, among them Daimler-Benz, Dynamit Nobel, and Krauss-Maffei (which made Leopard tanks). As Germany's richest man, he received, and kept, the Federal Grand Order of Merit with Cross and Sash.

In what became the "Flick Affair," his son in 1983 sold his holdings in Daimler-Benz and other giants to Deutsche Bank but somehow neglected to pay almost a billion marks in taxes before absconding to the family's huge estate in low-tax Austria. To cover up this incredible rip-off, the firm bribed top German parties and politicians with sums ranging from 30,000 to 565,000 marks for Bavarian boss Franz Josef Strauss, ex-president Walter Scheel, a few cabinet ministers, and Helmut Kohl, later to become chancellor. In the end, two cabinet ministers were sentenced to negligible fines.

Krupp and Thyssen merged in 1999. Every day I see their logo in my elevator and on escalators in Berlin's train stations, but I am aware that not all their products are so harmlessly uplifting. Their shipyards, for example, are international leaders in producing submarines.

Behind all of them, influencing every aspect of financial and political life, are institutions like Allianz insurance, the Commerzbank and, on the highest rung, as criminally guilty as any and a true world power, Deutsche Bank.

On July 10, 1945, a U.S. Senate Subcommittee headed by Harley Kilgore (D-WV.) reported:

> Hitler and the Nazis were latecomers in these preparations. It was the cartels and monopoly powers—the leaders of the coal, iron and steel, chemicals and armament combines—who at first secretly and then openly supported Hitler in order to accelerate their ruthless plans for world conquest . . . Your Subcommittee finds that the German economy was developed as a war economy, and that its vast industrial potential remains largely undamaged by the war: that Germany has a worldwide network—including even the United States—of

commercial relationships and economic, political espionage out-
posts which she could mobilize for another war; that the leading
German industrialists are not only as responsible for war crimes
as the German General Staff and the Nazi Party, but that they were
among the earliest and most active supporters of the Nazis, whom
they used to accelerate their plans for world conquest, and that these
industrialists remain the principal custodians of Germany's plans for
renewed aggression. (U.S. Senate, Report by Kilgore Subcommittee
on War Mobilization, November 22, 1946.)

These ugly, blood-besmirched characters, still very much alive when
I worked in East Berlin, helped shape my picture of West Germany,
the traditions it built upon, and the powers behind its politicians, from
Bonn to Munich and West Berlin. A share of them had not been active
Nazis—or Nazis at all, especially on the Social Democratic side of the
aisle. But only a very few in the Bundestag or state legislatures had
been active anti-fascists; the small Communist Party delegation, almost
all of whose members were survivors of Nazi camps and prisons, was
outlawed in 1956.

Of course, my heart went out to all the good people in West Germany
who were trying courageously to change the direction. In McCarthy-
era America I had learned how difficult resistance could be, and in West
Germany, with the East-West dividing line so close, it was undoubtedly
worse. Had I somehow landed in the Federal Republic, I would have
joined their resistance. But I had not.

18—Defying Stacked Deck

I happened to land in a new republic where the factories, mines, and
landed estates of those mighty guilt-ridden men had become public
property and a barrier against their powerful rule as job-givers and
decision makers. Their refusal to accept these losses in this divided
country and city and their active hatred of the GDR demanded a
choice. While socialism and capitalism were fairly abstract issues in

the United States in the 1960s, chewed over in many theoretical variations, here, in my new home, the dividing line was far sharper, with
echoes of fateful events in 1919, 1933, 1938, 1939, and 1945 resounding in almost every street we trod. "Which side are you on?" was not
just a good union song but an almost daily decision. Until the Wall was
built in August 1961, that other side was only one stop away on the
subway, one step away on unchecked street borders. Many sought to
evade a choice in some agreeable, unpolitical niche. But for a "political
animal" like myself, this was never an option. And how in hell could I
ever accept the rule of an Adenauer, Globke, Krupp, or Thyssen?

Yet how should I look upon this alternative Germany? How was it
developing? What doubts and burning problems were present?

From the start, all cards were stacked against little East Germany.
About the size of Ohio or Virginia, far smaller than the three zones
forming the Federal Republic, close to California in size, it had neither the iron and steel industry of its Ruhr Valley nor endless tons
of high-quality coal under its surface, but had to start off with one
steel plant, hardly any natural resources except potassium salt mines,
a little copper, and huge amounts of low-quality, damp, stinky lignite coal, its weak basis for electricity, fuel, and chemicals. Yet it was
saddled with almost 95 percent of reparation costs. France, Britain,
and the Benelux countries soon absolved West Germany from most
payments. But Poland and the USSR, immensely demolished, desperately needed their share of reparations, which came almost
exclusively from the Soviet-occupied zone. Whole factory complexes,
machinery, rail tracks, and a good share of emerging new production
were removed. To make matters worse, most industries in the East,
like machine tools or textiles, depended on raw materials from West
Germany, supplied in varying quantities or not supplied, depending
on how much pressure Bonn wished to exert in a changing political situation. Meanwhile, after 1947, West Germany was getting big
investments through the Marshall Plan, a key factor in its "economic
miracle."

There was another serious drawback. Large numbers of engineering
and managerial personnel, those most strongly infected with the Nazi

bacillus and fearful of punishment under Soviet occupation or left-wing rule, and hating nationalization with its ousting of their beloved industry leaders, disappeared westward, before the Red Army arrived if possible but also, in later years, often at crucial moments. Many took plans, patents, and documents with them plus their know-how on running factories. Their change of address involved no new language to learn and no risk. Their former employers, soon an integral part of the "economic miracle," were glad to offer them far higher pay than in the poorer, more egalitarian East. The young GDR economy thus faced not only wreckage, reparations (until 1953), and a cutoff from former resources but also had to rely on the thin ranks of engineers and managers willing to remain plus a new generation being trained in colleges that lacked professors and researchers who, having eagerly supported the Nazis, also had moved westward. Such luring of experts, including newly trained ones, was assiduously maintained through the years, even after the Wall made it far more difficult to "disappear." A former manager of a big GDR shipyard told me how half of his pre-1961 class of skilled machinist apprentices were regularly lured away by West German companies, but only after they had completed their expensive training. That meant big losses in the East and big savings in West German costs.

And yet, despite myriad difficulties and highly skeptical, even cynical sectors of the population, the economy had started up again, and here and there with genuine, new enthusiasm.

19—Volunteers to Cool a Steel Mill

In the first years after war's end, East Germany had to rely fully for its urgent reconstruction on the one single iron and steel plant with an indispensable rolling mill. In this Max-Hütte south of Weimar, named for one-time Bavarian King Maximilian and part of Friedrich Flick's immense empire, a thousand forced laborers toiled for military production. Twenty-six of their bodies, four of them girls, were found at one site after the war, fettered and shot in the head; another fifteen, also murdered, were found in a mass grave. Flick's title was annulled in June 1946. East Germany and the USSR shared ownership until July 1948 when it was nationalized, becoming a "people's owned enterprise," a VEB.

At this one available steel plant a fourth blast furnace was desperately needed. That required more cooling water; the one possible source, the river Saale, was six kilometers away—a craggy, hilly six kilometers. In 1949, there was little free manpower in this distant corner, so the Free German Youth organization (FDJ) called for volunteers for three summer months, with a slogan: "Max needs water!" Mostly college students responded, 2,700 of them, male and female. They moved into converted freight cars, received boots and padded jackets, and were soon loading or unloading sand and cement or hacking at the hard earth with pick and shovel. Some high school seniors joined up; one group voted at its new school Party group to resist their principal's objections, so fifteen boys and two girls moved in with college students from the philosophy, social science, and pharmacy departments, braving the heavy labor and primitive conditions but enjoying a cooperative spirit they never forgot. When the job was completed within the ninety-day plan, the volunteers celebrated with a big party featuring the GDR's best dance orchestra. Some of those volunteers joined in a nostalgic reunion party in 2014 to mark the job's 65th anniversary.

In 1955, the big plant, with a peak of 7,000 employees, opened its own "cultural palace," with fancy Greek columns outside and, inside, a theater with 700 seats, another with 200, a dance hall, rehearsal rooms, a library, meeting rooms, a restaurant, and a café. This soon became typical for large plants, but after 1990, like nearly all such palaces, it was closed down. The plant was purchased in 1992 by a Luxembourg company. In 2006, the remaining 650 employees worked for an Indian owner, in 2007 a Spanish group, and in 2012 a Brazilian corporation. Friedrich Flick, quickly amnestied after a postwar conviction, had become the richest, most powerful man in West Germany and was buried with the highest honors in 1972.

20—Rocks for Our Rostock

Here is another example from the early years on my side of the German dividing line.

Before the war, what was now East Germany had 200 miles of Baltic seacoast but few ports. Compared with Hamburg or Bremerhaven in the west, even its largest seaport, Rostock, was insignificant. Its five or six puny shipyards were almost completely destroyed. One yacht shipyard, where many of the city's allotment of 14,000 forced laborers and war prisoners and 2,000 concentration camp inmates had toiled, was wrecked by heavy bombing. The Kröger brothers who owned it, with close ties to the Nazi apparatus and the Gestapo, made a quick run for the West at war's end.

In the first months of Soviet occupation, some of the remains were demolished or removed as compensation. But by the end of 1945 it was realized how useful the shipyard might be and thus the first forty-eight workers began repairing Soviet fish cutters. Ownership was transferred to the city of Rostock. But in June 1946 voters in Saxony, East Germany's major industrial province, voted, with a majority of 77.56 percent, to dispossess war criminals and large-scale landowners. Their decision was extended to all of East Germany, and the shipyard was nationalized, becoming a "people's owned enterprise" (VEB) producing new cutters for the USSR. When one Kröger brother returned to reclaim the enterprise, a vote was taken in the shipyard. One man voted to give it back, fourteen abstained; 145 voted against him.

By 1953 all Soviet reparation claims had been fulfilled and total earnings now went to the GDR. A giant cable crane structure was erected, visible for miles around, which permitted construction of 10,000-ton ships. But a big problem emerged: Rostock's harbor wasn't deep enough. Weighty exports and imports had to be transferred at great cost to Polish Szczecin or West German Hamburg. Enlarging the harbor required a long protective breakwater, built quickly, if possible, so as not to lose another costly year.

In April 1957, an appeal for helpers and for stones brought in over

2,000 volunteer workers to join in hammering piles into the muddy
bottom and to place 50,000 tons of rocks that had been collected all
over the country "For Our Rostock." Within three months, new quays,
an office building, storage halls, motor repair works, and a fish cannery
finally provided the GDR with a modern deep-sea port connected with
all the world. Before long the shipyard was one of the largest and most
modern in Europe, busy making ships for the new GDR merchant
marine and for export, especially to the USSR and the Eastern Bloc
but also to neutral countries like Indonesia. Fifteen ships a year were
exported by 1971, including the first big container ships. (*DGR*, May
13, 1960, 75.)

21—Changing the Countryside

Conflicts and differences under the surface were never absent in the
ferment of GDR cities; for a few years they were far sharper in the
countryside. They began in the first postwar year in connection with
dividing up the landowners' estates, as I learned from my father-in-
law in my wife's village. He was a carpenter, and before Hitler a union
man, a Social Democrat. He was also a member of a Slavic minority
nationality in that region, the Sorbs, who had been oppressed for centuries, but especially by Hitler, and were seen as allies by the Soviets.
All street signs and shop or office signs were bilingual. His rural village,
even before the Nazis took power, had probably never known a single
Communist and not many Social Democrats either, which may explain
why the Occupation officers appointed him provisional mayor. Most
of the land confiscated from the owner (a titled lower-ranking prin-
cess who moved west) was split into new farms averaging twelve to fifty
acres. Non-farming village people like my father-in-law also received
small plots, just enough for urgently needed vegetables and, after a few
years, a number of small farm animals, maybe one hog, a nanny goat,
a ewe with lambs, some geese, chickens, and rabbits. For a majority,
especially in the cities but also for those rural mayors who remained
honest, the first years were extremely cold and hungry. Renate recalled

her family's luck, during a meager, hungry Christmastide, when her father found a rabbit frozen in the snow.

The mayor had no easy job, for on one hand the Soviets demanded full quotas from the farmers to feed hungry people in the cities, while relatively prosperous farmers wanted to sell as much as possible privately, at much higher, illegal, prices. Another crucial question, also involving the mayor and the Soviet staff, was determining who in the village had been a vicious brutal Nazi and who had simply gone along, as opportunists, doing little or no harm to others. All such matters made life for the mayor—and the Soviets—a series of tightrope acts.

After 1952, when the decision was made to move toward socialism, the first Agricultural Production Cooperatives (LPG) farms were started up, distinguished from Soviet "collective farms" because the members pooled land, farm buildings, and eventually herds but maintained ownership rights to the amount of acreage they had contributed. The growth of the LPGs was very slow; successful farmers tended to stay private whereas the cooperatives attracted less experienced or less industrious farmers, which meant that many of them failed to prosper. By 1960 at most a third had joined up. In that year the national leaders decided to force a solution to the problem of uncertain harvests and resulting shortages. It exerted strong, sometimes extreme pressure on all farmers to join the LPGs, including making it difficult for reluctant private farmers to get credit, charging them higher prices when they rented farm equipment, and even setting up loudspeakers near the homes of especially recalcitrant farmers. Some absconded westward. Others gnashed their teeth and joined.

And some were quite willing, like a woman I spoke to, a leader in starting an LPG in her village. She compared the effort with a horse and a repainted stable door. "It's new for him and he resists at first." She also used a metaphor about a cow giving birth: "Sometimes it's necessary to grab the emerging calf by the legs and give it a helping pull."

"And now," she told me, "as a member of a cooperative I can count on regular hours when I do farm work, and health and pensions are now covered. I get a regular paid vacation; for the first time since my honeymoon we can now visit the seaside—only 30 kilometers from here. I have a seat in the farm council where we make decisions and vote for the chair, a secretary and a treasurer."

At first, the going was not easy, and farm production slumped, worsened by two years of bad, wet weather. There were more shortages, even of Germany's staple food, potatoes, and people were not yet used to eating rice or pasta. There was a popular joke series in the Eastern Bloc in those years, resembling in its question-and-answer form the "knock, knock" jokes in the United States, but always involving "questions to Radio Yerevan" with naive biting responses. Like: "Question to Radio Yerevan: When we move past socialism to the higher goal of communism, will we still be using money?—Answer of Radio Yerevan: 'No, there won't be any of that either.'" Now there were farm-based additions: "What is the meaning of the word 'chaos'?—Sorry, Radio Yerevan does not deal with questions regarding agriculture!"

These shortages, probably a factor in the mass departure of so many people in 1961, may have been part of the reason it was found necessary to build the Berlin Wall—to save the GDR's existence.

There were also other mistakes along the way, like overstressing the cultivation of corn. And yet, perhaps surprisingly, farm families became so accustomed to the new cooperative teamwork methods that within two or three years they got to like them and produced more and more, surpluses of milk, butter, meat, and the customary fruits, vegetables, and grains. Though each member family could keep a cow and calf or pig and smaller animals, care of the herds became more hygienic, more efficient and more profitable. Farm families now had some leisure time, while the increasingly productive LPG farms had sufficient labor power for rewarding projects on the side, like horse-breeding, honey, hops, or weaving and basketry. A growing number of young farmers attended free agricultural colleges and became experts, and cooperative farmers in the GDR became an increasingly prosperous sector.

Another aspect was noteworthy. In West Germany, bad weather, the rivalry of mega-farms, and price pressure from discount chains forced many to give up their farms, less dramatically yet sadly reminiscent of John Steinbeck's great Dust Bowl Okie novel *Grapes of Wrath*. In the GDR, aside from that rough, tough year of change, 1960, purchases,

prices, and sales were guaranteed, assistance was provided when necessary, and no family was forced to give up farming against its will.

Thirty years later, after the demise of the GDR, most farmers
rejected the chance to regain their private fields and tried every way
to stay together in some legally permissible cooperative farm. It was
not made easy for them, though some old baronets and other lords got
friendly support in attempted comebacks.

22—More Defiance and More Progress

As the republic kept growing, its planned economy made it possible
to pay special attention to backward areas. Old Chancellor Otto von
Bismarck allegedly joked that "when the world goes under I want to
move to Mecklenburg because everything there happens fifty years
later." This region south of the Baltic had been the poorest and most
feudally backward in all Germany, until GDR planners altered its status
remarkably. New industries were developed based on growing supplies
of agricultural products from the new LPG farms, on shipyards like
the one described above, and other new sectors. In Eichsfelde, another
traditional poverty corner so down-and-out it was a world source of
organ-grinders and other oompah musical beggars, a large new cotton
spinning center offered thousands of job opportunities in the region,
especially to women previously cut off from almost any employment.

Big new industrial centers were constructed in many regions, north,
east, west, and south, with public transportation costing a pittance
connecting the jobs with high-rise homes. Young couples from all over
were attracted to such centers, with their clean, new nurseries, kindergartens, and schools, medical centers, cultural and sport facilities. The
supermarkets and department stores at these key project sites were also
better supplied with hard-to-get imported goods.

The concentration was on basic industries: mining, coke, iron and
steel, energy, transportation equipment, and machine tools. After a
rough start making simple plows the farm equipment industry was
developed until it could supply more and more complex machinery

for cultivating potatoes, grain, sugar beets, oilseed, and dairy products. But the concentration on basics and foodstuffs left less investment money or labor power for making consumer goods, an imbalance that gradually improved but was never able to meet demand, while too many well-designed, high-quality GDR-made goods—hair-dryers, sewing machines, vacuum cleaners—were exported to West Germany, where mail-order companies sold them at very low prices. That even included greatly desired delicacies like eel, calf's liver, and very good beer. Western wholesalers and retailers paid for these good things well below value in the hard "Western" marks or dollars so desperately needed for the import of vital raw materials—and, occasionally, limited imports of fashionable, modern goods to reduce the dissatisfaction of GDR consumers.

Yet undeniably, while always stumbling behind full-pocketed consumer demand, living standards moved upward. When we got married in 1955, I spoke to my wife about buying a refrigerator. "What for?" she asked. She had grown up without one, with a corner in the cellar and various tricks to keep foodstuffs cool. By the 1960s even villagers like her had learned what fridges and later freezers were good for. I was proud to have been quick and lucky enough to get one of the first new taller models. My consumerist pride was soon deflated, however, when my mother, on her first visit from New York, commented, "What a cute little fridge!" By the end of the decade almost every family also had at least such a "cute little fridge."

As for TV sets, their penetration, if somewhat later than in the United States or the FRG, was soon so swift that virtually every family had a set, except for those intellectuals who rejected them in favor of reading books or the like. For a while, there was a snag with color TV; most people wanted only the brand with two reception systems so they could pick up West German television. Such viewing was officially regarded as a "no-no" until well into the 1970s, but by then almost everybody watched such channels as much as they wanted. Only in two areas, around Greifswald in the northeast and Dresden in the southeast, was "West" reception technically difficult; as a result, until antennas got higher and more receptive, the latter area bore a sarcastic nickname: the "Valley of Blissful Ignorance." With most GDR viewers able to regularly watch both East and West news reports, some U.S. visitors found them most likely "the best informed people in the world."

As far as cars went, the little steel-frame, part-plastic bodied Trabants, or Trabis, were no rivals for Western brands. One Radio Yerevan joke I recall was: "Can a Trabi attain a speed of more than 110 km/h (about 68 mph)?"—The radio's answer: "It depends on how high you drop it from."

All the same, with few foreign cars available and all of them very expensive, the waiting time for a new GDR-made Trabant or a larger Wartburg was amazing, sometimes more than a decade, and a cause of plenty of anger and, as always, more jokes. In one, a wealthy American tells a friend: "You know, I was able to order this fancy German car called a Trabant. It must really be something! Just imagine, it's so sought after there's a ten-year waiting list! And when I mailed them the dollar sum they were kind enough to send me a small plastic model in advance—which actually works!"

Indeed, dollars could make a very big difference, and such gags caused as much teeth-gnashing as laughs. But used cars were easily available, often lined up on special parking lots with legible notes in each car detailing kilometer count, condition, price, and address. Oddly enough, a used car, at an unregulated bargaining price, often cost more than a new one, for which one had to wait so long but whose price, like nearly all prices, was nationally fixed. After finally getting a first new car, one could order the next one six years in advance, and with a spouse also ordering, it was possible to keep on trading old for new every three years if desired. That's how I came to own four Trabis, one after the other. Neither they nor the Wartburgs could match those glossy Western dream-cars so admired by Easterners when they zipped past, or inspected when parked at a curb by some visitor or, most frequently, envied in West German TV commercials. Renate never loved my Trabis, which were bumpy and loud, but I was happy with them; for simpletons like me they were easier to care for, requiring neither oil (which came mixed in with the gasoline at designated pumps) nor water, since the motor was air-cooled. Many East Germans grew attached to their little vehicles and took such good care of them, washing them assiduously every weekend (there were no carwash facilities as yet) that some cynics maintained that East German fathers spent more loving care on their Trabis than on their children.

Life did keep improving in the 1960s and 1970s. Though West German, American, and other media offered grim descriptions after brief, superficial visits, one leading West German journalist, Joachim Besser, no leftist, wrote surprisingly honestly about a two-week tour in 1966. Here are excerpts:

> The economy of the GDR is going through a boom period. Everywhere you go you hear about the labor shortage. Everywhere I read the "Help Wanted" placards—shop assistants, typists, garage hands, workers are sought. The phrase "economic miracle" is certainly applicable to the present state of affairs. . . .
>
> I visited Eisenhüttenstadt, with 40,000 inhabitants. There is the same picture here as in Schwedt, but here the picture is complete. The Eisenhüttenstadt combine turns out 1.5 million tons of pig iron annually. The ore comes from the Soviet Union, the coal from Poland. The new town is a fine town, a town which can be lived in. The buildings are light and friendly, there are good hotels and restaurants, a theater, cinemas and sports grounds. The shops too are good and tasteful.
>
> But . . . there is naturally a parallel expansion of the old industrial centers of Saxony. . . . Everywhere you go you see factories of a smaller size. . . . And new housing is not confined to the key points either. I saw the fascinating reconstruction work in Magdeburg, wandered through Chemnitz, today Karl-Marx-Stadt, and admired the modern form in which the center of the city is being rebuilt. Our modern town planners would be pleased to see what is being done, particularly in Chemnitz. Many of the mistakes made in West Germany have been avoided. There are no residential quarters right on the main roads, and new buildings are set well back, allowing space for the growing traffic of the future. Here it will not be necessary to tear

down the buildings again to widen the roads, as in so many West German cities. . . .

In restaurants I ate as well as in the Federal Republic, and in every case more cheaply. The menus in the luxury hotels are first-class; but I also ate in village inns, in quick-lunch restaurants, and in all cases the prices were between 10% and 30% lower than in West Germany. (Joachim Besser, *Kölner Stadtanzeiger*, December 3, 1966, trans. in *DGR*, December 23, 1966, 182–83.)

Besser goes on to describe the assortment of groceries on sale, generally good but varying from place to place, with a shortage of some items in some areas, and of oranges everywhere, but plenty of poultry, preserved foods, and, especially in the north, every variety of fish. In comparing standards with his own Federal Republic, he finds that "we are a decade ahead, but if you compare it with Poland or Czechoslovakia then it is the GDR which is well ahead."

Such improvement worried the men in Bonn. In December 1955, West Germany announced its "Hallstein Doctrine": "Formal recognition of the GDR by a state with which the Federal Republic entertains diplomatic relations would represent an unfriendly act." Tough consequences were threatened: a break in relations (except for the USSR, one of the "Occupation powers"). With West Germany economically far stronger than the GDR, the threat was effective. In 1957 Bonn broke relations with Yugoslavia after it rejected a secret bribe offer of big trade credits and recognized the GDR. Bonn broke with the new Castro government in Cuba for the same reason. But the threats worked well with Sri Lanka and newly independent Guinea, which had planned to establish relations with the GDR. When Bonn warned that all promised aid money was at stake, Guinea toed the line and quietly withdrew its diplomat from East Berlin. One side note was that recognition of West Germany required acceptance of its claims to "1937 borders," with slices of Poland and the USSR. Very few noticed that the Foreign Office official whose name was used, Walter Hallstein, had been a prestigious Hitler-era professor and member of various Nazi-front organizations, or that Wilhelm Grewe, who actually worked out the doctrine (and later became ambassador to Washington until John F. Kennedy threw him out) had been an enthusiastic Nazi Party member from 1933 until 1945.

The Hallstein Doctrine gradually became counterproductive; it cut Bonn off from Eastern Europe (except for its friend Romania) and increasingly from the Arab world which, after the Six Days War in 1967, objected to West German support for Israeli occupation of the Palestinian West Bank, East Jerusalem, and the Golan area. Arab-GDR connections grew closer and when, after a bloodless coup, a new government in Iraq decided to defy Hallstein in 1968, then-Foreign Minister Willy Brandt saw it as a warning omen and dropped the doctrine.

23—Nudity and Equality

Not only was a doctrine dropped in those days, but garments too, and by an amazing number of GDR citizens. I am referring to beach nudism, known as FKK, Freie Körperkultur, translated as Free Body Culture. After 1990 many of the West German vacationers who swarmed to the Baltic beaches of East Germany were often surprised if not greatly dismayed by the mass enjoyment of nakedness in the GDR—and they saw to it that it was strictly limited.

Nude bathing had formerly been forbidden everywhere. In the 1950s, as life improved, more and more people used vacation weeks to get away from towns and cities and the north's beautiful beaches attracted more and more. But in those days police in the East as in the West arrested those who tried to brave waves, wind, and sand without decent cover.

A large number of those enjoying the sandy beaches and Baltic waves in those early years were union vacationers. Big plants or industries like the miners or steel workers had their own hotels, but every factory or office had a supply of two-week vacation tickets to divide up among employees, most of them for an incredibly low 30 marks, including bed, all meals, evening dances, programs of music or talks about local history, and a morning half hour of beach calisthenics for those who wanted it (with loud music, even for those who did not want it). Sometimes there were only enough to grant employees such tickets every three, four, or five years, but many had luck more often, perhaps as a reward for good work or, it was whispered, thanks again to "Vitamin B" (*Beziehungen*, that is, pull). And then some employees did not apply for the tickets, preferring their own summer bungalows, camping, or visits with their families. Union hotels in the mountains or at a lake could be enjoyable, but the shores of the Baltic were always in greatest demand.

At the seaside hotels, most people used Germany's distinctive wicker "beach baskets," with seats for two, easy to turn so as to catch more or less sun or wind, with footrests, armrests for sandwiches or a book and, if your partner held up a bathrobe, a way to change modestly in and out of bathing suits (no bikinis as yet). But people were gradually getting less modest.

As times got better, and more and more, like us, had cars and tents, many did not wait for a union vacation ticket but went north on their own, either to a camping site with a fee for electricity, toilets, and showers or a "wild site" where, if they were thrown out, they could move on to another.

It was usually these wild site campers who decided that nudity was nicer. They defied the laws, first at small out-of-the-way beaches, then more and more belligerently. In the 1960s they won their way; local laws against nudity were relaxed or dropped. By 1968 a total of 50 kilometers (30 miles) were declared FKK beaches. By 1982, 40 beaches had obtained this official title, by 1988 it was 60, not just at the Baltic Sea but at lakes scattered through northern Mecklenburg. One site near the Berlin autobahn proved too distracting, hence dangerous, so a thick row of trees was planted to hide it from drivers.

Otherwise, FKK beaches were not hidden away but were open to everyone, including clothed "visitors," indistinguishable anyway since everyone was clothed when they arrived. Then they found a good spot, hollowing it out, often sticking a colorful cloth wind-shield in the sand but otherwise quite open. As the custom gained popularity, nudists grew more aggressive, expanding their section, often demarcated only

by the scribbled letters FKK on a piece of cardboard, into the neighboring "textile beach"—meaning clothed. This could lead to quarrels
with those opposed to nudity, but they usually got used to it, and some
beaches were even mixed.

Today's West German historians, almost daily occupied with deni-
grating everything about the GDR, insist that this custom was in protest
against strict authoritarian rule or at least a chance to get a small taste
of freedom for three or four weeks. Since nudity was no longer taboo,
the idea of protest carries little weight, but maybe some did see it as
freeing, which hardly differs from vacation feelings everywhere. Most
people I knew simply disliked wet bathing clothing, liked the sun, saw
no reason for shame and enjoyed the friendly spirit prevailing at every
FKK beach I knew. Our family was included, at the insistence of my
wife, who was, however, far more attractive than I, and did not suffer
like me from sunburn! Most people came as families, but even with
singles I heard of no harassing, stalking, or anything of the kind. It was
just a pleasantly free and easy way to spend a vacation. I would estimate
that about a third of all beach-goers were in the buff.

The prevailing good spirits certainly did not rule out almost inevitable jokes on the subject. Did this one (hopefully not objectionable to
anti-nudists) also contain a jab at commercialism?: An East German,
undressing at an FKK beach with his West German visitor, is amazed
at tattooed ads for a car brand on his back and a gasoline brand on his
chest. "I get paid a goodly sum for ads," the man explains. Then, looking rather lower, the East German says, "Oh, I'm so sad to see that you
have AIDS. But must you advertise that, too, and there of all places?
Who will ever pay you for that?" —"See that mixed game of volleyball
over there, with those good-looking players? Just wait till we get closer
to them and then take a look!" —"Aha! Not AIDS, but ADIDAS!"

Such jokes might be heard anywhere in Germany, but there were definite differences about sex in East and West. In the GDR there were no
porno magazines and only one magazine with a monthly artistic nude
photo; later on, there were art books of nude photography. Nor did I
ever see a single brothel or peep show; I was never once approached
by a prostitute. There were indeed amateurs who tried to befriend

foreign businessmen at trade fairs and the like. Western money was highly sought after because of luxuries it could buy in special stores labeled "Intershop," which sold Western goods for Western money (an unfortunate business—now still troubling Cuba). Was I too naive? I got around but never saw one single professional "sex worker" in all those GDR years. At the FKK beaches, expanding all along the coast and the lakeshores, I found an unself-conscious, unworried, friendly atmosphere, and not the slightest bit of commercialized sex.

In West Germany and West Berlin, brothels were legally permitted, often with neon lights inviting men to fancy "Eros Centers." In some well-known streets and neighborhoods—Hamburg's Reeperbahn was most famous—one neon marquee after another advertised sex shows inside, and insistent streetwalkers outside could become truly obnoxious. But non-commercial nudity with mixed sexes, outside the home, was almost completely restricted to saunas, and otherwise taboo.

Were there also differences in personal life? It seems so. A study made not long after German unification found that 19 percent of the mature population in West Germany was sexually active four to six times a week, but in East Germany twice as many, with 38 percent. In West Germany, 4 percent were sexually active at least once a day, in East Germany 13 percent. It was in the East that 83 percent of men and 86 percent of women said that the initiative to have sex "came from both." Seventy-eight percent of the Eastern women said that their partners had fulfilled their sexual wishes, often involving the frequency of orgasms.

In the GDR premarital sex was not frowned upon but accepted as normal. Contraceptives were free and available to sixteen-year-olds (or older), and the average age of marriage and having babies was much lower (though not at sixteen), despite the fact that over 90 percent of GDR women—but only about half of West German women—had a regular job.

Until 1958, West German law enabled a husband to nullify any job contract his wife signed, and until 1977 a wife needed her husband's permission to take a job, while he controlled any wages or salary she earned. Until 1962, a wife could not even have her own bank account. Married women did not have full status in any business dealings until

1969. And, as a side note, female teachers in Bavaria were for decades not allowed to keep their jobs if they were married.

All this contrasted strongly with the GDR, whose constitution demanded from the start absolute equal status for women in marriage and at work, with full and equal pay, as well as guarantees to enable those with families to continue employment. Advantages like paid leave when having a baby were there from the start, gradually increasing, as I describe in a later section. Availability of free nursery and kindergarten care also increased year by year until it was practically universal and, while German tradition has school classes ending at midday, GDR schools, after a warm lunch, offered afternoon activities, games, play, and time for homework, making it possible for both parents to work a full day.

It was impossible to abolish all injustices, bad habits, and minor forms of discrimination since, after all, people remained people, hence burdened with human frailties and habits. Miners or steelworkers, mostly male, still got better pay than office workers or retail sales clerks, mostly female. But within each trade pay was equal, and union contracts in every enterprise required a women's committee to check out complaints and work out plans for training and promoting female employees. This never applied at the very top of the Politburo (with only two women as "candidate members"), but it did on other levels, more and more. I recall what my American sister-in-law said to me during a family visit: "In all you've been telling us about your work and activities I've noticed how often you mention women in leadership jobs. They seem to play a much bigger role here." I had not been aware of it, certainly a good sign.

It would be wrong to minimize the problems and stress in the daily lives of single mothers and of working wives, too, balancing jobs, children, shopping, and housekeeping, while males, especially those of an older generation, were far too slow to grasp that they must bear a fair share in all the duties. Even the many benefits did not add up to a walk on Easy Street. What the GDR was able to do was provide women with a far greater feeling of equality, independence, and greater personal fulfillment.

I end this section with a last political nudist joke. One nude SED

official, meeting another, asks: "Have you read Marx?" The other
answers: "Yes, me too. Must be from the wicker beach baskets."

24—Problems Surface

In a book lent to me by John Peet, my boss, a bestseller by William L.
Shirer, I found the following:

> In November 1918 the Social Democrats, holding absolute power,
> might have quickly laid the foundation for a lasting democratic
> republic. But to have done so they would have had to suppress per-
> manently, or at least curb permanently, the forces which had propped
> up the Hohenzollern Empire and which would not loyally accept a
> democratic Germany; the feudal Junker landlords and other upper
> castes, the magnates who ruled over the great industrial cartels, the
> roving condottieri of the Free Corps, the ranking officials of the
> imperial civil service and, above all, the military caste and the mem-
> bers of the General Staff. They would have had to break up many
> of the great estates, which were wasteful and uneconomic, and the
> industrial monopolies and cartels, and clean out the bureaucracy, the
> judiciary, the police, the universities and the Army of all who would
> not loyally and honestly serve the new democratic regime. (William
> L. Shirer, *The Rise and Fall of the Third Reich*, Greenwich, CT:
> Fawcett Crest, 1959.)

Didn't these critical words, though describing the Weimar Republic
after 1918, apply all too closely to West Germany and West Berlin after
1945 —and to what was not done there? And wasn't this exactly what
had indeed been done in East Germany, under the pressure and protection of the Soviets, it is true, but led by highly motivated German
leftists? Why did the GDR's path, so close to that described by Shirer
and in many ways successful, end up in 1990 in failure? Was it due
to damaging pressures from the great power in the east? Or to pressures from the west? How much blame can be laid on devoted and

well-meaning leaders who were handed the reins after 1945 and then held them tightly till the end, marring their very remarkable achievements with blunders, autocracy, a lack of freedom and democracy? Or, as prevailing opinion-makers now maintain, was the whole damned system faulty to the core, just like its model in the USSR?

Another look at the cultural scene can provide a few hints at answers. I had discovered at the start that the basic anti-fascist, humanist foundation in the GDR was unquestionable, and for me decisive, but that problems enough remained, even when they were carefully swept under media carpets.

There was one place where the dust was not so well hidden and did cause some coughing—but also much laughter. Political cabarets in West Berlin had always aimed jabs at the GDR, hoping for guffaws from many in the audience who, before the Wall, crossed over for short visits. Then *Die Distel* (The Thistle), founded in 1953 as an East Berlin antidote, quickly became so popular that great luck, patience (sometimes measured in months), or a good supply of "Vitamin B" (that is, good connections) might be necessary to get tickets. At times tickets became a kind of currency, involved in swaps of hard-to-get items— no longer simple things like washrags or razor blades but rather blue bathroom tiles or rare car parts. *Die Distel* programs always included dutiful jabs at NATO armaments, at Adenauer, Franz Joseph Strauss, and other nasty targets, and some were quite telling. But Easterners laughed far louder at gags about problems within GDR boundaries, most commonly about the latest shortages, often goods that you could swear had always been available until you happened to need them. You might then get an almost scornful reply: "What, scissors? Why, scissors have been short for over three months!"

In one gag, soon part of the language, a polite salesman tells a customer: "I fear you are in the wrong shop, sir. This is where we don't have T-shirts. Next door is where they don't have tennis shoes."

Even when consumer supply had greatly improved (though with recurring surprises), there was no lack of complaints. Some gags reflected a lasting Eastern inferiority complex about almost every domestically made product, like one about a GDR engineer winning a U.S. competition to improve a new jet plane whose wings broke off at its top speed. "Simply bore a series of holes where the wings meet the fuselage," he submitted. "Are you crazy?" the media asked. But he offered to demonstrate it himself and proved his theory. "How did you ever get such an amazing idea?" they asked. "Where I come from I always noted one fact: even toilet paper never tears at the perforations!"

Here, again, jokes about the GDR's little part-plastic Trabi were inevitable, like "When does the Trabi reach peak speed?"—"When it's being towed."

The jokes could get sharper, to general delight, but I cannot swear that this one made it to the stage:

At the end of Prime Minister Grotewohl's official visit to China, he asked his host: "Honestly, Mao, just between us: how many still oppose your party's policies here?"—"Keep it to yourself, Otto, but we estimate about 16 or 17 million people."—"Oh," replied Grotewohl, "that's no more than in our GDR!" (population 17 million).

Hans Krause, the director of *Die Distel* until 1963, had a dramatic past; arrested as a soldier in 1943 for "undermining military morale," he fled and hid in a forest area until war's end. He had troubles later, too, though no longer life-threatening ones; his witty ensemble always balanced on the edges of what many leaders considered hostile. Jobs heading political cabarets could be short-lived; a gag about the fabled goatee of Party head Ulbricht, if not subtle enough, might mean an early end to a contract. Yet public support was so strong that most cabarets survived cuts, compromises, and management changes and kept people laughing.

Political cabaret was often closest to the brink, but filmmakers, authors, even artists and composers, were never immune. Unfriendly reviews in the official media, sarcastic "revelations" in West German radio and TV, or just word of mouth indicated that some happenings behind the scenes, after the applause died down and the crowds left for the subway, could be unhappier than some dramas on the stage, even marked by bitterness or tears.

A major achievement of the young GDR had been to win Bertolt Brecht, one of the century's best writers, after his nasty expulsion from the United States. But for some this coup was not wholly comfortable; in 1949 some influential critics had problems with his blindly defiant *Mother Courage*. In 1951, with that dispute largely forgotten, came his libretto for the opera *The Trial of Lucullus*, in which the Roman general is judged after death by fellow ghosts in the underworld. Did his military triumphs and culinary achievements, like introducing the cherry tree, outweigh his cruelty as a conqueror? A final decision was left to the audience. But recent war criminal trials in Nuremberg, and West German attempts to repudiate them, led official critics, even President Wilhelm Pieck, to call for certainty. Brecht altered the ending, judging Lucullus guilty and condemned to eternal oblivion, not for war in general, perhaps in self-defense, but for aggressive war. This was no great problem, as he often rewrote texts to keep up with developments. When reproached by a Western journalist for bowing to government interference, Brecht asked if he could name any other government that took such great interest in an opera performance.

Brecht was saved from overly sharp criticism by his world reputation and his run-in with the McCarthyite ghouls in Washington. Indeed, his Berliner Ensemble was granted a fine, well-financed theater. And with *Lucullus*, the main problem was really with the music. The twelve-tone score by Paul Dessau, who often worked with Brecht, with lots of drums and unusual percussion instruments but little melody, no strings, clarinets, or oboes, was not music to the ears of Walter Ulbricht, who huffily left the première as soon as the curtain fell, missing some catcalls but also a fifteen-minute ovation. Brecht's reply to critics who called it "dissonant, formalistic and decadent" was: "Gentlemen, in terms of music I have the impression that you are three hundred years behind the times."

Despite the altered ending and new name—*The Condemnation of Lucullus*—the opera was taboo until 1957, then produced in Leipzig and soon, for those gaining a taste for modern music, in over thirty GDR theaters. It was ignored in the West, which rejected almost everything from the "Soviet Zone" unless it could be labeled "dissident."

The GDR had many disagreements about the arts. Some, after spirited theoretical debates, faded and were happily forgotten. One, famously, was not. Again, an opera was involved, or rather its libretto, since the great composer Hanns Eisler never wrote the music. Brecht's close friend and collaborator, who composed the GDR national anthem, had also been forced to leave the United States by the Un-American Activities Committee. He had long planned an opera based on the story of Faust. Unlike Goethe, he placed his Johann Faustus in the midst of the Peasant Wars (1525), not as a hero but as an intellectual renegade seeking fame, selling out to the devil, betraying peasants and the poor, and symbolizing the sellout by many German intellectuals over the centuries, culminating in the Hitler era. Nor did those common people come off well who followed such a renegade.

But Faust, he discovered, was hallowed ground. His work, too, angered people like Ulbricht, who said: "In our struggle to preserve our German cultural heritage we must guarantee that one of the most important works by our great poet Goethe is not formalistically deformed, that the great ideals in Goethe's Faust are not reversed into a caricature." The Party newspaper called it "pessimistic, hopeless, anti-national, alien to the people." Eisler, deeply hurt, gave up the project and moved (temporarily) to Vienna, his hometown, while a basic theoretical discussion on art and theater began in the Academy of Arts. It ended abruptly with the "workers' uprising" on June 17, 1953.

Brecht's sarcastic poem concerning this event, "The Solution," is quoted over and over. Ridiculing one "official" author who said the people who had revolted might regain the government's confidence by redoubling their efforts on the job, Brecht responded as cleverly as ever: "Would it not be easier in that case for the government to dissolve the people and elect another?"

Rarely quoted are words, which, though highly critical, clearly iterate Brecht's basic support for the GDR. Despite disagreements and disappointments, I think this remained his position for the three remaining years of his life, during which his theater productions were always masterpieces. But because of his refusal to bash the GDR, his plays and writings were almost totally barred in Austria and West Germany. A top minister in Bonn compared his poetry with that of the thug, pimp, and Nazi "martyr" Horst Wessel, about whom the Nazi anthem was based (but who never wrote anything). The Bonn government even tried to prevent performances by the Berliner Ensemble in London. For them, Brecht was not a poet or dramatist but simply "a Communist"!

But why was there friction with top leaders of the young GDR, who like him, hated fascists and had hopes and plans for a happy future in a humane Germany, free of past evil influences?

They were obviously convinced that their duties included not only building a political and economic structure to this end but also guaranteeing that art and culture were doing the same. They saw themselves as revolutionaries, heading a vanguard party, and believed that in this struggle "art is a weapon." Their questionable manner of wielding this weapon was greatly affected by influences from their own past and pressures from the present.

Most of the Party leaders grew up in working-class backgrounds in the Kaiser Wilhelm era or early 1920s. A tradition in Social Democratic groups, before and after the Communist Party was founded in 1919, was the effort to raise working-class members' appreciation of the classics: Goethe, Schiller, Lessing, maybe Heine, music by Bach, Haydn, Mozart, and Beethoven, painters like Dürer, Rembrandt, maybe a few contemporaries like Max Liebermann. These artists all merited love and respect, but that often led to a mistrust of strange new trends like Expressionism or Cubism. That may help explain why many who became Communist leaders had middle-class, parlor-piano tastes and were suspicious of intellectual, individualist, or anarchist trends, even in pre-Hitler years when modernists like Brecht and Eisler took clearly left-wing positions, but were less "manageable."

But these attitudes did not always apply. Some leaders had intellectual backgrounds more attuned to experimenting; others, like President Pieck with working-class backgrounds, were quite open-minded. Contradictions and crosscurrents abounded, and views like those of Walter Ulbricht were strong: "We no longer want to see any abstract pictures in our art schools. Nor have we any need for paintings of lunar landscapes or rotting fish. Gray-in-gray painting, an expression of capitalist collapse, is in sharp contrast with present-day life in the GDR." Such views applied to all the arts.

A constant problem was the discord on the "German question." Adenauer, with the United States, wanted to establish his realm as the only legitimate Germany. His interest in its eastern region was to demonize and gobble it up as soon as possible. One way of disparaging it was to depict the GDR as not really German but diluted Russian, this at a time when West Germany was being saturated by American films, music, dance styles, and clothing fashions. GDR leaders, hoping to win Germans in East and West in opposing this, condemned Western fads and fashions, but also any frightening appeals to "proletarian internationalism." They stressed their own legitimacy as true preservers of good traditions, depicting German history as "a constant struggle between reactionary and progressive forces" in which they sought models, never in Nazi traditions but in those considered the "good guys." This is a clue to the efforts about avoiding both American and Russian uniform styles and seeking the "freedom-fighter" traditions of the struggle against Napoleon's occupation even when they leaned to some other aspects of Prussian tradition.

But then came people like Brecht and Eisler, stressing class militancy while recalling that Germany's past contained a long line of reactionary personalities: Luther in his later years, King Frederick, Schopenhauer, Nietzsche, Bismarck, and in many ways Wagner, all helping to pave the way to the national catastrophe with Hitler. Without denying this, the official GDR newspaper *Neues Deutschland* warned that such an aspect could hardly win friends among the general public, East or West: "Portraying German history as a line of uninterrupted misery is a reactionary and anti-national concept which serves objectively to destroy national self-respect and the national consciousness of the German people."

The emphasis on classics embodying enlightenment, humanitarianism, and internationalism certainly did have some positive results. Month-long commemoration of birth or death anniversaries introduced many in younger generations to the best of the past—Goethe Year in 1949, Bach Year in 1950, and Schiller Year in 1955—even when ties linking them to views of the GDR sometimes seemed overdone and led to sarcastic Western gags about adorning Goethe's statue with a red bandanna.

A celebrated guest at the Goethe and Schiller celebrations was Thomas Mann, Germany's most famous living author, who insisted on speaking in West and East; both writers, born in Western Germany, had undeniably moved to Weimar in the East. His visits caused chagrin to many West Germans; he was invited to ceremonies and banquets but also attacked and insulted in the right-wing media for leaving Germany in 1933, becoming a U.S. citizen, and opposing Hitler and Nazi aggression in wartime radio broadcasts. This, like his decision to speak in the GDR, was called treason. The attacks grew so hateful that in Stuttgart a four-man security guard was considered necessary. But in Weimar, on both visits, he received a hero's welcome, partly in gratitude for his defiance of anti-GDR taboos. During the second visit, public admiration was symbolized by an elderly man who asked for an autograph in a worn copy of Mann's Nobel Prize epic, *The Buddenbrooks*, carefully hidden away in the Nazi years.

Seeking a proper path between the many evil features and occasional episodes of great heroism in German history was never a simple matter. The GDR's clear rejection of racism and chauvinism toward other nations was always admirable, although, as the years went by, with few close contacts with people from other continents, its greatest early fervor did ebb, as became apparent after 1990. Some evil prejudices had never been completely conquered, but aspects of good influences have retained their strength at least into the present.

Joint attempts to find common grounds with West German writers, with or without the classics, played a diminishing role as the Cold War grew more tense at the dividing line. A main adherent of maintaining bonds was Johannes R. Becher, a noted writer in pre-Hitler Germany who had attracted emigrants like Brecht and Anna Seghers to the GDR after 1945 and become its first Minister of Culture. His death in October 1958 was almost symbolic. I had no idea of this when, shortly after my arrival in East Berlin from Leipzig, the publishing house I worked for delegated me and a few others to lay flowers at Becher's coffin and listen to the eulogies.

25—Attacks from the West

How much can that final maelstrom, the downfall of the GDR, be traced to Western opponents of any and every socialist dream? Regardless of mixed feelings among German writers East or West, perhaps divided in their views on dealing with "the other side," the basic political currents swept inexorably forward.

One twentieth-century source of this current sprang from Woodrow Wilson's fears of "red Bolshevism" after the Russian Revolution, when he led First World War victors in sending troops to crush it and, failing that, creating a "cordon sanitaire," or buffer zone, a ring of new states to "contain" the new Soviet Union, from Finland, the Baltic republics, Poland, Czechoslovakia, Yugoslavia, and Hungary to Romania. After 1945, the USSR was determined to prevent any repetition of this "cordon," which in 1941 had provided a starting ramp for murder and destruction of much of its territory. This was described by President John F. Kennedy as follows: "No nation in the history of battle ever suffered more than the Soviet Union suffered in the course of the Second World War. At least 20 million lost their lives. Countless millions of homes and farms were burned or sacked. A third of the nation's territory, including nearly two thirds of its industrial base, was turned into a wasteland—a loss equivalent to the devastation of this country east of Chicago." (John F. Kennedy, Commencement Address, American University, Washington, DC, June 10, 1963.)

Leftists, especially Communists, enjoyed respect, even great popularity after the Second World War, a result of the Red Army's major role in beating Nazi armies and the Communists' leadership and sacrifices in guerilla and underground struggles. This popularity was not shared by many in Washington and, after President Roosevelt's death, an offensive was mounted against it, aimed at forming a new cordon sanitaire. A few names stood out.

Jay Lovestone, once head of the Communist Party in the United

States, then a passionate anti-Communist, worked with the furthest right in the AFL and later the AFL-CIO as a connecting link with the CIA. The head of the FBI, J. Edgar Hoover, once said: "Lovestone is a rather sinister character, and it is a fact that he is being paid by the government in a kind of third-party activity to carry on certain intelligence work through the labor situation for the CIA." And if Hoover called a man sinister . . . !

Lovestone liked to work from his New York office; his "outside man," Irving Brown, set up shop in Paris in November 1945 and began splitting labor unions to counter Communist influence. His first success was organizing a right-wing split away from the French CGT, France's union federation since 1895, thus making it possible to oust the Communists from the government.

Brown then used his rich funding in Italy, splitting a strong central union and getting partisan leaders in the fight against Mussolini and Hitler, a majority of them Communists, thrown out of the coalition government in Rome. He did the same in Greece, then split independence movements in Africa, notably Algeria, and fighting unions in Latin America. In 1949, he helped break up the World Federation of Trade Unions and form a rival "pro-Western" federation.

In Germany, he countered all attempts at unified activities of the new East and West German unions, winning allies in those first hungry postwar years with money and food packages. One labor leader, later head of the West German union federation, complained bitterly in 1947 that "he had not received his CARE package for the month while others had gotten theirs."

Brown's millions came from the AFL treasury, the State Department, and firms like Exxon, GE, and Singer Sewing Machines with interests in Europe. After the United States launched its Marshall Plan in 1947, Brown got a good slice of its "special funds." When it was ended in 1950, the CIA took over funding.

Brown and Lovestone also organized a U.S. visit by the Social Democratic Party head in West Germany, Kurt Schumacher, and introduced him to "roll-back Russia" hardliner George Kennan, FBI boss J. Edgar Hoover, and Defense Secretary James Forrestal. Lovestone boasted to them about his Soviet Zone network of agents that supplied him with information and distributed menacing leaflets titled "Germany Under the Hammer and Sickle." According to some rumors Forrestal's fatal fall from his sixteen-story hospital window was either a jump caused by fear that "the Russians are coming"—or a push. I hope neither Lovestone nor Schumacher bore any moral responsibility for this fatal episode.

Unlike Forrestal or Schumacher, who died in 1952, Lovestone lived happily on. So did the Cold War. Weak efforts to maintain East-West labor contacts in Germany were thwarted by the Berlin Airlift and buried when the Berlin Wall went up. To celebrate such successes, Lovestone left his New York nest in 1963 with John F. Kennedy to visit West Berlin and even made a speech there—but refrained from claiming that he, too, was "ein Berliner."

But it was not all smooth sailing for the State Department and CIA. Many artists and writers kept opposing U.S. support for colonial powers suppressing independence movements and, even more, its threat with atomic weapons.

Washington was very unhappy about a big peace conference at the Waldorf-Astoria Hotel in March 1949, which I was lucky enough to attend as an usher, and shrewdly granted visas to Soviet delegates but not to anyone from Italy, England, or Latin America, making it look like a straight "red" gathering. But it was attended or supported by many leading Americans, from conductor Leonard Bernstein and dramatist Arthur Miller to Albert Einstein. In a corridor, I caught a close glimpse of one famous participant, Dmitri Shostakovich, despite attacks on his music in Moscow. Right-wing attempts to whip up angry picket lines, often directed at him, had only puny success.

A CIA attempt to spoil an even bigger peace conference in Paris also misfired. A third congress in Stockholm adopted the following petition, to be signed by people around the world:

We demand the outlawing of atomic weapons as instruments of intimidation and mass murder of peoples. We demand strict international control to enforce this measure. We believe that any government which first uses atomic weapons against any other country what-soever will be committing a crime against humanity and should be dealt with as a war criminal.

Famous people signed in many countries; so did over a million people in the United States (a few collected by me in Buffalo). But this soon required courage due to threats like this in the *Los Angeles Times*: "If anyone comes to your door with a petition sponsored by an association calling itself the Partisans for Peace don't sign it. . . . What should you do? Don't punch him in the nose or slam the door in his face. Reds are used to that. The thing to do is ask him for his identification; get his name and address if you can, take a good look at him, then telephone the FBI."

Chairing the petition drive in the United States was the world-famous sociologist Professor W. E. B. Du Bois who, though eighty-one years old, was arrested in handcuffs for being a "foreign agent." With no evidence against him and, by chance, a judge with courage, he was finally acquitted, but only after many onetime progressives, grown fearful, ducked out of any kind of support. He stated ruefully: "I never thought I would live to see the day that free speech and freedom of opinion would be so throttled in the United States as they are today, when students in our colleges may not hear or discuss the truth."

26—Spreading U.S. Culture

This worsening of the McCarthy era in the United States did not go over well in the outside world. So Washington stepped up its efforts. The CIA developed a propaganda network influencing over 800 newspapers, magazines, and news agencies and in 1950 set up an International Organizations Division (IOD) to subsidize tours of art exhibits, jazz musicians, opera stars, even the entire Boston Symphony Orchestra and an animated film of George Orwell's *Animal Farm*. It organized Committees for Cultural Freedom in thirty-five countries and, to counteract the peace congresses, decided on a Congress for Cultural Freedom in June 1950 in West Berlin.

Many Americans rejected German musicians with shady pasts. The Chicago Symphony Orchestra had to cancel a contract with conductor Wilhelm Furtwängler, and when his colleague Herbert von Karajan came to New York, it was recalled that he had opened concerts not too many years earlier with the Nazis' "Horst Wessel Lied" anthem. But a Committee for Cultural Freedom group intervened on his behalf; one of its leaders, writer James T. Farrell, said that Karajan's past was indeed "deplorable" but the protests "ignored the fact that the Berlin Philharmonic . . . symbolizes the courageous resistance of the people of Berlin to Communist totalitarianism." He won out —so West Berlin it was!

Over two hundred intellectuals attended the Congress, including John Dewey, Bertrand Russell, Arthur Koestler, Tennessee Williams, and Professor Sidney Hook of NYU, a leading anti-Communist theoretician since the 1930s. Visiting West Berlin for the first time, where he was encircled by his long-term "Red" foes, Hook feared the Russians might march in and "every delegate would have been a prisoner [of East German military police] within a few hours." But no, nobody marched in.

The views of the VIPs varied. Those of the ubiquitous Irving Brown, not exactly a cultural leader, were clear enough. Author James Burnham noted that the United States could wreck Russia in one day by dropping A-bombs on all major Russian cities. He was "against bombs now stored or to be stored later in Siberia or the Caucasus, designed for the destruction of Paris, London, New York, Chicago, Berlin and Western civilization generally. . . . But I am for bombs made in Los Alamos, Hanford and Oak Ridge . . . which for five years have been the sole defense of the liberties of Western Europe."

Others, distrustful about the luxury offered them amid a still very desolate Berlin, were dismayed by hearing little more than "Sock them!" Like British historian Hugh Trevor-Roper: "I regret to say that as I listened and as I heard the baying voices of approval from the huge audiences I felt, well, these are the same people who seven years ago were probably baying in the same way to similar denunciations of Communism coming from Dr. Goebbels in the Sports Palast." (Frances

Stonor Saunders, *Who Paid the Piper? The CIA and the Cultural Cold War*, London: Granta, 1999, 226, 74, 77, and 78.)

Regardless of any doubts, the Congress moved forward in defense of the Western World. It supported twenty prestigious magazines like *Encounter* in Britain, *Der Monat* in Germany, and the chic *Partisan Review* in the United States. Their clever "long leash" policy, avoiding crude polemics and even publishing critics of some U.S. policies as long as the trend against "Reds" and the Soviets was not violated, won authors like Hannah Arendt, Saul Bellow, Heinrich Böll, George Orwell, T. S. Eliot, Arthur Koestler, Irving Kristol, and even Thomas Mann.

27—Art Is a Weapon

The State Department, wanting to oppose long-held leftist views in European art circles that the United States was a cultural desert, organized a postwar European exhibition tour. But many leading Americans were as suspicious of modern art as Ulbricht or Khrushchev were. One congressman stated: "I am just a dumb American who pays taxes for this kind of trash." President Truman also hated such "lazy, nutty moderns" and declared: "If that's art then I'm a Hottentot." The tour was canceled. Such ideas and Senator McCarthy's attack on anyone who had ever leaned leftward made it difficult to sell America as a culturally sophisticated democracy.

To solve the problem, the CIA was called in, though its subsidies were camouflaged as support by foundations. Wealthy people were happy to let their names be used in such a good, and lucrative, cause. Or dummy names were used. Thomas Braden, leader of this project, said later: "We wanted to unite all the people who were writers, who were musicians, who were artists, to demonstrate that the West and the United States were devoted to freedom of expression and to intellectual achievement without any rigid barriers as to what you must write, what you must say, what you must do, and what you must paint, which was what was going on in the Soviet Union. I think it was the most important division that the agency had, and I think that it played an enormous role in the Cold War." (Frances Stonor Saunders, *Who Paid the Piper? The CIA and the Cultural Cold War*, London: Granta, 1999, 98.) But, he confided, "It was very difficult to get Congress to go along with some of the things we wanted to do—send art abroad, send symphonies abroad, publish magazines abroad. That's one of the reasons it had to be done covertly. It had to be a secret."

A main front was the Museum of Modern Art in New York (MoMA) whose president, oil heir Nelson Rockefeller, was also President Truman's Special Assistant for Psychological Warfare, and later New York governor and U.S. vice president. Other board members were connected with the Congress for Cultural Freedom. MoMA exhibition tours were able to win a dominant role for Abstract Expressionism in the Western world, forcing styles depicting real people and objects to retreat or give up. For twenty years it became the world's main promoter of Abstract Expressionism and the paintings of artists like Jackson Pollock, Robert Motherwell, Willem de Kooning, and Mark Rothko. One expert, Eva Cockcroft, wrote: "Links between cultural Cold War politics and the success of Abstract Expressionism are by no means coincidental. . . . They were consciously forged at the time by some of the most influential figures controlling museum policies and advocating enlightened Cold War tactics designed to woo European intellectuals. . . . In terms of cultural propaganda the functions of both the CIA's cultural apparatus and MoMA's international programs were similar and, in fact, mutually supportive." (Eva Cockcroft, "Abstract Impressionism, Weapon of the Cold War," *Artforum International* 12/10,1974.)

I recall an ironic note. The first painting I saw whenever I entered the MoMA as a youngster was Picasso's stirring *Guernica*. He was never an Abstract Impressionist but a dreaded Communist. But this painting could never be removed until Franco's death, when it was moved to Madrid.

The CIA, hoping also to prove American modernity in music, subsidized an International Conference of 20th-Century Music in Rome in 1954 to promote twelve-tone music. But that proved simply too far-out for hometown backers, and the matter was quietly shelved.

As Frances S. Saunders wrote: "Whether they liked it or not, whether they knew it or not, there were few writers, poets, artists, historians, scientists, or critics in postwar Europe whose names were not in some way linked to this covert enterprise." (Saunders, 2.)

She meant Western Europe. But those in the East were also greatly affected, especially at the confrontation line in Berlin and the GDR. Many, probably most, preferred figurative over abstract art, but pressures to be "modern" and join the "world art scene" were hard to ignore. Abstract art was increasingly viewed as progressive, avant-garde, daring, individualistic, and thus appealing. Figurative art was scorned as old-fashioned, regime-submissive, even linked to "heroic" fascist art and hardly worth looking at. Figurative art by East Germans showing people or places was often omitted from Western exhibitions; only abstract impressionism was "in," until it was replaced by new fashions like Pop Art.

So, on the one hand, the poor GDR artists faced authorities with conservative tastes and "anti-formalism, socialist realism" pressure from the USSR, making sales to GDR officialdom difficult. And, on the other hand, Western attacks on the GDR cultural scene and any figurative painting, also a tangible form of pressure, made chances for sales to Westerners even bleaker. The background split over politics and economics could make the cultural scene, and even personal lives, complex and difficult. Some, like composers Paul Dessau and Hanns Eisler, refrained from disparaging twelve-tone music or other modern trends in the arts, but rejected the accompanying politics and held clearly to their socialist convictions. For others, often younger and without as much experience or name recognition, hence not so decided in their views, the choice between the Western devil and the deep blue (or red) sea seemed clear and simple only to the shallow conformists or to the 100 percent pro-Westerners.

28—Hits to the CIA Fan

Not everything was silky-smooth on the other side either. The fabled fan of metaphor, though a carefully-guarded hush-hush fan, got hit very, very hard, and what hit it soiled many an illustrious name. In April 1966, the *New York Times* ran five sensational articles about the CIA: its connections, false fronts, dummy foundations, and subsidies granted for seemingly scientific inquiries, like the scholarly Center for International Studies. It was presumably independent, with MIT, Harvard, and other experts of renown objectively researching human rights, justice, and political economy, but was actually founded and funded by the CIA to help its Voice of America better pierce the Iron Curtain and upset the East. Its first project, on "Soviet Vulnerability," was led by Walt Rostow, a National Security Adviser.

In March 1967, the magazine *Ramparts* lobbed another load at the fan, revealing how the CIA funded and controlled the supposedly democratic National Student Association and a host of other organizations so as to woo and win over left-leaning liberals. Hardest hit were the Congress for Cultural Freedom branches, whose sophisticated, proudly independent publications were fully exposed.

In May, the *Saturday Evening Post* offered a kind of rebuttal. Thomas Braden admitted it all; he even confessed that the magazine *Encounter* was not only subsidized, a CIA agent was on its staff to prevent unwanted deviations. Braden, who mentioned that the headquarters of the Congress for Cultural Freedom had remained in West Berlin, defended the International Organizations Division that he had headed and proudly titled his article "I'm Glad the CIA is 'Immoral'"!

The confusion that followed almost deserved pity. Most editors and contributors to the allegedly independent magazines insisted that they had never known who was behind them. This made them either dupes or liars, especially after a few stated that "everyone knew." All U.S.-connected projects now came under suspicion, as did the Abstract Expressionism crusade, and this when world abhorrence of the bombing, burning, and Agent Orange poisoning in Vietnam was sharply rising.

Just before the soiled saddles of these "crusaders" were opened to view, President Eisenhower had praised MoMA as a bastion of freedom and democracy: "As long as artists are at liberty to feel with high personal intensity, as long as our artists are free to create with sincerity and conviction, there will be a healthy controversy and progress in art ... How different it is in tyranny, when artists are made the slaves and tools of the state, when artists become chief propagandists of a cause, progress is arrested and creation and genius are destroyed." How noble his words! (Frances Stonor Saunders, *Who Paid the Piper? The CIA and the Cultural Cold War*, London: Granta, 1999, 272.)

29—The Berlin Wall

The GDR's path, with its goal of socialism, always faced the unalterable fact that history had assigned it the disadvantaged, far weaker third of the country. Nor was its path less bumpy because of its sharp break with Nazi bigwigs and their system. The enforced isolation of the GDR by Bonn seriously damaged trade and made it difficult or impossible for its citizens to go to scientific conferences, compete in international sports events, or engage in many forms of cultural exchange. Some goods, like the optical products of Zeiss Jena, were barred from using their familiar, respected brand names, and Bonn, wielding its influence in Washington, got the GDR barred from the "most favored nation clause" whereby a country's products need pay no higher customs duties than even "the most favored nation." Washington awarded this almost universal right to Poland and Hungary, which it hoped to win over, but not to the GDR. The resulting heavier customs duties made it almost impossible to compete with West Germany in the valuable U.S. market.

Family ties with West Germany, the common language, and national feelings of German identity, with the constant lure and luring of West German prosperity, among the greatest in the world, made the GDR fearful about losing its experts and therefore highly selective in awarding exit visas. All these factors made it a vulnerable, tempting playing field for cloak-and-dagger gamesters and their backers, whose goal was its total defeat.

I wrote earlier of the efforts of Jay Lovestone and Irving Brown. Far more famous on this playing field was Allen Dulles, a past master in German underground doings whose law firm held hands, very grasping hands, with Nazi-era giants like I. G. Farben. As the first boss of the CIA, he helped topple democratically elected governments in Guatemala, Iran, and the Congo—and tried it again vainly in Cuba. In East Germany his agents, instead of assassinating leaders, tried hard to tempt them to defect. Heading the list was Otto Grotewohl, the top Social Democrat who had supported his party's merger with the Communists in the East in 1946 to form the Socialist Unity Party (SED). Their baits failed with him, however. He didn't bite, but became instead the first prime minister of the GDR.

The CIA never abandoned such efforts. A State Department document from 1956 reveals that the CIA joined other agencies in "operations aimed at weakening the economic structure of the Soviet Zone through the attraction of critically needed groups of technicians and scientists." And here, often enough, they did not fail; the Stasi saw the CIA as the "most successful intelligence service operating against the GDR." (*Secret Intelligence in the Twentieth Century*, ed. Heike Bungert, Jan G. Heitmann, Michael Wala, London: Frank Cass, 2003, 134–35.) As West German economic growth was encouraged, promoted, and built up, faster than the GDR could possibly match, this policy worked and threatened increasingly the economic structure of its smaller German sister.

After the CIA fiasco with the Bay of Pigs invasion of Cuba in April 1961, the new U.S. president, John F. Kennedy, angrily fired its boss, Allen Dulles, which made it possible to have a somewhat more relaxed meeting in Vienna in June with Soviet leader Khrushchev. But pressure by the latter to agree on an all-German peace treaty, ending the "Berlin problem" or, failing that, his threat to sign a separate Soviet-GDR treaty calling for the withdrawal of all occupation troops from Berlin, East and West, increased tensions again. So did Kennedy's request to Congress for an additional $3.25 billion for military spending, with a jump from 875,000 to approximately 1 million men, six new divisions for the Army and two for the Marines, a tripling of enlistment, calling up reserves, spending huge sums on fallout shelters stocked with survival essentials, with stepped-up air-raid warning and fallout detection systems. Kennedy proclaimed: "We seek peace, but we shall not surrender."

The heightened tension accelerated the number of those leaving East Germany through West Berlin. A kind of mass panic set in, based on "Who knows what's ahead?" and "Now or never" fears. I recall GDR shops closing down and hearing the same about assembly lines in factories. Again, this brain-drain hit hardest in the loss of engineers, technicians, physicians, and skilled workers, and everyone could see that the existence of the GDR was threatened. Should it flounder, there was a high likelihood of incidents that could all too easily lead to war, even atomic war. The future of Berlin had become a matter of life or death far beyond its narrow borders.

The day the Wall was built, on August 13, 1961, was my sixth wedding anniversary. We spent an innocently ignorant day at the Tierpark (zoo) with my sister-in-law and her fiancé, involved more with wildebeests or wallabies than with a wall, which we soon learned would change the lives of countless thousands and sadly cost the lives of some. Strangely enough, it brought me personally no disadvantages but actually made my life feel safer in a way, with no more fears, idle or not, of being spirited westward. But, month for month, we became aware of the huge contradictory changes it meant for the city, the country, and, in some ways, for the whole world.

Kennedy, who knew of the Wall plans in advance, luckily kept cool when it was built. His biographer, Michael O'Brien, wrote: "It surprised the President that no Soviet soldiers were seen in the streets; nor was there interference with access to West Berlin. The measures taken did not threaten vital interests of the Allies in West Berlin. . . . 'Why would Khrushchev put up a Wall if he really intended to seize West Berlin?' he said privately to his aides. 'There wouldn't be any need of a Wall if he occupied the whole city. This is his way out of his predicament. It's not a very nice solution, but a Wall is a hell of a lot better than a war.'"

That was sensible. But he was not the West's top man for nothing. "Kennedy urged [Secretary of State] Rusk to take steps 'to exploit politically propaganda-wise' the closing of the border. . . . It offers us a very good propaganda stick which, if the situation were reversed, would be well used in beating us. . . . It was an enormous plus for the West, an enormous minus for the Communist nations. . . . What he said was, everything must be done in terms of pictures—pictures particularly . . . to describe what a dreadful thing this was in terms of bottling up a whole nation and preventing them from leaving." (Michael O'Brien, *President Kennedy and the Berlin Wall*, *The History Reader*, New York: St. Martin's Press, 2011.)

In October, things looked menacing again—after a minor dispute about border checks, the U.S. Army moved tanks right up to Checkpoint Charlie at the East Berlin line. From our office balcony only six blocks away, we could almost look into their muzzles; we were right in the line of fire. The next day Soviet tanks clanked around the corner, passed us and faced them, stopping only when the tank guns of the two sides were literally inches apart. Luckily that confrontation, too, was settled peacefully.

30—Hearts and Minds

The Berlin Wall, abhorred by so many and presenting huge propaganda advantages to GDR opponents and very stiff questions to its friends, was praised by few outside the official GDR media, and by John F. Kennedy, who preferred it to war. It altered the entire German situation, often in unexpected ways. For example, the Woodrow Wilson International Center for Scholars in Washington noted that while Berlin's formerly open frontier had made work easy for Western activities, "the closing of the border offered the communist state more security."

The basic Western direction remained the same. But Adenauer's hardheaded confrontational approach had to be changed. This occurred when Social Democrat Willy Brandt moved in, first as foreign minister, in a coalition with the ex-Nazi Kurt Kiesinger, and then as chancellor with his brainy sidekick Egon Bahr, once RIAS head in West Berlin.

Bahr explained the new strategy. Since a revolt by East Germans was now more unlikely than ever, he said, and with Soviet troops just as present in the East as American troops in the West, further isolating the GDR would lead nowhere.

> In the Soviet Union the demand for consumer goods has grown and has led to positive developments. Why shouldn't this hold true for the Zone [the GDR, VG]. The USSR is determined to catch up with and overtake the West, especially in living standards, in which the West is strongest. Aside from this being a goal which presents the West as a model and represents an orientation to western accomplishments, it is clear that the Zone should not be excluded from this policy in the East Bloc. . . .
>
> We have said that the Wall is a sign of weakness. One could also say it is a sign of angst and the instinct of self-preservation. The question is whether there might be chances of gradually decreasing these perfectly justified fears of the regime, bringing them to greater moderation at their borders and at the Wall as more practicable and since the risk becomes more tolerable. That is a policy which could be called Change by Moving Closer. (*Zeitschrift für Fragen der DDR und der Deutschlandpolitik*, No. 8, Cologne, 1973, 862–65.)

This new strategy no longer aimed at snapping up the GDR with sharp fangs, which were faced by sharp Soviet teeth, but rather by using homeopathic dosing, softening it up and easing ingestion with sweeter-tasting beverages like Coca-Cola. This new "Ostpolitik" (Eastern Policy) included a long overdue recognition of the border with Poland, Brandt kneeling at the Ghetto Monument in Warsaw, and diplomatic dealings with GDR representatives, with mutual visits and easing of travel difficulties. But there was no real recognition of the GDR.

For the GDR government, the Berlin Wall required attempts, largely in vain, to counteract both the bad press and the anger and frustration of East Berliners. Especially East Berliners, whose "privileged status" with West Berlin shopping and entertainment possibilities had always caused envy in other GDR regions, especially Prussia's historical rival Saxony, so that the sudden end of this status caused not a little schadenfreude.

The Berlin Wall also demanded lots of new thinking in the GDR, most importantly in regard to the economy. Walter Ulbricht, tough when beating down possible rivals (luckily without death sentences), and interested but limited in his views on art, music, and literature, was realist enough to see the urgent need of improvements. He got experts to develop a New Economic System of Planning and Management (with an equally awkward acronym, NÖSPL), providing more independence for the factories, fewer umbilical ties to the Party headquarters in Berlin, genuine inducements and rewards for good work, and an interest in profit—not private profit, of course, since enterprises were nationally owned, but closer ties to market demands with increased reliance on trained economists rather than Party officialdom.

Some improvements began to be felt, but so was the heavier hand of Leonid Brezhnev in Moscow after Nikita Khrushchev was ousted in October 1964. Economic experiments were viewed in Moscow as false, perhaps even impertinent, from a country that the Brezhnev people surely looked upon as subordinate. Who knows how successful Ulbricht's plans might have been?

The engineer-economist who developed NÖSPL, Erich Apel, head of the Planning Commission, also tried to get better trade deals from the big sister in the East: higher prices for top-quality exports like ships, railroad cars, and consumer goods, lower prices for crucial imports. But Moscow rejected what it considered subsidies for a GDR that enjoyed far higher living standards than its own. When Ulbricht bit into this sour apple, accepting its logic, or its pressure, and insisted that Erich Apel sign an unequal deal with the USSR, he felt betrayed and, choosing another option, shot himself.

THE BERLIN WALL also led to some not so tragic effects in unexpected ways, including the cultural scene. There was less preoccupation with West Germany, with whether to stay here or go there, since it was now much more difficult, and hence more attention was paid to GDR problems, not only in factories or on farms but in schools, colleges, hospitals. on vacations.

This could be seen in pictures, not the kind of photos that Kennedy called for, but in pictorial art. Every five years, Dresden featured a month-long art exhibition, visited by hundreds of thousands. Entire factory teams, office staffs, and countless individuals came by the busload and trainload and spent a day viewing new paintings, prints, applied art, and design. Renate and I never missed a one. I cannot recall seeing abstract art, which I think was found only in small private galleries, but the early abundance of happily energetic, smiling working people at their jobs and an occasional soldier or two was displaced more and more by a wide variety of individual styles, with landscapes, cityscapes, ordinary people with their problems, events in Vietnam, Nicaragua, Cuba, or elsewhere in the world, and portraits of actors, scientists, or foreign personalities like Martin Luther King Jr. In the 1970s and even more in the 1980s, art reflected GDR problems, often with a critical brush. It was not always clear whether some paintings expressed "positive" criticism, aimed at improvement and humanization, or a veiled rejection of the whole GDR. The amazing number of people who visited these shows discussed such questions widely, also questions about art influences from the Western world, and chose their favorites or ones they disliked.

There were similar developments in other spheres. The annual international documentary film week in Leipzig was at first almost ignored by the local population, who suspected shallow hurrah films about successful socialist construction. But gradually they discovered not only dramatic films direct from the world's hotspots—Vietnam, Chile, Nicaragua—or dramatic conflicts in Western countries, but also critical films about problems in the Eastern Bloc, including the GDR. It became increasingly difficult to obtain seats, even in the central 1000-seat movie theater.

It was no different with the annual festivals of political songs, every February in East Berlin. Some of the world's best singers could be seen and heard, like the Quilapayun Octet from Chile, the Argentinian Mercedes Sosa, Pete Seeger, Billy Bragg, or stirring chorus groups from

Italy, Finland, South Africa. Also featured were young GDR groups, searching for musical paths between the docile expectations of youth organization officialdom (who paid the bills, after all) and a desire to sing out what was on their mind about GDR problems close at hand.

One question was always involved: how could hearts and minds be reached? The sharp line represented by the Wall led to renewed efforts to develop more of a "GDR consciousness," as opposed to an all-German one, in a campaign that could easily be overdone, often stupidly. Even traditional folksongs were dropped from music broadcasts if they included West German place names. City maps of Berlin ended carefully at the sector borders, showing only East Berlin—not even a single West Berlin alleyway. Almost amusingly, the text of the gracefully melodic, very un-Prussian GDR anthem was played but no longer sung in public because it called for a peaceful—but unified—Germany. Again, gags were rife, for example about the young teacher who rejects the school globe offered him in a shop, explaining, "I really wanted only a GDR globe!"

In 1959, the "Bitterfeld Way" campaign had been launched, promoted by Walter Ulbricht and named after a chemical plant at whose big clubhouse authors and artists met to discuss ways to overcome gaps between them and industrial workers. This led a few writers to take factory jobs; many more visited workers' brigades to encourage or advise after-work amateur art or writing clubs. I became a small part of this campaign and met with workers and apprentices in the maintenance department of the immense Buna chemical plant. Several hundred art or writing clubs were formed, more working people did gain interest in cultural matters, and some authors wrote about industrial themes, now often avoiding rose-colored superficiality and honestly portraying life in the working world with all its problems and contradictions. A few books became bestsellers.

As with films and painting, books with critical content led to many discussions about their authors' true intent. Most seemed motivated by a wish to expand democracy and improve conditions, to attack coldness, indifference, sloppiness, or disregard for human values and move the GDR closer to socialist goals. In a few, though veiled to survive the blue pencils of Party censorship, one sensed opposition to everything in the GDR and a longing for the blessings of a prosperous market economy on the other side of the Wall. And in a few, there seemed to be a "plague on both your houses" attitude. The subtle differences evoked reactions varying with readers' own views, and it was just this thought-provoking complexity that made GDR literature so many-sided, so searching, and often so good. It was augmented by similarly nuanced books from other countries, East and West, including many modern American offerings. The printers with their tight paper limits could never satisfy the demand of growing throngs of readers. In many book-shops customers picked up shopping baskets on entering and often filled them, hardly looking at the extremely low prices. This created the phenomenon of "stoop goods": the most desired books, not displayed on shelves or tables, were kept below and behind the counter, reserved for friends and favored customers unwilling to face long waiting lists in the libraries.

31—Worried Watchdogs

But so much critical honesty in books, on canvas, stage, or screen began to worry the usual watchdogs. A play by the provocative Peter Hacks, who had moved east to the GDR in 1955, tying a love story to conflicts between two factories, was found to be too frank about contradictions within the ruling SED Party. It did not run long, but we were lucky to see, and enjoy, one performance. A novel by a former miner about drifters, ex-cons, and ex-Nazis in GDR uranium mines, run jointly with the Soviets to challenge the U.S. atomic monopoly, contained descrip-tions, characters, and "Wild West" language that were found to be overly realistic. Only one chapter was published.

Such contradictions also reached the theaters, which were blossom-ing with a new generation of wonderful actors and directors. In 1959 the Volksbühne risked staging *The Bathhouse* by Vladimir Mayakovsky, whom Stalin had called "the best, most talented poet of our Soviet epoch" (though only after his suicide in 1930). The play is a sparkling attack on bourgeois, platitude-threshing bureaucrats, so to play safe a Russian director was engaged. But he pulled no punches; my boss John Peet described the big shots in the front rows at the premiere, squirming and uncertain whether to laugh and applaud like everyone else or look indignant and maybe walk out in protest. When I tried to buy tickets a few days later, a note regretted that the performance had been "called off due to the illness of a main actor." Somehow that "main actor" never regained health; the play, dropped for many years, was just too bitingly critical.

Six years later, however, in 1965, another Russian play was a magnificent success. I saw *The Dragon* with an experienced U.S. actor who was enraptured by the stage design, the costumes, and the masterful acting. Written during the siege of Leningrad by Yevgeni Schwarz, its giant three-headed dragon provided gasps and laughs. Had its sharply sarcastic attack on fascist tyranny and those accommodating themselves to it also implied criticism of Stalin and his methods? And if so, how much applied "here and now"? Packed audiences would reflect and debate about this, and enjoy it, for sixteen years and 580 performances, not only in East Berlin but in sold-out performances in Paris.

Films and TV usually had larger audiences than plays and books and therefore attracted more scrutiny. The television scene was also the most visible East-West battlefield. Despite official discouragement, ever more GDR viewers turned to the growing number of West German channels, public and private; some did so almost exclusively. All were, of course, more or less subtly anti-GDR. "East-TV" had only one channel, and then much later two. While always burdened by dull news and official statements, it also offered finely acted and directed versions of great books and historical series and, after a while, action films, whose heroes were mostly members of the People's Police. These might be followed by moral sermons against crime, but were, all the same, well-made and full of suspense. Miniseries with six or seven episodes, clearly partisan but highly dramatic, were discussed and debated by large portions of the population. Many viewers rewarded such improvements by not turning dials so quickly westward. Even music, dance, and humor shows were increasingly competing, though

less luridly or lasciviously, with the Hollywood films, mass-appeal slap-
stick, sex, and violence on West German channels.

I HAVE PRAISED early productions of the GDR's one and only film
company, DEFA, especially its wonderful films on anti-fascist themes.
According to my private theory about film quantity and quality,
most countries produced about one really good film for every fifteen
released, which meant about one a year for the GDR and, at that ratio,
a correspondingly higher number from Hollywood.

But in the Stalin era, both the USSR and the GDR had inhibited
their best filmmakers and slid (or been pushed) into shallow cliché
hurrah-boosters whose audiences consisted largely of groups from
schools or factories who had been given free tickets. But in the late
1950s and early 1960s, during the Khrushchev years, more and more
films ventured bravely, or recklessly, onto delicate terrains now far less
troubled by political smog. A series of highly critical, highly controversial DEFA films were produced or begun in 1964 and 1965.

But the usual critics in leading positions worried that "compromises" signaled a drift away from the ideal of developing "socialist
consciousness" and leaned toward Western ways on the political compass. Standards were being diluted, they claimed. Criticism of aspects
of GDR life, now more frequent, aided and abetted the adversary across
the divide. Once again, they insisted, the compass needed correcting.

In October 1964, Khrushchev was ousted and the far heavier hand
of Leonid Brezhnev was felt, supported by similarly minded East
German adherents. What followed was the notorious 11th Plenum of
the ruling SED Party, December 16–18, 1965. Instead of the debate on
economic improvements projected by Ulbricht, center stage was stolen
by his up-and-coming lieutenant, Erich Honecker, who chose instead
to attack in the sphere of "culture and youth" with angry accusations of
"skepticism," "nihilism," even "pornography." "Our GDR is a cleanly
state," he maintained, "based on irrevocable standards of ethics and
morals, of decency and good customs."

One writer noted sarcastically: "In other words, writers are guilty of
ethically dehumanizing young people—with destructive actions, brutal

descriptions, Western influence, sex orgies, the devil only knows what else—and of course that nasty hankering for doubting. We writers are just griping away from the outside while our good working people are building up socialism."

Another writer, Christa Wolf, though a member of the Central Committee (although not for much longer), was the only one with the guts to disagree, clearly if obliquely, at the 11th Plenum. It was "our lack of an intellectually forward-looking attractiveness which opened up vacuums for some sectors of young people into which, quite naturally, alien and hostile ideologies were able to intrude." She criticized a stress on "economism," propagating no other goals than prosperity, and urged a dialogue between East and West. Her words were disregarded—or worse.

Enormous harm was done. The popularity of GDR-TV channels dipped accordingly. The films of 1965 were buried for years and although many ascents and descents followed and, after a while, not a few new, top-rate films were made (at that 15-to-1 ratio, sometimes even better), some broken parts in the bonds between leadership and the creative cultural scene could never be fully repaired.

Six years later, Erich Honecker was able to push out the aging Walter Ulbricht. What followed at first, to general surprise, was another relaxation in nearly every field, cultural and political, with far less worrying about Western influences. But this new mild wave hit another reef in 1976. Wolf Biermann, originally from West German Hamburg, a talented, satirically critical, guitar-playing poet and long a sharp thorn in the side of the GDR leadership, gave a hugely ballyhooed concert in western Cologne, largely anti-GDR in substance and larded with sharp denunciations of Party leaders. It was shown over and over—and over—on West German TV, several times a day, I think, for at least a week. Honecker's angry response was to bar Biermann from returning to the GDR. I feel certain that the episode was a well-planned trap arranged between Bonn and Biermann, which the top GDR leader fell right into, with fateful consequences. The pressures that followed were extremely polarizing, some condemning Biermann as demanded by the SED, others refusing to do so. This caused another split among writers, actors,

and intellectuals and led many to request, successfully, to move westward. Support for the GDR among intellectuals, once very strong, never
fully recuperated, and a dissident underground blossomed, mostly tolerated but closely observed by the Party and its security apparatus. As for
Biermann, always first and foremost an extreme egoist, he has since then
and until today moved further and further to the right.

The many campaigns and debates on art and literature almost
always involved the question of censorship, which could hardly be
separated from developments in the big Soviet patron, where changing influences and political pressures brought results reminiscent of a
rollercoaster. This close relationship certainly needs scrutiny if one is
to understand GDR developments.

32—The GDR and the Soviets

Soviet-East German relations at war's end were inevitably complicated. Terrible wreckage, ruin, and misery were everywhere. German
atrocities had been most fearsome by far in the USSR; their campaign
of genocide cost up to 27 million lives, more than four times that of the
Shoah. It was not hard to understand the desire for revenge by Red
Army soldiers, who, while fighting for four bitter years, often heard of
the loss of their families to flames, frost, hunger, or execution inflicted
by the SS and Wehrmacht; also of the organized starvation of over 3
million Red Army prisoners. A result, in the first days or weeks before
they were halted by higher officers, was confiscation and rape.

The Red Army took swift action to distribute bread, soup, and
other necessities and restore some kind of normality, but much political damage had been done. And years of anti-Soviet propaganda had
been effective. German casualties had been worst by far on the Eastern
Front; most Germans did not know or did not want to know what
mass war crimes their sons, husbands, or fathers had committed there
as occupying invaders. A result was often sullen hostility and sometimes worse.

Then too, Red Army occupation troops could hardly win over the

population, due to continuing German nationalism and cultural differences, with many Soviet troops coming from areas where living
standards were more fair and equal but also far lower than Germany's
relative wartime prosperity (at least until its final year). Unlike GI
occupiers, the Soviets had neither handsome uniforms nor aromatic
Lucky Strikes or Wrigley chewing gum to hand out. Even in language
terms, Russian has a different alphabet, and English, much closer to
German, is far easier to learn, at least in a pidgin-English way. The
United States soon began spreading its glistening cultural fads and
offerings, not always superior to what the Soviets had to offer, but
certainly more digestible, infectious, and easier to copy and take as a
model. Even in East Germany, how often had I attempted a polite smile
at proud attempts to sing, in heavily accented English, "Chattanooga
Choo-Choo" or other great songs? And the easygoing air of many GIs
appealed, especially to women and children.

But experiences varied greatly. Renate told of the first Russian soldier she encountered while she, her mother, and her sisters, one a baby,
were fleeing from the front lines. He asked in sign language if they
had a knife. Terrified, they said no. He left but returned ten minutes
later with a knife and cut a big portion of ham and bread from his own
rations to give to them.

A friend told me of a quite different encounter when he was fourteen. His "first" Russian soldier demanded his wristwatch. But when
he showed that he had none, the soldier rolled up his own sleeve, took
one of the five he had already "gathered" and gave it to him. But then,
alas, when the second Russian soldier came along, he was no longer a
fellow proletarian—and lost his new present.

The confiscation not only of wristwatches but of large amounts of
machinery, train tracks, and other property as reparations, though
agreed upon by all victorious powers, did not improve the relationship.
Neither did tough treatment of some lesser Nazis and Nazi-inspired
juvenile resisters known as "Werewolves"—but also of any unwelcome
opposition.

Yet, weak at first, other currents began to emerge, led by Soviet officers with knowledge of German culture, such as Lt. Col. Alexander

Dymschitz, and by Germans, some of them emigrants, with knowledge of Russian or Soviet culture. While French, British, and American endeavors along similar lines were emerging in their occupation areas, East Germans learned of writers like Pushkin or Tolstoy along with the knowledge, equally new to many, about the immense German atrocities in the USSR.

But stress was laid on building human bridges; music by Shostakovich and Prokofiev, Sergei Eisenstein's wonderful films, modern writers like Gorki, Sholokhov, Ilya Ehrenburg, and Daniil Granin, along with other often enthusiastic but easily forgettable ones. Many enjoyed *The Road to Life* and other humane books by Anton Makarenko about his work with wild street kids. Then there were performances by the Moisseyev folk dance ensemble, the graceful ballet mastery of Galina Ulanova as Juliet and top soloists and ensembles. Most memorable, on August 18, 1948, was a legendary concert by the Alexandrov Red Army Choir in Berlin's most beautiful square, the Gendarmenmarkt, singing "Kalinka" and other catchy songs, dancing, and then offering, as a gentle solo, "Sah ein Knab' ein Röslein steh'n," offered in Goethe's German, a song loved by most of the 30,000 Berliners crowding around the broad stairway of the bombed-out but still imposing Schauspielhaus Theater.

This gradual improvement suffered a nasty dip after 1948 with a campaign against "formalism"—instead of sticking to content, best of all happy socialist workers or courageous and heroic combatants, a stress rather on forms and colors, as in Abstract Expressionism. This was spread to the whole Eastern Bloc. Led by Andrei Zhdanov, commander in Leningrad during its long siege, then Stalin's cultural deputy and presumed successor, the prewar attack on all Western influences increased sharply. Some saw this as a reaction to the icier atmosphere of a Cold War, begun, they felt, with the demonstration of awful power at Hiroshima and Nagasaki and verbalized in Winston Churchill's provocative "Iron Curtain" speech in Fulton, Missouri, on March 5, 1946, and in a less-known message by U.S. diplomat George Kennan calling for "containment" of a "Soviet threat" that was "impervious to logic of reason," but "highly sensitive to the logic of force" and would back down "when strong resistance is encountered at any point." Such logic led in 1947 to the Marshall Plan and its military complement, the Truman Doctrine, both aimed bluntly eastward.

In contrast with such call-to-arms bluster, I believe the basic Soviet goal was to rebuild and unite its wrecked country as quickly as possible and secure its borders so that no attack could ever again be launched from a neighboring country. But for Stalin and Zhdanov this also demanded a stress on traditional Russian values and against "individualistic, introspective, formalist" trends then gaining ever greater authority in the Western world, as typified by abstract art and the writings of James Joyce. Zhdanov called for "democratic" art and culture, summed up as "socialist realism," free of what were seen as pro-U.S. "imperialist" influences. For a few years this was labeled "cosmopolitism," a word carrying anti-Semitic nuances.

Among the worst manifestations of this campaign, in February 1948, was the condemnation of the music of Soviet composers Dmitri Shostakovich, Sergei Prokofiev, and Aram Khachaturian for alleged "formalism, for turning away from popular culture and traditions to the purely individualistic preferences of a small group of elitist aesthetes." This implied that Party leaders, above all Stalin, could judge music more correctly than three of the world's best living composers.

Such attitudes, with the disparagement of "non-realistic" works by artists like Marc Chagall, Piet Mondrian, or even the communist Pablo Picasso, were dictated to the whole Eastern Bloc. The resulting turns of the screw hurt the young cultural scene in the GDR; I have mentioned in an earlier chapter how attacks against formalist influences hit Western emigrants, all too often with anti-Semitic overtones, and led to the downgrading, or departure, of some good, talented people. This bad era ended, almost in its entirety, with the death of Stalin. After a brief interregnum, his successor, Nikita Khrushchev, though no modernist in his tastes, ushered in that far more relaxed era called the "thaw," which soon reached the GDR.

While still in the United States, I had worriedly followed the earlier developments. In the army I was largely cut off from such problems, and during my first two years in the GDR, in an out-of-the-way town and in contact mostly with uninterested ex-soldiers, I was hardly affected and only vaguely aware of them. By the time I reached Leipzig in September 1954, the climate had fully changed. Most of those pushed off to the sidelines now again held respected, often leading positions, like Hermann Budzislavski, the dean of my Journalism School. (I might add that in all my GDR years, aside from a few harmless language leftovers, I was confronted with anti-Semitism on only one occasion, receiving the drunken blows of one of the British Army deserters in Bautzen.)

With the thaw, book-lovers could rejoice at the publication of wonderful Soviet books. Older ones were now rescued from oblivion, such as *Red Cavalry* and *Tales of Odessa* by Isaac Babel and the hilarious, fascinating, mystical and critical *The Master and Margarita* by Mikhail Bulgakov. And new authors were published. Our great favorite was the Kirghiz writer, Chingiz Aitmatov, whose short story "Jamila" was called by the French writer Louis Aragon the "most beautiful love story in the world," Also beautiful, also tragic, and treasured by Renate, was his "Farewell Gulsary," a sensitive story of a racehorse and its owner.

A series of moving films, often about the war and clear departures from all clichés, influenced many people's thinking about the USSR. Most successful, in 1957, was the tragic *The Cranes Are Flying*, which won the top prize in Cannes; a leading French film critic positively contrasted its female lead, Tatyana Samoilova, with Brigitte Bardot. It was a great film, three million moviegoers saw it in the GDR, 350,000 in East Berlin alone. Samoilova received a present from one East German fan with a note: "Finally, on the Soviet screen, we see a face, not a mask." Other fine films soon followed.

DESPITE THE UPS and downs, the negatives and positives, the Soviet presence in East Germany before I arrived was crucial in overcoming fascism and erasing fascist views, at least from all public walks of life. What was left of the mills and factories of bloody dynasties like Krupp, Flick, Siemens, and the big banks was entirely confiscated, a historic step (if it had only lasted). Junker estates had been divided up and given to agricultural laborers, poor farmers, and families that had to leave Poland and Czechoslovakia. Such giant steps in a wrecked, chaotic economy certainly involved injustices, but titled landowners had been exploiting poor farmers and German or Polish laborers for centuries, much like Mexican braceros, and most had willingly joined in all Nazi war crimes, profiting from the toil of millions of slave workers.

These sweeping measures represented a clear sharp turn in German history, aimed at realizing the dreams of reformers and revolutionaries from Thomas Müntzer in 1525 to Heinrich Heine, Marx and Engels, or Karl Liebknecht and Rosa Luxemburg before their murder—dreams of breaking the chokehold of cartels, banks, chauvinist press lords, and arrogant Junkers. All this was only possible because of the Red Army's presence. Many West Germans also hoped for such changes in 1945; their efforts were quickly aborted.

Soviet troops played a key part in ending the uprising of June 17, 1953, which they had unsuccessfully tried to head off. Their tanks, deployed but ordered not to fire, had perhaps saved the GDR for three and a half more decades. Despite doubts and criticism, many, like me, were grateful; those leading the uprisings looked increasingly frightening. As a follow-up the USSR helped out with things like butter, then in short supply, and with new modern tractors and combines.

The next event of great importance was the so-called secret speech by Nikita Khrushchev in February 1956, supplying countless details on the terrible cruelties of the Stalin era, and causing great upheavals in Poland, Hungary, and in Communist parties and circles throughout the world. The catastrophe was sadly understandable; these were facts that had been denied and rejected for decades; countless people saw their deepest beliefs shattered. But somehow my reactions were more complicated; I had long suspected some of this. Now we knew the worst—and the truth. Couldn't these revelations presage a break with past distortions and evils, a return to the principles and directions that had been so precious to us? Somehow, alongside anger and disillusionment with so many of our slogans and affirmations, this seemed to me to offer new hope, a message comparable to messages we later found in the words and deeds of people like Ho Chi Minh, Fidel Castro, Che, and Salvador Allende.

But Nikita Khrushchev came and went, for better or for worse, and problems between the USSR and the GDR increased, based largely on external pressures and economic problems in both countries. They led too rarely to fraternal, mutual assistance and too often to attempts to overcome domestic problems without regard for others. A major example was the Soviet petroleum price increase in 1982, which forced the GDR back to ecologically awful lignite as its main source of energy and chemicals. Later, with Gorbachev in leadership, there were Soviet negotiations with the Bonn government behind the back of the GDR, involving its possible sacrifice, as well as GDR attempts, despite Soviet disapproval, to negotiate on its own with Bonn. All these developments ended with the demise of both.

33—The USSR and Me

Soviet developments were always important to me. Even as a young- ster I admired Foreign Minister Maxim Litvinov's role in the League of Nations, the predecessor of the UN, where his eloquent calls for "col- lective security" against the rise of Hitler were sadly ignored. British prime minister Neville Chamberlain rather liked fascism, especially the Mussolini kind, and then saw the rise of Hitler as a welcome bar- rier against communism or anything remotely resembling it. After the putsch by Franco in Spain, Chamberlain enforced a phony all- European policy of allegedly neutral "non-intervention," preventing the elected Spanish government from buying weapons to defend itself while letting Hitler and Mussolini send unlimited shipments of planes, tanks, troops, and experts via Portugal to Franco. A reluctant and later regretful President Roosevelt was also caught up in this betrayal, with only two countries refusing to go along and supporting Spain—Mexico and the USSR. The assistance of two alone was in vain, but millions, including me, were grateful all the same.

When Hitler saw that the British government, faced by a choice, chose the fascists, even though their victory would almost encircle France in a fatal three-sided vise, he moved on in 1938–1939 and seized Austria and Czechoslovakia with hardly a disapproving murmur from the Western democracies. One exception, U.S. Assistant Secretary of State George S. Messersmith, warned in vain: "Czechoslovakia was no more Hitler's last demand than Austria had been.... The stronger Germany became, and the more statesmen conceded to Hitler, the more he would push German expansion." (George S. Messersmith, "Appeasing Fascism," *Wayne State University Conference on Munich*, ed. Melvin Small and Otto Feinstein, Lanham, MD: University Press of America, 1992, 66.)

The Soviets had to conclude that the West would do nothing against further German advance eastward, against them. The resulting Hitler-Stalin Pact, though unexpected and nasty in many ways and still roundly condemned today, was a desperate response to such collusion, with Britain and France supporting Germany as a crude but potent battering ram, with a Hitler attack eastward destroying the hated USSR and maybe ruining the Nazi Third Reich as an added bonus. Stalin's self-defensive countermove was aimed at dividing these foes, creating a buffer zone and winning time.

In June 1941, Hitler did attack the Soviet Union, after conquering nearly all of Europe, including France. As a high school student I followed the front lines on the map, with the greatest fear, as the Wehrmacht pushed to within sight of Moscow before it could be halted, and a year later to the Volga and across the Caucasus Mountains, threatening to join up with its army moving through North Africa and conquer all of Eurasia. Then, again in great suspense, only vaguely aware of a gigantic cost in lives far worse than all other nations, I traced the Red Army as it fought back westward, month by month, finally ending the Hitler plague in the city in which I would later live. Three monuments remain in Berlin to honor the thousands who died in that last battle. Had they not fought so bitterly—and successfully—I and countless more would have been sent off to fight and perhaps, like my cousin Jerry, to die at the hands of the racist Nazis. Those events help explain my feelings about the USSR.

"Were you really a Stalinist?" I've been asked. Few today know that in the 1930s and early 1940s the Communists were leaders in organizing powerful unions and winning basic rights for working people.. They were decades ahead in fighting for the rights of African Americans, as symbolized by their worldwide campaign to save the lives of the nine Scottsboro lads sentenced to death in Alabama on false charges. They led in fights to halt evictions of families onto the streets and the auctioning off of insolvent farms. Communist or pro-communist writers, artists, and composers were key to invigorating the entire cultural scene in the United States, and they stood out in the fight against fascists, domestic or foreign. The emotions involved extended to the USSR, which was then seen and praised by countless wise men and women for being the only country not hit by the Great Depression, and which had done away with joblessness, with illiteracy, with racism, as well as opposing fascism.

Yes, I also had private doubts about Stalin, about the trials with their confessions of guilt and their death sentences, and with the twenty-two months of the Hitler-Stalin Pact. But people, not only on the left, tend to think and believe what they want to believe, and play down any doubts. There was so much repression in the world by Britain, France, and the United States in dozens of colonies, half-colonies and at home, that many of the world's most brilliant, admirable people weighed the scales in the same way I did. Indeed, viewing the role of the USSR from an anti-fascist, anti-Nazi perspective, we found no contradiction between admiration for it and humanitarianism or genuine U.S. patriotism. The course of the Second World War reinforced such a position.

After 1945, the pressure to forget and reject all this grew so strong that fewer and fewer held to it. I was one who was stubborn, and seven years later took a risk, making the fateful decision to put myself into Soviet hands. Looking back, I must say that they, seeing in me a friend, treated me well and heartily. And I saw their presence in the GDR as a guarantee of my own personal liberty.

I visited the USSR (and later Russia) six times. On my trip with my mother in 1964, we first saw beautiful Leningrad with its amazing long days, making it possible to read a newspaper outside at 11 p.m., its ballet, with audiences throwing dozens of little bouquets onto the stage in appreciation, its monuments, its handsome, broad river Neva but also, in many faces, traces of that terrible siege, nearly 900 days long, with a million and a half deaths, mostly civilians, dying of hunger and cold. Then we visited Samarkand, with its magnificent mausoleums and Registan Square with its madrassas, schools but really temples, and the remains of an advanced astronomy center from the fifteenth century. Tashkent, also in Uzbekistan, was full of contrasts. We saw modern, boring new buildings and a mediocre Russian opera, but then, at a wonderful evening in a big arena, saw whole families enjoying songs, dances, and clearly hilarious remarks by the moderators. Uzbek women wore their vivid flame-pattern dresses and black braids, and, if I recall correctly, not one with a niqab or such a head covering. Our guide finally stopped showing us heroic statues and took us outside town, past earthen homes with goats chewing grass on their roofs, to an outdoor tea house at a riverside, with friendly, elderly men cutting onions and carrots for pilaf and sipping tea from little cups.

In 1965, after three years with Radio Berlin International, writing and producing broadcasts for ham radio enthusiasts in North America, I became director of a new Paul Robeson Archive at East Berlin's Academy of Arts. For me Robeson was far more than just a great singer, actor, and athlete, he was a truly great Renaissance mensch, one of the century's greatest! In 1967, I visited Moscow, hunting for material on his visits to the USSR for an exhibition to mark his seventieth birthday the following year. Among many impressions, far more than as a tourist, I found a relative normality and open discussion, sometimes surprising (like the intellectual who displayed a heroic poster of John F. Kennedy in his home). I also visited an American and his Russian family in their pleasant apartment. An exile like myself (from the 1930s), he spoke of his life's ups and downs. In answer to my questions, he said that in previous years his Party group had quickly acted on any anti-Semitic incidents, but it had recently become neglectful in this matter. Through him I met Lily Golden, a professor of African Studies, the daughter of an African-American agronomist and his Jewish-American wife who helped develop the cotton industry in the early Soviet years. I also recall one young man who interpreted for me, a doctorate student at the Academy of Sciences, who spoke of his pride that he, a Turkoman, could achieve an honored career while his father, before the Revolution, had faced nothing but discrimination.

In 1974, I visited Karelia as interpreter for an American actor and singer, Dean Reed, from Colorado, who had moved to East Berlin. For a Gold Rush film based on Jack London stories, GDR filmmakers used a long, narrow lake up in the Soviet north country as a substitute for the Yukon River. Aside from long truck drives over the ice-bound water-way and a fascinating group of Yakutians from farthest Siberia, hired on with sleds and dogs for the racing scenes, I was most interested in one extra of Finnish descent, recruited during the Depression in Canada to help build up "Soviet Karelia" (Karelian is a dialect of Finnish). He only hinted at the extremely difficult war years when he had been a soldier and a POW; thanks to his ability with an accordion he got a job at the bilingual Karelian-Russian theater and was then hired on as a regular actor. At his request, I later sent his daughter, who played in the local symphony orchestra, a score of Ernest Bloch's *Rhapsodie Hébraïque* for solo cello.

In 1971, at the invitation of Berlin neighbors working in Moscow who offered us a temporarily empty apartment, we four took the long, pleasant train trip in our own private compartment from Berlin to Moscow, with no meals offered but all the free tea we wanted. We spent two weeks there, enjoying especially the delicious pelmeni, ice cream and dairy and bakery goods, the speedboat trip down the Moscow River, and the preferential treatment given children, as in the Moscow subway, where adults stood up to give children a seat. In Berlin, the opposite is expected.

In 1988, Renate and I had a two-week vacation at the Black Sea near Sochi. We grew accustomed to the pebble beach, liked the good food (but not very friendly service—perhaps for guests from Germany) and rejoiced at the far friendlier dolphins jumping up and down to watch us swimming. We could not fail to notice that while neon lights cele-brated Gorbachev's "perestroika" reconstruction plan, it had evidently not had much effect. Shops and the downtown department store were miserably understocked. Without marked improvement, this could not last much longer, I concluded. On my last visit, in 2016, I found our

Cassandra predictions confirmed in a now-capitalist Moscow. I noted some of the results: a cluster of modern skyscraper business buildings, gold-domed churches now seemingly everywhere, and banks and retail shops like never before, from fast-food to IKEA. But there too, luckily, the Kremlin, always impressive, and the beautiful Basilius Cathedral and Novodevichy Convent, the latter with its amazing cemetery, crowded with graves of famous people, recent or long gone. And, a still vital remaining reminder of the old days, a handsome children's center for sports and hobbies, founded by Soviet Young Pioneers.

Behind the Kremlin were simple monuments to the major battles of 1941 to 1945, Stalingrad, Kursk, Leningrad, the Dnepr River crossing, Berlin—all so deeply inscribed in my memory and heart from my high school days that I could not restrain some tears. Also poignant for me were urns in the Kremlin wall with ashes of Harvard man John Reed, famous chronicler of the Russian Revolution, of Charles Ruthenberg, also a founder of the U.S. Communist Party in 1919, and of "Big Bill" Haywood, the leader of the IWW "Wobblies" and many tough strikes in the early twentieth century, lesser-known heroes of my homeland's history!

THE TWENTIETH CENTURY had witnessed a giant experiment, a form of socialism with world-changing influence. Beginning in 1917, it spread new hope, and then again, in 1945, after fascism was defeated and so many in Asia and Africa sought independence. The USSR made enormous advances in industrializing, in achieving literacy, health care, and other benefits for many millions, Much of it went down the drain after 1990. Many saw this as democratic liberation; there were indeed new freedoms, recompenses, and improvements. But some like me saw the years 1989–94 as a reversion to the past, a step backwards. I assign much of the blame, along with many other factors, to the rule of Stalin, his methods, his minions and his legacy, some of which can probably be traced to age-old Russian traditions of autocracy and cruelty plus the effects of a terrible civil war and devastating invasions. I see his cruel reign as a distortion, and not inevitable. Another slice of responsibility can be attributed to heavy-handed Party boss Leonid

Brezhnev (1964–82); some prefer to blame Khrushchev (1954–64) or Gorbachev (1985–91), or, often enough, the whole top-heavy system. No matter how blame is apportioned—and by no means only from the East—influences and pressures from the Kremlin closely affected GDR development, very positively in some ways, but increasingly negatively with every year.

DURING MY FIRST visit to my United States homeland in 1994 I was asked: "How could you ever live with those Russians in East Germany?" I had to smile; they certainly had many troops stationed here, but aside from a few garrison towns they were hardly visible, with almost no contact with the civilian population, no doubt to avoid problems, also of a sexual nature, negative or positive, and envy, for the standard of living averaged well above that in the USSR. Almost the only place to see Soviet soldiers in Berlin was either at the zoo (the Tierpark), where there were few linguistic difficulties, or on memorial ceremonies at the impressive monuments to those who had died. A Russian civilian from the embassy staff once kindly drove me home from some gathering; on the way he pointed to a building near the river: "That's where the Nazis killed my best friend—in the last week of the war!"

Two Russian families, with trade organizations in Berlin, lived in our building. The eight-year-old son of one of them became so fluent in Berlin German by playing with the other kids that he corrected his embarrassed Russian teacher's grammar. The other couple, childless, sometimes invited all the kids in the house to tea and cookies and once presented them with the husband's weekend fish catch. A neighbor got a shock one evening when she found one (a fish), alive, in the bathtub, also full of wet bread (as fodder!). But these people were civilians; Red Army uniforms were seldom seen away from the zoo. At the Leipzig Fair I was an interpreter for a businessman from Iceland. "I've never seen a Russian," he said. "Are there any here? Can you point one out?" By chance we did come upon just one, a very short young lieutenant. The Icelander stared at him for a moment with obvious surprise and then asked: "Tell me, are all Russians so short?"

34—Stasi

Aside from "the Russians" and the "Berlin Wall," the term most associ-
ated with the GDR in Western minds, especially West German ones,
was certainly "Stasi," and with it every imaginable evil. But owing to my
experience in the icy Cold War United States, my judgments about the
Stasi were more complex. I could never approve of their often stupid or
nasty methods or their very ubiquity. But unlike most of those around
me, I could compare and evaluate political smog levels in more than
just one country.

For one, I perceived very well the unceasing attempts to smother
the GDR child, if not in the cradle, then before it could attain durable
maturity or worrisome competitiveness. The attacks were not restricted
to painting and literature, or to radio and TV, but involved a wide
network of people who supplied constant information on economic,
military, cultural, and political matters to West German, American, and
British centers in West Berlin. And every presumed freedom-seeker
who succeeded in crossing to West Berlin or chose to stay in the West
after a visit was thoroughly pumped on all such matters as well as for
tips on others to lure or blackmail into taking the same path. Rejecting
such grilling in a "reception center" meant forfeiting assistance in finding a job, a home, financial help, or even a flight from West Berlin to
West Germany, and rail and road routes were checked by East German
authorities.

A major force in the early years of hostile activity was the
Kampfgruppe gegen Unmenschlichkeit (KgU), the Combat Group
Against Inhumanity, which was linked to the espionage network of
former Nazi Eastern Front expert Reinhard Gehlen and to the Senate
of West Berlin, with financial aid from the Ford Foundation and the
Red Cross, since it was officially described as a humanitarian organization. Its aim was to destabilize or wreck the GDR. In the 1950s this
included exploding railroad and highway bridges, igniting a fire in a
Leipzig department store, storing poisons to be used against Soviet
soldiers, and tricks to disrupt food transports. Those actions, in any
case, were planned—but stymied. By 1959 the KgU was no longer

considered a match for the Stasi and was closed down, replaced by methods like encouraging and supporting attempts to burrow under or otherwise surmount the Wall, aimed at grabbing headlines just when major GDR celebrations were scheduled.

This all helps to explain the widespread network of the Ministry of State Security, known as the Stasi (short for Staats-Sicherheit). Wilhelm Zaisser, who commanded the Thirteenth International Brigade in the Spanish War (under the pseudonym General Gómez), headed it first, but after he was blamed for not foreseeing or properly coping with the revolt of June 17, 1953, he was replaced by another former hero, Ernst Wollweber, who had organized seamen internationally to support the Spanish Republic. But he too was ousted, for joining in a palace revolt against Walter Ulbricht, and was followed by Erich Mielke, also a former International Brigader, who had fled Germany in 1931 after allegedly shooting a policeman during a riot in Berlin. Sixty years later, after the demise of the GDR, he was condemned to six years in prison for the shooting and served four of them. He was eighty-eight when he was released on parole.

Mielke's long rule as Stasi boss demonstrated how such activities can too easily fall into the hands of the kind of men who like to administer "countermeasures" in any society, some with an FBI badge or a blue uniform with Taser, nightstick, and revolver, some with a Supreme Court robe approving an execution, and some with an ID card of the NKVD or Stasi.

Mielke was generally ridiculed or despised, and certainly does not seem to have been sympathetic in any way. But despite that, I find it a purposeful and deliberate lie to equate even the Stasi's worst activities with the tens of thousands of cases of Nazi torture, hanging, and execution—over 16,000 by guillotine—mostly Communists and other leftists, even before their killers stormed through Europe and began mass annihilation. Was this false equation propagated in part to distract from the great numbers of SS and Gestapo killers hired by equivalent West German institutions, often for leadership positions?

This distorted "Stasi-Nazi" campaign, especially after the death of the GDR, was reflected in many films, and never more cleverly than in an excellently written, directed, and acted but exceedingly deceitful 2006 German Oscar-winner, *The Lives of Others*. Its main villain is a sinister, lecherous, and brutal Minister of Culture. How many of its audience knew anything about the six men who held that GDR position? The first one, Johannes R. Becher, a prominent poet and writer during the pre-Hitler years, also wrote the moving text of the GDR national anthem. Another, a Parisian exile, helped compile the famous Brown Book indictment of Hitler in 1933 and led anti-fascist activity among German ex-patriots in wartime Mexico. A third, after studies at the Sorbonne and Oxford, fought Hitler in the underground. He later became the first and only Jewish ambassador to Italy and Vatican City (for the GDR). A fourth escaped to England in the last transport of Jewish children in 1939. All six were highly educated, cultivated men, absolute opposites of the type shown in the film.

The film shows how a meticulous Stasi examination of the keyboard letters of a typewriter enables them to nab the film's hero after he secretly sent exposés about the GDR to a West German magazine. The same exact study of typewriter letters was at the center of the Washington trial in 1949 of the U.S. diplomat Alger Hiss. Richard Nixon, gaining his first fame as a Communist hunter, used the keyboard letters to convict Hess, a leading architect of the United Nations, as a Soviet spy. I cannot believe this similarity was coincidental, but surmise that the film's author, in turning this scene on its head politically, felt confident that few if any would recall the original story.

This film, like those not so well made, gave a baleful picture of the GDR and especially the Stasi. It was no pleasant organization, certainly, and snooped into all aspects of public and private life. In the very first postwar years, people did indeed avoid critical jokes, at least in public—and wisely so. And till the end, for anyone involved in organized dissent, or planning a break over or under the Berlin Wall, it could indeed be threatening. But the vast majority of GDR citizens, not involved in such activities, knew about the Stasi but did not take it so terribly seriously. In fact, it was frequently, and certainly fearlessly, joked about. In our building, with twenty-four families, most neighbors assumed that two men worked for the Stasi, one a taciturn fellow whom nobody liked or saw much of, the other a friendly fellow who joined in activities of house inhabitants, like our biannual clean-ups of lawns and shrubbery around the house. Neither ever asked prying or otherwise dubious questions.

The widespread network of paid and unpaid agents within the GDR aimed not only at keeping tabs on all activities seen as subversive, but also was tasked at closely and objectively observing the thinking trends and general atmosphere within the population. It now seems clear that their reports were not sufficiently believed or not effectively acted upon by the men—or man—at the top.

As elsewhere in the world, every method was seen as legitimate if considered necessary to save the system. Organized opposition, especially, was to be nipped in the bud as quickly as possible, or, if that was difficult, then closely observed and controlled. Such buds ripened apace in the small, disadvantaged GDR, so greatly overshadowed by its wealthy next-door neighbor. A vicious circle ensued; the greater the perceived danger, the bigger the control apparatus, which made it more disliked, leading to growing dissent and to further Stasi expansion.

I do not wish to prettify the picture of the organization; it could certainly be obnoxious. But in the case of the three men I knew who were employed by the Stasi, I am convinced they were motivated by an allegiance to the progressive aims of the GDR and a repudiation of Western efforts to undermine it. My one-semester roommate at Leipzig was one of them (as I learned later, which led me to wonder if his connection may have been why he happened to be my roommate). When we met by chance years after the end of the GDR, he spoke about his former job, taken on in gratitude for the good treatment and career chances offered him, a forlorn war orphan from East Prussia. With many, no doubt, regardless of motivation—like those who join the U.S. police, FBI, or CIA because of patriotism, perhaps to unearth Nazi wartime spies —power often corrupts. This certainly was true of the Stasi's last, longest, and most abhorrent boss. I might add, without generalizing, that the one active dissident I knew personally who was imprisoned by the Stasi (before he was expelled against his will to West Germany) said that the only torture he knew of, based on conduct judged cooperative or stubborn, was a corresponding increase or decrease in the number of allotted cigarettes. But I cannot generalize.

A few years ago, *Der Spiegel* quoted a historian, recently employed by the Stasi Investigation Authority, who insisted that the publicized numbers on Stasi employees and informers had been extremely exaggerated, counting many people twice, including over ten thousand who worked for the GDR in West Germany or elsewhere but never spied on GDR citizens, and falsely listing many thousands who never did any spying or informing. (Ilko-Sascha Kowalczuk, "Die schlanke Stasi," *SpiegelOnline*, February 21, 2013.) Another exposé in the same magazine reveals that in September 1960 Chancellor Konrad Adenauer assigned Reinhard Gehlen, the same superspy of Hitler who organized the BND, the offshoot of the CIA in West Germany, to spy on his political rival Willy Brandt and check on his activities as an anti-fascist exile during the Nazi years. How many GDR lives after the demise of the GDR were wrecked or driven to suicide for doing far less snooping— or none at all? (Klaus Wiegriefe, "Adenauer Has Gehlen Spy on Willy Brandt," *SpiegelOnline,* April 7, 2017.)

The East German equivalent of the BND, the "external division" of the State Security Ministry working outside the GDR, was headed by Markus Wolf, a son of the writer Friedrich and brother of the film director Konrad Wolf. He was famous for its amazing success, largely thanks to relationships based on his political conviction that West Germany and its ally in Washington endangered the cause of world peace. Its one calamity was Willy Brandt's retirement as chancellor after his close collaborator was discovered to be working with Markus Wolf. Its biggest success was Rainer Rupp, who under the alias "Topaz" reached a high-level position in the NATO military planning structure. During a NATO Europe-wide war exercise called Able Archer, in November 1983, which simulated an atomic war, Rupp assured the Soviets that the maneuver was not, as they feared, a preparation for an actual attack, and that may have saved the world from atomic war. After unification, Rupp was sentenced to a ten-year prison term.

I too was approached by the Stasi with requests for assistance. After the United States set up its embassy and consulate in East Berlin in 1974, the latter asked me to visit to "clarify my status and that of my sons." I telephoned the local police to ask if I need have any fears about going there. No, I was assured. But a little later I got a visit from two gentlemen who asked if I would help them by going to film evenings now being offered by the embassy and "make friends there." I responded very honestly that I felt nervous just going near that location with its two big Marine guards, and they wrote me off, as they did on two other occasions when I was able to convince them, always very politely, that I was of no use to them.

Of course, being one of a very few Americans in the GDR, it was not surprising that I, too, was observed. As I later learned, world-famous anti-Nazis like Thomas Mann and Bertolt Brecht, being German, were always observed in wartime United States, not to mention the plight of even the most loyal Japanese Americans. The exhaustive checks on me by the FBI were, after all, in a country never really threatened, neither from Canada nor Mexico, and with two big oceans to the east and west, while the GDR faced a very explicit foe right next door, not one yard away, which was able to win out in the end.

Among the Stasi reports on me that I have read were also a few odd notes, for example that I spoke fluent English, German, French, and Russian (unfortunately, only the first two are correct). The files, probably incomplete, were less interesting than the FBI files.

For most people in the GDR, I think, the Stasi, though certainly unloved and by many despised, was hardly the ghastly monster so often portrayed in today's media. Common causes of laughter (or ridicule) were the duos of casually dressed men, about 100 or 200 yards apart who tried to look nonchalant as they lined the routes of visiting state dignitaries.

Here's a little side note: One section of a building a few blocks away from us was said to be only for Stasi employees and their families. My son, rather curious at seventeen, saw a little boy on a tricycle in front of it. "Where does your daddy work?" he asked. "I'm not allowed to say," the lad lisped, and I always got a laugh not a shudder when I told the story.

I have thought of writing a book about some idiocies by both the

FBI and the Stasi, and calling it "Cosi fan tutti"—Indeed, they all do it! What country doesn't?

35—Normalcy

After the Wall was built in 1961, there had been a definite improvement in GDR living standards. Some tensions eased, but others grew. Many young people, without problems like finding job training or full-pay jobs, were unhappy about taboos regarding matters like clothing, music, even male hairstyles. The relationship between them and the government recalled a sailboat, feeling the strength of currents from below its keel, derived from young people's pressures, but also ruled by winds from above. And colder blasts were blowing in from the east after Brezhnev replaced Khrushchev and were further frosted by some stern local authorities. But other winds, hot as any sirocco from the Sahara, were closing in from the West via radio, TV, or smuggled records and tapes. They blew in Elvis, the Beatles, the Stones . . .

When the Rolling Stones arrived in western Dusseldorf, 5,000 hysterical fans at the airport supplied a kind of omen for their coming concert in West Berlin's beautiful outdoor Waldbühne on September 15, 1965. All hell broke loose. The first battles were with groups who invaded without tickets but tried to seize the best reserved seats. Before long, lights were torn down, all the lighting went out, cops rode in on horses—and were often pulled off them by the crowd. Autos, city train coaches, and countless nearby windows were demolished, almost ninety were arrested, a similar number injured.

It was hard to say who could still sing happily the Stones' favorite "I Can't Get No Satisfaction." Hardly the GDR leaders across the border. Seized by a great fear of possible contagion, their over-quick reaction was to ban nearly fifty of the larger and smaller "beat groups" in Leipzig that had formed in the prevailing tolerant atmosphere. The protest against this ban in a major city square was heated up by attempts to prevent it. That only provided more publicity and was met with a rough reaction by police fearing a repeat of the Waldbühne devastation. This conflict was an important reason for tightening the screws on music and the cultural scene at the 11th Plenum Congress of the SED. It took about six years for the pressures on musicians and audiences to relax in the East and seven years before the Waldbühne in West Berlin could be opened for concerts again, this time for more peaceable singers like Joan Baez.

Yet despite occasional excitement on the youthful musical scene and strife in sectors of the general cultural scene, life was different from what newspaper readers in Milwaukee or TV viewers in Munich may have imagined. Despite bad spots, some true and unfortunate but many superficially magnified in the hostile West German press, we led by and large normal lives. There was always some shortage or other to bother people and some were angered by stuffy slogans and clichés in the media. But most of us just ignored them and hardly even noticed the near disappearance in public places of those white-lettered slogans on red cloth calling for lasting peace, more socialism, or more production. There were still a few jokes regarding those, like the one about the banner that said "We pledge overfulfillment of our annual quota" over the public cemetery. Or the universal jest that "Our economy has only four more problems to deal with—winter, summer, spring and fall."

But most people went to work in the morning, raised their kids as best they knew how, went to the movies, sometimes the theater or opera, far more often to the soccer stadium, and took part in a host of weekend and after-work sports, hobbies, and amusements. Whenever I traveled outside the cities in the warmer months, I passed countless dachas (one of the few Russian words generally adopted); about half the population had some bungalow, simple or fancy, with lawns, with or without fruit trees and gardens, more and more often with small swimming pools. In the evening hours, I saw people at such houses happily grilling steaks or burgers, consuming potato salad or other homemade delicacies, drinking, mostly beer, listening to music, mostly of Western origin, chatting and enjoying themselves, while the young set, as soon as they were old enough, were off to the nearest disco on their motorbikes or motorcycles, the plebeians on bicycles, and almost none with cars, since eighteen years was the requirement for a license or car ownership.

Almost every lake around East Berlin (and there are very many) was full of boats, from canoes and rowboats to elegant sailboats and yachts. In icy winter days, still frequent in those years, parks were full of kids and parents on sleds, skates, or skis, while ardent skiers saved a week or two of their annual vacations and drove to the low mountains in the south. Perhaps, like a far smaller number of mountain-climbers, they dreamed of Alpine slopes or peaks. But they enjoyed what they had.

Many Western visitors who took brief looks at East Berlin or the GDR noted the shabbiness of building facades and the decrepit look of many neighborhoods. They may not have seen the big white high-rise housing developments, usually off tourist routes on city outskirts. These new buildings were rarely architectural masterpieces, though here and there I saw attempts at handsome designs. Relatively few city-dwellers had separate homes. But new or old, shabby or recent pre-fab, behind the facades I almost always found comfortably furnished homes, some with a hankering for consumerist ostentation, others with simpler good taste. The often shabby exteriors of privately owned buildings and the plain city-owned pre-fabs were more easily accepted by tenants who paid only an eighth or a tenth of their income on rent.

36—Police Gags

Fashions in jokes often change as much as fashions in heels or hose. I already wrote of the joke wave in the Eastern Bloc based on "questions to Radio Yerevan" and its double-pronged responses. Some joke waves, sadly, are directed against people of specific national origin or dialect, as in West Germany against supposedly stupid East Friesians. They can be racist with a long-lasting effect, like those about "lazy Mexicans." If they are about people in some trade or profession, they are usually less painful. There was once a wave in the United States against economists, starting with their skill, or lack of it, with screwing in ceiling light bulbs. (It takes five of them; four to turn the table around which the fifth man with the bulb is standing on!) I doubt that it brought bitter tears to that target group.

Are the waves of policemen gags international? For years they were widespread in the GDR, always involving a presumed low IQ level. I will offer up a number of such jokes here, favorites of mine, partly to indicate that the forces of law and order were not looked upon with awe and fear, not even in the GDR, and partly just to lighten the atmosphere before the coming sadder chapters of the book (sadder for me, anyway).

The commonest gags involved two cops on a beat. Why always two? Because together they had eight years of schooling. Or because at least one could read and the other write.

Or about the two cops who were asked directions by a tourist: "Do you speak English?" he asked. They shrugged. "Parlez-vous français?" The same response. He stutters the same question in Russian but has no more luck and drives away, shaking his head. One cop says: "Gee, he must be smart. He knows lots of languages!" The other responds, "Yeah. But what good did it do him?"

In a longer joke, a teacher tries to get acquainted with her new fifth-grade class: "Tell me, children, what would you like to be when you grow up?" There were no answers. "What, haven't any of you thought about what you'd like to do?" Still no answer. "Oh, I can't believe that. You, the little girl over there, What's your name?" —"Susi Schmidt, Frau Lehrerin." (The proper title for a teacher).

"What would you like to do, Susi?"—"I don't know, Frau Lehrerin."

"Oh dear. How about you? And what's your name?"—"Hans Müller."—"And what would you like to be, Hans?"—"I don't know, Frau Lehrerin."

"Really, nobody at all?" One hand at the back is raised timidly. "Well, at last, here's a lad who's thought about the future. And what would you like to be?"—"A policeman."

"How nice! We do need friendly policemen to help and protect us. And what is your name?" —"I don't know, Frau Lehrerin."

One of my favorites: The chief stops as he drives past a cop on the corner. "Are you crazy? You're wearing one black boot and one white one! Get home in a hurry and come back properly dressed!" "I'm sorry, boss," came the answer. "At home I also have only one white boot and one black one!"

Or, finally, one about the policeman who finds a live penguin in the street, all alone. "What shall I do with him?" he asks the captain. "Why, take him to the zoo, you idiot!" Late that afternoon, as the captain leaves to go home, he sees the cop walking with the penguin, hand-in-flipper. "Didn't I tell you to take him to the zoo, you damned fool?" —"But yes, I did! And now I'm taking him to the movies!"

But as the next chapter indicates, cops were not only assigned to dealing with friendly penguins!

37—Loud Notes at the Wall

When Mikhail Gorbachev took over in Moscow after three superannuated leaders, at what seemed by comparison a youthful fifty-four, his vigor and freshness, his abandonment of outmoded protocol methods, and above all his surprising offers of peaceful disarmament made him popular almost everywhere, including the GDR. It forced Ronald Reagan to break at least his open pursuit of military domination and take a seat at the negotiating table. But Gorbachev's restructuring policy, called "perestroika," did not achieve any real results, whereas his transparency policy, "glasnost," opened the doors for critics determined to change the entire socialist system. This, at least, is how the GDR Party leaders saw it and, for the first time, they faced the problem of contradicting Moscow. They, too, wanted rapprochement between the United States and the USSR and a reduction in disastrous armament costs, but not if the agreement between the giants was to be at their expense.

And now, in mid-June 1987, Ronald Reagan was coming to Berlin to make a speech. Kennedy's famous "Ich bin ein Berliner" words twenty-four years earlier were still a legend. Would this very different president's words enhance the world's new hopes?

And could it be pure coincidence that, less than a week before Reagan's speech, three days of rock music concerts were planned, just a stone's throw from the Berlin Wall, directly on the Western side of the Brandenburg Gate where he was going to speak?

On the first day, David Bowie sang from a specially built giant platform; he was followed on subsequent days by the Eurythmics and Genesis, with Phil Collins. Sixty thousand West Berliners were at the concerts, but they were aimed at another audience; huge amplifiers blasted the music over the Wall, deep into East Berlin, so loud it caused real alarm among patients in the big Charité hospital not far enough away.

It was hardly generosity that motivated the free concerts. In the two years that followed, famous singers like Bob Dylan, Joe Cocker, and Bruce Springsteen would have great success in East Berlin, but none had as yet. As one young fellow told me, "There are plenty here who'd sell their grannies for a chance to see such musicians!" It was crystal clear: lots of young East Berliners were to be lured as close to the Wall as possible and, who knows, maybe even to try storming it. A tough reaction by the GDR police seemed just as inevitable, with arrests and no doubt injuries. It had happened once or twice before but never at this most neuralgic spot. No matter what the outcome, a rebellion of young people, maybe a battle, would supply exactly the right prelude to Reagan's famous and belligerent call, "Mr. Gorbachev, tear down this wall!"

The CIA radio station RIAS did all it could to reach a wider GDR audience, more than ever before. It considered the event, as later recalled by a main editor, a "mosaic stone" on the road to November 9, 1989 (the fall of the Wall) and the end of the GDR.

But as Scotland's Bobby Burns once rhymed, regarding unexpected results, "The best laid schemes o' Mice an' Men, Gang aft agley." Nothing turned out quite as it had clearly been planned.

Hundreds of young East Berliners did indeed swarm toward the blaring music. And yes, the police, and no doubt Stasi, were there to keep them from getting too close to the Wall and provoking a truly dangerous situation. But they were clearly under strict orders; no police weapons, no tear gas. Even when a few firecrackers and bottles were thrown, especially on the third night, they just linked arms in a tight line. In close-up TV reports—West-TV, since GDR-TV barely covered the event—I could see real fear in the eyes of men in that line, but no weapons in their hands.

I watched on TV how, east of the Brandenburg Gate on the Boulevard Unter den Linden, six or seven sheepish-looking young East Berliners called "Down with the Wall" or "Gorby," whom they now championed as a counterweight to GDR leaders. But it was obvious that some West-TV "maestro" behind the camera was waving for a crescendo, and perhaps waving a handful of desirable 10 West-marks as well, but with anemic results. One Western reporter, almost in tears, told of nasty police violence against him, a journalist, and displayed a barely discernible blue mark on his shin. There had indeed been a threat of danger at the border. But the East German side, obviously under strict orders to avoid trouble, was successful; aside from a few scuffles and a few arrests, there was no riot.

The exact opposite was true in West Berlin. On the eve of Reagan's appearance, 150 parties and organizations rallied downtown to protest his support for the bloody "Contra" attacks against Nicaragua, defying UN resolutions and even rulings of the U.S. Congress. But their main demand was for an end to the U.S. military buildup and an agreement with the Soviets on disarmament. It all went peacefully, with a crowd of perhaps 50,000, until one small masked bloc broke windows of the big KaDeWe department store. As if by command and careful planning, the police suddenly appeared. Wild chases, with frisking and beatings for anyone whose clothes or hair length looked suspicious, lasted that night and the day that followed, when Reagan spoke so eloquently of freedom. Again, nightsticks fell, tear gas spread, homes and a bar were broken into, all subway and bus traffic to and from a part of the borough of Kreuzberg known as "oppositional" was completely halted, shutting it off from the rest of the city. As a climax, five hundred people were "kettled" from 3 p.m. to 8.30 p.m., not allowed to leave the police encirclement even during a rain shower. There were 366 arrests and countless injuries, also to passers-by and journalists; one man required hospital care.

The scuffles in East Berlin had been more like a Sunday School picnic in comparison. But not for the Western media, for whom it had been the scene of angry, rebellious battles, described almost hysterically, while the West Berlin events, outside the local press, were hardly mentioned and Reagan's emotional words got the main headlines.

38—Hope with Honecker in Bonn

All kinds of things happened in 1987. Five days after Reagan's speech, the GDR government officially conformed to UN recommendations by abolishing the death penalty, which it had not used for many years anyway. Even bigger news was its general amnesty for criminal and political prison inmates in the GDR, excepting only those convicted of sexual violence, other violent crimes, or Nazi war crimes. By the end of the year 32,500 inmates were released, leaving only 5,300 behind bars. This also put an end to the more than dubious method of letting political prisoners leave for West Germany for a sum paid by the government there.

This was not the first such amnesty in the GDR, but it was the biggest. Many believed that the two decisions, both praised by Amnesty International, were a prelude to an event Erich Honecker had long been dreaming of, an official visit to the Federal Republic as accepted head of state with all the usual honors, and thus recognition of the coexistence of the GDR as a second German state. Diplomatic relations had long been established with almost every country in the world, but Erich Honecker still yearned for a "free and equal" visit to West Germany. For some years this had been hindered, or outright forbidden, by the Soviet leaders, but with the growing estrangement between the top men of the GDR and the Gorbachev team, who were negotiating with Helmut Kohl and his West German team on their own accord, Honecker defied them and flew to Bonn, then the capital.

He rejoiced proudly to see the GDR flag hoisted at the ceremony (both flags had the same colors but the GDR flag had at its center its official emblem, a hammer and compass encircled by a wreath of grain), also to hear both anthems played, and to pace past the honor guard. He carefully ignored petty deficiencies, like the smaller motorcycle escort, shorter red carpet, and lack of a gun salute, since Bonn slated this as a "work meeting" and not a "meeting of state." Chancellor Kohl insisted—and won—uncut TV coverage of both leaders' banquet speeches, in East as well as West, and used his speech to get his digs in about German unity, while Honecker more tactfully stressed the need for mutual work for peace.

During his day with Honecker, Chancellor Kohl visibly displayed a lack of any enthusiasm whatsoever; indeed, you could often wonder if he was chewing on a lemon. But the rest of the five-day trip went off well. Honecker was treated almost royally in Munich, where the Bavarian boss, Franz-Josef Strauss, once an implacable foe, now helped the GDR economy with big, urgently needed credit advances.

Honecker was most warmly welcomed in his little hometown in Saarland, where he met his sister, visited his parents' graves, and got a warm welcome from the minister president, Oskar Lafontaine, a Social Democrat who, twenty years later, would co-found and co-chair the left-wing party Die Linke.

It was here that Honecker set tongues wagging when he said that since the two states belonged to different military alliances "it is only too understandable that the border is clearly not as it should be." But he felt confident that if cooperation between them continued "then the day will come when the borders will not separate us but will unite us, like the border between the German Democratic Republic and the Polish People's Republic." That border had neither a Wall nor other barriers, except the Oder and Neisse rivers.

Many viewed this visit as the pinnacle of Honecker's career. It raised many hopes, some for a friendlier, more open relationship that would make travel easier and bring more and better commodities into the shops, and others for joining the two states together, a goal that dreamers could hardly have imagined was only three years away. Behind the victorious spirit he displayed, troubles were increasing in the GDR and the economy was no longer in the steady climb of so many previous years.

39—Broken Dreams

Some people were doing more than just dreaming about a major change; they were actively trying to undo any hopes aroused by Honecker's Western travels that the two states might get along and achieve a more equal relationship. A lengthy West German TV presentation soon introduced a number of GDR dissidents, hitherto almost unknown but now presented in glowing terms. The aim was neither ambiguous nor original but seemed to me more clearly purposeful in its defiant opposition than ever before.

A few months later, I saw the same faces again on my TV screen. Every January in Berlin there is a march, or rather a walk, honoring the memory of Rosa Luxemburg and Karl Liebknecht, both still loved for their opposition to the First World War and their fight for working people, and both murdered in January 1919 in Berlin two weeks after they helped found the Communist Party. The monument by Mies van der Rohe marking their former gravesite was destroyed by the Nazis, but a new site was constructed, also for other famous leftists. The annual walk there by many thousands is a lasting tradition to this day, interrupted only by the Nazi years. I always took part, during the more formal GDR years and in the years since. A majority take the subway and walk seven or eight blocks to lay red carnations on the gravesites. More militant leftist groups from all over Germany and beyond walk several kilometers down Karl-Marx-Allee with banners, flags, and sound trucks and then join and mix with the main, usually older group.

In the 1980s I always walked with other members of the Writers' Association and had a chance to chat for a few hours on all kinds of interesting subjects. But in January 1988 things were suddenly different. Another writer and I arrived five minutes late for our group, usually no problem, since we had never moved off till about twenty minutes after the official starting time. This time, however, our colleagues were already gone. We tried to join another group, any group. That had always been possible. But not this time. We were told to keep to our own group, which was now long gone. So instead we turned around and went home.

On West-TV, I learned what the problem was. A group of dissidents had stationed themselves at one point along the route, holding up "unapproved" banners, many citing that famous quotation of Rosa Luxemburg: "Freedom is always the freedom for those who think differently." These words, repeated so frequently since then, were not okay for the GDR leaders, especially since those holding the banners up, or trying to, had been most actively attacking them, with the assistance of the West German media. Yes, I had seen them on West-TV a few months earlier. Some people clearly opposed any East-West détente.

Those with the banners were arrested, while muscular hands tried to cover the front of the lenses of Western journalists, just what the latter wanted, for they already had pictures enough. I was almost amused to realize that both sides, the Western journalists and the Stasi, knew well in advance that something was planned, which also explained the strict measures that kept us from joining the march.

This time the authorities were smarter than during the fiasco after the banning of the singer Wolf Biermann twelve years earlier. The dissidents had clearly expected to get arrested and then to turn the incident into a big protest campaign inside and outside the country, with candles in windows calling for their freedom and a big Western media campaign. But instead, they were persuaded—or tricked, as they maintained—to avoid imprisonment by agreeing to get expelled from the GDR, at least temporarily. They switched their angry activities to West Berlin or England, but their plans for big candle-light protests and the like had been stymied.

By this time, despite the seeming success of Honecker's Western travels, despite new possibilities for two million GDR citizens to follow suit and visit their Western relatives—a million more than the million pensioners who went every year—and despite the huge amnesty of prisoners, the problems of the GDR had increased so visibly that many sensed that "the writing is on the wall," as in the biblical Book of Daniel where a mysterious hand warned that the kingdom would be split up. This time the warning lay in just the opposite direction and was not that mysterious. But here, too, as with Daniel in the lions' den, hungry carnivores were involved!

It might be worth mentioning that those who so frequently quote that wise sentence by Rosa rarely quote countless other words of hers. Like these from *The Junius Pamphlet*, written in prison in 1915: "We stand today . . . before the awful proposition: either the triumph of imperialism and the destruction of all culture and, as in ancient Rome, depopulation, desolation, degeneration, a vast cemetery; or the victory of socialism."

THUS, DESPITE HONECKER'S travels, the GDR remained the target of Western oligarchs with a dogged resolve to regain former wealth and power between the Elbe and the Oder.

And those who were helping them, including the ones who had waved the Luxemburg banners, stressed three major themes as repeatedly and vigorously as any performers with the motifs of a Richard Wagner opera. Of course, their motifs sang out on issues where the GDR was most vulnerable.

One related to the National People's Army, its unwelcome "preparedness" programs in the schools, its pressures on young men to enlist in officers' training programs for longer than the required eighteen months, and its treatment of conscientious objectors, rough and only gradually moderated in later years under Church influence. The GDR armaments and those of the Soviet troops were strongly condemned, especially after Soviet missile launchers were brought in as part of the tit-for-tat U.S.-USSR atomic competition, which, most unusually, Honecker once dared to criticize as "devil's ware." Somehow the dissident critics always hit most heavily by far at the East side of the rivalry.

A second target involved the environment. The GDR organized a remarkably effective system of recycling garbage, paper, and bottles and used no beverage cans. It created good national parks and preserves. But its reliance on its awful lignite half-coal was a curse, poisoning whole districts. Attempts to switch to less damaging fossil fuels (sun and wind energy were hardly known then) were cut abruptly by sharp price increases in Soviet oil and gas. Hugely expensive moves toward atomic energy, seen as a clean alternative, ended with the Chernobyl disaster. So it was stuck with lignite for heating, power, fuel, and its vital chemical industry. Leaders were highly sensitive about any criticism in this respect.

And thirdly, the very delicate questions of free speech and freedom of the press were stressed. Every relaxation in pressure from above in these matters was followed by demands for further steps, which others feared would lead down the slippery ramp to "glasnost" as in the USSR—and political suicide.

I was friendly with some of the so-called dissidents and could easily sympathize with much of what they said. Often honest and sincere, devoted to human rights, peace, or the environment, they could and sometimes did play as positive a role as in other societies. But in the prevailing situation, I felt, whether consciously or not, that they were being misused. And I found their thinking so concentrated on GDR criticism that they had neither eyes nor ears for the wider world. In contrast with the rulers in Bonn, the GDR generously aided the ANC in South Africa, SWAPO in Namibia, Ho Chi Minh's Vietnamese, the Sandinistas, and the anti-Pinochet forces. What would success of those dissidents, whose motivation was implacable anti-GDR hostility, mean to their struggles? "Human rights" were demanded by people often totally uninterested in Mandela, Leonard Peltier, or even the "Berufsverbote" in West Germany, where some were jailed, many were fired, and 1.4 million people were investigated by the equivalent of the FBI because of their undesirable views.

40—Education Questions

Before turning to the decline and fall of the GDR, I want to discuss one of its very best, though in some ways faulty, sectors, the education system. There were only public schools, no private or church schools. Nor were there differences based on class background, tracking the better twelve- or even ten-year-old pupils by sending them to a college preparation school (called a "gymnasium") and leaving most working-class kids behind. In the GDR, except for pupils talented in music, mathematics, languages and especially sports who could if they wished go to specialized schools, all pupils stayed together until they were fourteen—later changed to sixteen. Only then did some go to college prep schools and the majority to apprenticeship schooling. This sharp break with German tradition is today being fought over in many German states, with some urging the GDR solution, though rarely identifying it as such.

School quality depended greatly on principals and teachers, but not on their location, since all the schools in the country used the same curriculum. This may sound like uniformity, which it was, of course, for better or for worse. It was aimed at that other main evil of German education. No longer would some children be disadvantaged by the equivalents of a "little red schoolhouse." Youngsters from rural villages had the same education as their peers in Berlin, Leipzig, or Dresden.

In addition to German, math, history, geography, civics, art and music, they all studied biology, chemistry, and physics, with nary a word about "intelligent design," "divine creation of the earth" 6,000 years ago, or squeezing all wildlife (except the poor old dinosaurs) into Noah's ark! Russian classes began in the fifth grade (usually not too successfully) and in French or the far more popular English optionally in the seventh. Some youngsters near the borders could take Polish or Czech, and in the Slavic minority areas the Sorbs or Wends could learn their language. All pupils had sports every week, and all had to learn to swim.

A special feature was "polytechnical education." Younger children cultivated a school garden and learned skills like sewing, drilling, technical drawing, and reading industrial plans. As of the seventh grade they spent one day every two weeks in a factory or, in rural areas, a cooperative farm, to learn about working conditions, the "socialist production" system, and various trades, perhaps finding one that appealed to them, and also to gain respect for working people, the proclaimed foundation of GDR society. The older pupils might also help in simpler production processes. This system was studied and partially adopted by Finland, whose schools are now among the world's best.

At sixteen, after the tenth grade, a large majority became apprentices for two years, often in trade school dormitories attached to industrial complexes. This was free; they received a monthly allowance, and learned any of three hundred trades, from baker, barber, well-trained cook or skilled waitress to electrician or precision mechanic, usually with another related trade to permit later switches. The courses included basic technology, electronics, data processing, and industry economics, two hours weekly for sports and often more foreign language training. There were chances, with one additional year, to switch over to college preparation.

The apprenticeships led to guaranteed jobs at the same wage scale as for adults, and those with ambition could keep on learning and earn "master" licenses. Good electricians, masons, plumbers, or carpenters, aside from regular jobs, were always in demand "after hours" for private work on weekend dachas, and usually became very prosperous. There were frequent West German comments after unification that "in spite of everything," GDR schools must have been pretty good; their pupils had not only learned reading, writing, math, and science well but had become skilled and resourceful craftspeople.

GDR HISTORY AND civics classes always contained a clear anti-Nazi character. Unsurprisingly, there was great stress on capitalist responsibility for fascism and war, based on the sad truth, and also on the resistance by an extremely courageous underground, which was often led by Communists, who were especially victimized and especially committed, but sadly unable ever to stop the Nazi juggernaut, which was only defeated in the end by the Allied armies. It was proper, I think, to pass on to students the heroic heritage of men and women who risked and sacrificed their lives fighting the Nazis in those armies, in Spain, as partisans, but especially within Germany, in the belly of the monster. Many schools were named after them, and history clubs researched their lives and their deaths. This helped counteract stories by fathers or grandfathers about their "heroism in battle," while they were bringing extreme suffering to all of Europe.

I think schoolbooks in most countries like to stress heroes rather than victims, George Washington, Abe Lincoln, General Eisenhower or Patton, more than those who suffered along the way. The GDR did the same.

It was very wrong, however, to devote too little time to the Holocaust, the horrifying details about those millions of Jewish and Roma (Gypsy) victims killed in work-to-death factories and annihilation camps at Auschwitz, Majdanek, Treblinka, or Sobibor in occupied Poland. And though the heroes stressed in the East were usually ignored or even maligned in the West, both Eastern and Western schools far too often neglected those other victims: the handicapped, the religious anti-fascists, and the homosexuals. One-sidedness of any kind, I believe, was and is a serious mistake.

Another factor, no doubt, was the GDR's growing estrangement with Israel, founded one year before either German state. At first, the USSR and its bloc supported and armed Israel. GDR President Wilhelm Pieck stated: "We view the creation of a Jewish state as an essential contribution toward enabling thousands of people, who were subjected to the most extreme suffering under Hitler fascism, to build up a new life for themselves."

But the atmosphere changed as Israel moved ever closer to the United States and the West and, as both cause and consequence of this, Stalin's policy turned viciously anti-Semitic or, as it was called, "anti-Zionist" and "against cosmopolitanism." This led to the tragic trials and executions of veteran anti-fascist fighters like László Rajk in Hungary and Rudolf Slánský in Czechoslovakia, and in the GDR to many dismissals but, thank the lord, no big show trials or executions. After Stalin's death, the situation improved swiftly; I never found anti-Semitic caricatures or the like, even when Israeli policies and wars were strongly opposed. Victims of the Nazis living in the GDR received many benefits: longer vacations, free transportation, earlier and bigger pensions. But in official publications and schools a tendency was present, until nearly the end, to avoid discussion in depth of specifically anti-Jewish oppression and genocide.

West Germany also forbade the Hitler salute, the swastika, and denial of the Holocaust, but though its leaders publicly and almost exclusively stressed the anti-Semitic side of Nazi rule, veiled adulation of the past and acceptance of so many of its former enthusiasts, dead or active, was accepted by the ton. The GDR did not pay reparation money to people outside its borders or to Israel, but it had no public space whatsoever for racists and pro-Nazis. And, though history classes had definite weaknesses, literature classes assigned *The Seventh Cross* by Anna Seghers, *The Diary of Anne Frank*, and Bruno Apitz's extremely popular *Naked Among Wolves*, about a Jewish child dramatically rescued in Buchenwald. When this true-to-life child was finally traced and found by a popular newspaper, already a student and active Israeli basketball player, his visit to the GDR was met with a magnificent welcome.

In many ways, a humanitarian atmosphere prevailed. Many older classics were assigned, the Germans first of all, some of the best Soviet authors, but also *Robinson Crusoe, Hamlet*, or *Romeo and Juliet*, as well as books by Jack London, Mark Twain, and Victor Hugo. Modern Western authors were rarely taught but were, if you were early and lucky, available in the bookshops in a wide variety. I wondered at times how many of the best GDR books were sold, read, or taught in West Germany, not to speak of the United States. Hardly a handful, I fear, and usually only those classified as "dissidents."

When they were fourteen, GDR pupils spent a day visiting the concentration camp sites and monuments at Buchenwald or Sachsenhausen. Teachers, best of all those dedicated, enthusiastic "New Teachers" from the early years, put their hearts into getting across anti-fascist ideas and feelings of international friendship and solidarity—for Algerian independence fighters, for those fighting apartheid in southern Africa, for the Vietnamese, and for imprisoned militants like Manolis Glezos, the hero of Greek defiance against the Nazis, then imprisoned by Greek putschists. There was a campaign for the Wilmington Ten, framed on a murder charge in North Carolina and, most dramatically, for Angela Davis, facing a possible death sentence in California. The virtual avalanche of protest cards and letters from GDR youngsters, including those sent directly to her, filled literally truckloads of post bags, astonishing the presiding judge and possibly helping her just a little in gaining freedom.

A teacher friend in a small town near the hilly southern border showed me the place where, in the last days of the war, a starved dark-skinned soldier, a prisoner of war, was trying to escape. Villagers who found him went to get food and medical aid, but before they got back Nazi soldiers had arrived and killed him. Was he American or French-African? They didn't know. But every year, my friend told each new class the story and led them in a few anti-fascist songs and a recitation at a grove of trees they had planted around a little monument where he was buried. He held a similar ceremony nearby where two Red Army soldiers had died in battle. I doubt that the pupils ever forgot these simple experiences.

Of course, memories faded with the years, good ones and many bad ones; younger teacher generations had not been hit emotionally by the Nazis and the war years, making it harder to pass on that original strong anti-fascist spirit. But some of it remained. With my family I visited the stony construction site where my cousin Jerry, with many enslaved Jewish American and Italian prisoners-of-war, had been worked to death by toil, hunger, and lack of medical care. A young man volunteered to show us the way, and he told us that in GDR days every school class visited the little monument on a hill, left flowers, and saw to it that all was clean and neat. Now, sadly, it was being neglected and forgotten.

WHAT ABOUT THE pressing political questions of the day? They always provided difficulties. Apprentices were supposed to become good at their trade but also, in official language, become "class-conscious working people" and "socialist patriots and proletarian international-ists." This was easier said than done.

Teachers of very young children could point out good things in their surroundings without much fear of skepticism. But by the fourth or fifth grade, comparisons with the system across the border led to troublesome contradictions. Despite endless admonishments, parents not only watched Western TV channels but let their children watch, too, where they were treated to an exactly contrary picture, presented in a very shiny wrapping. For many adolescents, the extolled merits of GDR society, with no joblessness, no tuition fees, without poverty or greedy capitalists exploiting workers and supporting reactionary regimes, were simply not as interesting or as attractive as forbidden pleasures.

When Aunt Minna in Hamburg sent packages with items hard to get or as yet unknown in the GDR—the latest chic jeans, colored felt-tip pencils or just shopping bags with pretty designs—and TV showed the adventurous life of young people with loud, Harley-Davidson motor-cycle tours, crazy dances, weird clothes, and even the hush-hush drug scene, their own all-too-normal life seemed dull and made it hard for them to take the teachers' words very seriously.

Some teachers faced such problems squarely and frankly. A small-town teacher in Thuringia, a former principal, told me his formula: 1. If you are convinced yourself, you must not fear conveying heartfelt feelings with genuine, contagious enthusiasm; 2. You must not keep repeating yourself, boring all those who are listening (or no longer listening); and 3. Most important, if you want youngsters to believe descriptions of conflicts or hard times faced by people in the capitalist past or present, "over there," you must also be honest in discussing deficits and difficulties at home, which your students experience personally. Only then will they trust your words about past or distant problems.

I found this very sensible. But for Education Minister Margaret Honecker, wife of the GDR's top man, and for her staff, debating GDR problems was considered far too risky. Teachers were not credited with the flexibility needed to manage free, open discussions of problems that might well lead to criticism of their own policies. This lack of trust, also for media audiences in general, was an important factor in the GDR's decline.

But many questions were truly tricky, also some from the East, as when Polish shipyard workers went on strike. Or when the stout Soviet leader Nikita Khrushchev, famed for that "secret report" in 1956 about Stalin's multiple crimes, and for reports, correct or not, of his angry shoe-banging at the UN. Actually, he became rather popular in the GDR; it was even said that Walter Ulbricht got along well with him. But when, in October 1964, "Nikita" was suddenly and unceremoniously bounced, for "health reasons," which no one believed, how could a poor schoolteacher explain such an event troubling our faultless mentors? In one ninth-grade class, I heard, students badgered the teacher so much, demanding an explanation, that he broke down and fled the classroom.

Such situations, doubtless causing turmoil at the highest levels as well, help explain why political controversy or debate was discouraged and took place afterward, outside school walls.

Sadly, it was often pro-GDR children from left-wing families, the most interested in politics, who were discouraged from open discussion by insecure teachers. This could cause the despair of such pupils, while the majority simply went along, saying all the things the teacher wanted to hear, causing no problems but leading to hypocrisy and political uninterest.

A third kind of pupil grew rebellious, rejecting all ideas being taught, including important ones against fascism and racism. This may have reflected a deep-seated fascist residue in some families, repressed sharply in the GDR but impossible to completely overcome. Such youngsters were ripe for fascist views imported from West Berlin and West Germany even before the Wall fell. After it was gone such views could bubble up undisturbed and in bulk from their slimy breeding-grounds.

I will close this long section with two anecdotes illustrating the contradictions of those years. An elderly teacher I knew, rather like a schoolmarm of the past, laughed about her son-in-law, a dogmatic education "apparatchik" in the Leipzig school system. His daughter's high school had been hit by a rare, unpleasant problem: head lice! Anyone afflicted was sent home on quarantine for a week or so. Now, the girl said, stories circulated that victims were offering living specimens for sale—as get-out-of-school passes! The class joked about demanding a two-week quarantine for everyone. But when his wife told this stuffy bureaucrat about these jokes his stiff response was: "How can they even joke about missing one day of their fine socialist education?"!

The other recollection is about a book by Alfred Wellm, a teacher turned writer. *Pause für Wanzka*, published in 1968, was an attack on school system ills and problems, a plea for more humanity and warmth, especially for children who had trouble adapting to discipline or conformity but might be very talented in their own way. But basically, for all children, who all deserved plenty of love and attention.

This critical little novel was attacked by Education Minister Honecker and her bureaucrats. It was printed despite her objections and had magnificent success. In a country of less than 17 million, it sold a quarter of a million copies, mostly to parents but also to large numbers of teachers. It was finally filmed, but not until 1990 when GDR films, like GDR books, almost completely disappeared.

Renate and I loved this book, which reflected an aspect of education we felt was too often neglected. Young people, more than ever in
adolescent years, do want to learn things, but do not want to be well-
mannered, obedient pupils all the time, figuratively sitting with folded
hands on their desks. Many want to be rebellious in their thinking and
sometimes in their actions. They seek not only romance but a share of
the Romantic, or the Adventurous. There were many clubs and hobby
groups for youngsters in the GDR and almost no limit on athletic
possibilities, free of charge. But I wished for more understanding of
these other needs, breaking with polite conformity and prim behavior,
more in the tradition of the German rebel Thomas Müntzer, or Rosa
Luxemburg, Harriet Tubman, John Brown, Amilcar Cabral in West
Africa, the underground in South Africa, and, of course, Che Guevara.
And occasional less directly political romantics and adventures in fic-
tion and in their lives as well would not have hurt; indeed, more of
this might have brought far greater bonds to the GDR and perhaps
more heartening results in those final days. Perhaps, too, it would
have enjoyed greater success in preserving many good traditions, as
opposed to the kind of "adventure" romantics seeping in too often
toward the end, with stirring tones from the evil past. Such conflicts
reflect the contradictions, the opposing trends and movements within
the complicated, ill-fated society of the GDR.

41—How It Was Done in Poland

The field of literature, so important to so many GDR citizens, was
never neglected by hostile West German institutions and media. New
GDR books seen as critical were praised and their authors flattered by
Western reviewers. The authors were invited for lucrative book tours
or to accept prizes or honors. If the GDR authorities viewed this as
undesirable meddling and recruiting, they sometimes refused to grant
an exit visa and were then angrily denounced for limiting literary freedom. If visas were granted, such authors were often wined, dined, and
feted and urged either to remain in the West, or, more likely, encouraged

to return to the GDR, maintain connections and step up their criticism. And West German editions of their books were promoted, which brought those desirable West-marks.

Different strategies were developed for each Eastern Bloc country, such as Poland and Hungary, where visas were easily available. But in all of them, writers, directors, or musicians seen as dissidents or potential dissidents were praised in the media and especially on the eastward-aimed Voice of America, RIAS in West Berlin, or similar outlets for defending democracy and human rights. Oppositional groups were cultivated and free publication rights demanded. If they were restricted, a "freedom of the press" outcry was unleashed; if restrictions were relaxed the stakes were raised, perhaps with demands for independent organizations or parties openly opposing the government. If achieved, these could lambast every weakness, every shortage, every quarrel, and every limitation. They commonly targeted corruption—and what country is completely free of that ill? Such muckraking is generally a praiseworthy endeavor, but in the Cold War paradigm, the dragon to be bested was not really corruption. From East Berlin to the furthest tip of Siberia, and also in Cuba and China to this day, the targets and the stakes were far higher.

A classic example of this was described by reporter Carl Bernstein, famous with Bob Woodward for exposing Watergate and finally getting Richard Nixon thrown out. In a lengthy article in *Time* magazine, Bernstein wrote of a meeting between President Reagan and Pope John Paul II at the Vatican on June 7, 1982, when they agreed on a joint, secret campaign against the Eastern Bloc. According to National Security Adviser Richard Allen, this was "one of the great secret alliances of all time":

> The operation was focused on Poland . . . the birthplace of John Paul II. Both the Pope and the President were convinced that Poland could be broken out of the Soviet orbit if the Vatican and the U.S. committed their resources to destabilizing the Polish government and keeping the outlawed Solidarity movement alive after the declaration of martial law in 1981.

Until Solidarity's legal status was restored in 1989 it flourished underground, supplied, nurtured and advised largely by the network established under the auspices of Reagan and John Paul II. Tons of equipment—fax machines (the first in Poland), printing presses, transmitters, telephones, shortwave radios, video cameras, photocopiers, telex machines, computers, word processors—were smuggled into Poland via channels established by priests and American agents and representatives of the AFL-CIO and European labor movements. Money for the banned union came from CIA funds, the National Endowment for Democracy, secret accounts in the Vatican and western trade unions.

Lech Walesa and other leaders of Solidarity received strategic advice—often conveyed by priests or American and European labor experts working undercover in Poland. . . . As the effectiveness of the resistance grew, the stream of information to the West about the internal decisions of the Polish government and the contents of Warsaw's communications with Moscow became a flood. The details came not only from priests but also from spies within the Polish government. . . .

A free, non-communist Poland, they were convinced, would be a dagger to the heart of the Soviet empire; and if Poland became democratic, other Eastern European states would follow. (Carl Bernstein, "The Holy Alliance," *Time*, February 24, 1992.)

A side note: The go-between who connected Reagan with the Pope was none other than the seasoned, multilingual Gen. Vernon Walters, who was deeply involved for decades in regime changes from Brasilia to Suva in the Fiji Republic, from Warsaw and, as his final triumph, to Berlin.

Sometimes banged pots and pans were effective, sometimes symbolic colors or clever logos, and economic pressures were almost always involved, for it was with them that dissatisfaction could be encouraged and built upon. In every case true weaknesses and blunders of the target country were hunted up and worked on—that is how crowds could be won over. This strategy, which finally paid off in

152 A SOCIALIST DEFECTOR

Eastern Europe in 1989–93, has remained the operating manual and, dog-eared but still applicable, is still being applied, with more or less success, in Ukraine and many other countries—in Cuba, Venezuela, Bolivia, and other places as far apart as China and Belarus.

42—Boring from Within: The Church

Among those involved in the dissident movement of the GDR were various Lutheran Church leaders. Some religious dignitaries were GDR-friendly or neutral, but most leaned politically toward their strong, wealthy base across the Elbe and joined attempts to unroll this impertinent little republic, in spite of the declining number of church-goers. This was described in detail in 1990 by a leading actor in the drama, Vera Lengsfeld:

> The revolutionary movement of last autumn in the GDR did not spring from thin air. It had been preceded by ten years of building an opposition movement for peace, human rights and the environment under the protection of the Lutheran Church. This was possible because of the special nature of church-state relations in the GDR, which were unique in the Eastern Bloc.
>
> The peace groups developed all their activities on church premises. They met there and held seminars, workshops and conferences. Exhibitions traveled throughout the country going from church to church. Many church representatives provided not only protection for the movement but participated actively, as organizers, speakers and advisers. The first independent newspapers were produced on church duplicating machines. Libraries were set up in church rooms from which people could read and borrow publications which were inaccessible or forbidden in state libraries. These libraries quickly developed into informal meeting places. By the mid-1980s the independent groups were well connected to each other and annual meetings of delegates and large events regularly attracted thousands of visitors.

The church regularly defended the opposition in its conflicts with the state. As a result the church gained much moral credibility and became a significant political factor in the country. Three years before it fell, the Honecker government was already unable to make a decision without considering how it would be received by the opposition and the church. (Pamphlet from the United States, collection of author.)

After Vera Lengsfeld's dreams had been fulfilled and the GDR dispatched, she became a Bundestag delegate, first with the Greens, then, moving to the right, with the Christian Democrats. After losing that seat as well, in the most disastrous local defeat that party had ever experienced, she withdrew to freelance journalism and moved, ever further and ever more venomously, to her current approval of the neo-fascist positions of the Alternative for Germany Party (AfD), which stresses hatred toward immigrants, especially Muslims (and the "Islamization of Europe") and, less loudly, an increase in German armaments, opposition to same-gender marriage and abortion, and lower taxes for the wealthy. She has moved a long way since the 1980s—or has she really?

There is another interesting example of how poor Jesus Christ was dragged into oppositional politics. Rev. Rainer Eppelmann can't be blamed for his mother, a Nazi Party member, or his father, an SS guard at Buchenwald and Sachsenhausen concentration camps, who nourished a bitter hatred of Communists as long as he lived. But son Rainer either inherited or imbibed this last trait, and that led to great difficulties with the GDR, which he was later able to avenge.

In 1979, he organized, first in one church, then in a second and third one, so-called Blues Masses, cool musical events for mostly unreligious young people with an unambiguous anti-GDR tilt but garnished with just enough brief Bible references or texts to receive reluctant clearance from the authorities as "religious services." There were twenty such Blues Masses until 1986, when they became too confrontational even for church leaders in the GDR.

One of Eppelmann's main messages, like Vera Lengsfeld's, was "beat swords into plowshares," a noble biblical message frowned upon by GDR leaders. Their feeling that it was aimed primarily at their National People's Army or its Soviet allies was not unfounded, but it would have been far wiser, I thought at the time, not to make taboo or even forbid these words but to officially adopt and propagate them like other official peace messages had been, thus removing their provocative effect. I fear my advice again went unheeded.

In the last months of the GDR, no longer governed by the SED, Rev. Eppelmann was appointed Minister for Defense and Disarmament, a newly renamed position. His job entailed dismantling the National People's Army while saving its planes, tanks, and other equipment, which was then often sold to Indonesia or Turkey to oppress Papuans, Kurds, or other "dissenters." He was also kept busy purging barracks of the names of anti-Nazi fighters if, as was often the case, they had also been Communists. There was cruel irony in this, since his father had been an SS guard in camps where some of the same people had been prisoners.

After the end of the GDR, Eppelmann became a Christian Democratic Union deputy to the Bundestag, where, no longer mindful of his onetime vigorous pacifist ideals (for the GDR), he joined in approving eleven weeks of reconnoitering and then bombing military and civilian targets in Serbia in 1999, including sensitive chemical factories. This deployment of Tornado planes, made possible by reunification, involved the first military gunfire by German military men outside national borders since the Second World War.

After Eppelmann, like Lengsfeld, failed to get reelected, he was chosen to chair the Bundestag's grandiosely titled "Inquest Commission for the Evaluation of the History and Consequences of the SED Dictatorship," dedicated to the same goal, enunciated by Justice Minister Klaus Kinkel, of "delegitimizing the SED regime." Eppelmann's vita became even more mottled when it was discovered that, for many GDR years, he had been in close contact with CIA agents, or "people from the U.S. Embassy" as he preferred to call them, to whom he provided detailed information on discussions in church circles, on the growing dissident movement he was promoting, and on developments generally. During a trip to West Germany, permitted for clergy by GDR authorities in 1987, the relationship became so close that there were claims that he gave advice to President Reagan for his "Mr. Gorbachev, Tear Down This Wall" speech. (Klaus Eichner and Andreas Dobbert, "Headquarters Germany: Die U.S.-Geheimdienste in Deutschland," *Edition Ost*, Berlin: Das Neue Berlin Verlag, 2008.)

43—Causes of the Downfall

Dissidents like Eppelmann and Lengsfeld lost favor in later years because of their far-right swing and general nastiness, but in 1989 and 1990 they acted as yeast in the sourdough bread of dissatisfaction.

The three main motifs they reiterated under protective church steeples were indeed important, if not always sincere. The first, environmental issues, extremely important though they were, tended mainly to disturb only intellectuals in those early days, and perhaps also those living in lignite coal areas, although some may have grown accustomed to living there, and to getting well paid.

Their second issue, the right to voice opposing views loudly in public or in print, interested those intellectuals who had plenty to say and sometimes wanted to be heard. But for the majority, I think, this was not a truly burning problem and only grew hotter toward the end.

As for military questions, the issues taken up by the dissidents affected most directly eleventh- and twelfth-grade youngsters at college preparatory schools who were pressured to enlist for three years of officers' training. Most males, after ten years of schooling and two years of apprenticeship, largely accepted the eighteen months of military service as fate, like those in West Germany. There were not many conscientious objectors.

But in another way, the military sphere was indeed deeply involved in the downslide in the 1980s, when almost everyone sensed that things were no longer moving ahead economically and seemed, more and more clearly, to be slipping backward.

True, Soviet troops and weapons were here, perhaps with a mixture of comradely friendship as well as some caution toward Eastern as well as Western Germans. But GDR leaders, watching that menacing threat from across the Elbe, felt that the NVA forces must try to balance the Bundeswehr as much as possible, without leaving the USSR to do the entire job alone. This was also probably expected, or stressed, by Moscow.

It was no easy matter. In fact, it was impossible. The Bundeswehr had far, far deeper pockets when shopping for its nearly 500,000 soldiers under arms and 1.3 million in reserve. In 1980, it purchased ultra-modern Tornado warplanes and anti-tank helicopters. In 1981, the first Roland armored anti-aircraft missile tanks rolled in and in 1982 eight frigates were launched. In 1983, the first Jaguar 2 tank destroyers clanked into training positions. In 1986, it was Skorpion mine-laying tanks and, later that year, Patriot surface-to-air missile systems from Raytheon and Lockheed. One year later, MARS middle-range missile launchers were added. Then came the armored reconnaissance vehicles and amphibious transport tanks of Thyssen and Rheinmetall, companies with long wartime experience. Armored weapons platforms were due by August 1990; by then, however, the NVA no longer existed.

But as long as the NVA did exist, it tried to maintain modernity with planes, tanks, and other weapons for its 173,000 armed men and 323,500 in reserve, an increasingly heavy and ultimately useless burden.

A second challenge to the economy involved industrial production. The Ulbricht-sponsored experiments with more customer-based planning and production and fewer umbilical ties to Party central in Berlin had been dropped after Leonid Brezhnev took over from Nikita Khrushchev in Moscow. One can only speculate as to their possible success. But one thing became increasingly clear; swift progress was urgent, and in no field more than electronics. The quality of GDR-made machine tools and a number of other products was near that of the best in the world. But to stay competitive, electronic steering was now necessary. How was the GDR to keep up?

The USSR, in a global race of its own in armaments and space research, could or did not offer much help at all. Even less could be expected from Eastern Europe, and the Western "COCOM List" embargo forbade sales of anything of possible military value to the East, which meant almost everything. Sometimes the GDR could slip around this Verbot and buy a few items from companies willing to buck the rules, but only at steep prices in Western money, of which the GDR had far too little. So it was a David-Goliath struggle against giants like IBM and Sony. A few remaining old-timers and a younger research and engineering staff built up new development centers in Frankfurt/Oder and Erfurt (where my physicist daughter-in-law was offered a very high-paying job). By 1968, a logic circuit model and in 1978 a 1 megabyte bit of memory hardware was achieved. This was celebrated with jubila-tion in the GDR media but was noteworthy only because it had been achieved by an isolated GDR, almost completely on its own. Though always behind in the race, the GDR had to keep sprinting; it spent nearly 30 billion marks on electronics alone between 1986 and 1990, which meant cutting into investments aimed at satisfying consumer demands.

A third major problem was economic and human. Wartime bomb-ing and the large influx of Germans from former East Prussia, Silesia, and former-German parts of Czechoslovakia created an abysmal housing shortage. Renate and I had experienced the involuntary apartment-sharing that this required but which got us a roof over our heads. About 1951, after the first years of clearing rubble and repairing damaged buildings, new construction got underway, most famously with the wide, two-kilometer white, tree-lined Stalin Allee in East Berlin, later renamed Karl-Marx-Allee. About 111,000 new apartments were built by 1970, but except for some city centers and key industrial sites this was far too slow. In crowded old buildings, dissatisfaction was on the rise.

At the Party Congress in 1971, Erich Honecker, after ousting Walter Ulbricht and striving to gain popularity as new leader, promised a giant program with three million new or renovated apartments. By 1990, all would have a modern apartment or home, eliminating the housing problem forever!

There was nothing like a new apartment to satisfy people often living like I did when I first arrived: cold water, no tubs or showers, no flush toilets or central heating. Few worried about architectural beauty or lack of it, even after budget cuts reduced earlier plans for many statues, murals, portals, or other embellishments, though here and there bolder architects varied pre-fab patterns and colors and created pleasant vistas.

Replacing old brick-on-brick methods with cranes and pre-fabricated panels made for quick construction. Almost every town got new apartment houses. New city boroughs arose, with schools, kindergartens, clinics, shops, restaurants, and theaters. In East Berlin in 1976, it was decided to modernize 100,000 older apartments and build over 200,000 new ones, mostly in the suburbs (thus rarely seen by Western tourists). In rural areas, low-interest credit made it easier to build private homes. By July 1978, Honecker was able to ceremoniously cut the ribbon opening the door of the one-millionth new GDR apartment since 1971.

Younger people were happy to "improve," just as we had been some years earlier. Old folks, who often stayed on, were dying out. Even handsome half-timbered houses in central areas with their long traditions were often falling apart and getting replaced since installing modern heating and plumbing behind old facades cost far more than new construction. With the GDR always short of investment money, materials, and labor power, this meant tough decisions that varied from one town to another.

But rent, even in the new buildings, was kept at an incredibly low 1.25 marks/m^2, with heating and hot water included and the state making up the difference. Since this amount hardly ever exceeded 10 percent of income, it meant that tenants were a mix from many sectors— factory workers next to civil servants or even professors. Wonderful as this rate was for us tenants, it was an ever greater burden nationally, but Honecker & Co. rejected some economists' calls to ease the strain on the economy by raising the rents, carfares, and prices for staple commodities. It was clearly feared, no doubt correctly, that such increases would backfire politically, like the increase in the price of Wartburg cars, which caused an uproar. So the housing program, wonderful as it was, burdened the economy, like electronics and the army, while it struggled to reach the almost incredible goal of 3 million homes.

The biggest political problem was travel. Men over sixty-five and women over sixty could visit relatives in the West for one month each year. Even the few who decided to remain there meant no loss to the economy. It was youngsters who were most unhappy; they watched tempting travelogues on West-TV. In the 1970s I had begun giving talks all over the GDR, most frequently to young audiences and basically about U.S. political developments. But increasingly, in the question period after my talks, I was asked "Why must I wait until I'm sixty-five to see the Mona Lisa or the Golden Gate Bridge?"

In the mid-1980s many more were able to visit relatives in the West, not just pensioners but over two million annually. New problems developed, however. At the factory I sometimes visited, part of the "Bitterfeld" writers-meeting-workers-movement, one woman complained to me, "Yes, now I can visit relatives for birthdays, weddings or funerals. But I can only exchange enough to take fifteen West-marks with me. What good is such a measly amount? My aunt is sick of treating me every time!"

The government was in a quandary. The economy was always extremely short of the Western money needed for urgent imports of raw materials, all kinds of equipment and consumer goods, from oranges to Italian shoes. Everything possible was sold to get such money. In one old seaport town, Wismar, even picturesque cobblestones were to be sacrificed, but after they were dug up from the streets, the wise mayor saw to it that they were not sold but hidden.

But how, then, could more millions of GDR travelers be further subsidized, not only for the expensive West German railroad fares which they could buy with East-marks at low Eastern prices, but with more spending money in West-marks as well? It was economically impossible to increase the allowed exchange to the more than 15 of the coveted West-marks allowance.

One prevailing problem was that those in top leadership, like Honecker, were products of an earlier age and never learned, but rather feared, that coming clean with the population about problems and how to deal with them as well as possible was difficult but necessary. Instead, they kept announcing successful statistics as if all was well, even when no one believed them. In May 1989, they manipulated election figures, fearful of an even slightly legitimate result instead of a ludicrous figure over 98.8 percent. This blunder lost them support even from those happy to get a handsome new apartment at last.

Such ups and downs, with so many crosscurrents and contradictions, were illustrated by a kind of joke, full of both truths and exaggerations, and sometimes titled "The GDR Miracle":

"How come everyone in the GDR has a job but only half do any work? How come only half do any work but production quotas are always overfulfilled? How come quotas are always overfulfilled but there's never enough in the shops? How come there's never enough in the shops but everyone has everything they need? How come everyone has everything they need but they never stop grumbling? How come they never stop grumbling but 99 percent still vote for the National Front?"

This last miracle would soon be fatally frayed. It would take the rest down with it.

Some like me hoped, indeed almost prayed, that the next Party congress would finally see the old guard step down. But even if they did, by no means a certainty, who would be replacing them? Those old men were out of touch, yet most of them had truly worthy résumés, had fought the Nazis, and often suffered terribly in prisons, camps, in Spain, in the underground, or in difficult, troubled exile. Most of them, I was convinced, though dogmatic and stagnant in their thinking, still cherished hopes and plans for a world free of war, exploitation, and misery. Would new men (and maybe some more women) also be devoted to these hopes? Might they be careerists? Ever a Quixote disciple, I sent long letters with my views and suggestions to top people I thought needed to be warned, saying (politely) that they must change their methods or go under. But Quixotes commonly go unheeded.

44—Liberation—or What?

By July 1989 the signals were unmistakable. Thousands of GDR citizens, not the usual kind of Lake Balaton vacationers and Budapest sightseers, were gathering in no-longer so sisterly Hungary, hoping to cross into West Germany's ally Austria—and eventually succeeding. Others gathered in the West German Embassy in Prague.

As for me and my family, we were genuine vacationers, first at the Baltic seashore where thousands, swimming and cavorting with or without clothing, worried, if at all, more about the water temperature than about borders in the south. Shortly afterward, we flew off for three weeks at the international journalists' hotel on the Black Sea coast of Bulgaria. The beach was beautiful (here only available with clothes), the food delicious, the rooms elegant, and at a price for three full weeks that the travel agency charged for two weeks and with far less noble conditions. Delicious grapes, peaches, tomatoes, and figs were everywhere, and on outings we passed pretty villages with bright flower beds along the roads. Herds of sheep added to an almost idyllic picture, spoiled only once by a side visit to a poor, sad Romany (Roma/Gypsy) settlement.

But omens increased. Vacationing Polish journalists learned to their dismay that their zloty had lost half its value overnight. When I asked Russian colleagues when and how the USSR would overcome current difficulties, they answered: "It can't and it won't." I wondered, was their seemingly cynical tone tinged with despair or gratification? Since foreign newspapers arrived a week late and we had none of today's electronic communications, we knew nothing of events in Dresden, Leipzig, or Berlin.

On our return we faced a genuine shock! Elaborate celebrations of the GDR's 40th anniversary had been spoiled by "Gorby, Gorby" cheers for the visiting Russian leader, who stole the show from an aging Honecker, trying to get over a three-month illness and an operation for what turned out to be cancer. The military march and youth parade with torches were followed by a small riot, based in a dissident church and broken up by police proving they could get just as tough as West Berlin cops.

Honecker had left the Party rudderless at a time of its worst disarray, helpless to cope with the thousands now climbing into buses at the open Hungarian-Austrian border and being whisked away to their dreamed-of West German goal. Many of them came from the Dresden area, where TV from West Germany was hard to get, causing "blissful ignorance" that there were problems over there, too. Those who had jammed the West German embassy in Prague were permitted to "go west," but only, Berlin decided, incredibly, in trains passing through the GDR at Dresden, where there were riots by those trying to jump aboard.

We heard of Monday protest marches in Leipzig, starting at a dissident church (where Bach was once organist) and challenging the Stasi men in such numbers that only gunfire could have stopped them, a bloody alternative that Honecker's presumed successor, Egon Krenz, had luckily rejected.

On October 18, Politburo members led by Krenz finally had the guts to throw out Honecker and two buddies, one a former good journalist who had become an obsequious marionette, enforcing the deadly boredom of much of the media, the other largely responsible for the failing economy. In the next amazing weeks, one by one, nearly all the other deadwood was dispersed.

Like most GDR citizens, I stayed glued to our TV news reports and, for the first time, so did countless West Germans. The GDR media, often taken over by its own staffs, no longer faced Party pressures; journalists were excited and their reports hot and controversial.

Back in 1980, after achieving the minimum requirement of writing two books, I had joined the Writers' Association. Its meetings, too, were now exciting. Inner tensions, formerly below the surface, broke out openly with three main groupings: one, a small remnant, still opposed any criticism of the SED; a majority opposed the stultifying pressures of the past but hoped to save the GDR; and a third group loudly rejected it altogether and was eager to avenge past injustices, genuine or exaggerated. The exchanges grew ever more hostile, and many supported the recently formed, semi-legal New Forum.

It was essentially the New Forum that organized the giant demonstration on November 4, 1989. When I reached it near Alexanderplatz I was amazed to see the countless banners and posters, angry, witty, and all opposed to the status quo, including Egon Krenz, the new Party leader and head of state, whose toothy smile was often caricatured. Criticism, or even originality, had been unknown in GDR posters; I had yearned for signs not dictated from on high but with personal, witty messages like those I recalled from the United States before they were frozen by an icy Cold War. Yes, these offered new, fresh air. But my feelings were divided. I felt that the Party had fully lost control and worried about who might now take over. Was this a "Fight for Freedom" or was it "the Counter-Revolution"? I met two colleagues who, like me, had been sharply critical of the leadership but supportive of the GDR and its basic system. They were smiling joyously and looked surprised when I spoke of my fears.

I worked my way to the front, not among but next to the marchers. Almost no police were visible, perhaps by agreement for a non-official parade, which, a great novelty, had been permitted. Theater people, who helped organize it, stood around wearing signs saying "No Violence." I wondered, what if, instead of turning, the crowd kept marching right down Unter den Linden to the Brandenburg Gate and perhaps past it and over the Wall? Who would or could stop them?

But the crowd did make a turn and returned to Alexanderplatz, now jammed with a hundred thousand people, perhaps many more. From a makeshift stage on a truck, a long roster of celebrities was making speeches with varied messages, and a wholly unknown crowd response—not the usual applause at indicated pauses but laughter, whistles, approval, rejection, derision.

Two apologetic yet defensive speeches by Berlin's Party secretary, Günter Schabowski, and the famous counterintelligence master, Markus Wolf, who had quit the Stasi three years earlier, were met with boos and shouts. A few speakers who seemed to be completely rejecting the GDR got mixed reactions. Most applause went to people like the writers Christa Wolf and Stefan Heym, known for confrontation with top leaders, who demanded major changes, democratic openings, new values, and new leaders, but not rejection of the basic GDR goal of socialism. As I headed back to my family, I was deeply disturbed, but this balance, without assuaging all my worries, had put my worst fears to rest.

A week later came the crowning event. At a press conference, Günter Schabowski, head of the SED in Berlin and roundly booed at Alexanderplatz, took a paper from his breast pocket and read off-handedly that the Berlin Wall was open—"right now." East Berlin immediately stood on its head; huge crowds, some driving Trabis but most on foot, poured past dazed border guards and spread out over West Berlin, never neglecting to go first to the nearest bank and pick up their "welcome gift" of 100 West-marks for everyone, even in utero babies if body shapes seemed convincing. One cartoon showed a man, holding a big tomcat dressed in baby clothes in his arms, warning a bevy of kids, "Don't tell them you were already here with your mama!" It was hard to figure out how those 100 marks could be picked up by 20 million people; the GDR only had about 16 million and many, especially older people, did not come to Berlin and cross over. But who cared? Renate and our two sons were also in the crowds and took and spent the money. As for me, I neither wanted nor dared to go, and especially not to show my ID, as long as the U.S. Army was stationed there.

I empathized with the rejoicing, the visits, and parties with friends and relatives; for weeks my son told of sightseeing in places known to us only per TV or hearsay, like the West Berlin Opera House and Symphony Hall, the fancy Ku'damm shopping street, the war-damaged Kaiser Wilhelm Memorial Church, the Aquarium, Botanical Gardens, and famous Zoo—with its giant panda! And not to forget the famous KaDeWe department store with its consumers' dream, foods from all the world.

Could I be like the Grinch in the face of such universal joy? Could I disparage freedom or lament the loss of that terrible, worldwide abhorred Berlin Wall, now being broken into a seemingly infinite number of chips, painted only on the Western side, for sale to tourists? Why wasn't I just as happy?

In late November, I attended the International Documentary Film Week in Leipzig, my annual chance to get glimpses of action in the wide world—Vietnam, Chile, Nicaragua, Iran, Palestine, Afghanistan, southern Africa, the United States. But like most of those attending, foreigner or not, I skipped the movies one evening to see a local world event, Leipzig's famous Monday demonstration, which had started the new ball rolling. The square was completely full, there were a few speeches with no hindrance from anyone, and people chanted the now famous slogan, "Wir sind das Volk!"—"We are the people!"

But then we saw groups of tough-looking young men scattered through the crowd and loudly changing one word of the slogan to: "Wir sind ein Volk!"—"We are one people," a clear call to bury the GDR. When a young West German speaker warned against reunification, the young men booed him loudly. The majority seemed rather baffled at this word change, but none objected—or dared object. On leaving the square, I saw a van with a West German license passing packages of far-right pamphlets to waiting young men, perhaps the same ones I had seen and heard in the crowd.

A week later, I read of a female Ethiopian student in Leipzig forced to flee from attackers and a group of students with a GDR flag being rescued by a Protestant pastor in his home from a similar attack. For the first time, we heard of bomb explosions, even in a kindergarten.

I found two bright spots. On November 13, Hans Modrow was elected, almost unanimously, as new prime minister. I knew him (briefly, personally) to be an unusually integral party official. As top SED man in Dresden, he rejected the usual handsome villa and lived in a normal three-room apartment. He was seen hanging up clothes on the clothesline, not too common for any husband but amazing for a big shot. He angrily rejected those little "presents" given by factory managers during inspections. I had even seen him standing on line for fresh rolls on Saturday mornings. How many Party bigwigs did that? But his multi-party cabinet, after a few good deeds, could last only until the coming elections.

The second bright spot was the unusual, early Party congress on December 8 and 9, demanded by a newly outspoken if rapidly diminishing membership. Almost all the old leaders were dropped or even expelled. The gallant new Sir Galahad was little Gregor Gysi, a witty, eloquent, now politically active lawyer whose speech was enthusiastically acclaimed at Alexanderplatz a month earlier. In the seventeen-hour meeting, he urged and won the decision to save the

Party. It would change its ways, apologize for past misdeeds, reject dictatorial "Stalinist" practices and claims to predominance, but would not dissolve (which would have lost all Party property and its organized structure). It would keep the name Socialist Unity Party, not trying to conceal its past, but add Party of Democratic Socialism with a hyphen, SED-PDS—and later drop the first half.

Soon afterward, the New Forum, the SED-PDS, the once tame, now rebellious "bloc parties," and a few new parties, meeting in a church-organized Round Table, decided to write a new constitution and call free elections. The constitution was soon forgotten; the elections were not. First set for May, they were moved up to March 18, 1990. Currents were shifting, the tide of forming a free, democratic GDR was rapidly receding as the media mounted endless attacks against corrupt GDR leaders and Stasi crimes. One high point was achieved when some groups, now ascendant, called for an attack on Stasi headquarters; the leaflets said "No Violence" but added "Bring bricks to block up the entrance." Much of the building was sacked, while out in the back, almost unnoticed, mysterious trucks spirited away tons of documents. Some claim (and others deny) that these were the mysterious secret GDR "Rosenholz" documents that landed with the CIA, with names of those who had secretly helped the Stasi outside its borders.

Election suspense mounted and though officially requested to refrain from electioneering within the GDR, West German leaders, including Kohl and Willy Brandt, swooped in defiantly like arrogant, quarrelsome vultures, feeding on the remains of the dying republic. They offered a sunny future with unlimited travel, cars of every brand, all the Cokes people could drink, all the bananas they could eat, and above all the miraculous West-mark, now increasingly demanded by street dealers. And above all, freedom in a united Germany and, in Kohl's oft-quoted words, "blossoming landscapes" for all East Germans. His eloquence, enhanced by magnanimous giveaways of Cokes and similar gifts, reached deeper into the hearts, minds, and perhaps stomachs of tempted East Germans. Some, like me, yearned for a miracle—a strong SED-PDS vote, despite the immense dissing of it and the GDR.

My older son Thomas and I went to watch the election results at the temporary headquarters of the SED-PDS, once the carefully guarded, almost holy Central Committee building of the SED, now open to the public. But the unhappy public soon dispersed. With an amazing voter turnout of 93 percent, Kohl's Christian Democrats led the field as triumphant victor and were thus able to head the new government. The Social Democrats suffered, surprisingly with only 22 percent, and our favorite, the SED-PDS, got 16.4 percent—about the proportion of truly faithful GDR supporters I had always estimated.

The path was now free for rapid steps toward reunification. The Social Democrats joined the new government as junior partners, then quit, but went along with the GDR burial preparations, leaving the SED-PDS fully isolated. Among the new brood of Christian Democrats, as yet in an inconspicuous job as deputy spokesperson, was a young physicist who later gained prominence, Angela Merkel.

45—New Brooms Sweep Clean

Conversation in those days centered largely on one question: How many new West-marks would you get for your soon obsolete East-marks? Would the rate be a desirable 1:1 ratio? Or a 2:1 ratio, cutting your bank account in half? It was finally decided: the desirable 1:1 rate would apply to 6,000 marks for senior citizens, 2,000 for each child, but 4,000 for everyone else, and the rest only half-rate, 2:1. There was a wild hunt for seniors or parents with enough to spare and ready to make deals, while endless sidewalk lines at jammed banks hastened, if possible, to improve their accounts.

After that settled down, the momentous day arrived for the new banknotes to be handed out: Saturday, July 1. One branch of the Deutsche Bank, reopened in East Berlin after forty-five years, was allowed to start on the stroke of midnight. A small riot ensued, a few bank windows and someone's rib got broken and a few fainted in the wild jam as eager hands grasped and waved the new miracle bills. Cars raced past our windows, West German flags waving, horns hooping, all

168A SOCIALIST DEFECTOR

louder than a soccer victory. For days, lines blocked sidewalks at the banks again as a decades-old dream came true!

On Monday morning, walking past the shop windows, we found ourselves in a new world, a Western world. In one shop after another we saw rearranged interiors with masses of new Western commodities, sparkling, tempting, modern! Fancier refrigerators, washing machines, dryers, sofas, armchairs, tools, utensils, household goods.

Most noteworthy for me were the bookshops, with Western publications gracing every window. Most prominent were how-to advisers, esoteric books, travel guides for regions one could now visit, enticingly sexy paperbacks, and political books by hitherto taboo political writers like Orwell, Koestler and, very copiously, Leon Trotsky.

Renate, a very good (and very popular) librarian, loved books, as I did, and we looked at this new selection with some curiosity. But before long, we learned of the bitter reverse side of the picture. To make room for these new books—and prevent competition—80 million GDR books were destroyed. The publicly owned wholesale company that supplied GDR bookshops, located in the traditional book city of Leipzig, threw its entire stock, 50,000 tons of newly printed books, into dumpsters and onto a big garbage dump.

Among them were certainly some dull Party-inspired tracts and government treatises, and some "factory productivity" and party-line novels, aiming at approval from on high, rarely read but given as awards on official occasions. They would hardly be missed. There were also the so-called classics, by Marx, Engels, and Lenin, which not too many would miss. But such categories were a tiny fraction of what was destroyed. Aside from all GDR authors, good and bad, there were literary classics by Mark Twain, Jack London, and Pushkin, by Bertolt Brecht, Heinrich and Thomas Mann, even by Schiller and Goethe. There were high-quality translations of modern authors from Hemingway and James Baldwin to John Updike, Gabriel Marquez, and Chingiz Aitmatov, who was discovered for the wider world by GDR literary experts. There were books on fine arts, nude art photo collections, and beautifully illustrated albums on architectural gems like the Merseburger Cathedral, founded in the eleventh century. Common to all of them was one characteristic; they had been published and printed in the GDR.

One book was by me, my history of American songs and singers from Yankee Doodle to Bruce Springsteen, with emphasis on Woody Guthrie, Leadbelly, and Pete Seeger. Its first edition, 8,000 copies, sold out immediately, and a second edition had just been delivered. But all landed in a dumpster; the small, respected publishing house quickly paid me my share in old GDR marks just when that currency lost half its value. Then, like many GDR publishers, it went bankrupt. This term, bankruptcy, according to a majority of the last People's Chamber, elected in March 1990, applied to the whole German Democratic Republic as well. They proceeded to act accordingly, just as with the books.

Hand in deathly hand with this book massacre was the demise of libraries. Till then, thanks to public financing, every town, city, borough, and all but the smallest villages, schools, factories, and hospitals had libraries. In West Germany there were no such binding regulations; a town might or might not choose to have a library, and books were far more expensive. Now this system arrived in the East. At the time of the *Wende*—the GDR term for the 1989–90 "turnaround" or "U-turn"— the region of Halle alone had about 250 full-time libraries. Within two decades less than ninety were left.

Near my home, there was a wonderful children's library at the back of a large movie theater with attractive show windows appealing to different ages, interests and hobby groups, with weekend readings for the youngest. With the new age, and sharply reduced subsidies, it could no longer pay exploding rent charges. At about the same time it closed, a fancy brothel was opened above a restaurant across the street, "with fountains and whirlpools." Now it too has closed and today, many years later, both remain empty and unused.

Reading books did and still does continue, with some assistance from the handy electronic method. And the "blossoming landscapes" promised the Ossies (from Osten = East) in a unified future now also include those circular, revolving airport-style book stands, full of whodunits, horror, and "erotica" paperbacks, usually with lovely ladies sprawled colorfully across the covers. A large number are imports from the United States, but West German authors had long since proved capable of jumping into this market, and no doubt East German authors soon caught up. I am afraid I have not kept up with this development.

46—Germany—United at Last!

The People's Chamber, elected in March, came to its final decision in August with only die-hard SED-PDS deputies opposing the death penalty of a republic just over forty-one years old. The vote was: YES 294, NO 62, ABSTAINING 7. And so, on October 3, 1990, President Weizsäcker, Chancellor Kohl, and all the other dignitaries gathered on the steps of the old Reichstag building in front of a giant crowd, and with no references to the fateful burning of that same building in February 1933, leading to Hitler's dictatorship, they rejoiced at what they eulogized as a rebirth of democracy in a united Germany, enjoyed an explosive fireworks display and the triumphant singing of the "Deutschland über alles" anthem, finally resounding once again right up to the Polish border, with flags waving everywhere, their black, red, and gold stripes finally rid of the added hammer-compass-grain insignia that had disfigured their centers here in the East. The newly enlarged state seemed headed gloriously forward toward a new life of unity and prosperity.

ONE OF MY first samples of this new life was hearing someone preaching loudly at Alexanderplatz. As I pushed through a circle of puzzled or amused onlookers, I saw, around the preacher, people lying, and a few even rolling, on the pavement. Have we really come to this, I wondered, recalling Joe Hill's famous "Pie in the Sky" song in which "Holy Rollers and Jumpers come out / And they holler, they jump and they shout." Minutes later, on the same big square, I saw costumed Hare Krishna people pacing around in a circle and mumbling while someone sold the appropriate books.

I never saw the rollers again and only rarely the Krishna people. With the Wall barrier down, Scientology folk also tried to do some convert-ing. I had to sympathize with a friend whose son joined a sect, probably Scientology, and disappeared, but I don't think they had much great luck in the East.

Neither, for that matter, did the established churches, Roman Catholic and Lutheran (called "Evangelic" in Germany), which were greatly disappointed. They had expected that East German freedom would bring pious swarms into their now privileged churches. But the increase was modest; most Ossies remained unrepentant pagans. A partial explanation was the 8 or 9 percent "church tax" subtracted from every church member's paycheck. And disinterest. Renate had quit years ago out of anger at one very nasty right-wing pastor in an icy church, and her whole family had followed suit. As for me, though a non-believer, I had friendly feelings toward morally motivated Christians—or Jews or Muslims—but very unfriendly feelings toward fanatics of any religion and I was glad when obligatory Religion class was dropped from the Berlin school curriculum. I wondered, when I passed highway signs directing drivers to church services, whether church membership would continue to decline, even in West Germany. Was Eastern paganism contagious?

Less spiritual but more conspicuous in the first post-Wall years were all the fancy consumer goods, including one phenomenon fully new to people here: fruit and vegetable stands, which appeared on many East Berlin corners, usually run by people of Turkish or Kurdish origin. There and in the supermarkets, we Ossies (and despite my strong United States accent I too was an Ossie) could now admire a bewil-dering display of fruits and vegetables in ordered rows of polished exactitude. Some we knew well, and some, like pineapples or coco-nuts, had been Yuletime rarities. But kiwis and avocados were new to a majority, and mangos, persimmons, pawpaws, and passion fruits were fully unknown. Most impressive, almost dramatic, was the unlimited supply of beautiful bananas, which had been so greatly missed. East Germans became far and away the best customers in all Europe of these curved, tasty symbols of our great "banana revolution"!

Most fruits came from far away. We heard complaints that apples were being imported from Chile or New Zealand, while good orchards in Berlin's outskirts were forced out of business and chopped down. There were louder complaints that beautifully packaged, bright red tomatoes from Holland or Spain tasted like paper or like nothing at all. But ah, how we could rejoice at yoghurt, no longer simply plain and white, but now in a dozen sweet and colorful flavors! And the variety of sugary breakfast cereals, in all shapes, was overwhelming!

Fully new in East Berlin was the Turkish döner kebab, a kind of open baguette filled high with meat sliced from a pressed meat cone in a bed of lettuce, tomato, pickle, onion. Though almost impossible to eat without spillage, it was very tasty. Over the years the number of döner and fruit stands would greatly decrease; also to decrease in numbers were the sad-looking young Vietnamese men at subway entrances, trying to act nonchalant while offering smuggled, untaxed American cigarettes, with the likely approval of the manufacturers and rare interference by the police. Most had come by government agreement to work in the GDR for four or five years. When the Wende shut their workplaces, many chose to stay here and began to gradually climb the social ladder—to legal sales of clothing at market stands, restaurants, and then handsome supermarkets for Asian specialties.

One welcome feature in post-Wende Berlin was the opening of foreign food restaurants. I had missed them greatly in the GDR where there were only a handful, true rarities. The waves of GDR people now visiting more and more foreign sites, in West Germany—we, too, soon visited Hamburg—all parts of Western Europe, the beaches of the Mediterranean from Turkey and Greece to Tunisia, Spain, and then on to the Canaries and beyond, helped hitherto skeptical East Germans to know and enjoy foreign foods. Streets in East Berlin began to fill up with foreign signs and menus, Chinese and Italian, then Vietnamese, Indian, Arabic, Croatian, Mexican, Afghan, and many others, mostly small and often short-lived—I mean the eating-places, not the staff or customers. Even the frequent opening and closing of small restaurants was a new phenomenon to Ossies.

When I first visited the West Berlin boroughs of Kreuzberg, Neukölln, or Wedding I was happy to find an international atmosphere recalling New York and its great variety, not just the restaurants but skin colors, languages, and clothing. How much nicer than almost totally white East German uniformity!

Now East Berlin kept changing. Its many streetcars were no longer plain yellow but displayed a wide variety of advertisements. There had been a great lack of advertising in the GDR, none at all in radio or on TV, no alluring billboards, few neon lights. Now more and more sidewalk cafés—also rare in the GDR, perhaps for lack of willing waiters and waitresses—sported wide umbrellas over their tables with bright ads for Camels or Lucky Strikes.

With world travel now possible, there were many travel agencies, also a novelty at first, with offers for group tours to all those foreign sites and sunny beaches, and also sun-tanning "studios," perhaps for those who couldn't afford even semi-tropical beaches but wanted to look as if they could. New additions were fingernail designers, often Vietnamese, and, as fashions evolved, body piercers and inky squadrons of tattoo artists. Most of the video renters who flourished with the Wende gradually dropped out, to be replaced by healthier additions like bicycle renters, as habits in East and West Berlin approached those in Copenhagen or Amsterdam.

Also possibly connected with health were the hitherto unknown massage parlors, though it was not always clear, except in some ads showing temptingly lovely East Asian masseuses, which sphere of health enhancement they were most concerned with. This question was even less ambiguous with the peepshows and their "private cabins," but I know of only two in East Berlin, both ironically on Rosa Luxemburg Strasse. Clearly defined brothels were even less visible on this side of the former Wall, but were probably easy to find on the Internet or with the aid of knowledgeable taxi drivers.

Encouragement in these directions was offered by a wide selection of colorfully explicit magazines on every newsstand. The famous, now ubiquitous newspaper *BILD*, a godsend for subway readers who like simple words, very brief news items, lots of sensations, and sports gossip, also offered a daily nudie photo on page 1. A big shop displaying enticing lingerie, dildos, and related paraphernalia was opened in East

Berlin by the chain of the famous Beate Uhse, perhaps the only woman pilot in the war and then the queen of erotica, who was even awarded a Federal Cross of Merit for her efforts. But before long, her East Berlin affiliate closed shop and, later, so did her central shop in West Berlin and its Erotica Museum, pushed out by new building construction. Perhaps Internet possibilities were a factor in reducing success; it was hardly because of prudery. But prudery did seem involved when many nude Free Body Culture beaches were closed, with the remainder banished to smaller areas off near the "dog beaches" and out of sight of "decent" West German family vacationers.

More important were the changes in our homes. Generous though obviously politically motivated tax and subsidy policies led with surprising speed to improvement and bright new colors for the shabby, crumbling facades of countless East Berlin buildings (and led also to Berlin's near bankruptcy and huge debts for years). Even our building, erected in 1961, got its interior heating, plumbing and weather insulation renovated. After a few difficult months of construction these improvements motivated us, at last, to improve our lives with a dryer and a dishwasher. Of course, such building renovation caused rent increases, in our case from the 114 East-marks we had paid in all those GDR years to the escalating bill currently standing at 600 euros (1,200 West-marks), and no longer inclusive of water, hot water, heating, and electricity. Rent, usually about a tenth of my GDR average earnings, today eats up over a third to half of my pension. Barring further big increases I can still afford it, but a lot of people can't, which means forcing long-term tenants out of central boroughs and to the cheaper outskirts. Fancy modern gentrification, often for wealthy Berlin newcomers, is conspicuous on street after street.

Unlike half of the GDR's city dwellers, we never had a bungalow—or dacha—in the suburbs or out in the countryside and were not affected by thousands of quarrels involving West Germans, often people who had left the GDR years or decades earlier and now claimed bungalows they had left behind, but which had been assigned to people who had since then put years of effort into repairing and improving the buildings and the gardens. It was a shock for many, who often knew nothing of earlier owners, when a fancy West German car suddenly drove up and an often impolite, even arrogant "Wessie" insisted on taking meter measurements inside and outside what he called his "private property." The legal situation was very sticky, and very political.

With no such bungalow to visit (or quarrel over) and grown-up offspring, we could well manage without a car in the city's now choked streets and rare parking spots. I gave my inexpensive used car to my son Thomas, while carefully keeping it in my name; if it were in his name he might find a sharp decrease or worse in the unemployment pay he was often forced to rely on. This made me the innocent recipient of fines for false parking or exceeding speed limits; luckily, they were rare.

We occasionally paid the steeply increased fares to see, and often enjoy, plays, concerts, and museums in West Berlin, such as the little museum with works of the great Weimar-era sculptor and artist Käthe Kollwitz. With our grandchildren we also enjoyed the West Berlin Zoo, less spacious than East Berlin's Tierpark with its broad expanses for the animals and the visitors but with the largest variety of species in the world, including that widowed giant panda. Such a subway excursion was truly worth the price.

47—The Economy: Changes

Promised prosperity seemed assured, at least for the producers of the countless brightly packaged products now on sale everywhere, with their enticing brand names, long known and yearned for in the East thanks to West-TV ads. Who would now buy GDR products? People preferred nicely packed eggs from the West, even though they were more expensive and not nearly as fresh as "Eastern" eggs. Who would buy Eastern cheese or sausage rather than vacuum-packaged Western products, especially attractive under special lighting and delicately layered in what proved to be the thinnest of slices? Only slowly did people come to realize that GDR sausage or cheese, even when sold without any packaging, usually tasted better. But these products virtually disappeared from the counters of the supermarket chains that replaced the GDR's publicly or cooperatively owned supermarkets and small private shops. Within half a year, 60 percent of East German commodity production had almost literally bit the dust. Today, twenty-eight years later, special sales of those "East products" that modestly survived are jammed with nostalgic customers.

Cars had not been so necessary in the GDR. A visiting American professor, after a research trip, told me: "I don't see why so many people here want cars. With that close-knit network of trains, buses and streetcars you can get almost everywhere you want without long waits." And it cost only 15 or 20 pfennigs in town and 8 pfennigs per railroad kilometer.

Nevertheless, GDR families did want cars. By 1989, about half of them had one, but rarely the kind they yearned for: VW, Opel, Fiat, Renault, or even BMW or Mercedes. Now at last the dream became reality. It need not always be new; Ossies began to realize that though it was great to proudly peel West-marks from your wallet, it was not always so simple to replenish the supply. So they sought bargains. As West Germans discovered, from this hunger a jolly little rhyme made the rounds: "Fängt's an zu rosten, verkauf's im Osten"—"If it starts to rust, sell it in the East." Even I fell for this in a one-sided trade with a curious Wessie. For my Trabi (and too much cash) I got a brightly painted Opel, whose rusty underparts caused it to flunk the first checkup.

In those euphoric months, discarded GDR furniture filled the streets and so did discarded cars, simply abandoned. The two-stroke Trabis and Wartburgs had been no models ecologically, but I wondered how tripling or quadrupling the number of larger, speedier cars after 1990, with jammed streets and parking space and cutting up the landscape with ever wider Autobahn highways, often with no speed limits, affected the environment. Yet each year it became more desirable to own a car, since village shops closed, local rail lines shut down, and train fares soared. So did urban fares for the subway, el, streetcar, and bus, rocketing to 25 times the old GDR rates, which had always been kept, amazingly, at 1945 levels. Fearsome fines, fifty euros and more, now threatened any transgressors caught without valid, punched tick-ets—there are no turnstiles here, only "punching machines"—to punch tickets, not delinquent travelers. Of course, we knew nothing in those years about the poisoning of the atmosphere by purposely deceptive diesel emission trickery. Nor were we yet aware that exalted crooks of that kind, even when caught red-handed, were seldom if ever punished as fearsomely as subway ticket deceivers.

The whole scene was all so new and different. We Ossies were besieged by impressive but more than deceptive insurance offers and mailed "no-risk" opportunities to win bundles of money, by dirt-cheap bus tours to alluring tourist sites that then meant hours of sales blurbs at obscure stop-offs. Even I, the American, was as naive as most East Germans. To the amusement of my family, I fell for two dodges, one a free one-month newspaper subscription that then proved very hard to cancel, and a wonderful bargain from a traveling salesman, a suede leather jacket handsome to look at, but never again wearable after the first light rainfall.

Our whole money picture had to change. A bank employee recalled cash deliveries before the Wende: "We had a ten-year-old Wartburg car which simply drove around Eisenach and supplied all our branches. Either the manager or just the driver were alone in the car with 500,000 to even a million marks in the trunk."

Now, armored vans with two armed security men take countless precautions, sometimes even then in vain. And we too changed our attitudes. In the GDR, the publicly owned banks all offered a 3.25 per-cent interest rate, stable from 1971 to the end. Only one big installment plan purchase was allowed at a time. (Was that an infringement of free-dom? I guess so, but for many a salutary one.) Cars were sold only for immediate payment, and with rent so low, it was not easy to get in debt or have banking problems, and few did. After the Wende, what with checking accounts separate from savings accounts, with installment payments on the car, the new fridge or washing machine, the chic sofa or bedroom set, people had to balance any money left over in a careful assortment of banks, all of them "your best friend and adviser" and probably none of them honest. Difficult choices were also necessary among a confusing assortment of offers by many all too loud, well-meaning competitors for health care, household, and life insurance. Editorials in the newspapers, now taken over by West German press giants, liked to praise all this as "newly won individual freedom and responsibility in a democracy." Cynics viewed it as a multiple rip-off!

The money switch, celebrated with triumphant whooping and general hoopla, forced all enterprises to pay their staffs with the new West-marks, of which they had very few. Nor could they easily earn more, since the USSR and Eastern Europe, until then the main trade partners and which had paid for imports with a common currency ("transfer rubles"), now had to pay in tough Western money. The products, though often as good and more durable than those of Western rivals, were usually less fashionable, had no famous brand names and logos, and were suddenly more expensive. "No, thanks!" was the obvious response. With the domestic market vanishing because their products were disdained or unavailable, it was very difficult for GDR companies to keep their heads above water.

And, like us private citizens, the companies had banking problems, far bigger ones. Publicly owned GDR enterprises always received credit from publicly owned banks, which was recompensed with a percentage of the earnings. It just went from one pocket to the other, a harmless kind of Peter-Paul relationship. Those amounts had not represented debts. But they did now! With GDR banks sold off to private Western banks, these were now "claims," to be paid off in West-marks. The Western banks had paid only 900 million marks to buy the Eastern banks but now demanded that the enterprises pay up all those "claims," which were calculated as worth up to 43 billion marks, plus rapidly climbing interest amounts often higher than the purchase sums. According to an official report of the Federal Inspection Authority, this granted the private West German banking system, at one blow, economic domination over virtually the entire East German economy. A well-calculated avalanche, it buried nearly all industrial survivors. Even successful, state-of-the-art factory complexes were suffocated and sold off for a song (in German "für ein Apfel und ein Ei"—"for an apple and an egg"). Eastern competition with Western products, seldom strong but often an unwanted factor, had become a thing of the past, a jolly result of unification only one side could enjoy.

THE "ROUND TABLE" of all East German parties, chaired by the churches, which decided on the fateful March 1990 elections, had also proposed an institution to be called the *Treuhand*, or "Trust Agency." Originally it was touted as a way to retain the value of GDR industry for the benefit of the East German citizenry, even after it was privatized.

After the elections were won by a "one Germany" majority, negotiations on unification were assigned to a hitherto unknown, crafty, gimlet-eyed Christian Democrat named Günter Krause. His West German counterpart, tough Interior Minister Wolfgang Schäuble, who would retain his tough, nasty role in German and European politics until very recently, had far stronger cards in his hand. But he hardly needed them. Krause, looking ahead, was more than compliant, and was later duly rewarded, twice, with Cabinet posts in the unified government. After flubbing both of them, he founded two private companies that both went broke, and garnered several indictments for assorted dirty work. But that came later. In 1990, his basic job was to sell out the GDR.

The Treuhand's alleged aim, recompensing East Germans for incurred losses, was quickly transmogrified: how to privatize the whole economy quickly and make sure that not a bit of value of the 8,000 state-owned companies, built up with the sweat, sacrifice, and dedication of the people, should revert to them. Nor should over four million employees be included in any decisions about their lives. Not even the elected Bundestag should have a say, only the new Treuhand, made up, with one short-lived exception, Günter Krause, exclusively of Wessies. Everything was to be hocked off or scrapped. That included, aside from all of industry, nearly 10,000 square miles of publicly owned farmland and forests, large sections of public housing, much of the army's buildings and equipment, everything the Stasi had owned, the property of parties and organizations, and, to round off the picture, the state pharmacy network. In other words, almost everything of any value, from fields and forests, railroads, and new steel works to insulin supplies and the famous Babelsberg Film Studios. The first 3,713 factories, 43 percent of the total, were shut down within twenty months, costing the jobs of almost three million employees.

In the Treuhand's bargain basement sellout, big, successful factory complexes were sold, not for their genuine value but for sums shrewdly diminished by subtracting the impossible new bank claims and calculating the immediate loss of sales possibilities. They were frequently split up and sold piecemeal as real estate, sometimes for one symbolic mark per section, often to West German competitors or fly-by-night entrepreneurs who removed all saleable machinery and simply let the rest go to ruin. The huge Ernst Thälmann Works in Magdeburg, with 35,000 employees, was carved into five parts and then, one after the other, abandoned. From a train window, I saw the brick ruins, usually with smashed windows.

Christa Luft, economics minister in the brief interim cabinet of Hans Modrow, said scornfully: "They accepted anyone who knocked on the door to get something; the main thing was that he have a West German zip code. Even if he had had three or four bankruptcies—that didn't matter. It was really evil. . . . We had hundreds of books in the GDR in which we learned how to switch from a market economy to a planned economy, but unfortunately not a single one on how to move back again."

Her words were borne out by the final facts: 85 percent of the publicly owned property was sold to West German people or companies, 10 percent to foreign buyers, and only 5 percent to East Germans.

A rare honest TV report exposed one example. An East Berlin factory, whose 1,200 employees made all of the GDR's large-size heating equipment, was valued at about 68 million marks, plus 150 million in liquid assets and valuable real estate. The main Western producer of industrial steam boilers, Deutsche Babcock, sent an expert to check on buying its former competitor. But Michael Rottmann, lying to his boss that it was worthless, hitched up with two Swiss buddies, whose bankrupt little firm had a resonant name, and bought it at a fantastically tiny price of 2 million marks. No one checked their credentials. After selling the real estate and letting the factory go to pot, they pocketed

150 million marks and Rottmann absconded to a high life abroad. Ten years later, in 2009, he was finally extradited to Germany, sentenced to three and a half years, but not fined since he claimed he had no money left. The Federal Appeals Court soon reversed his sentence because of the statute of limitations and he was set free. The 1,200 employees became jobless.

48—Freezing Times

That almost picturesque case was symbolic for the bribery and corruption from top to bottom. Another story is even more illustrative. Tucked away in the southern mountains, near a beautiful castle built in 1250, was a factory employing 5,500 people; it had been the biggest producer of refrigerators in the entire Eastern Bloc. When the Wende hit, ruining nearly all sales possibilities, every one of the last remaining 630 "was fearful for a whole year, from morning to evening" that the Treuhand would soon turn 1992 into their last year with a job— and where else were there jobs in this picturesque but out-of-the way region?

Then something clicked. At a meeting in Montreal every country pledged to phase out all appliances emitting FCKW chlorofluorocarbons, which endangered the ozone layer. Refrigerators were among the major sinners. But a variant, fluorohydrocarbon or FKW, was permitted, so manufacturers turned to it, even though it too caused atmospheric warming.

An expert from Greenpeace was not satisfied. A scientist friend discovered how to substitute perfectly harmless carbides, thus avoiding all nasty chemicals. But alas, not one of the seven big Western manufacturers was willing to change its ways. Then he discovered the East German company, which, unable to afford FKW, was on the brink of Treuhand dissolution. After working speedily with its main engineer and with a small subsidy from Greenpeace, a new safe and harmless fridge was developed.

The first product came off the line in March 1993, and after a publicity tour by the Greenpeace enthusiast there were soon orders for 65,000 "Greenfreeze" fridges. The Treuhand reluctantly agreed to give it a chance, so, at the last minute, hundreds of jobs were saved.

Not everyone was happy. One of the Big Seven firms spread the word that the new product ate up 30 percent more electricity. An independent study disproved this. The rivals spread gossip that it might explode. Greenpeace replied that there was no more gas involved than in three cigarette lighters; all tests proved it safe. And then it came out that the chemical FKW substitute being used by the Big Seven was harmful environmentally. Now even Bosch-Siemens, the biggest rival of "Greenfreeze," admitted publicly that it was indeed "a sensational success" or, as one newspaper wrote, "a revolution." Experts from all over visited the little town to take a look. A big battle, it seemed, really a triumph, had been won.

But its success was its undoing. Within months, copycat versions were developed. Since the Greenpeace man, in the interests of the environment, had counseled against patenting it, the biggies were easily able to push it to the wall. A Dutch company that bought the plant in 1996 also went bankrupt, and the factory was shut down. The walls are left but none of the jobs. (Christoph Gunkel, "Öko-Coup aus Ostdeutschland," Der Spiegel, March 13, 2013.)

This, the only plant in town, was one of thousands to shut down, many here in hilly southern Saxony. Is it surprising that pro-Nazis, quickly moving in from the West, found good hunting grounds and built varying networks of disappointed and disoriented Ossies?

One leading GDR dissident, Werner Schulz, a founder of the New Forum and proponent of the Treuhand, saw things differently in later years, calling it the biggest fraud in German history: "They had no desire to have another car manufacturer in East Germany. They had no desire to have a producer of FCKW-free refrigerators in the East. They closed these plants down very deliberately because they were competitors. All they wanted was subsidiaries, workshops as extended auxiliaries. At one blow, the entire industrial capital of the GDR was demolished." (Channel ZDF, "Beutezug Ost," September 10, 2010.)

All in all, when the Treuhand started off, it assessed the value of the GDR enterprises it took over arbitrarily at close to 600 billion marks. When it closed up shop four years later, not a pfennig of that was left, but instead a 250 billion–mark mountain of debt. Where, oh where did it all disappear?

The fateful decision to switch so swiftly away from GDR money was evidently made by Chancellor Helmut Kohl and his Christian Democrats in order to win the votes of all those Ossies who had a feverish craving for magic West-marks and all the goodies connected with them—but no idea of the consequences. The strategy had worked, helping Kohl and his allies to win in a landslide and gain control of the unification process but devastating whole regions and sending waves of young people to the West in a hunt for jobs.

TWICE A YEAR, I had taught English improvement courses for the GDR Academy of Sciences with all its many research institutes. My students included a few professors, many doctors of science, but mainly younger scientists working their way up in every field of natural and social sciences—from enzymes, anthropological pollen research, or astrophysics to Middle East developments or early German authors. For me, with my high school science background, it was a demanding but fascinating job.

Locking up the GDR Academy of Sciences with all its institutes and closing down the industrial combines with their research centers ended all GDR scientific work; most of my former students lost their jobs at one stroke. A few of the best-known professors found berths in foreign universities; a very few got jobs in industry. Most had to start hunting for some other way to make a living.

I am still friends with one scientist, the daughter of a couple who, since both were Jewish, fled from the Nazis to the United States after he fought in Spain. When they were harassed during the McCarthy era, they moved to the GDR and did important medical work. Their daughter was engaged in experimental research at the famous Charité hospital. But when the Wende came, neither her parents' past nor her own accomplishments helped her. She and countless other

East Berliners were simply pushed out, with a variety of transparent excuses. They were Ossies, their opinions were disapproved, and their jobs were sought after.

A couple I knew, in their late fifties, experts in Sanskrit and other languages, lost their jobs as professors at Humboldt University. Almost entire staffs in the social sciences—law, languages, history, sociology, and, of course, political science—were thrown out. Those in the natural sciences were rated by a panel of West German colleagues, often rivals in the same fields, on their abilities and "moral qualities" above all, on possible contacts with the Stasi, which was almost unavoidable for scientists who visited Western countries or tried to obtain Western equipment. Their membership and degree of activity in the SED was also a theme. I was told that more academics were fired after 1990 than in the Nazi years of barring Jews and burning books.

The picture was similar at the schools of the crushed little republic. Civics teachers, history teachers, or any who had been active in a school's SED organization, regardless of their subject, were almost sure to go. Some may have been no great loss, though the manner of ousting them was nasty. But also excluded were the last of that enthusiastic generation of "New Teachers" who jumped in to replace Nazis after 1945 and were often among the best, but were now themselves replaced, in a kind of reverse vengeance, just before their pension age.

The Wessies moved in to top jobs in all fields of life, from judge's benches and organizing traffic to controlling sewage, and always claimed to know far better than the backward locals how things were done properly. Thanks to their sacrifice and magnanimity in coming to help poor ignorant Eastern "brothers and sisters," they received what was known as a "bush bonus" in their paychecks, even though many were so-called "DiMiDos"—that is, those who worked DIenstag, MIttwoch, and DOnnerstag before returning westward on Friday for their super-long weekends.

What about journalists? A friend and colleague was a top journalist at a GDR magazine whose good photos, skilled reporting, and, except for the editorials, avoidance of heavy-handed lecturing made it very popular. Soon after the Wende, he found himself facing, as new superior, a young journalist from Hamburg without a clue about East Berlin, the GDR, or what readers here liked or disliked. Of course, despite his many years at the job, she got higher pay. But his melancholy at being demoted by a clueless newcomer soon lost meaning: the magazine was shut down.

In the same press building, the popular women's magazine *Für Dich* (For You) was forced by its new owners to abandon its well-written, intelligent articles on a wide range of subjects in favor of "more appropriate" themes: fashions, cosmetics, and tricks or devices to capture a husband or, when captured, to hold on to him in defiance of wrinkles, weight increase, or rivals. Then it too was shut down.

I had many friends at radio headquarters, where I had worked for a few years. In the final GDR months, the radio and TV staffs threw out disliked "dogmatists" and some who had worked too visibly with the Stasi. TV began to have commercials again, but the staffs, not cut too sharply in number, created something of a new spirit.

Then, an official group of Wessies descended on the radio center, led by a retired right-wing Bavarian journalist. A questionnaire they used immediately recalled my fateful questionnaire in the U.S. Army; this one asked about connections, not just with the Stasi but also with the SED, to which many radio and TV journalists had belonged, as did over 2 million adults out of a population of 16 million. A former colleague described waiting in line on the stairway until he was called into an office where one or two panel members looked at his record and questionnaire, put a question or two, and then, figuratively speaking, raised or lowered a thumb, like Nero in the Colosseum. Out of 13,000 employees about 4,000 were kept on, mostly from the kitchen, car park, canteen, or janitorial staff, plus some musicians, dancers, and technicians. Almost all radio and TV programs, good, bad, popular, or boring, were dropped. A rare exception was *The Sandman*, a kiddies' bedtime series, for years more popular than a Western copycat. Nine thousand employees were given a skimpy compensation for their broken contracts and sent off to fend for themselves.

49—*Rawhide* and More Raw Times

What about our family? Nearly all my income sources as a freelancer were gone with the Wende. Who now wanted to hear an over-sixty ex-pat talk about the United States when people could buy all the glamorous and exciting books about it they wanted, from Tom Clancy's right-wing thrillers to Stephen King's horror? And if they could afford it they could go there and see for themselves! There were three-day New York tours: Statue of Liberty, Times Square, Empire State Building, quick looks at Greenwich Village and Harlem, and a double-decker trip down Fifth Avenue. Or take expensive looks at the whole country: Niagara Falls, the Capitol and White House, then all the way to the Golden Gate, a Chinatown cable car ride and, crowning it all, Grand Canyon and the Las Vegas Strip. So why listen to me? There were few if any periodicals for my left-leaning analyses, no teachers' clubs, cultural, or union clubs had survived the political earthquake. New high school and college staff had never heard of me or, if by chance they had, did not like me. I was off most shopping lists, and funds were scarce.

And yet I had luck. A West German TV channel discovered a popular U.S. cowboy series from the 1960s, *Rawhide*, with a debonair young Clint Eastwood as a hero in its 217 episodes. It was decided to have them dubbed at the excellent but now reeling, hence inexpensive, GDR synching studio. Since the translators had trouble with Western lingo, I was offered the job of collating written dialogue and spoken lines, which often differed. I shared the job with two friends and took on only a small share of the episodes, but they paid so well that I was rescued for the two years until my pension payments began, better than average thanks to an agreement won some years earlier by our writers' association. And I was surprised to find that *Rawhide* was fun, well-made, and even had a progressive slant.

Renate was also lucky. When the Wall went down, the higher pay rates in West Berlin hospitals forced Eastern ones to pay more or lose their entire staffs, and this also applied to her in the patients' library of a major hospital. But other rules were rigid; when she turned sixty in 1992, she was obliged to retire, against her wishes, since she loved

the job. Her pension was far lower than mine but better than nothing, so we managed okay financially, even when our rent began soaring
upward.

Our sons had less luck. Thomas, unhappily, was a journalist, now
the worst trade imaginable, and had to keep punching in a tough, endless bout up to the present. Timothy lost his job at the now defunct
GDR film company DEFA, but after a while was able to beat out rivals
and win the management of a cinema theater. But he, too, had to learn
that the free enterprise system involves punching—or really kick-fight-
ing. Not a few scars remain.

Masses of people were not lucky. A colleague at the studio job working on *Rawhide* told me that these episodes marked her last weeks at
this job, and she had no idea where she would then turn for herself
and her little daughter. The common German greeting, "Wie geht's?"
(How are things?) was often answered in those days by the words, "I
won't ask you if you don't ask me!"

In the supermarket, before the Wende, Renate and I sometimes chatted with the woman at the cheese counter. Always friendly, she tipped
us off on the day's best and tastiest bargains. In her early forties perhaps, somewhat dumpy, she had a plain but usually smiling face. Some
months after a giant national chain replaced the store's GDR public
ownership, she spoke to us, not to offer a cheese specialty but to tell us
that her usual vacation application was rejected and another date dictated. Since it failed to match school holidays, making it impossible to
holiday with her little son, she had asked if it could be altered, a request
that in GDR days, while not always fulfilled, would have always been
considered. Now she got the snappy answer: "You'll take your vacation
when we tell you to!"

Not long thereafter, we met her again. This time, she confided, the
manager had not spoken of the vacation but told her she was no longer
needed; she would soon be out of a job. She looked at us sadly and
asked, this time with tears, "Is this what we all voted for?"

A few months later we saw her in a drafty train station, peddling
cheeses from a small portable table, on her own we guessed, seeing no
company logo.

50—Life in Utopia

My feelings about the Wende were not improved when a giant Coca-Cola structure was erected on the roof of a thirteen-story building across the street. Bright red and white neon curtains soon flashed into my living room every evening, opening and shutting, rising and falling, to remind me about that refreshing pause. Those lights knew no such pause! This had formerly been the House of the Child, offering children's toys and apparel, a delightful puppet theater, and a café on the top floor—"Adults allowed only if accompanied by children." That was gone. Luckily, after a few months, so was Coca-Cola. Yet, in a way, it had been a symbol of my own life cycle.

Some people could never reconcile themselves to the loss of the GDR; a few small groups still wave its flag at left-wing parades and even put on the blue shirts of the Free German Youth organization.

Renate, too, never lost her despondency or bitterness at the change. She was never too interested in "politics," least of all in far-flung world developments so important to me (partly, no doubt, because geography had not been part of her meager schooling). She had been as impatient as I at phrase-mongering speeches, full of worn-out straw, with the difference that she never listened to them or read the even lengthier articles. But she had strong feelings on a human, personal, less abstract level, a warm bonding toward the GDR, mourning its death and loathing those she saw as part of the change, like Kohl, Reagan, or G. H. W. Bush in the West, Václav Havel and Lech Wałęsa in the East, and dissidents like Eppelmann and Lengsfeld in the GDR.

As for me, though also bitter to this day, with a few tears when I watch the best old DEFA films, I tried to maintain resiliency. Perhaps my mixed background helped, or maybe my genes. Lamenting would get us nowhere; it was necessary to adjust to a new vista no longer ending at the Elbe but extending to the Rhine, or beyond, and attempt a fair appraisal of this new world that seemed to bring an improved life for some, at least for those who kept their jobs or soon found new ones, while bringing disappointment to others.

51—Two Palaces

Not religion but perhaps monarchism was involved in one bitter defeat. In 1951, the huge central palace of Prussian kings and kaisers, heavily damaged by bombs, was not preserved but demolished. Was this because reconstruction, at that time clearly impossible, would always be fantastically expensive, requiring sums, material, and manpower needed for far more urgent tasks, or was it because it was a symbol of Prussian rule and expansion? Perhaps both.

In the 1970s, on the same site, a modern "Palace of the Republic" was erected in something like Bauhaus style. One third was for the GDR parliament, or *Volkskammer*. The rest was for everyone: an auditorium, which, in less than an hour, could switch from an open dance floor to modern seating for up to 5,000, and which hosted political congresses, popular TV shows, and concerts, with guests ranging from pop singers to Harry Belafonte, Mercedes Sosa, Miriam Makeba, Mikis Theodorakis, Santana, or Pete Seeger. There was also a small theater, a disco club, bowling alley, a post office (open on Sundays), and ten restaurants and bars for espresso, beer, wine, or ice-cream drinks, all moderately priced and inviting. Best of all was the spacious two-story foyer, full of comfortable sofas and armchairs, sixteen big paintings by the GDR's best-known artists, and many lamps, giving it the nickname "Erich's lamp shop" (for Honecker). Open from early to late, free of charge, it was a place to escape hot sun, rain, or snow, meet friends or just relax. Most East Berliners loved it.

A close friend, a safety inspector, told me of an interesting difference. During three years of difficult construction, there were two fatal accidents. Munich's Olympic Stadium, on the other hand, with a roughly similar construction time and number of workers, cost nearly one hundred lives.

During the Wende, unfortunately, it was found that fire-resistant materials with asbestos had been used. Other prominent buildings, some in West Berlin, were successfully cleansed of them. But a blue-blooded businessman, Wilhelm Dietrich Gotthard Hans Oskar von

Boddien, whose company had gone broke, saw a chance for his big project: rebuilding the Kaiser's palace, or as huge a building with the same outer facade. International architects like Renzo Piano tried to save the GDR building as an impressive historical landmark, loved by so many. But winners take all, and this symbol of the GDR had to go, even though rebuilding the Kaiser's palace cost over a billion euros. Rumors had it that Helmut Kohl wanted no GDR Palace of the Republic at the other end of Unter den Linden from its Brandenburg Gate. The Bundestag agreed, although no one knew what the rebuilt giant would be good for. Today, after years of pleading and demonstrations, then tearing down and rebuilding, the royal exterior is almost complete, with its stout tower, its uppermost cross, and all its stone Prussian eagles. It will probably offer a library and a museum of indigenous arts and crafts from former colonies in Africa and the South Pacific. In a few years we shall know. Many people, like me, cannot pass the giant new structure without heartache.

The TV tower in East Berlin, one of the tallest in Europe, was hated even more than the Palace of the Republic, since it can be seen from almost everywhere in East and West Berlin and for many miles around. But it has no asbestos and is too big and prominent to tear down. There are attempts, partly realized, to construct buildings around it, obscuring it for people in nearby streets.

As little as possible must remain of the GDR. As author Hermann Kant commented: "For some people it can't be gotten rid of often enough, they still want to be victorious again." Even after twenty-eight years, many leading people fear it like a zombie and boil at all but the most negative recollections or legends. The mildest praise of the GDR, even objective analysis, is quickly attacked by a hornet swarm of op-ed writers, historians, and politicians. Some also demand such attacks from leaders of the Linke Party in an attempt, since they were unable to destroy the party, to tame it instead, much as the Greens had been tamed and, far earlier, the SPD. In a speech to West German judges in 1991 (with the last ex-Nazis gone by then, either to comfortable retirement or to their graves), Justice Minister Klaus Kinkel put it this way: "I am relying on the German judiciary. It must be possible to delegitimize the

GDR system, which justified itself till the bitter end with its anti-fascist beliefs, its professedly higher values and its asserted absolute humanism while, under the cover of its Marxism-Leninism, it built up a state in many aspects just as inhumane and frightful as fascist Germany."

This effort, a part of official policy, was voiced by a man who, as foreign minister, had bonded with the Turkish secret service against the Kurds, with fascist Ustashi elements in Croatia, with the Israeli Mossad against Palestinian prisoners in German prisons, with Saddam Hussein in Iraq, and had declared: "There are two parallel tasks we must master; within our country we must again become one single people [*Volk*], outside it we must complete something we have twice previously failed to achieve: finding a role, in agreement with our neighbors, which corresponds with our wishes and our potential."

What Kinkel demanded recalls fearsomely the wishes and the deeds of Kaiser Wilhelm, who last ruled in the palace now being restored, and of Hitler, who was responsible for its destruction, along with that of much of Berlin and all Europe.

Kinkel's demand for delegitimation reflected the ongoing fear that memories of the GDR are still not fully erased, even after the Palace of the Republic is torn down and countless army camps, schools, and streets have been renamed. There must be no more Communist names, even for those executed by the Nazis. The horse is simply not dead enough—could it still be capable of a kick or a bite? Do some people have the wrong memories? Who knows when they may recall them enough to reject such wishes for "one single *Volk*," as the Kaiser and Hitler phrased it, or should again strive for that deadly "potential"? Might another economic crash like 2008, or maybe worse, act as a defi-brillator and revive the dead horse? Is that why the GDR—again and again and again, ad nauseam—must be delegitimized?

52—Home Again

While unification sped ahead and the GDR slid into oblivion, I had personal worries to think about. How would I be treated? Would the

Bonn authorities, when they took over, send me to my U.S. Army fate? Where could we escape to? No East European country, not even the USSR, was a possibility anymore. Cuba teetered on the brink; at that time few would have bet a dime on the survival of the Castro government. North Korea did not seem a tempting prospect. I asked a friend in Vienna about a possible niche for me in neutral Austria. No, he answered frankly. What should I do?

I did nothing. Happily, my case got routine treatment and I was given an FRG document. There were only two brief hitches: when I thoughtlessly wrote "Brown" for hair color the clerk looked at me and politely altered it. And then a stamp in the new pass forbade me as a foreign citizen from any gainful employment. After I offered proof that my diploma, my apartment, income, and wife were all quite German, the limitation was removed. It might have been tougher if I were from Izmir, not Manhattan!

But what about seeing Manhattan again? In 1975, the official in the new U.S. consulate in East Berlin had urged me to return, assuring me that I need have no great fears. I had not trusted his assurances. In 1989, a letter I wrote to the Class of 1949 bulletin about my story was printed, then reprinted in the big glossy *Harvard Magazine* for all alumni. I received a flood of mail and even visits, leading to some lasting friendships, and also a letter from a prominent Republican on the class committee who, despite his expressed differences with my views, invited me to attend our 40th class reunion. I hastened, with high hopes, to the current U.S. consul in East Berlin. At first, she saw no difficulties; I had never become a GDR citizen or otherwise given up my U.S. citizenship. But when I returned two days later with the necessary photographs, she advised me otherwise. "The U.S. Army has a long memory," she warned. I was both grateful and disappointed, and went on with my life.

During one of my mother's visits, she told me that the family had used an old connection with someone from the CIA (a former schoolmate of my brother) to ask whether I could return unscathed. "Yes, anytime," they were told, but he would have to blast the GDR when he arrived. Certain of my response, she had not even told me about it.

Some years later, after her death, I mentioned this to my brother, who said: "Oh, I guess she didn't tell you the other part of the bargain. You would have had to stay in East Berlin for a while and work for them before coming home!"

I recalled this years later. Another American at the radio station where I had worked for a while, also a deserter, had once phoned and told me he was going to visit his ill father in the United States. "Can you do that without ending up behind bars?" I asked. "Yes, it will now be possible," he said. I asked him how long he would be gone. "About six weeks." He never returned, but I heard that he was not jailed. Years later a former colleague told me that after the death of the German ex-wife of that American a letter was found in her desk from their son in California, requesting the dates of his work at the radio station so he could get his pension money for the time he had worked there— for the CIA! A similar course is obviously what was intended for me.

Even after the fall of the Wall, but with the consul's words well in mind, I still feared the U.S. Army and refrained from visiting West Berlin. But a friend in the United States had found a law firm in Washington that dealt with military matters like mine. In April 1994, I sent it the renewed invitation to the Harvard class reunion, now the 45th.

One evening a lawyer called. "You can come back," she said. "You may have to spend a night or two behind bars, but then it will be okay!"

I turned to Renate: "*Jetzt oder nie!*"—"Now or never!," I said. Practical as ever, almost her first reaction was: "But if you attend a reunion you will have to buy a new suit!"

I called my brother. "You're crazy," he said. "Do you trust some unknown woman in Washington?" I said "Yes" and then mentioned my wife's first worry. "A new suit?" he snorted. "You better buy one with stripes!"

But go we did. My stomach felt queasy and my mouth dry when I spotted Long Island under the plane wing and headed down. We were picked up at the airport, as expected, taken past the good old Statue of Liberty to Fort Dix and discharged from the U.S. Army after forty-two years, with no time behind bars or any punishment. Two months later, after some delays, I received a regular passport.

It was truly an adventure, for Renate at least as much as for me. A first stop the next day was the big bus terminal on Manhattan's West Side. I soon noticed her fears in that confusing rush of people after hearing so many stories of crime in the big cities, and she didn't let me release my hold on our luggage for a second, hardly even to go to the men's room, leaving her to wait, huddled in a corner. But then she went to the ladies' room and told me how, while washing her hands, her eyes strayed to the next mirror and met those of a young African American tidying her lipstick. They smiled at each other at this womanly moment and this broke a knot for Renate, who now began to enjoy the trip.

We spent eleven weeks there, had fine reunions with my grown-up niece and nephews and some old friends, and I tried to understand menus with foreign foods I had never heard of, while Renate never quite trusted the idea of leaving the tip on the table, where "anyone could grab it." We greatly enjoyed our first lobster dinner with my nephews and then spent almost a week at the class reunion, getting a reception that ranged from polite to very friendly, with one minor exception from a former room neighbor who scolded briefly but nastily that I had never revealed my radical views to him back in Dunster House. Actually, he had never asked; as I recalled, his main interest then had been capturing chunks of the football goal posts. The Newport location where we first gathered was almost regal: a former millionaire's mansion. Aided by some good wine, I danced a livelier jitterbug than in decades, to Renate's amazed but happy surprise. And at a lobster dinner, we were now almost experts. Moving on to Cambridge, there were many recollections for me, including a visit to my old room in Dunster House, now on a co-ed basis which I could never have dreamed of. At the final dinner, we somehow landed at what turned out to be the VIP table, next to all kinds of "class enemies" with whom we got along quite well, thanks in great measure, I am sure, to Renate's charm.

Most noteworthy for me were not so much the changes—films, radio, books, and correspondence had kept me more or less up to date—but simply the pleasure of being surrounded by people who spoke my mother tongue. No longer was I the foreigner with the charming but amusing accent but now a native, even though I amazed fellow New

Yorkers by talking good New Yorkish but displaying ignorance about altered subway turnstiles, how to dial people on the telephone, how to ask fellow passengers for help in getting change for the bus fare, or finding a "yellow strip" whose touch opened the exit door. Before we found it, the bus had started up again. But I soon got used to most of the changed routes and ways, and Manhattan's street grid system made it easy to find any address.

Surely one of my greatest pleasures after so many years was, as a passionate birdwatcher, to see old feathered friends I had missed so much in Germany, even the common robin, blue jay, cardinal, thrasher, and catbird. Above all were the hummingbirds, which live only in America. They were a source of the purest delight; these tiny creatures made my heart jump to see them again.

53—More Trips Home

I did not stay, but returned for visits every few years, with Renate as long as she lived. The first aura, enhanced by stays in my family's homes in beautiful Connecticut, Maryland, and New Mexico, and Cambridge for every reunion, became more normal, and we almost grew used even to the mind-boggling rows and rows of overfilled shelves in the big supermarkets. Who could count the varieties of breakfast cereals, cheeses, even packaged toothpaste or shaving cream? Most relatives and old classmates lived comfortably, a few not quite so well, a few of them luxuriously. But we had no feelings of envy.

Most interesting, and most strenuous, was our book tour around the country in 2003 with my autobiography, *Crossing the River*. It took us to twenty-three different places, from Providence, Rhode Island, to Portland, Oregon, to bookshops, colleges, radio stations, a union group, a synagogue, and one church gathering, at the First Parish Church near Harvard Square in Cambridge.

During this trip, without that first aura, we could not fail to notice some of the problems. Two old friends, in New Jersey and upstate New York, voiced fears of losing their quite simple, time-worn private homes due to high taxes. A cousin could not afford the thousands demanded for cataract operations like those I had undergone in an out-patient clinic in Berlin for 100 marks each (and which would have been free in GDR days). Although we had enough money with us and were often treated, we came to note that some items were easier to swallow than their prices, and decided to leave some attractive cheese brands on their shelves.

Two things worried Renate most; the widespread obesity—not yet so frequent in Berlin—and the poverty. We saw so many people in need, pushing shopping carts with all their possessions, still a rare sight in Berlin. Worst of all, the many, many poor people sleeping on every second park bench along Central Park West or Riverside Drive, and one, in a cardboard container, on the sidewalk three blocks from the UN building. Renate and I could never grow accustomed to this, or the conviction that it was criminal immorality to let people suffer in this way. There was lots for us to chew over, not only lobster.

54—Investments

My travels compelled constant reflections and constant comparisons, especially on the book tour in 2003 when I spoke and answered questions about just such comparisons. After my talk at the First Parish Church near Harvard Square, the first comment was from a man who sputtered angrily about East Germany and walked out. Happily, no one followed him. He was a rare exception; most audiences on the tour were curious and friendly—or at least polite.

The second to speak up, an engineer, told of his dealings with a GDR factory near Halle and more recently with its privately owned successor. In former days, over 2,000 were employed there. Its present staff, about 600, now produced far more. What, he asked politely, did I have to say to that? To this basic question, relating to my life's three eras and to my long-lasting beliefs, I still have no simple answers. Were achievements of the GDR, despite its failings and final failure, worth the long effort? Were the huge successes of the United States

and present-day Germany so decisive that all questions or comparisons were ridiculous? The questions and the debates have not come
to an end.

A first approach was easy: high productivity requires time-saving,
labor-saving equipment, which requires investment—lots of it. Where
does the money come from?

One retort was easy to make. The United States, blessed geographi-
cally and historically, owed its early growth to massive, bloody seizure
of the lands and riches of the native indigenous population, and building an economy whose trade and much of whose industry rested on the
backs of several million whip-driven slaves in merciless hot fields. After
that, it had had no war on its own territory since the mid-nineteenth
century, but it profited from those abroad.

The massive investment advantages of West Germany were more
recent but no less tainted. They derived for the most part from industrial and financial giants like Volkswagen, Daimler, Siemens, BASF,
and Deutsche Bank. Some of their property had been bombed, some
in the East had been confiscated and nationalized, but huge sums
remained from their wartime exploitation of forced foreign laborers,
captured soldiers, and cheaply purchased concentration camp prisoners. Thousands had died of overwork, brutality, hunger, and illness,
but after 1945 and a few gentle slaps on the wrist the giants regained
their might, wealth, cozy global connections, and high productivity.
Volkswagen became the world's biggest automaker, and BASF, despite
its Auschwitz crematoria, the world's biggest chemicals company,
recently overtaken by the equally guilty Bayer.

In addition, West Germany received millions of Marshall Plan dollars to get its industry off to a flying start. They were accompanied
by noble words about generously rebuilding war-torn countries and
less noble intentions regarding America's erstwhile ally. In 1949–50,
40 percent of the investments in the West German coal industry came
from Marshall Plan funds. Such investments are great stimuli to high
productivity.

Worth mentioning is that the manager of Marshall Plan funds
for Germany, Hermann Josef Abs, started out in the Hitler years by

"Aryanizing" Jewish firms, then led the grab by Deutsche Bank of one company after the other in every country the Nazis conquered. In 1945, after a few months in easy internment and completing the Marshall Plan job, he became Germany's most powerful and influential banker.

Smaller, poorer East Germany had paid off over 90 percent of the heavy reparations burden. It could then use whatever war criminal property had survived the war, but with none of the war profits and little of the valuable know-how. Nor could it squeeze investment money from Third World trade victims or grossly underpaid sectors at home. All the same, starting almost from scratch and forced to concentrate its limited resources on basic needs like energy sources, it had within a few decades achieved a genuine economic miracle, thanks to the sweat and diligent learning process of its people plus, in part, some very good overall planning. But the necessary concentration of its limited resources on modern, top-quality industrial complexes in the most crucial fields left far too little for satisfactory productivity levels in other fields, especially consumer goods, where it always lagged behind. The solo move to electronics proved unattainable.

55—Productivity East and West

Deeper-lying problems were also involved. Socialist enterprises (and that's what I consider them) lacked not only investment sources but two valuable tools: the carrot and the stick. On one hand, there was none of that tough, competitive lust of owners and managers to grab ever larger slices of the market, beating competitors with new cost-cutting techniques or some doohickey to win new customers and make another million. Such motivation meant higher productivity plus a stream of new doohickeys, big or small, useful or useless, some even harmful, but always attractive and well-packaged.

Many GDR workers with blue, white, or pink collars did try to improve the work process and increase production as the posters urged; ambitious workers or managers took evening courses, hoping to get ahead; women were encouraged to move up into management. But the GDR offered no juicy carrot dreams of big profits and great wealth. Some, nourishing such dreams, risked fleeing over the Berlin Wall. Others were simply happy to fulfill quotas and not break their backs or any other part of their anatomy.

The second missing tool was the stick. This could be brutal elsewhere to judge by reports like this one from the United States, written by a fired government whistle-blower who had to take an underpaid sales job for a while:

Some employees at Bullseye [an invented name] had been yelled at too many times or were too afraid of losing their jobs. They were not only broke, but broken. People—like dogs—don't get that way quickly, only by a process of erosion eating away at whatever self-esteem they may still possess. Then one day, if a supervisor tells them by mistake to hang a sign upside down, they'll be too afraid of contradicting the boss not to do it.

I'd see employees rushing in early, terrified, to stand by the time clock so as not to be late. One of my fellow workers broke down in tears when she accidentally dropped something, afraid she'd be fired on the spot. And what a lousy way to live that is, your only incentive for doing good work being the desperate need to hang on to a job guaranteed to make you hate yourself for another day. Nobody cared about the work, only keeping the job. That was how management set things up.

About 30 million Americans work this way, live this way, at McJobs. . . . After all, Walmart has more than two million employees. . . . It is, in fact, the largest overall employer in the country and the biggest employer in 25 states. (Peter Van Buren, "An Apartheid of Dollars," *TomDispatch.com*, April 24, 2014.)

This report would have amazed GDR working people. They would have to punch in totally drunk for weeks on end or conk the boss with a crowbar to get fired, and, even then, only with the union's okay. Knowledge of available jobs elsewhere removed any fears of displeasing bosses.

This lack of big sticks was truly humane, but not always conducive to high productivity. When contact with the public was involved, as in retail shops and restaurants, it could mean an absence of unctuous subservience and toadying to arrogant or lustful customers, but also produce insensitive waiter haughtiness. That often depended on the management and the work atmosphere.

The general result was a more relaxed atmosphere, less grim racing against time, often against the other worker, shift, or department such as I had seen in Buffalo. People went to the doctor on work time, to the dentist, even the hairdresser; some went shopping in little co-operative stores. I was visiting one factory when word got around that juicy fresh tomatoes from Bulgaria had just arrived; two workers took orders from the others and hastened down so as not to miss out on them. I also discovered humane work rules in a steel mill I visited; those working with hot iron and steel had ten-minute breaks after twenty minutes of work. Is this common elsewhere? It is possibly less productive.

This was also joked about, as with the little rhyme among white collar workers: "*Freitag nach eins, Jeder macht seins*," which means (unrhymed): "Friday after one everyone's on his own."

How could a lack of fervent ambition or greed on one hand, and fear on the other, be compensated? Perhaps never completely. Revolutionary enthusiasm is difficult to maintain for more than a generation or two, and even harder in the GDR where, due to history, revolutionary factors were rarer, though not fully absent. Attempts to encourage feelings of responsibility and belongingness with painted slogans and rousing speeches, never too successful, bounced off most workers' souls the more they were repeated. There were inducements and moral pressures to meet production quotas or improve on them and frequent competitions for the "best brigade" or department or the best new ideas. This had a certain effect, especially when rewarded not only with pennants and bulletin board photos but financially as well. Yet over the years such inducements produced only limited enthusiastic fervor. I heard of a few inspiring cases where a clear challenge was involved: a Japanese firm designed and fitted out an important new factory in the GDR at a special low cost if finished by a deadline date so tight they were sure it was unachievable. But it was achieved, and the success was not won with a stick but by the strong, collective will of all concerned (though maybe with some carrot nibbles afterward). But such successes did not occur every day, while tempting West-TV pictures and distorted news stories came over every evening to dampen any possible enthusiasm.

That comparison between before and after by the Cambridge engineer made me think over my visits to GDR enterprises and my job at one of them. Why were so many employed in GDR days? I recalled all those who were not directly productive. Every medium-size factory had one or two SED organizers, a union secretary or two, someone to work with apprentices, and one for promoting women. Others, chosen by the union, helped employees find housing, organized vacation offers, and perhaps staffed the union's vacation hotels. The kitchen staff usually had a dietician in charge. The clinic, aside from treating accidents, ran checkups on occupational illnesses and arranged stays at spas. Factories had kindergartens, libraries, and bookshops with technical books but also novels, even poetry; in some, an "artotheque" lent out reproductions to decorate office walls and breakfast rooms. Every big plant had a House of Culture with music and dance groups, writing, art, and hobby clubs from filmmaking to auto mechanics. All had sports programs; the bigger the plant the more it offered: soccer, handball, track and field, even gymnastics and fencing if in demand. And all free of charge. I have a photo of myself at the House of Culture of the big Rostock shipyard, with its skilled staff of twenty-six.

Such office or clubhouse jobs were part of the staff mentioned by the engineer in Cambridge. Some may have been seen as a way to switch from a greasy machine to a clean office with green plants and even a chance, if unobserved, to catch forty winks. Perhaps they could have been held by fewer or unpaid employees. Like the general atmosphere, such staffing seemed crazy in terms of competition between social systems. But was it so wrong? Are we really on this earth to produce, produce, produce, faster and faster, filling shops with articles hardly necessary for pleasant living but a little more modern than those of a competitor? Many are even designed to wear out soon after the guarantee time. Is keeping up with the Joneses and owning the very latest model with the most apps really beneficial to the individual, or to the world? Mountainous junk piles, worldwide, are part of the result.

Germany's great writer Goethe wrote of a sorcerer's apprentice who learned a magic formula to carry in more and more water to scrub the floor, saving him the work. But alas, he did not know the second half of the formula, how to end a menacing overflow. Only the sorcerer's return in the nick of time brought the magic words and prevented a catastrophic surplus. In a fairy tale of the Grimm Brothers there is a similar overflow, again thanks to magic words, but of sweet porridge. The mother knows only the words to produce more and more. After a while the whole village swims in sweet porridge. Again, just in time, the daughter returns with the word to end overproduction. The villagers are saved but must now eat their way back into their smothered cottages. Such stories might remind us of melting polar icecaps; I see them as omens of technological advances deluging the world with more of everything, except vital jobs for humans. Science and technology have moved far too swiftly, while the achievement of a decent society is too slow in arriving. And what are today's magic words?

Perhaps the more easygoing GDR alternative, if paired with sufficient discipline and order, is better in the long run for bones and tendons, for blood circulation, and especially for nervous systems. People spend so much of their lives at the workplace. Why should they be happy only when they can go home and forget their job? Or fear losing it? I might have said to the engineer in Cambridge that some aspects of life may be more important than productivity, or asked him whether it was harmful when jobs are made more pleasant. For example, when plant employees pay birthday visits to pensioned workers, tell them plant news, or gossip and bring flowers, sweets, and a little cash present. My father-in-law looked forward to every such visit.

56—Keeping People Happy and Satisfied

Keeping people happy or at least satisfied is extremely important in every society. The levels differ from region to region but always require certain minimums of food, shelter, school, and medical care.

A chief interest of leaders in every country, no matter what its political or economic system, is in safeguarding not just their immediate positions and possessions but also the economic and political system that guarantees them. Like nearly every organism, animal, vegetable, or human, their basic motivation is self-preservation. If a fair proportion of the population in their country is more or less satisfied, they sit safe in their saddles and the saddles stay firm. If not, they begin to get worried and plan countermeasures.

Ever since the Second World War, most Western democracies have been quite stable. For years, or decades, large sectors attained a fairly secure job, a home with a good, non-leaky roof, little or no fear of eviction, enough to buy what they want to eat, a car, perhaps more than one, a modern kitchen, household and other electronic appliances, and, in the United States, enough to travel a bit, perhaps to Yosemite or the sunny Caribbean. For years and years, a majority had little fear of losing everything and becoming paupers.

With so many satisfied, most Western governments felt secure enough to tolerate the unpleasantly shrill voices of a small, angry minority and to conclude: "If they find joy in it let a few radicals shoot off their mouths about greedy plutocrats. Let them publish their little bulletins, manifestos, and impoverished newspapers or journals. Who reads such cliché-stuffed gibberish? A few hundred? Maybe a few thousand? No threat—no sweat! How many citizens will listen to their protests at London's Hyde Park Corner or similar 'bastions of freedom,' or ever dream of seizing muskets and pikestaffs?'"

Despite my sarcasm, even the right to speak at a street corner or publish a little leaflet (in the age before "social media") were never magnanimously granted a free people but were rather part of long, often tough struggles. It was victories like the Magna Carta in England, the Bill of Rights in the United States, and the Declaration of the Rights of Man in France that created traditions permitting them, and such rights require constant vigilance, sometimes active defense. They are limited or absent in countries whose rulers fear imminent threats to their system, but even in traditional democracies, when foundations seem to tremble, the firmest freedoms may be curtailed and the rustiest of screws tightened. No matter what system is in power, it wants to stay there and acts accordingly.

How was it possible to achieve a level of satisfaction in the Western democracies, high enough to convince those in power that the reins can be held loosely and boast worldwide about it? How are needs satisfied, and hopes for luxuries as well?

In the United States, as I have mentioned, the seizure of the land of the indigenous peoples was followed by the cotton industry on the backs of slaves. In Germany, an important base was carried over from the suffering of slave laborers before 1945. Regardless of such ugly origins, highly efficient levels of productivity were undeniably achieved and export success helped maintain a high proportion of employment, hence more sales of consumer goods and more jobs, all leading to that key criterion, a high proportion of satisfied people, proud of their freedom and democracy.

Especially in wealthy Germany this made it acceptable to occasionally tolerate small, far-left parties. When the Linke (Left Party) came along in 2007, after an East-West party merger, it too was tolerated; in the East where it was not easy to squelch, and in the West, where it was hardly a threat. Revolutionary fervor, even angry dissidence, was rare after the downfall of a socialist state and with the prosperity promised the East German states and achieved in the West German ones.

But another factor is usually ignored, forgotten, or covered over. How many realize or, if they do, really care that such well-being is not only a result of workers' skill or managerial efficiency but also of conditions in countries supplying raw materials and consumer goods at ridiculously low prices?

57—The Best from All the World

I have mentioned the shiny displays of fruit rewarding us Ossies after unification. I tried nearly all of them, like apples labeled Granny Smith, Golden Delicious, Pink Lady, Royal Gala, and, my favorite, Braeburn. But when I got curious about their origin, I came across a report from South Africa: "Putting enough food on the table is seasonal worker Aruna Morrison's biggest struggle. Aruna can find work for only six months of the year sorting apples on a farm in Ceres. . . . Providing enough food for the family is a daily challenge. 'We only eat bread and butter. It's very difficult. It's not enough.' . . . It's sad when her child cries for bread, but there is nothing to give." (Kate Raworth, "Rotten fruit," OXFAM, *ActionAid International*, Johannesburg, April 1, 2004.)

Many varieties of delicious chocolate, unavailable in the GDR, were now just the thing when visiting or on birthdays and holidays. But then I read this:

> In Western Africa, cocoa is a commodity crop grown primarily for export; 60 percent of the Ivory Coast's export revenue comes from its cocoa. As the chocolate industry has grown over the years, so has the demand for cheap cocoa. On average, cocoa farmers earn less than $2 per day, an income below the poverty line. As a result, they often resort to the use of child labor to keep their prices competitive. Most of the children laboring on cocoa farms are between the ages of 12 and 16. (Humphrey Hawkesley, "Ivory Coast Cocoa Farms Child Labour," BBC News, November 10, 2011.)

Or take coffee:

> In Guatemala, coffee pickers have to pick a 100-pound quota in order to get the minimum wage of less than $3 a day. A recent study . . . showed that over half of all coffee pickers don't receive the minimum wage. . . . Because of this situation, many coffee workers bring their children to help them in the fields in order to pick the daily quota. . . . A February 4 investigative report revealed children as young as 6 or 8 years old at work in the fields. (Julie Hjerl Hansen, "Gourmet Coffee Picked by Young Children," *Danwatch*, Copenhagen, 2016.)

After the Wall came down, what attractive possibilities we Ossies enjoyed when purchasing apparel!

> More than four million people work in Bangladesh's garment industry. . . . But the relentless demand for ever-cheaper clothes from high-street stores and supermarket chains in the West is keeping workers' wages at levels as low as $68 a month. . . . The Rana Plaza disaster in 2013, in which 1,130 people died and 2,500 were injured when a run-down eight-story factory complex making clothes for Primark, Benetton, Walmart, and other Western brands collapsed, highlighted the dangers of the industry in Bangladesh. One former worker recalled: "Since the disaster, employees have to work harder. . . .They have higher production targets. If they cannot fulfill them they have to work extra hours but with no overtime. It is very tough; they cannot go for toilet breaks or to drink water. They become sick. They are getting the minimum wage as per legal requirements but they are not getting a living wage." (Simon Parry, "The True Cost of Your Cheap Clothes," *South China Morning Post Magazine*, Hong Kong, June 11, 2016.)

The products of giants like Colgate, Nestlé, and Unilever fill shelves all over the world. The names of Unilever's billion-dollar products are household words: Lux and Lynx, Hellmann's, Knorr, Promise, Lipton, Magnum, Vaseline, Popsicle, Good Humor, and Ben & Jerry. All three giants use palm oil from Indonesia, and those millions of trees, steadily replacing rain forests, need the best of care: A woman who works in a unit caring for palm plants told Amnesty International how she was pressured to work longer hours with implicit and explicit threats:

> If I don't finish my target, they ask me to keep working but I don't get paid for the extra time . . . my friend and I told the foreman that we were very tired and wanted to leave. The foreman told us if you don't want to work, go home and don't come again. It is difficult work because the target is horrifying. . . . My feet hurt, my hands hurt and my back hurts after doing the work. . . .

A TEN-YEAR-OLD boy who quit school to help his father when he was eight gets up at 6:00 a.m. to gather and carry away loose palm fruit. He said he works for six hours every day, except Sunday: "I carry the sack with the loose fruit by myself but can only carry it half full. It is difficult to carry it, it is heavy. I do it in the rain as well but it is difficult . . . My hands hurt and my body aches."

Amnesty International comments:

> Something is wrong when nine companies turning over a combined revenue of $325 billion in 2015 are unable to do something about the atrocious treatment of palm oil workers earning a pittance. (Meghna Abraham, "Palm Oil: Global Brands Profiting from Child and Forced Labour," Amnesty International Multimedia Newsroom, London, November 30, 2016.)

Long eager lines wait to buy every novelty in electronic goods. Here, too, I read reports like this:

> Many sources mention coltan's importance in the production of mobile phones, but tantalum capacitors are used in almost every kind of electronic device. . . . For the Congolese, mining is the easiest source of income, because the work is consistent, albeit for only $1 per day. It is laborious, as miners walk for days in the forest to the ore, scratch it with hand tools and pan it. . . . Austrian journalist Klaus Werner has documented links between multi-national companies like Bayer and the illegal coltan traffic. A United Nations committee . . . listed approximately 125 companies and individuals involved in business activities breaching international norms. . . . Because of uncontrolled mining . . . the land is being eroded and is polluting lakes and rivers . . . The eastern mountain gorilla's population has diminished as well. Miners are far from food sources and have been hunting gorillas. (Wikipedia: "Coltan.")

On one hand, brutally low, brutally enforced wages don't only wreck rain forests for gorillas, orangutans, and world environment but also wreck the lives of men, women, and children. On the other hand, they permit low prices and higher living standards for Northern consumers, and thus keep the doors there open for more political tolerance, freedom of speech, and the press. How might proper wages in coffee plantations, coltan diggings, or clothing sweatshops affect satisfaction levels in the North and West? And what might that mean in connection with freedom and democracy?

Such thoughts—or facts of life—lead to reflections about the GDR. It had few trade relations with the southern continents, and those it did have often meant more giving than taking: rebuilding after bombing damage in Vietnam, organizing the amazing Carlos Marx clinic for the poor of Nicaragua, helping Cuba increase modern, efficient milk farming, teaching handicraft trades to young people in southern Africa. But it had little or no access to the cheap cocoa and chocolate, coffee, and bananas, so often burdened with fears and tears. This was one important reason it could not reach the same levels of consumer satisfaction found in the advantaged countries of triumphant free enterprise. And that affected the willingness of leaders to tolerate opposition.

The scenery has long since been altered. Many in Eastern Europe, with their products shut out of the marketplace, have seen their economic chances lowered. Their young people use membership in the European Union to move to Western Europe. Since this chance is not available to the young people of Africa and Asia, they can only escape military threats and deprivation by risking their lives in tiny nutshell vessels crossing the Mediterranean, akin to the dangers at the Mexican-U.S. border before it is totally walled up. It is ironic that simple makers of clothes, shoes, and household products in Africa are forced to flee thanks to the import of cheap products, often second-hand, made by poor workers in Southeast Asia, and that the luscious Bulgarian melons and tomatoes we once enjoyed have been pushed from their markets by mass products from Spain or the Netherlands, delicious-looking, uniform in size, color, and shape, harvested by people forced to leave their own fields in more southern areas, but also in Bulgaria and Romania. And these bright tomatoes, so beautifully packaged, are often tasteless. In consumer products as in politics, packaging is very important.

Conditions differ from region to region, but a rebellious spirit is rising in some of them. What is done to contain such feelings, hinder rebellion, and counteract any potential threats to the ruling systems?

58—System-Saving Media

The media can play an important role in deflecting opposition. In Western countries, college-educated recipients are treated to clever op-ed authors who warn against "risky experiments" and "extremists on the right and left," though extremists on the right generally worry them less. Their cherry-picking of world news reinforces convictions that "our forces of freedom and democracy" (and of course private enterprise) must solve world problems even when, unfortunately, this means using Agent Orange in Vietnam, "shock and awe" missiles on Baghdad air raid shelters, bombers in Libya, helicopters in Somalia, drones in Afghanistan, and a gunboat or two for smaller menaces like Grenada. The media are there to explain why they're needed.

The "broader masses" must also be informed, at least about those major events where soldiers are involved and sometimes even killed. But the press or broadcasts of the tabloid variety tend to offer less on serious matters; their task is not so much to encourage false thinking as to discourage any real thinking at all. For some, there are reports on weddings, births, divorces, and scandals involving kings, queens, princes, and princesses, with lots about their garments, coiffures, and other juicy details.

For more typically masculine tastes, extensive reporting on spectator sports is offered: in the United States football, basketball, and baseball, also hockey, racing, and "wrestling." Elsewhere it is soccer, or cricket in more British-based regions. Spectator sports, though full of human interest and useful for betting, somehow seem to me (when I'm in a cynical mood) to bear a resemblance to flatulence: short-lived suspense about an uncertain result, then, if no bad result, a good, harmless pleasure, enjoyed but quickly forgotten until the next occurrence and with no effect at all in the world. Of course, I don't mean to disparage rah-rah emotions that help good people forget weekday pressures and let off weekend steam. If no violent hooligan clashes occur, commercialized sports hurt nobody. True devotees have amazing knowledge and make keen analyses of endless statistics and details. But I still have a sneaky suspicion that a clever media goal is to get people to look first, last, and sometimes only at the sports pages.

Other sections good at hindering rebellious thoughts cover fashion fads or surefire health and diet novelties. Stories about animals and small children are always good for a laugh or a tear. The automobile world, especially novelties and bargains, is a sure bet. Constant attention-getters are the latest flood, earthquake, massacre, and, above all, crime, the bloodier the better. I see nothing reprehensible in all this, attention to human-interest subjects is, as the term suggests, very human. People are unhappy or angry when it is downplayed, as in dry GDR media when people joked that the news report "Australia sinks into the Indian Ocean" would probably get a short mention on page 5 after the reports on plan fulfillment in steel or wheat. Human interest items only become questionable for me when they grab the most space and attention and force news of war and peace, of giant wealth and tragic poverty, of growing, greedy power, and, above all, of active opposition, into the smallest corners of the page, screen, and smartphone—or off entirely—in order to help save our system.

In the United States a few powerful companies became masters in making people addictive to juicy, easily digestible, mental fast food— cola diets with an inconspicuously far-right bias. A *Forbes* magazine headline listed "15 billionaires who own America's news media companies," with 90 percent controlled by six corporations: Comcast, News Corp, Disney, Viacom, Time-Warner, and CBS. News Corp, founded by Rupert Murdoch, has a media empire that started in Australia, made a big jump to Britain, and another to the United States, where it takes first prize in a tough race for most successful right-wing distortion. Several of the biggest wheels in his TV garage were disqualified (and sacked) as sexual predators, but Murdoch's vehicles keep wheeling down their odoriferous Fox tracks.

This scene can change with varying rivals, but some things stay the same, as described in an article in the magazine *Jacobin*:

> Throughout American history, wealthy elites have attempted to control the news — from Southern slaveholders and their allies trying to quell abolitionist journalism to press barons like William Randolph Hearst and Robert McCormick opposing FDR's New Deal. . . . Now, as readers and advertisers have migrated to the web . . . online advertising revenue is largely going to Google and Facebook. As they become our primary news sources, these new digital gatekeepers and their algorithms increasingly determine what information society receives. . . . In this media landscape . . . rich people and corporations can say what they want, but nearly everyone else is censored by market forces. . . . Left entirely to the market, anything that doesn't attract advertisers and wealthy interests is likely to go unsaid. (Victor Pickard, "When Billionaires Rule: How the Rich and Powerful Shape Our Media," *Jacobin*, August 30, 2016.)

In West Germany, a similar concentration took place, most famously in the callous hands of the right-winger Axel Springer, with his highbrow broadsheet *Die Welt* and his lowbrow street sales rag *Bild*. Even more powerful is the Bertelsmann company, once the major publisher of books for the Nazi SS, a fact it suppressed or denied for years. With its originally German base now extended and widely spread from New York to Beijing, it controls the RTL and VOX television networks, the illustrated magazine *Stern,* and the merged Penguin-Random House-Doubleday-Bantam, Crown publishing house, making it the biggest in the United States. If you're reading a book, the chances are good that a few quarters or euros from the price land in Bertelsmann vaults.

59—Media Battles

The media were always a key arena for the conflict between the two

German states, with one side largely aggressive, and the one where I lived mostly on the defensive, trying its best to save its system. Neutral journalism, despite some claims, was never genuine; each side had an ax to grind.

I found to my regret that the ax wielded by the other side was sharper. Many surviving disciples of Dr. Goebbels in West Germany had absorbed his lessons well. Younger journalists added lessons from the theoretician Edward L. Bernays (1891–1995[!]), who wrote in 1928: "The conscious and intelligent manipulation of the organized habits and opinions of the masses is an important element in democratic society. Those who manipulate this unseen mechanism of society constitute an invisible government which is the true ruling power of our country. We are governed, our minds are molded, our tastes formed, our ideas suggested, largely by men we have never heard of." It was Bernays who replaced the unpleasant word "propaganda" with the nicer "public relations"—or PR. (Edward L. Bernays, *Propaganda*, New York: Horace Liveright, 1928.)

Bernays's disciples, often working on New York's Madison Avenue, extended sales of "the world's very best anti-caries toothpaste" to pushing "the truly most able, honest candidate," and then, for us benighted people behind the Iron Curtain, to extolling "our great freedom and democracy"—as ever with that frank little add-on "and its free market economy." In this German lumberjacking contest GDR journalists wielded far too many blunt hatchets, heavy-handed pronouncements and angry polemics when finely honed savvy and quality efforts were needed.

A number of GDR journalists had picked up some Journalism 101 truisms: that even highly educated people sympathize sooner with a sweet seal pup, a bewildered polar bear mother, an ailing killer whale, and certainly a little girl who falls down a well than with long-enduring strikers in Buenos Aires or the hunger and need of a million people in Nigeria or Bangladesh, unless these too can be shown in individual, human terms. At times, GDR media offered truly informative reports on freedom struggles in southern continents by courageous reporters, some of them my former journalism classmates in Leipzig, which were far superior to those by Western reporters who often flailed in false waters, from the Bay of Pigs to the Gulf of Tonkin.

Yet, in reporting on Western countries, above all West Germany, GDR journalists were not just critical, as might be expected, but simplistic, unsophisticated, and limited to worn, official vocabulary, wielding axes instead of épées. As for reporting on domestic matters, to call it "one-sided" was a euphemism, and few dared trespass into delicate areas more hallowed even than Goethe's *Faust*. It seemed that "our GDR," as it was often called (not seldom with a sarcastic undertone), had no problems at all except maybe the weather and, of course, "the West." Everything was always boringly hunky-dory, the economic situation was like a one-way cable-car, always ascending, ever higher and higher, until, that is, the final GDR weeks when the cables broke.

Some better journalists, unhappy at strict rule from on high in the official party press, switched into better-quality, less "official" weeklies and monthlies. A few became top favorites, like one witty, fearless film critic who panned bad films no matter who made them and awaited praise for their "great political value." Or the clever reporter who amused or disturbed us with lively details from court cases, mostly but not only in West Berlin. A satirical magazine risked cartoons and sketches as close to the critical edge as the political cabarets, and then there was the magazine that included an artistic nude photo every month, the only one available in the media (and thus in the "stoop goods" category), and also offered high-quality literary journalism.

Why couldn't the men at the top see something so obvious and lift their heavy hands from the main news writers in those days? This almost invited people to switch to pleasant, easy-to-digest West-TV fare. Why did they cling to tools so blunt, hence so boring?

One explanation lay in the journalistic background of those who still viewed the gray Russian *Pravda* as a model. They also worried about any criticism that might "help the enemy who can use it against us." Then there were some, less dedicated, chiefly interested in their own careers or simply incompetent (these qualities often overlapped) and hardly eager for critical reporting that might cause personal disadvantages.

Discouraging as this was, and despite my scorn and my sorrow at the results, one basic question remained: what timber were those sharp axes directed at, who wielded or sponsored them and which trees did they aim to fell?

60— Censorship

Until the Wall was erected in August 1961, censorship was difficult with thousands crossing daily between East and West Berlin. "Objectionable" books or publications could be lambasted but not kept out. Visiting or working in West Berlin, many purchased the sensational *Bild*, with its nudie every day on the front page, less artistic than provocative, and with short, easy-to-read, effective distortions of the most vicious nature. And if you saw anyone with a thick paperback wrapped in brown paper in those years, you could bet she was reading a West German edition of the pro-slavery epic *Gone with the Wind*.

After the Wall was erected, visitors from the West or GDR citizens returning from visits there were checked for taboo publications, which gained rarity value. But radio and TV pressure could not be kept out, a very sensitive matter in the GDR where, well before social media arrived, political gossip whizzed from one group and one end of the country to the other in no time. Fences are higher in the United States, I think: a hellfire "born-againer" in Pocatello or a stars-and-bars waver in Lubbock who watches only Fox News and listens lovingly to Limbaugh will hardly know what Katrina vanden Heuvel is writing in *The Nation*—and that works both ways. But in the GDR managers, professors, and research scientists commonly came from working class or farm families, which they often visited, so rumors and gossip spread like brush fires to all circles, from the Baltic north to the Thuringian south, especially if started or fanned by Western TV.

This frightened the country's leaders. Any GDR publication uttering even the most cautious criticism of acts or decisions by the ruling SED could expect immediate propaganda support in West-TV, and the slightest easing of top-level pressure led to calls in the West for a further move toward press freedom, like Mikhail Gorbachev's policy in Moscow of *glasnost* transparency. If it occurred, then came the next step, and the next, supported or even subsidized from without. Ultimately, in Poland and Hungary, in 1990 in the GDR and 1993 in the USSR, the desired goals were achieved.

Historically, besieged fortresses have rarely been noted for tolerance. When the Goths laid siege to Rome in AD 537, there was the strictest censorship. During the Prussian siege of Paris in 1871 "the papers print only what the ministry dictates, and they all print the same thing. . . . The public is forbidden under penalty of arrest to repeat anything which is not in the papers."

The GDR, led by men whose traditions derived mostly from the Soviet Union with its own bitter past and who had themselves been engaged in life-and-death struggle against the Nazis, was besieged daily by its foes via radio and TV. Far deadlier weapons stared in from across its long western border. This was hardly conducive to an easygoing political atmosphere. And GDR leaders were well aware of the bloody end of Allende and his supporters in 1973 in Chile, who had chosen to reject censorship despite threats like the following:

> Throughout the 1960s the CIA poured funds into Chile's largest—and staunchly right-wing—newspaper, *El Mercurio*, putting reporters and editors on the payroll, writing articles and columns for placement and providing additional funds for operating expenses. After the paper's owner, Agustín Edwards, came to Washington in September 1970 to lobby Nixon for action against Allende, the CIA used *El Mercurio* as a key outlet for a massive propaganda campaign, running countless virulent, inflammatory articles and editorials exhorting opposition against—and at times even calling for the overthrow of—the Popular Unity government. (Peter Kornbluh, *The Pinochet File: A Declassified Dossier on Atrocity and Accountability*, New York: New Press, 2013, 91–92.)

Was Allende's tolerant policy a wise one? Did it finally cost him— and thousands—their lives? The question was not disregarded in East

Berlin. Nor by me. But then, censorship had not saved Rome from the Goths or Paris from the Prussians. Nor, in the end, did it save the GDR.

Perhaps a more daring, more open journalism would have had greater success against that "other side." The rarity of unvarnished information, wit, and originality in news reports added only to the growing dissatisfaction; the price paid for the lack of rapport and credibility finally proved fatal.

61—Me and Censorship

What about me? In 1968, I had just turned forty. I had left my job as director of the Robeson Archive; I was really no archivist. The switch was a fortunate one. I quickly found work translating into English; many could translate well into German, but very few in the other direction. Then I began writing articles, always about events in the United States or historical articles inspired by anniversaries, like that of the execution of Joe Hill in 1915 or of Sacco and Vanzetti in 1927. Their stories and many of the current conflicts were close to my heart, and there were hardly a handful who understood and could write about them. No GDR correspondents were yet permitted in the United States, but I could keep up with developments thanks to hourly news reports and other programs on AFN, the soldiers' radio channel in West Berlin, plus my left-wing newspaper subscriptions, U.S. films on TV or in the movie houses, and my correspondence. In the ten years since I graduated at Leipzig, my classmates had spread into every section of the media, from local newspapers to TV. I needed only to call a friend and ask, "Could you use an article about the Chicago Eight trial or the Native American fight at Wounded Knee?" And there was so much to write about: the anti-Vietnam War movement, the Black Panthers, Kent State, Watergate, Angela Davis, miners' strikes, the Bicentennial, Jimmy Carter, Ronald Reagan, Muhammed Ali.

My views about the United States, if not exactly the same as official views, almost never collided with them. Therefore, by and large, I was not troubled by censorship. Once, with a book I wrote about U.S.

history (something like Howard Zinn's), I ran into a few disagreements with the publishing authorities (the equivalent of censors) on some angles on world events. I made a few painless changes in wording, or I ignored the requests for alterations, and never heard any more about the matter. I doubt they looked at the pages again.

Official SED newspapers, local or national, were cautious about slipping off official lines or even vocabulary, but I hardly encountered problems with them when opposing Ronald Reagan or the Pentagon, supporting Martin Luther King Jr., or fighting to free Angela Davis. Nor was I inclined to paint any unsullied halo over Richard Nixon. Some editors couldn't quite grasp my attempts to add human interest, suspense, and even humor to reports. But others could. And there were those good weekly or monthly publications, edited by sensible journalists, with strong leftist principles but without blinders, often with experience as exiles in Western countries, who tended to pay attention not only to the authorities above them in the political ladder but to the wishes and intelligence of grateful readers. I got along best writing for them.

My greatest success was with my two years of radio broadcasts on American folk music in 1966–67. The first series introduced GDR listeners to singers I loved, like Pete Seeger, Leadbelly, Woody Guthrie. When I translated texts in voice-over over the singers, I got complaints from people taping the music, so I translated only before the songs started. As new names became known to me—I got their LPs from friends and relatives—I introduced Phil Ochs, Tom Paxton, Joan Baez, Peter, Paul and Mary, Odetta, and that strange newcomer, Bob Dylan. My second series attempted a loose history of the United States in song, starting with "Yankee Doodle," with song programs on the Gold Rush, abolitionist and Civil War songs, Appalachian ballads, hobo songs, songs for and against U.S. wars, and union songs of later years.

Thanks to this series, I started corresponding with Pete Seeger and was his interpreter when he came to sing in East Berlin. Before the concert in the jammed Volksbühne, the largest theater, he wondered how this German audience—his second in Germany, his first in the GDR—would receive his anti-fascist songs. During "Shtil di nakht," the song in Yiddish by the Vilna poet Hirsch Glik about a Jewish partisan woman's fight against the Nazis, there was total, moved silence. Then Pete sang "Peat Bog Soldiers," created by imprisoned German anti-fascists, and the entire audience joined in! I think Pete and Toshi were greatly moved. So was I.

At a meal before the concert, Pete found a beautifully folded napkin on his plate with a note asking if it were possible to get a ticket, since they were all sold out; it was signed by "an apprentice waiter." The local concert manager at the table with us said "Impossible!" But Pete looked at Toshi, she nodded, and he said, "He'll get in if he has to carry my banjo through the stage entrance!" Which is what happened!

In the broadcasts, in my articles and the rapidly increasing number of talks I was invited to give in all parts of the country, occasionally with music, I always avoided the crude "drugs-jobless-repression-suffering" reportage on the United States so widespread in the earlier GDR years and still reflected in all-too-common clichés—a counterpart to the crudely simplistic nonsense about the GDR in the Western media. I tried to depict a complicated United States, favored by history and geography and with a high average living standard but marked from the start by conflicts between the forces of the greedy and those fighting for a better country and a better world in a constant struggle to improve life for the many who were hard hit. Some editors, school principals, or local bigwigs still preferred a simple "East-West, Good-Evil" worldview, each side labeled in big letters. If such people did not like what I wrote or said, they could refrain from printing or engaging me. I always found more than enough of the other kind to keep me off the minus side of my bank account.

While traveling around the GDR as a wandering American, I disappointed some by driving up not in a Chrysler but in my Trabi. From the start, I confessed to my audiences that I had not just arrived from New York but had long been living in the GDR. When I told them I would not be describing how terrible everything was in the United States, since that was not true, that alone made audiences perk up and listen with more interest. But, I added, I would also not be painting the picture of ease and luxury they saw in TV series like *Dallas*, the Texas oil baron series so popular in East and West in those years and believed by many to be a true reflection of normal U.S. life. That too would be false. Instead, as in my articles, I offered realistic information on the dramatic conflicts then taking place. I always tried to include some humor, a rarity in GDR political discourse, especially when it came to leading personalities, even U.S. presidents. But those years offered jokes enough about Nixon, Ford, Carter, and Reagan. Like how Ronald Reagan could easily count to ten—up to twenty when barefoot—and in the shower to twenty-one. Duller audiences occasionally needed longer to wake up, grasp that they were hearing a joke and laugh, but all were happily amazed at such irreverence from a podium. (Trump and De Vos were as yet unknown, of course!)

My criticism of GDR weaknesses, the narrow, dull news reports, for example, also got surprised laughs and applause, which I balanced with my support for the basic meaning of the GDR and its aim of achieving a fair society. I sometimes threw in a couple of provocative, rarely mentioned quotations from the "mentors"—Marx, Engels, Lenin. My style got me invitations from all over the country and the few I lost because of my criticism didn't worry me; I used and enjoyed the privileges of a freelancing court jester. Perhaps I should have used them more, and I think that others could well have shown more courage. Even today, decades later, I occasionally receive thanks from former listeners and readers for the good songs, the jokes, but most of all for my frank words.

Once, at a public forum in East Berlin, I answered an audience question with a few of my usual critical remarks about aspects of GDR life, perhaps on the media. I spied a little man in the fifth row holding in his lap one of the big taping machines of those days. I asked the speaker next to me whether the Stasi always worked so overtly here. He laughed and said, "No, we know him well. He's a radio journalist from West Berlin. If you tune in to RIAS tomorrow at noon you may get a surprise." And indeed, there was my voice from West Berlin's CIA channel—but only my critical words, taken out of context and with a heading like "East Berlin American Slams GDR Politics!" The little man had not wanted to do me a favor!

62—System-Saving Elections and Democracy

In the Western democracies the election process, a hard-fought product of many struggles, can also serve as a response to dissatisfaction. It
was obvious that the GDR did not place much value on elections as a
method for achieving this, and the lack of free elections in Communist-
ruled countries was one of the most common reasons for opposing
them.

True, there were five parties in the GDR. The Christian Democratic
Union was akin to the West German party of the same name only in
the first postwar years and again at the very end of the GDR. There
was a Democratic Farmers' Union, a Liberal Democratic Party, mostly
for shopkeepers and other small businesspeople, and a National
Democratic Party, largely for non-guilty and repentant low-level Hitler
supporters and reformed "old soldiers" and aiming at winning support
for the GDR and its anti-fascist system away from the story-swapping
traditions so prevalent in West German circles and publications, about
youthful military "heroism" at Warsaw, Crete, Smolensk, or Leningrad.

Almost from the start, these "bloc parties" had little independence,
however. They offered advice in matters affecting their varied constitu-
encies and were represented at every level of government, but they all
recognized the Socialist Unity Party (SED), the "party of the working
class" (called, not quite accurately, the Communist Party) as determining force, and delivered cooperation, not opposition. In elections the
only slate offered was that of the National Front, with candidates from
all five parties plus organizations like the Union Federation, the Free
German Youth, and the Cultural Association (Kulturbund). It was possible to reject this single ticket, but few used the available booths and
just folded the ballot paper and put it in the slot. Who could know?
Why risk a marred reputation and possible disadvantages with vacation spots, job promotion, or an okay on a trip to West Germany?
Some did—but not many. And results were always in the ridiculously
high 90 percent range.

Sometimes this procedure was (unofficially) justified by recalling
that free elections had once enabled Hitler to gain power, a theme

recently recurring again with the rise of the far-right Alternative for Germany (AfD).

I was not a citizen and didn't vote, but I had my own explanation for what was basically a periodic, useless rigmarole. I felt sure that in a truly secret vote with more than one list or candidate, even if all were equally GDR-faithful in their programs, West Germany would immediately unleash an artful media campaign conjuring up some differences, genuine or invented, hinting that anyone wishing to "oppose the Communists" should vote for Candidate B rather than any other, especially Candidate A. This would create a crack in the political structure and could be expanded, step by step, with ever newer demands leading to the obvious final goal. Fear of such a likelihood and a determination to stay on top were surely the basic reasons for keeping elections the way they were, even in years when a majority of the voters, though not an overwhelming majority, would most likely have supported Candidate A. The risk was simply too great, as the March 1990 election proved. This logic prevailed elsewhere, and still does in Cuba or China.

Only once did one of the bloc parties oppose a law in the People's Chamber, legalizing abortion in March 1972. Religious members of the Christian Democratic Union disapproved, fourteen of their delegates voted "No" and seven abstained. It was a small protest—by general agreement, I surmise—that did not affect the outcome but was, in this one break with unanimity, a minor sensation.

As with censorship, I perceived the thinking behind such elections but could not feel happy with them or their ridiculous results, with party officials in each district vying for the smallest number of "dissident" points short of the 100 percent level. It was indeed a farce with one justification—the social system had to be saved—against any attacks, against any opposition! Here, as elsewhere, that was top priority!

But democracy is a far more complex matter. Despite the odd no-choice elections, the GDR certainly had its democratic elements. A certain back-and-forth communication between people and government was enhanced by a rule that written complaints to government, party leaders or elected delegates had to be answered and, whenever possible, dealt with. Many people obtained satisfaction in questions of unfair treatment or malpractices, especially in the personal or local sphere.

More important, general pressure "from below" often had a real effect. The law permitting abortion, for example, followed years of pressure by troubled women wanting to control their own lives. Improvements for young couples and new laws strengthening gender equality in job promotion and qualification reflected wishes and pressures of working people, most especially women with children. Young people's anger at various restrictions in the field of music and recreation led to a whole new Youth Code.

I recall with a smile how new advantages for young couples caused grumbling and sarcasm among older people, who complained that it was they who had toiled and sacrificed in overcoming war damage and building up a new economy in the hard early years, but it was "young upstarts" who were now reaping all the fruits. One nasty joke made the rounds: "Have you heard? Thanks to the complaints by us seniors that we have been forgotten, the SED Party Congress has decided to think of us, too. After January 1st all pensioners over 65 will have the right to cross the street anytime, even against a red light. And those over 75 will be obliged to cross the street against the red light!"

Before long, changes were made in favor of seniors as well. One I recall was that workloads were to be reduced during the last five years before retirement without cuts in pay. Again and again, as the economy strengthened, new measures were taken to resolve weaknesses and improve life for as many as possible. In 1957, thanks to democratic pressures, the courts ended the already almost nonexistent prosecution of gay men, and in 1968 the old German law against homosexuals was totally annulled (but not until 1994 in West Germany). Unfortunately, many people's thinking on the matter was not automatically altered by a change in the laws. *Coming Out*, a fine GDR film, truly able to reach minds and hearts, was unfortunately not released until 1989. By unhappy coincidence, its premiere was on the same evening the Wall came down, and it was therefore largely overlooked.

The question of democracy for working people was also a complex matter. Of course, there were unions in every shop and office, on something like a "closed-shop" basis. After his trip through the GDR, the West German journalist Joachim Besser wrote the following surprisingly fair description:

> In the big nationally owned factories which I visited, the individual workers have no greater influences on the big decisions than anywhere else in the world. Decisions such as enlarging the factory, new production lines and so on, are taken by the factory management in cooperation with the local or central planning agencies.
>
> But when it comes to the question of how the work has to be done, the workers have a lot to say. From this point on, inner-factory democracy is very effective. The workers and their trade union representatives have great influence on the wage structure, on bonuses and on the social services. They all cooperate in improving working conditions and in discovering more rational ways of doing the work. For good suggestions individual workers or whole brigades can receive large bonuses and distinctions such as the title "Hero of Labor." (Joachim Besser, *Kölner Stadtanzeiger*, December 3, 1966, trans. in *DGR*, January 13, 1967, 7.)

I got a similar impression, although some workers told me that the influence of the union varied from factory to factory, depending on the degree of involvement of employees and the quality of the union leaders they chose. For many or most people, quitting time meant getting home to the spouse, the kids, and the TV screen. Sitting after hours in a meeting room was not to everyone's taste. And the unions were also committed to increasing production, fulfilling quotas, and meeting plans, which could lead to contradictory intentions and pressures.

But I found one factor very important in assessing the degree of democracy in practice. Because of the constant labor shortage, the GDR working class, especially in key production sectors, was strong enough to thwart heavy pressures or high-handed measures and win out in many a grievance. Strikes were basically taboo, but if they felt their interests were neglected, workers did on occasion resort to slow-downs or other methods to get what they wanted. They knew that, aside from extreme cases where sabotage directed from the "other side" was suspected (and I might add that I knew personally of no such case), they were needed and protected.

Almost everyone in management up to the very top came from a working-class background and thus had a certain common ground with all employees. Everywhere in the world, some people in higher positions may get conceited or try to carve out undue perks for themselves. People are people, some have human failings, and only rarely are saints or angels. But here there could be no amassing of profits, there were no aristocrats or exploiters, no millionaires, no "idle rich," or family dynasties. For me, this was of major, essential importance.

A few years after the Wende, a bon mot made the rounds among working people: "In GDR days, to avoid difficulties, it was wiser not to say anything against Erich Honecker or other Party bigwigs. But you could answer back and say whatever you wanted against the foreman, the department boss or the manager! Today it is the other way around. You can say anything you want against Chancellor Kohl and political big shots, but you damned well better be careful what you say about your foreman or any other factory boss!"

63—Elections in the Western Democracies

Those words contain true wisdom about the presence and absence of differing freedoms in different systems. Democracy and freedom are not attached to free enterprise, free market economy, capitalism, or whatever you call it. There are so many capitalist countries with little freedom or democracy, which, I am convinced, are not absolute qualities, totally present or absent, but vary and differ from one society to the other and can increase or decline with time and circumstances.

Looking westward across the Atlantic, I saw free, secret elections, almost always with two or more slates and two or more candidates. This was a great achievement and required vigilance and resistance to

frequent attacks such as photo identification demands and other chi-
canery. It had sometimes permitted important gains when it reflected
popular pressures such as the big strike movements in the 1930s that
led to Roosevelt's New Deal or the resistance to police dogs and water
cannon in Montgomery and to police truncheons on the bridge at
Selma in the 1960s that led to advances for the Black Freedom movement, even with Texan Lyndon Johnson as president.

But when it comes to labor laws, affordable housing, a good, equal
education, medical care, or women's rights, the wishes of the people,
especially working people, are rarely reflected, and the super-wealthy
forces opposing such improvements can usually celebrate the most
victories. Best represented in Washington are the NRA and its hand
weapons lobby, the pharmaceutical lobby with its sadistic prices, the
energy lobby with its leaky pipelines and fracking, a growing inter-
net-control lobby, the food and agriculture industry, moving along to
destroy honey bees, monarch butterflies, and wild fauna and flora generally, its related poisonous soft drink and fast-food lobbies, and, most
dangerously, the bomber-drone-warship lobby. Their powerful influence reaffirms the reality that freedom and democracy are never pure
and undiluted, even in the pillared halls or learned op-ed pages where
they are most frequently invoked. Where big money rules, freedom and
democracy can be pushed to the back seat or out the door completely.

A common method is the two-party system, which is based on a
tried and true formula. If jobs get scarce, if prices soar, if a recession or
an unpopular war angers the citizenry, it can simply place the blame on
the party in office and vote for its rival. One party often cultivates a less
reactionary image than the other; it may establish ties with labor leaders, speak on friendlier terms with minorities, and loudly defend "the
little fellow." But with much the same backers, its record for delivering
on election promises has rarely been encouraging. And with no genuine alternatives, voters keep bumping up and down on the old red-blue
donkey-elephant carousel. Or refrain from voting at all!

Of course, politicians try to keep their own party in power in
Washington, which brings countless perks and opportunities. But they
are seldom heartbroken when voted out of office. Their party may well

226 A SOCIALIST DEFECTOR

return to office in two or four years. Even if it doesn't, highly paid jobs beckon to all ex-politicians with connections. There is great flexibility between the two main parties; though they are not twins, for one is much older after all, and certainly not identical twins, they are siblings all the same. Industrial and financial giants behind them may have a favorite child, like some parents, but maintain family ties with both. And if it ever comes to preserving their "free enterprise" system, family feelings would be paramount, with both parties equally committed.

Are rebellious new parties possible? Since 1860 with Abe Lincoln, not one could break the two-party vise! Not Victoria Woodhull in 1872 with her Equality Party for women's rights and suffrage, not the Populists with many farmers but too few workers, not the Socialist Party led by railroad worker Eugene V. Debs, which got over 900,000 votes in 1920, then split and faded, nor Robert La Follette, whose Progressive Party won his own Wisconsin in 1924 and 6 percent nationally but disappeared with his death.

As a college student, I took part in one bold attempt and learned how high the hurdles are. In 1948, we built up a new Progressive Party with ex-vice-president Henry Wallace—for union rights, against racism and Harry Truman's aggressive foreign policy. But first we had to get onto the state ballots.

Only 10,000 signatures were needed in North Carolina, but the state had few Progressives. Since African Americans were rarely registered, they could not sign petitions. Five of us drove down for a week to help. It was my first visit to the South; I can never forget the desperate poverty I saw, both black and white but strictly separated. In the end, however, the NC Progressives did somehow squeeze onto the ballot!

In Massachusetts, 56,000 signatures were required. Double that number were needed, however, since half were always rejected because of an address change, "illegibility," or an initial instead of a written-out middle name. Yet somehow, we made it, there and in all but three states. But the giant effort had exhausted our little teams when it came to campaigning, getting out voters, and preventing crookery with the ballot counting. The media bad-mouthed us mercilessly; red-baiting ruled the roost in a tense world, with the Berlin Airlift in full swing. Even Wallace enthusiasts, seeing the name of the reactionary Republican Thomas Dewey on the ballot, held their noses and voted for the Democrat Harry Truman instead. Wallace got only 2.37 percent, once again burying hopes of unlacing the two-party corset. That defeat largely ended what was left of the 1930s leftist movement, opening the door to a right-wing era at home and abroad that lasted until the 1960s. The Save Our System crowd had won again with their old "lesser evil" syndrome, crushing alternatives in the bud. New people's parties, if not impossible to start, are very, very difficult!

Around 1900, the wealthy lawyer, writer, and philanthropist Frederick Townsend Martin summed up the election situation in his time:

> It matters not one iota what political party is in power, or what President holds the reins of office. We are not politicians, or public thinkers; we are the rich; we own America; we got it, God knows how; but we intend to keep it if we can by throwing all the tremendous weight of our support, our influence, our money, our political connection, our purchased senators, our hungry congressmen, and our public-speaking demagogues into the scale against any legislation, any political platform, any Presidential campaign, that threatens the integrity of our estate.
>
> I have said that the class I represent cares nothing for politics. In a single season a plutocratic leader hurled his influence and his money onto the scale to elect a Republican governor on the Pacific Coast and a Democratic governor on the Atlantic. The same moneyed interest that he represented has held undisputed sway through many administrations, Republican and Democratic. . . . Truly can I say that wealth has no politics save its own interests. (Frederick Townsend Martin, *The Passing of the Idle Rich*, Garden City, NY: 1911, 149.)

Over a century later the following words by Princeton professor Martin Gilens suggest that not much has changed:

> The degree of inequality in influence over government policy is enormous. I didn't expect low-income Americans or the middle class to

have as much influence as the affluent. Nevertheless, the extent of the inequality is enormous and when preferences diverge—so when the policy preferences of the affluent differ from those of the middle class or the poor—what you see is significant influence by affluent Americans over policy outcomes and essentially no influence by people with less income. (Martin Gilens, *Affluence and Influence: Economic Inequality and Political Power in America*, Princeton: Princeton University Press, 2014.)

With the election of Donald Trump, the situation took an unusual turn but seems, in essence, hardly changed and hardly more democratic!

THE BRITISH SYSTEM, for years, involved not two but three major parties. The effects of the Second World War enabled the more left-leaning Labour Party to win true victories like the National Health System, but then it became increasingly tame and respectable and, abandoning the fight for basic changes, returned to its position as a "lesser evil" domestically while taking part in a series of military attacks against the people of other countries. For those who died or lost loved ones, its missiles and bombs were anything but "lesser evils." The real rebels were forced out into the damp British cold. The system was fairly similar in Canada, Australia, and New Zealand.

Then, almost suddenly, the elderly socialist Jeremy Corbyn dared to buck this system and achieved surprising success. All those who still oppose any real change are currently waging a nasty fight against him, outside and inside his party, and various struggles seem to lie ahead within all three parties, Labour, Conservative, and Liberal Democratic. But for the first time in many years there are hopes of making some progress despite all the big guns aimed against it.

Every country has its own election methods. With proportional representation, common in Europe, any party that can overcome an election hurdle, usually 5 percent of the total vote, gets seats in the legislature based on its percentage. This has meant that six parties are currently represented in the German Bundestag. It is more complicated but surely more democratic than the methods in the United

States or Britain where only the "first horse past the post" in each district gets seated and all other votes are lost, even if a party can get many votes nationally, but never a majority in any one electoral district. Yet despite this fairer system, grand-scale financial support and one-sided media coverage almost always guarantee that no parties win out that might really make a big difference and cannot be bought or, if necessary, tamed.

In its early years, West Germany used every method to squelch the disturbingly oppositional Communist Party, even though its members had been by far the most active and tragically self-sacrificing in fighting the Nazis. Then it was outlawed completely in 1956, and only readmitted under an altered name in 1968 when it had become so weak as to present no political threat worth mentioning. It could never get close to that necessary 5 percent level.

I have already mentioned that after the downfall of the GDR, a new left-wing party had emerged in East Germany, built on the remains of the former ruling party, the Socialist Unity Party, but with a completely altered political basis, apologizing for the misdeeds of its predecessor and rejecting what was called "Stalinism." In 2007, it joined with an angry new oppositional party in West Germany to form Die Linke (The Left), which, though constantly discriminated against, gradually established itself as one of four lesser parties, getting about 10 percent of the vote, to challenge the two main German parties, the Christian "Union" caucus and the Social Democrats. Another latecomer is the party of the Greens, which is far more conservative than the Green Party in the United States. The latest addition is a menacing party of the far right, the Alternative for Germany (AfD), which was soon able to win many dissatisfied voters, fearful of the future but opposed to the ruling "establishment," not convinced by Die Linke but rather misled into blaming all their woes, present or future, on the Muslims and all refugees and immigrants who arrived in great number in Germany, especially in 2015 and 2016. Its biggest gains were in economically neglected and disadvantaged ex-GDR states; it even seems to have attained first place in one of them, Saxony. Its growth and the possibility of even swifter increase in case of any economic crisis could not fail to recall the growth of the Nazi Party during the Depression years after 1929. How should this party be treated—accepted as one of the "normal" parties or kept as a pariah, avoided and isolated like someone with Ebola or leprosy? According to people on the left, anti-human, potentially murderous positions like those taken by AfD politicians were fascist in nature and therefore "not an opinion but a felony." But its murderous nationalist position of favoring the wealthy and building the armed forces hardly varies from that of most other parties, and it is now gaining ever more acceptance.

Democracy in different societies has always been a complex matter, with changing definitions, hopes, interpretations—and sometimes perils.

64—System-Saving Hate and Jingoism

What if distrust of both the media and the most carefully kneaded, well-greased elections in the Western democracies keeps rising, with increasing dissatisfaction or even anger?

A determined archer has many arrows in his quiver. One of them has proved effective for centuries: foster hostility between various groups. Maybe geographic groups, like South versus North, with their varying dialects. Or religious ones: Catholics, Baptists, Jews or Muslims loathing all others as heretics or, worst of all, those atheist infidels. Many find "commandments" in their Holy Books against same-sex marriage, abortion, even evolution, or fear a shadowy "Sharia law." Such faiths involve resentment of any who differ as snobby, doubt-laden "intellectual elites" or worse!

Another arrow may be feathered by the date of arrival. In the United States, citizens with four, three, or just two generations behind them but who speak English without a foreign accent look down their possibly shorter or longer noses at successive waves of funny-talking but "menacing" newer arrivals. How many generations of hopeful people have suffered under these arrogant assertions of superiority: "We have been here longer; we belong—and not those inferior Irish, German,

Swedish, Chinese, Italian, Jewish, Balkan, Japanese, Latino, or, most recently, Muslim invaders!"

The sharpest dividing line is based on born differences like skin color. This contagious epidemic has extended far beyond the United States, where countless white generations were raised from childhood to look down at people with African forebears and accept or often consider their misery as slaves, sharecroppers, or jobless, underprivileged victims of discrimination and mass incarceration to be deserved or inevitable. They blame the victims for their problems. This black-white split was a key driving force in all of U.S. history, from the cotton trade, benefiting traders, banks, even universities in the North as much as plantation owners in the South. Some politicians today still encourage the worst-paid white laborer, the poorest white dirt farmer or jobless sufferer to think: "It's all the fault of that lazy black food packer, or dirt farmer, or jobless relief sufferer who, for doing nothing, gets money due to me. But at least I'm better than him! And it damn better stay that way!" And when he comes to fear that even this last remnant of "superiority" is being "taken from him," then look out! This strategy, setting one group against the other, is the main weapon of the AfD party, and some far better established politicians, most notably those with the word "Christian" in their party name, have always kept it at the ready and used it when considered useful—or necessary. And as long as so many blame "those others" for their problems instead of the true perpetrators, then the powers that be can slip each night untroubled into their silky monogrammed bed clothing.

A related method spreads the idea that all problems, from a lack of fuel at the gas pump to terrorist attacks, can be blamed on those strange people from across the Rio Grande, the ocean, or in Europe the Mediterranean. Isn't it obvious, they ask repeatedly, that they envy us, hate us, for no good reason, and want to destroy us? People of color are mostly blamed, but also included are the Russkies, clearly waiting to pounce any day now. The Chinese, already ruining our livelihoods, are not far behind as a potential danger (now augmented by those North Koreans). Latinos steal our jobs, sell us poisonous drugs, or ogle our poor womenfolk, maybe all three. And they even want medical treatment when they get ill! The Muslims are now worst of all; for God's sake, most of them can't even speak our language! And just look at what they wear! Veils! Beards! We must all unite (if white) to defend our values from those other worlds! Build more bombs! Build more bases! Build higher walls! Stop the caravans! Stop the boats! And God bless America! Or Deutschland!

Back in 1918, the journalist H. L. Mencken wrote: "Civilization, in fact, grows more and more maudlin and hysterical. . . . The whole aim of practical politics is to keep the populace alarmed (and hence clamorous to be led to safety) by menacing it with an endless series of hobgoblins, most of them imaginary." (H. L. Mencken, *In Defense of Women*, New York: Cosimi, 1918.)

All too often, this trick ended not just with words and imprecations but with bloodshed, terrible bloodshed, directed and determined in Washington, from Guatemala to Hue and Hanoi, from little Grenada to big Somalia, from Kabul to Baghdad, and Tripoli. And too often, since 1990, Germany has also jumped in.

THE GDR, TRULY threatened, with growing dissatisfaction due to a host of problems, both internal and forced upon it from all sides, and in the end overwhelmed by them, certainly resorted to some very unpleasant methods to save itself, like the Wall or the Stasi network. But it did not resort to racism, setting one region against the other, jingoism, or hatred of other nationalities. It discouraged all regional rivalries rooted in long-forgotten wars, like those between Prussia and Saxony, and integrated Germans from the "lost regions" of Silesia, East Prussia or Sudetenland as quickly as possible, always referring to them (if at all) as "re-settlers," never as refugees or by their former regional names. Toward the end, when Poland showed signs of sliding out of the Eastern Bloc, isolating the GDR, I did note an unfortunate lessening in the usual stress on German-Polish friendship. But this was short-lived and hardly dented the lasting emphasis on internationalism, from kindergarten onward, with special insistence on recognizing the Oder-Neisse line as a permanent "border of peace" with Poland.

65—Keeping America Safe

I must again look backward. From 1945 to 1949, I was in college; Germany and Mussolini's Italy had been defeated, and we rejoiced at the idea of a world at peace, with progress for the citizens of our United States and the world. But alas, all was not well. Very soon came the signals that our country was sliding to the right into an era known as the (Joseph) McCarthy era even before that U.S. senator emerged from the lower depths and long after he drank himself into obscurity and an early death.

On March 21, 1947, President Truman signed United States Executive Order 9835, sometimes known as the "Loyalty Order," allegedly designed to root out Communist influence in the government but also to rally public opinion behind his Cold War policy, the Truman Doctrine, and to demonstrate that Democrats were not "soft on Communism." This program investigated over 3 million government employees; about 300 were fired.

The Taft-Hartley Law of 1947 banned Communists from any leadership positions in the CIO unions they had done so much to organize, from GM's Flint plant in Michigan to the black and white cigarette makers in Winston-Salem, and broke most other organizations connected with them.

In October 1947, the House Un-American Activities Committee subpoenaed a number of persons working in the Hollywood film industry to testify at hearings; it had decided to investigate whether Communists were planting propaganda in U.S. films. A group of Hollywood bigwigs helped out; their Motion Picture Alliance for the Preservation of American Ideals, with Communist-fighters like Walt Disney, Clark Gable, Gary Cooper, and Ronald Reagan, asked the writer Ayn Rand for a guide. She gladly obliged, and so did they in the films that followed. It warned filmmakers: "Don't smear the free-enterprise system . . . Don't smear industrialists . . . Don't smear wealth . . . Don't smear the profit motive . . . Don't deify the 'common man.' . . Don't glorify the collective." (Colin Marshall, *Film*, Open Culture, Mountain View, CA, May 27, 2016.)

Dozens were subpoenaed, and hundreds blacklisted. The hearings opened with rapid statements by Disney and Ronald Reagan, then president of the Screen Actors Guild. Then the "unfriendly witnesses" were hauled up in full view of the TV cameras and asked the frightening question, "Are you now or have you ever been a member of the Communist Party?" Actually, this had never been illegal, and during the "fighting 1930s" tens of thousands had become members—like me in 1945—mostly because of its leading role in organizing unions and standing up for the rights of African Americans, as well as Soviet and Communist support for Spain. But even those who said "Yes, I once was a member, but I quit and regret my blunder" were ordered to prove their repentance: "Who else was? Name all names!"

Thus denunciation of former friends and associates became the only way to save their own livelihoods. Many succumbed to this trap, some of them in tears. The actor Larry Parks said: "Don't present me with the choice of either being in contempt of this committee and going to jail or forcing me to really crawl through the mud to be an informer. I don't think it is a choice at all. I don't think this is American. I don't think this is American justice." But after two days of pressure, he too succumbed. (James Robert Parish, *The Hollywood Book of Scandals*, New York: McGraw Hill, 2004, 92.)

A decade later the actor Sterling Hayden said: "I was a rat, a stoolie, and the names I named of those close friends were blacklisted and deprived of their livelihood." Hayden "was widely believed to have drunk himself into a near-suicidal depression decades before his 1986 death." (Paul Buhle and Dave Wagner, *Hide in Plain Sight*, New York: Palgrave Macmillan, 2004, 251.)

Long lists denouncing progressive celebrities were sent to the media and the studios. The most notorious report, *Red Channels*, cost hundreds their jobs; careers were wrecked for years, often forever. Vicious media blasts led to ostracism, even for their families, to depression, divorces, early deaths, and suicides. Those with foreign passports like Charlie Chaplin, Bertolt Brecht, and Hanns Eisler were forced to leave the United States; those under attack but without this possibility included Leonard Bernstein (conductor, composer of *West Side Story*), composer Aaron Copland, and mystery writer Dashiell Hammett, who, though a veteran of both world wars and very ill, served a prison sentence.

Like Hammett, playwright Arthur Miller, singers Pete Seeger and Josh White, actors Ossie Davis, Ruby Dee, Zero Mostel, Orson Welles, and singer-actor Paul Robeson defied the inquisitionists. Most were too famous to lock up. The first group, which started things off in 1947, was the "Hollywood Ten," screenwriters and directors who refused to crawl and name names, and were sent to the penitentiary for up to a year. Alvah Bessie, who became a friend of mine, had been one of the oldest American volunteers to fight in Spain. He too spent ten months in prison and never regained a job as film writer. Most famous was Dalton Trumbo, who wrote further under false names and won two Oscars. In 1960, when no one came to the stage to claim an Oscar (with an invented name), the truth was revealed and the ban finally broken. In 2016, an excellent film, called *Trumbo*, told the story.

The effect on Hollywood was disastrous. Fear was everywhere. "Patriotic," right-wing clichés prevailed in an oligarchy ruled by men like Disney and Reagan, who crowed most loudly.

One exception deserves mention. After his prison term, director Herbert Biberman and others blacklisted in Hollywood made a film about a miners' strike in New Mexico. In it Mexican Americans fought for equal rights with the "Anglos" and, thanks to the newly discovered courage and strength of their wives, finally won out. Every method was used to sabotage the film: deporting the main actress to her home in Mexico, flying a plane over the filming sites, shooting at and slugging actors, and forcing all cutting and dubbing to be done in secret, makeshift studios. Congressmen and film moguls joined the attack; a corrupt projectionists' union prohibited its members from showing the film. The film was shown in only one theater in New York and twelve in the United States, but in Europe, *Salt of the Earth* was awarded the International Grand Prize of the Académie du Cinema in Paris in 1955. As for me, I loved it!

One of the world's most beloved actors and singers was the African American, Paul Robeson. His patriotic "Ballad for Americans" was a giant hit all over the United States in 1940. I was lucky enough to see him in *Othello* in 1943, one of Broadway's greatest Shakespeare successes, and join in twenty minutes of applause. His "Ol' Man River" in *Show Boat* became a world hit (he later altered a few words and turned it into a "fighting song"). But when Robeson refused to disavow his unpopular views, like friendly relations with the USSR, and defied the House Committee, all that changed. I described earlier how, after his giant outdoor concert for 20,000 people in Peekskill, New York, in September 1949, the state police had redirected our cars and buses down a side road where racists shattered almost every window in our buses. Robeson, blamed for the damage and injuries incurred, was kept out of every stage or concert hall, and banned from producing any but private records, from acting in any film. His passport was seized; he was even forbidden to visit Canada where no passports were required (though his Freedom Arch concerts, from a truck right at the border, drew thousands of enthusiastic Canadians). It took nine years of legal and public struggle before he was able to travel again, to his miner friends in Wales and Scotland, to Stratford for another *Othello* performance, to most of Europe and far Australia. But his name was erased from the U.S. mass media, even from the All-America Football Team lists of 1917 and 1918. Few know that he was the prime mover in the fight to get black baseball players into the major leagues and led in supporting the fight against apartheid and colonial rule in Africa.

The trials and pressures of those years, aimed most conspicuously at the dwindling Communist Party, were meant to destroy all remnants of the "fighting left" of the 1930s. By 1959, they had largely succeeded.

66—J. Edgar vs. Black Liberation

A key man in the witchhunts was J. Edgar Hoover, the bulldoggish FBI head who had organized the "Palmer Raids" against Communists in 1920. By the end of the McCarthy era a very ill Paul Robeson had been forced to retire (his son thinks he was poisoned by the CIA to prevent a trip to Cuba) and the equally legendary Professor Du Bois moved to

Ghana. But Hoover found new enemies to occupy his thoughts and actions; in 1968 he sent a memo to all FBI offices:

> "An effective coalition of black nationalist groups might be the first step toward a real 'Mau Mau' in America, the beginning of a true black revolution." They must "prevent the rise of a 'MESSIAH' who could unify, and electrify, the militant black nationalist movement. . . . Pinpoint potential troublemakers and neutralize them before they exercise their potential for violence . . . the long-range GROWTH of militant black organizations, especially among youth." (David Wallechinsky and Irving Wallace, *The People's Almanac*, Garden City, NY: Doubleday, 1975, 253.)

A main target of Hoover's was the Black Muslim preacher Malcolm X. After visiting Mecca, Europe, and Africa in 1965, the gifted orator dropped his rejection of joint action with anti-racist whites, thus becoming far more worrisome. Worse yet (for Hoover), Malcolm called on new African countries in the UN to support the freedom movement in the United States. That made him a major "troublemaker." Shortly thereafter, his house was burned to the ground; he and his family barely escaped. A week later, during a speech in Harlem, he was gunned down. The murder is still a mystery; the FBI denied "direct" involvement but still refuses to release any records.

Hoover then turned his attention to Martin Luther King, whom he called the "most notorious liar" in the United States. He had King's hotel rooms bugged, partly to record any extramarital doings. When some were discovered, his agents "anonymously" sent the audio evidence to King with obvious threats: "Look into your heart. The American people would know you for what you are—an evil, abnormal beast. There is only one way out for you. You better take it before your filthy, abnormal fraudulent self is bared to the nation." (Beverly Gage, "What an Uncensored Letter to M.L.K. Reveals," *New York Times Magazine*, November 11, 2014.)

King neither committed the recommended suicide nor abandoned his program. Instead, he established contacts with unions and in

1968 marched with striking black garbage collectors in Memphis. Far more alarmingly for system-saving zealots, he planned a Poor People's Campaign—white, Latino, Native American, and black—in a tent city to "occupy" Washington and demand economic justice. The FBI did all it could to undermine such plans, but King continued, pausing only to support the strikers in Memphis. That break became his death warrant. Was it an FBI death warrant?

The Black Panther Party was founded in Oakland in 1966 to defend the rights and lives of black Americans, also with guns, allowed by a law that definitely was not meant to include black people. With a romantic flair—black berets, leather jackets, and disciplined training—it also organized free breakfasts for children in poverty-stricken black neighborhoods and free medical care for young and old. By 1970, it had about a hundred chapters across the country.

Once again, Hoover was hatchet man. In Chicago the talented young Black Panther Fred Hampton was convincing black, Latino, and white youth gangs to stop killing each other about "turf" and join together to fight for the rights of all of them. But an FBI spy infiltrated Hampton's group, described the apartment layout to the police, and drugged Hampton into a heavy sleep. The cops' unprovoked night raid on December 4, 1969, killed him and another man and wounded six, including his eight-months' pregnant life partner.

Four days later, two hundred heavily armed policemen aided by helicopters besieged six Black Panther members in their Los Angeles office. All in all, within a few years, at least twenty-five Black Panthers were killed and many were arrested, forced into long, expensive legal battles and often sentenced, sometimes for life. By forging letters to set one region against the other, it was possible to split the organization in 1971 and soon wreck it.

67—Break-In, Breakup, Breakdown

Once in a while the FBI also took a hit, long before the possibilities offered by electronic hacking. March 8, 1971, was a special night for millions. Billed as the "Fight of the Century," Mohammed Ali was attempting a comeback after a three-year ban for refusing to serve in the war against the Vietnamese. Though no boxing fan, but a onetime deserter from that same army, I too was rooting for him even in far-off Berlin!

On that night, eight people, sure that guards would be absorbed in watching the fight, broke into the FBI office in Media, Pennsylvania, and absconded with about a thousand letters and documents. Even before driving off in several cars, to make any chase difficult, they found an order signed by Hoover instructing his agents to visit and badger antiwar activists to "enhance the paranoia endemic in these circles and further serve to get the point across, there is an FBI agent behind every mailbox." After sifting through the papers, the group, grandly calling itself Citizens' Commission to Investigate the FBI, mailed its findings to the media. Most chickened out, alleging "moral principles." But the *Washington Post* and then its rival, the *New York Times*, despite efforts by Attorney General Mitchell to stop them, printed some of the damaging papers.

Years later one of the raiders, Bonnie Raines, published the details, writing, "We broke laws to reveal something that was more dangerous. We wanted to hold J. Edgar Hoover accountable. . . . You could accuse us of being criminals—and Hoover did just that: he was apoplectic and sent 200 agents to try and find us in Philadelphia. 'Find me that woman!' he screamed at them." (Bonnie Raines, "Democracy Needs Whistleblowers," *The Guardian* [International Edition], January 7, 2014.)

Not one was ever caught. Why was he so furious and what did they discover—and uncover?

It was called COINTELPRO, short for COunter INTELligence PROgram. Begun in 1956, this top-secret, illegal FBI section spied on and subverted organizations it didn't like. Originally aimed at Marxists, and highly successful against the Communist Party, its later targets included anti-Vietnam War groups, feminist organizations, and solidarity movements for Puerto Rico and against apartheid. More and more, it was directed against anti-racist groups like the Southern

Christian Leadership Conference, the Congress of Racial Equality (CORE), the Student Nonviolent Coordinating Committee (SNCC), and activists like Malcolm X, Dr. King, and the Black Panther Party. Its methods were to infiltrate, burglarize, set up illegal wiretaps, plant forged documents, spread false rumors inciting one group or leader against the other, even involving violence and murder.

When the black comedian and activist Dick Gregory attacked the FBI during an election campaign in 1968 as "the filthiest snakes that live on this earth," Hoover, seeking revenge, wrote his special agent in Chicago to "consider using this statement in developing a counter-intelligence operation to alert La Costra [*sic*] Nostra to Gregory's attack on LCN." The Cosa Nostra was the American version of the Mafia underground. Hoover urged that "sophisticated, completely untraceable means of neutralizing Gregory should be developed." In other words, he wanted to incite the Mafia to "take care" of Gregory—like Fred Hampton was taken care of by the FBI itself. Luckily, it didn't happen. (Kim Janssen, "When J. Edgar Hoover Told Chicago FBI to Set the Outfit on Dick Gregory," *Chicago Tribune*, August 22, 2017.)

Even President Harry Truman, no slouch himself in fighting presumed or real "leftists," found that Hoover went too far. He said, "We want no Gestapo or secret police. The FBI is tending in that direction. They are dabbling in sex-life scandals and plain blackmail. J. Edgar Hoover would give his right eye to take over, and all Congressmen and Senators are afraid of him."

Blackmail was indeed a favorite method of Hoover, who had agents collect items like the following, about a U.S. senator. The FBI man found a woman who tattled about her sex session "on the couch in the senator's office." At a later date, when he was planning hearings on the FBI, focusing on its illegal electronic eavesdropping, an aide described what happened: "A couple of Hoover men visited him and said: 'Senator, I think you ought to read this file that we have on you. You know we would never use it, because you're a friend of ours. . . . We just thought you ought to know the type of stuff that might get around and might be harmful to you . . .' They handed him the folder . . . he read it for a few minutes. [Then] they went on their way. The next thing I knew we had orders to skip over the FBI inquiries." Somehow there was almost never any criticism of the FBI in Congress. After Hoover's death, locked cabinets were found in his office with 883 such files on senators and 722 on representatives, at least 12 on Supreme Court justices, and even a few on presidents. (Anthony Summers, "The Secret Life of J. Edgar Hoover," *The Guardian* [International Edition], January 1, 2012.)

Hoover was evidently hit by blackmail himself. Although loud and nasty in attacking gay people, many accounts assert that Hoover was also gay. Some of his Mafia acquaintances were said to have pictures of him in women's clothing; one Mafia leader is quoted boasting that Hoover is "in our pocket." True or not, for decades he hindered all investigation of Mafia activities, preferring always to "go after Reds" or people like Dick Gregory and Martin Luther King.

The raid into the FBI office in 1971 plus the earlier exposés of the CIA and its cultural activities by *Ramparts* and the *New York Times*, then the ouster of President Nixon after his lies and illegal break-ins such as at Watergate all led, during a short-lived, more open period in 1975, to Senate Committee investigations led by Frank Church (D, Idaho). It was found that COINTELPRO operations, even those against communist and socialist groups, had exceeded legal limits and violated constitutional guarantees of freedom of speech and association. COINTELPRO was officially suspended.

How many of its methods were really abandoned is anybody's guess. Repression by the FBI and local police units certainly did not cease. One example was the jailing and life imprisonment of the Native American activist Leonard Peltier in 1977 after the siege of Indian protesters at Wounded Knee. Another was the lifelong jailing of the black journalist Mumia Abu-Jamal in 1981. In both cases, allegedly for murder; fair trials or revisions were denied. Countless young black people get appalling prison sentences, serving to "keep them in their place"—away from the rebelliousness that increasingly alarmed circles fearful of losing a white majority—and power. Mass incarceration, especially of young black Americans, made the United States the country with the largest prison population in the world, absolutely and proportionately, while the private employment of prisoners at low or no pay disturbingly recalled slavery. Mass ownership of video cameras now showed how many innocent black people were getting shot by racist cops.

Out-of-line white rebels could also get hit, as evidenced in police break-ups of OCCUPY groups, most notoriously on November 18, 2011, at the University of California, Davis, when police in riot gear sprayed military-grade pepper spray at close range into the faces of peaceful, seated students.

Thanks to the famous exiled whistleblower Edward Snowden we have an increased awareness of the power of those who "protect our freedom" so diligently. Modern electronics permit any ruling power to know what each and every one of us is saying on a phone, in email, Facebook or Twitter, and even, with almost perfect exactitude, where almost any one of us is sitting, driving, defecating, or, God help us, demonstrating. Peaceful protesters can be spied on with Stingray cellphone interceptors, tracked with biometric facial recognition, and followed with license-plate readers. Spying isn't limited to black activists. And the Save Our Society crowd seems to agree fully on locking up anyone who lifts even a corner of their snooping camouflage cover or opens a window on their torture and the killing of anyone in their way.

Lest my critical remarks about my homeland seem to be one-sided dissing, thus worsening even further a bad reputation based on the sins of my younger days, I wish to stress that in my eyes every American villain, past or present, has been outbalanced in the scales of history. For every Jefferson Davis, Stonewall Jackson, or John Wilkes Booth we know of a John Brown, a Frederick Douglass, and a Harriet Tubman; for every greedy octopus like Jay Gould, J. P. Morgan, or John D. Rockefeller there have been saintly personalities like Mother Jones, Pete Seeger, or Martin Luther King; for every nasty and brutal clown like J. Edgar Hoover, George W. Bush and many recent additions there has been a witty, humane wonder like Woody Guthrie or Charlie Chaplin. And loving them and fighting alongside them, without headlines, there have always been many, many good people, trudging along, ringing doorbells, carrying picket signs (and occasionally rifles), also endangering their lives to the tune of "Yankee Doodle," "The Battle Hymn of the Republic," "Solidarity Forever" or "We Shall Overcome"!

It is because of them that I consider myself a patriot. I am not "proud to be an American"—which was due to no accomplishment of my own—nor do I see the United States as closer to heaven or God's blessing than any other country. Indeed, I feel love for most people in all countries, whether I've been there or not, since they are human, hence brothers and sisters.

I have come to feel very close to rebellious Germans, too, from the fighting preacher Thomas Müntzer and the courageous writers Lessing and Heine, my favorites, to Marx and Engels, Rosa Luxemburg and Karl Liebknecht and those who fought and died opposing the Nazis. But the United States is my original home. I love the good in its past, and I love my mother tongue, which can be misused or neglected, but is also so flexible, humorous, and simply familiar. And that extends to many people—from Tom Paine and John Brown to Herman Melville and Mark Twain, even those like the very independent Sweet Betsy from Pike or Tom Joad and Woody's Union Maid.

68—Personal Run-Ins

As a politically active student and then a factory worker, I sometimes felt the hot breath of that other kind of American. During the Progressive Party campaign in 1948, my friend Jack Lee and I were distributing leaflets calling on young men (like myself) to comply with a new draft law and register but to join us in trying to repeal it. Within ten minutes, we were threatened by a bunch of right-wing toughs, then arrested by the police, who did nothing against our attackers. We were only behind bars for a few hours (I'm still proud of those hours), but a week later, this time with about twenty-five fellow protesters, male and female, young and old, we were assailed by a mob, promoted by the media, protected by the police, and armed with a surprisingly large, well-packed supply of tomatoes and eggs. When I complained to one big cop, he said, "What tomatoes?" and then got hit himself right on the rear end of his nicely pressed uniform. When we left, some mob member slugged me on the back of the head, hard enough to make me go blank for a second and feel tooth gratings. The only reaction I got from the cop standing next to me was an icy stare.

In the summer of 1945, after joining the Party, I helped found a Communist student branch at Harvard. It was a jolly bunch, mostly top students, and all devoted to achieving a world of peace, equality, and justice, without racism or anti-union repression. We were active in good causes. Our members organized a picket line outside a plushy student bar that excluded the handful of black students then studying at Harvard, and we kept at it, evening for evening, till we won open admission. We joined a protest against a Boston department store hiring only white employees, and, at ungodly early hours, we handed out leaflets at plant gates to help union organizing. But we were a hush-hush group, secretive about our branch because of growingly malevolent rejection of our views and possible consequences for our futures.

Thus, when we phoned the Party secretary who helped us connect with union, African American, and other leftists in Boston, most of us worried about the gentlemen who, we surmised, might be listening in on our conversations, a worry later found to be all too justified. So we never used our names when calling. But what could we do about the woman's sweet four-year-old daughter who often answered the phone and, recognizing our voices, loudly identified us when calling her mother to the phone. Those of us who called more often chose nicknames as a protective measure, like Peach, Apple, or Strawberry. One of the first to try this out, the one most worried about his future legal career, was met by the little girl's loud, happy voice: "Mommy, it's for you, it's Apricot Manny Goodman!" Some of our group later had great difficulties (like me). In later years, after the atmosphere eased, six or seven of our little group became leading professors in their fields— sociology, Far Eastern languages, philosophy, mathematics, linguistics.

Two years later, as the political ice was frightfully hardening, I had a very different telephone experience. While working in a factory in Buffalo (at the suggestion of that same mother), I lived in a furnished room where the husband seemed very cool and his wife, my landlady, rather too sweet. One day, when they were out, the phone rang. Being alone—my work shift did not begin until 4 p.m.—I decided to answer for them and take a message. Then, at the other end, I heard a voice say the dreaded letters "FBI." As soon as he heard it was me, he hung up. I needed no further explanation.

Years later, thanks to the Freedom of Information Act I discovered (after a seven-year wait) that the 1,100 pages of FBI reports on me— quite a large pile—included quotations of harmless remarks I had made at a left-wing picnic in Buffalo and details on my subscription and financial contributions to the Communist Party's *Daily Worker* newspaper and to the organization that helped Spanish refugees.

Looking through those 1,100 pages I sometimes had to smile. The FBI somehow discovered a "second marriage" of my mother to some-one nobody in the family has ever heard of. And because I had not only changed my name (at my own request) when arriving in the GDR but also my date and place of birth, I read how some poor FBI man vainly searched for birth records in the wrong month and city (Buffalo). The authorities worked hard to find out who I really was; after one fully false path they succeeded, with the help of my college yearbook photo. They then followed the path of Victor Grossman, aka Steve Wechsler, all through my further life and career, even translating an unimportant little article about me in a local Leipzig newspaper.

In those FOIA papers I also found a letter from some Harvard fellow student (his name redacted) who denounced me as a leftist radical. I wondered if this was what started the ball rolling toward the Army checkup that changed my life and cost me my native country for so many years. In 1994, at the first reunion I attended of our Harvard Class of 1949, my Dunster House roommate confided that two FBI men had questioned him about me. This was no surprise; they ques-tioned all relatives and undoubtedly many friends and acquaintances. But what was surprising is that they quoted conversations held within our rooms. I was never able to ask our two other roommates about this. I'm sure no mechanical bugs were involved.

69—System-Saving Force and Violence

What usually happens when people in powerful positions can no longer rely on media blandishments and distractions, unconvincing electoral choices, or jingoistic calls for patriotic support of "our brave boys" (and now "our brave girls") abroad, or on various domestic pressures? When all such methods fail, to help modern-day King Canutes roll back angry waves, what do they do then?

A main resort is violence. In young, less developed nations the margins of toleration are thin. Leaders who lose out may face imprisonment, a bullet, or a noose. Politics can get very bloody. In lands with established traditions, there is usually a silent understanding. Well-established parties, in agreement on basic questions, can usually get along in peaceful alternation.

But rough situations can arise anywhere, anytime, even in my own United States, which, like France or Britain, is highly reputed as a stable democracy with traditions of liberty. Or was, more or less, until November 8, 2016. Was violence never needed to rescue our system? I leafed through the history books.

IT WAS INDEED a key part of the earliest settlements, driving Native Americans from their lands and decimating them in the process. In the same era, starting in 1619, millions of West Africans were kidnapped to pick cotton, tobacco, or rice under the whip, making some people very wealthy.

THE REVOLUTION HAD barely been won in 1786 when Daniel Shays led about four thousand veterans and poor farmers in Massachusetts in armed protest against being cheated out of their pay, getting forced from their land by wealthy landowners, and thrown into debtors' prisons. After some skirmishes, and nearly capturing an armory in Springfield, they were beaten and jailed. But Shays's Rebellion was a key reason for a quick convention in Philadelphia, a strict new constitution, and for George Washington to leave retirement and run, unopposed, for president.

BETWEEN 1835 AND 1848, Mexico was robbed by force of arms of a third of its territory, creating the Southwest of the United States and California. That was called "Manifest Destiny."

IN THE SOUTH, many rebellions challenged slavery. One, led by Nat Turner in Virginia in 1831, resulted in the death of over fifty members of slave-owning families and more than 200 black people, including fifty-seven rebels who were executed. Turner could read and write, so southern states quickly enacted laws forbidding all schooling for slaves or free blacks, restricting any rights of assembly for free blacks, and requiring the presence of white ministers at all black worship services.

THE MOST FAMOUS rebellion was that of the fiery abolitionist John Brown at Harpers Ferry in October 1859. Though smashed in a day, with Brown and other fighters soon hanged, it polarized the nation and led to the greatest insurrection of them all, an attempt to keep slavery by quitting the Union. Thus the Civil War was an example of violence as a final resort in saving a system. On both sides.

THE RAPID INDUSTRIALIZATION that followed brought strike struggles often seen as insurrection. The Great Railroad Strike of 1877 against the Baltimore & Ohio Railroad, after new cuts in wages that were already well below hunger level, spread across the United States, with 100,000 workers fighting private railroad company militias and National Guard units. After twenty men, women, and children were killed and thirty wounded in Pittsburgh, angry strikers burned railroad cars, locomotives, and finally the freight depot.

The *New York World* wrote: "Pittsburgh has been seized. The city is fully under the control of a howling mob." The Chicago press headlined "A Revolt of Vagabonds and Communists" like the Paris Commune six years earlier and demanded they be shot down like "wild beasts." One journalist wrote: "If they're hungry give them a diet of lead." Then cavalrymen, withdrawn from battling Sitting Bull, slashed at strikers, killing fifty and wounding nearly a hundred. In St. Louis a newspaper barked, "This is no longer a strike, it's a workers' revolution." In the end, military strength prevailed, with very visible results: new, well-fortified armories in many cities. (Richard O. Boyer, Dr. Herbert M. Morais, *Labor's Untold Story*, New York: Cameron & Kahn, 1955, 61–62.)

ON MAY 1, 1886, thousands struck peacefully for an eight-hour working day, not ten or twelve hours like most of them labored. When police killed some strikers in Chicago, a protest rally was held at Haymarket Square. Suddenly a squad of cops marched in and someone—his identity is still a mystery—threw a bomb, killing and injuring police and participants. Eight union or anarchist leaders were sentenced, all but one to death, though not one had been involved with the bomb. Two were later pardoned, one committed suicide, but four "Haymarket Martyrs" were hanged. A huge anti-union, anti-foreigner campaign engulfed the country, but a whole generation of working people was inspired to step up the fight. In 1890, in Paris, the Second Socialist International chose May 1st as "a day of international workers' struggle and solidarity" in memory of the executed men.

IN 1892, THE powerful tycoon Andrew Carnegie and Henry Frick, who managed his giant steelworks at Homestead near Pittsburgh, decided to break the union and worsen conditions. When a strike was called they had sniper towers with searchlights erected, connected by twelve-foot-high fences with water cannon capable of spraying boiling-hot liquid.

The strikers organized a human ring on land and small boats along the river to keep scabs out. When Frick got the Pinkerton Detective Agency to send in goons on barges thousands of people, often whole families, lined the shore to support (and win) a genuine sea battle. Then Alexander Berkman shot and stabbed Frick in his office; Berkman and his lover, Emma Goldman, both anarchists, were not connected with the strike and Frick survived, but the event brought a great loss of sympathy for the workers. The state helped Carnegie with troops while the conservative American Federation of Labor (AFL) refused any support. To get scabs, European immigrants were recruited almost before they left the ships and black workers were brought up from the South. Neither group had any experience with union struggles; they were not told what they were doing and were kept separate from the local people. As intended, the result was hatred between the groups. After five and a half months of hunger the strike was broken, a "blacklist" kept active strikers from getting jobs anywhere and those rehired were no longer paid $4 hourly for eight hours but $2 hourly on twelve-hour shifts and seven-day weeks. Steelworkers did not recover from this defeat until the CIO came along in 1936.

IN CHICAGO, IN 1905, the railway man and Socialist Eugene V. Debs, the Haymarket Martyr widow Lucie Parsons, and coal miner organizer "Mother" Jones joined to found the Industrial Workers of the World (IWW). Western ore miner "Big Bill" Haywood opened the first meeting with defiant words: "This is the Continental Congress of the working class. We are here to confederate the workers of this country into a movement that shall have for its purpose the emancipation of the working class from the slave bondage of capitalism." (Howard Zinn, *A People's History of the USA*, New York: Harper & Row, 1980, 158.)

The IWW preamble reflected his words: "The working class and the employing class have nothing in common . . . Between these two classes a struggle must go on until all the workers come together on the political as well as on the industrial field and take and hold . . . the industries of the country." (Len De Caux, *The Living Spirit of the Wobblies*, International Publishers: New York, 1978, 22)

The IWW, or Wobblies, rejected the racism of the American Federation of Labor and welcomed every worker, regardless of "race, creed, color, sex or previous condition of servitude." It started to bring black and white workers in the South to meet and fight together for their rights, and, unlike the AFL, which organized on a basis of skills, usually meaning only better-paid United States—born workers, the IWW tried to unite all workers in a factory or industry, skilled or unskilled, so owners could not pit one group against the other. It was for "One Big Union"!

The IWW also fought for free speech in the western states. Barred from speaking on street corners, then almost the only way to recruit workers moving around for seasonal jobs, a member would defy the law and start speaking from a soap box or platform. When he was arrested, another man climbed up, if only to read from the Declaration of Independence. And then another, as long as possible, with more "free-speechers" arriving on freight trains, singing rousing hymns with witty new union texts by the Wobblies' poet Joe Hill. Hundreds were arrested, beaten, stuffed into crowded jails, but in the end they won out and the laws were annulled.

By 1912, Wobblies had led some 150 strikes of dockworkers, farm laborers, loggers, and miners. Then came their most famous fight. In Lawrence, Massachusetts, woolen mills hired female immigrants, who, speaking over twenty-five languages but knowing little English, could, they were sure, never unite against their hunger wages. But the IWW, led by Haywood and the young, dynamic Elizabeth Gurley Flynn, overcame language problems and marched singing through the streets, 25,000 strong, defying all attacks by men in uniform (and conservative Harvard students). When they were hosed with icy water in the sub-zero weather, they grabbed one cop, stripped him, and tossed him into the river. It was here in Lawrence that a poem and song gained fame: "Yes, it is bread we fight for, but we fight for roses, too." "Bread and Roses" is still a slogan today. (James Oppenheim, "Bread and Roses," *The American Magazine*, New York, December 1911.)

Increasingly desperate, wrathful mill owners and police attacked mothers and children, dressed thinly in an icy winter in a city of woolen goods, and threw them into police trucks. This made the public turn so strongly against the owners that they had to accept defeat.

WHEN IT WENT to war, the U.S. government took its revenge. On September 5, 1917, President Wilson sent federal agents to raid forty-eight meeting halls and arrest 165 IWW members, Bill Haywood among them, for "conspiring to hinder the draft, encourage deser-tion, and intimidate others in connection with labor disputes." After five months, in the country's longest criminal trial thus far, 101 Wobblies were found guilty and sentenced to prison, some for twenty years. Haywood, ill with diabetes, skipped bail and fled to the Soviet Union, where he died in 1928. An urn with half of his ashes is in the Kremlin wall, the other half near the Haymarket Martyrs' Monument in Chicago. Other IWW men were shot, maimed, and lynched. Though IWW remnants exist to this day, its impact as a strong "working-class menace" in industry was largely destroyed.

THE SOCIALIST PARTY also opposed U.S. entry into the First World War. It was strong, with thirty-four elected mayors (the one in Milwaukee served for over twenty-five years), and U.S. Congressman Victor Berger, who called capitalism a malaria swamp "and the speculators are the mosquitos. We should have to drain the swamp—change the capitalist system—if we want to get rid of those mosquitos." (Victor L. Berger, *Berger's Broadsides*, Milwaukee, 1912.)

The main Socialist leader was that grand old locomotive fireman, Eugene Debs. Outraged by attacks against war opponents—two Socialist Party leaders had recently been hanged by their wrists from a prison rafter—he thundered against the war at a rally in June 1917 in Canton, Ohio: "The master class has always declared the wars; the subject class has always fought the battles. The master class has had all to gain and nothing to lose, while the subject class has had nothing to gain and all to lose." He was indicted two weeks later for "violating the Espionage Act."

At the trial, Debs made his dramatic statement: "I have been accused of having obstructed the war. I admit it. Gentlemen, I abhor war. . . . Your Honor, years ago I recognized my kinship with all living beings, and I made up my mind that I was not one bit better than the meanest on earth. I said then, and I say now, that while there is a lower class, I am in it, and while there is a criminal element I am of it, and while there is a soul in prison, I am not free." (Richard O. Boyer, Dr. Herbert M. Morais, *Labor's Untold Story,* New York: Cameron & Kahn, 1955, 200–201.)

Debs, sixty-three, was then sentenced to ten years. Although locked up in Atlanta with five other men in a small, hot jail cell, and restricted to a single sheet of paper per week, he ran for U.S. president in 1920

and got over 900,000 votes. He was finally pardoned, aged and ill, at
Christmas 1921.

SIMILAR METHODS WERE used against those who carried on IWW
and Socialist Party militancy: the Communists. Nine weeks after their
founding (into two separate parties at first, later united), hundreds
were suddenly nabbed while marking the second anniversary of the
Russian Revolution. Two months later, after "fake news" of plans for a
revolution on May Day 1920, over 6,000 were arrested in thirty-three
cities. In Boston 400 were shoved through the streets in shackles. In
Detroit 800 were held for six days in a narrow corridor with hardly
enough air and little to eat or drink. Many were beaten and tortured,
and over 500, who were not U.S. citizens, were deported on a ship
to Russia. Planning these raids was an up-and-coming young man, J.
Edgar Hoover, who soon formed and headed a new institution, the
FBI.

THE FOLLOWING YEARS were full of violence. When thousands of
unemployed hunger marchers tried to present petitions to Ford Motor
Company in Dearborn, Michigan, in March 1932, police and Ford
security guards fired on them with machine guns, killing four and
wounding over sixty.

The West Coast waterfront strike in 1934 lasted eighty-three days,
with a four-day general strike in San Francisco after the shooting of
two workers. Countless tough conflicts, often involving bloodshed,
led to the new Congress of Industrial Organizations, the CIO, unit-
ing millions of ethnically varied, semi-skilled producers of steel, cars,
tires, electrical appliances, cigarettes, with seamen, subway and truck
drivers, even barbers. Woolworth clerks took part, not just sitting—
occupying—but singing and dancing in the aisles. Most were organized
by left-wingers of various shades, especially Communists.

A major event was the GM workers' sit-down strike in Flint,
Michigan, six weeks in unheated, bitter-cold factory halls. Wives and
girlfriends, some in a red beret unit, defied police tear gas attacks to
supply the men inside with food. The first newsreel I can recall—I was

eight—showed the sit-downers of Flint, unshaven and triumphant, waving from the factory windows.

A few months later, at the "Memorial Day Massacre," Chicago police killed ten and injured thirty unarmed steelworkers and their supporters. Bloody repression of striking coal miners in Kentucky and West Virginia, most famously in Harlan County, Kentucky, flared up in the 1920s and 1930s and again in the 1980s. All those countless fights, involving strikers, the jobless, and those evicted during the Depression, were the base for New Deal victories: Social Security, the forty-hour week, unemployment pay, and, above all, the legal right to organize into unions. It was an irony of history; these victories, the basis for a higher standard of living after the war and a model in the fight against the "Red menace," were largely achieved under the leadership of Communists and other leftists in the 1930s and early 1940s, the same people who were vilified, expelled, and even imprisoned in the 1950s.

EVENTS ABROAD COULD be just as nasty, and far bloodier. The United States jumped in as a world power in 1898, when it wrested the Philippines, Guam, Puerto Rico, and in all but official terminology Cuba from Spain by force of arms, and took Hawaii by intrigue. Its further expansion was graphically described by rueful, retired Marine Corps Major-General Smedley D. Butler (1881–1940):

I spent 33 years and four months in active military service and during that period I spent most of my time as a high-class muscle man for Big Business, for Wall Street and the bankers. In short, I was a racketeer, a gangster for capitalism. I helped make Mexico and especially Tampico safe for American oil interests in 1914. I helped make Haiti and Cuba a decent place for the National City Bank boys to collect revenues in. I helped in the raping of half a dozen Central American republics for the benefit of Wall Street. I helped purify Nicaragua for the International Banking House of Brown Brothers in 1902-1912. I brought light to the Dominican Republic for the American sugar interests in 1916. I helped make Honduras right for the American fruit companies in 1903. In China in 1927 I helped see to it that Standard Oil went on its way unmolested. Looking back on it, I might have given Al Capone a few hints. The best he could do was to operate his racket in three districts. I operated on three continents. (Smedley Butler, "America's Armed Forces," *Common Sense*, November 1935, 8.)

70—Fascist Violence

Major-General Butler had not yet made such revelations nor expressed such views but was known for his great popularity with veterans of the First World War. That explains a mysterious, almost forgotten episode of U.S. history. In 1933 a group of very wealthy businessmen from a major bank, a giant chemical concern, and an armaments company among others, were alarmed at a few social moves early in the presidency of Franklin Roosevelt and tried to win Butler for a fascist coup. Allegedly led by a patriotic "veterans' organization," it would set up Butler as dictator with Roosevelt (maligned as an "invalid" because of his enforced use of a wheelchair) as a pure figurehead. This so-called "Business Plot" or "White House Coup" was exposed by Butler before a committee of Congress and got first-page media coverage, until, very suddenly, it was labeled a "gigantic hoax" and disappeared from view. Most of the congressional records were destroyed. No one was prosecuted.

But William Dodd, the U.S. ambassador to Germany, stated in a message to Roosevelt:

A clique of U.S. industrialists is hell-bent to bring a fascist state to supplant our democratic government and is working closely with the fascist regime in Germany and Italy. I have had plenty of opportunity in my post in Berlin to witness how close some of our American ruling families are to the Nazi regime.... A prominent executive of one of the largest corporations told me point blank that he would be ready to take definite action to bring fascism into America if

President Roosevelt continued his progressive policies. Certain American industrialists had a great deal to do with bringing fascist regimes into being in both Germany and Italy. They extended aid to help Fascism occupy the seat of power, and they are helping to keep it there. Propagandists for fascist groups try to dismiss the fascist scare. We should be aware of the symptoms. (Richard Sanders, "Facing the Corporate Roots of American Fascism," *Press for Conversion* 53, Coalition to Oppose the Arms Trade, COAT, Ottawa, April 2004.)

WHICH CAME FIRST, the fascist chicken in Europe or the rotten egg of U.S. big business? Since few knew anything about the involvement of American industrialists, the eyes of everyone interested in world developments—including my young eyes—were directed with growing anxiety at the growth of that nasty European rooster, especially the German subspecies.

In 1919, after defeat in the First World War, Germany had adopted one of the world's most democratic constitutions. But when the Great Depression hit ten years later, in October 1929, and millions of angry, often hungry, men and women turned to the Social Democratic Party or, increasingly, the smaller, rapidly growing Communist Party, this frightened the Junker landowners, banks, and industrialists, big ones like Krupp, Siemens, and Deutsche Bank and small ones like Bechstein, the piano-maker. So they threw their money and backing to a mob that offered to save their system—Hitler and the Nazis. With the left parties disunited and lacking giant media presence, the Social Democrats supported the old right-wing General Paul von Hindenburg for president—as a lesser evil against Hitler—rather than the Communist Ernst Thälmann. But almost as soon as Hindenburg won, he chose Hitler to take over the government as chancellor. With new jobs created by a giant rearmament program, including the militarily valuable new highway system, the Autobahn, and by quickly and brutally crushing resistance, Hitler's Nazis were able to rally most Germans behind them and expand their influence and control further and further through much of Europe, jailing and murdering first

Communists, then left-wing Social Democrats, anti-fascist Christians, Roma (Gypsies), disabled persons, gay men, and above all, almost the entire Jewish population.

This extreme example demonstrated that even in societies proud of their reputations as freedom-loving democracies, the powers behind the throne may accept free elections and permit unwelcome, even rebellious views, but only until dissatisfaction seems to be getting out of hand. When progressive new governments are attempted or seem possible, they react fast and toughly, using the entire keyboard of violence.

THIS WAS DEMONSTRATED again three years later in what I see as the most heroic and one of the most tragic episodes of the twentieth century. In Spain, in February 1936, ninety-nine Socialists, three anti-royalist parties with 162 seats, and seventeen Communists were democratically elected to the Cortes. The strong anarchists also supported the resulting "People's Front," enabling it to form a government. Unlike in Germany, they were all able to join together, and they began to improve the miserable lives of the great majority in Spain, ruled till then by giant landowners, immensely wealthy corporations, a bloated, top-heavy church apparatus and officers' caste, and foreign owners. But even their moderate measures crossed the red lines of the ruling caste, which turned to extreme violence, led by General Francisco Franco. Its plans to seize power in a day or two misfired as many Spaniards, especially workers, seized whatever weapons they could and stopped them. Some 40,000 volunteers from over fifty countries came to help them, risking and often losing their lives to save the republic and stop the spread of fascism. German exiles were among the most numerous; nearly 3,000 were U.S. Americans. Most volunteers had to brave dangerous mountain passes simply to enter Spain, which the French government had forbidden.

The Spanish people and the foreign volunteers fought heroically, but Hitler and Mussolini sent in far more planes, tanks, weapons of all kinds, troops, and advisers than the republic could cope with, while the rulers of Britain, France, and, sadly, the United States, not only rejected its passionate requests to buy military equipment for its defense, but did everything to prevent aid from arriving from Mexico and the USSR, the only two countries supporting Spain. The defenders of Madrid, Valencia, Barcelona, and a shrinking region of the country, about a third near the end, defied the conquest for nearly thirty months before finally being betrayed. Well over 300,000 died during the war; Franco had 100,000 POWs executed; at least 35,000 died in his concentration camps; an unknown number were dumped into mass graves, often killed because they were elected mayors or teachers in pro-government villages or sometimes simply because they wore glasses and were thus suspected "intellectuals." The fascists ruled for thirty-six more years, until Franco's death in 1975, while the defeat of Spain—thus surrounding France from three sides—encouraged Hitler to start the Second World War with all its misery, with Warsaw, Coventry, Dresden, and Auschwitz.

A MAN WITH the notable name Sosthenes Behn was founder and CEO for many years of the giant U.S. company International Telephone & Telegraph (ITT), which also controlled the Spanish telephone system. When the war began there, and afraid of losing its huge profits, ITT not only supported Franco, but its boss was especially tough in pressuring Washington to keep boycotting the legitimate government. Behn told later how he had observed the first bloody attack on Madrid from the top of his Telefonica tower and prematurely prepared a victory banquet for General Franco. (Dr. Paul Schmidt, *Statist auf diplomatischer Bühne*, Bonn: Athenäum-Verlag, 1950, 170.)

Three years earlier, in his first meeting with U.S. businessmen in August 1933, Adolf Hitler had offered a friendly welcome to Sosthenes Behn, who not only headed ITT but was the biggest shareholder in the Focke-Wulf aircraft company, whose bombers hit Allied convoys in the Atlantic in the Second World War and scouted out information about their routes for submarine attacks. (My brother, a ship's officer, was lucky enough to live through them.) ITT, which also owned shares in companies making radar and other equipment for the Nazis, later had the chutzpah to sue for damage done to its German aircraft factories by British and U.S. planes.

THE CAUSE OF the Spanish Civil War was always close to my heart, and in 1946 I took part with enthusiasm in a march through Harvard Yard opposing U.S. recognition of Franco Spain and its inclusion in the UN (and also Churchill's Cold War threats with atomic undertones). I followed with great emotion what the worsening atmosphere meant for those who had supported a democratic Spain. Dr. Edward Barsky, volunteering in Spain as a surgeon, had worked almost directly on the front lines. "Operating under heavy bombing, at times using flashlights when the power failed, Dr. Barsky and his associates set a record of sorts in December 1937, when they operated for 50 hours without a break." In 1950 Barsky was indicted and jailed for refusing to divulge names of beneficiaries or contributors to his organization helping Spanish survivors. Ernest Hemingway, whose best-known book was about Spain, commented: "Eddie is a saint. That's where we put our saints in this country—in jail." ("Edward Barsky, Surgeon, Dies," *New York Times*, February 13, 1975.)

Robert Thompson, also a volunteer in Spain, became a battalion commander and survived some of the deadliest battles. Five years later, he was again fighting, in New Guinea on the Pacific front: "Volunteering to lead a small patrol in an attempt to establish a foothold on the opposite shore, Staff Sergeant Thompson swam the swollen and rapid Konembi River in broad daylight and under heavy enemy fire. Armed only with a pistol and hand grenades, he assisted in towing a rope to the other shore where he remained under cover of the bank and directed the crossing of his platoon. Staff Sergeant Thompson then led the platoon against two enemy machine-gun emplacements that dominated the crossing and wiped them out. The success of this action permitted the advance of the entire company and secured a bridgehead for the advance of the following units." Again, he survived, got a battlefield commission, and received the Distinguished Service Cross. (Alan M. Wald, *Trinity of Passion: The Literary Left and the Antifascist Crusade*, Chapel Hill: University of North Carolina Press, 2007, 20–21.)

Six years later, Thompson was sentenced to three years in prison, one of the first of over 100 people prosecuted and often jailed for being Communists. While on a lunch line in prison, he was attacked by a group of Yugoslav fascists, jailed for jumping ship. One of them cracked Thompson's skull with a metal pipe. Once again lucky, he survived, but just barely.

In the next group sentenced for this same crime was Elizabeth Gurley Flynn, a legendary leader of the famous "Bread and Roses" strike led by the Wobblies in Lawrence, Massachusetts. A founder of the American Civil Liberties Union, and a fighter for the rights of the Spain vets, her speech at the start of the nine-month trial is considered one of the greatest in U.S. history. But, sixty-five years old and diabetic, she landed in a federal prison for twenty-eight months.

The famous novelist Howard Fast was jailed for three months in 1950 because, like Barsky, he refused to tell the Un-American Activities Committee the names of contributors to a fund for Spanish War orphans. His best-known novel, *Spartacus*, begun in prison, had to be printed privately because publishers, bookshops, and libraries blacklisted him. (It later became an Oscar-winning movie, but only after he had retracted his Communist views.)

Sosthenes Behn, who maintained ties with old Nazi friends back in power in Bonn, died, wealthy and untroubled, in 1957.

DOWN THROUGH HISTORY, when governments or systems considered themselves threatened, they resorted to any and all countermeasures, including violence. The GDR was notably rough at its strictly guarded border, the Wall, trying to stanch the hemorrhaging of its skilled citizenry. But in 1989, despite clearly impending downfall, it did not experience more than a few relatively minor skirmishes. The Wende itself was totally free of bloodshed.

71—A Festival and Roosevelt's Four Freedoms

I had always been deeply interested in foreign policy. All of us leftists at Harvard had joined in organizing that memorable Harvard Yard protest march in 1946. But even the other Communists joked that I was more emotionally involved with an election in distant Bolivia or a revolt in Madagascar than with events in Cambridge or discussions in my economics seminar. They were not far from the truth.

A year later, in line with just such emotions, I had great luck. I became a delegate to the first World Festival of Youth and Students in the Czechoslovak capital of Prague and was able to meet and converse, in one way or another, with young people from half the world. At the opening ceremony, our American delegation, about 250 strong, stood next to a group with copper complexions and bright-colored robes. It was the Mongolian delegation, about which we were almost totally ignorant. We couldn't speak much, but soon found that they were great archers—and skilled film documentarists. Most of the 20,000 who came to Prague had, as adolescents, been hit in some way by the Second World War; many had taken an active part in fighting the fascists up to two years earlier. Fresh flowers were still being placed and replaced below plaques in Prague where friends or family had died fighting the Nazi occupiers; street directions in German were still painted on many walls. But that nightmare was past; the festival spirit was optimistic, moved by many ongoing fights for independence, especially in Asia and Africa. During the festival, India and Pakistan gained their independence. I also recall how a group of young Greeks at a downtown street corner, all on furlough from their struggle against the rightist king and his U.K. and U.S. backers, came upon three Vietnamese fellows, also engaged in a fight for their freedom. Finding no common language, the Greeks, in exuberant solidarity, threw one surprised little Vietnamese fellow happily but carefully up in the air. Whether from Southeast Asia, South Africa. or the South Bronx, we shared hopes for a bright, free future without cannon fire or bombs!

And yet newer conflicts could not be overlooked, not on Harvard Square and certainly not on Wenceslas Square! At the international exhibition most of us Americans felt it impossible to display, like some other delegations, a big picture of their country's leader (then also including Stalin and Tito). Instead of a picture of Harry Truman, we decided to use one of the deceased Franklin Roosevelt.

Until I was seventeen, Roosevelt was the only president I had known, and I had greatly mourned his sudden death. I was aware of points of difference; one of his main missions, after all, was to rescue the status quo, the capitalist system. But he had an open ear for the needs of the people. He not only spoke wonderfully to them but listened to them as well, and after his tragic blunder in aiding Franco instead of the Spanish people, he turned to fighting fascism, and joined mightily in defeating Hitler, Mussolini, and the Japanese Tojo dictatorship.

On January 6, 1941, he had made a famous, stirring speech. Though only twelve at the time, I also felt its great impact. He declared that people in all parts of the world shared with Americans the rights to four basic freedoms: freedom of speech, freedom of religion, freedom from want, and freedom from fear. We thought about and discussed these matters constantly. Looking back after more than seventy-five years, I think about the extent of their realization in the different societies in which I have lived.

"The first," Roosevelt had stated, "is freedom of speech and expression—everywhere in the world." In this connection, unhappily, I could do no boasting about the GDR. There, in fact, lay its greatest failings. In earlier chapters I expressed my view that leaders in every country limit or permit freedom of speech and the press in proportion to their confidence or fears about preserving themselves and, above all, their system, with variations due to national traditions and the ebb or flow of dissatisfaction. It was the fears of GDR leaders about preserving their system that lay behind restrictive pressures in these key fields. As it turned out, their fears were more than justified.

But I also thought back to the twenty-four years in my own United States, a country whose leadership had hardly been threatened earnestly since 1865, and never fundamentally after 1945. This had not prevented the jailing of Howard Fast, Edward Barsky, Elizabeth Gurley Flynn, Bob Thompson, or the Hollywood Ten, the cruel repression of Paul Robeson, and of many more who were heartlessly ruined because of their views. Nor had this treatment been completely abandoned in later years, as shown by the treatment of several crusading "whistle-blowers" or the hard-hitting radio journalist Mumia Abu-Jamal, in 1982 sentenced to die, then to life in prison, without a fair trial. Such cases are rarely mentioned in schoolbooks. I thought of other censorship methods, not as dramatic as the ban on books like *Ulysses*, considered obscene (but later ruled permissible), but far more effective, like book sale boycotts or simply the silent treatment, as used against Bernie Sanders during crucial months of the 2016 primary campaign. Of course, that was very different from the journalistic monoculture of GDR days. But who knows what awaits us in coming years?

I also recalled that West Germany outlawed the Communist Party in 1956, shut down its press, seized its property, and jailed thirty-three of its leaders. With Willy Brandt's *Berufsverbote* (job bans) a decade later, 1.4 million possible "subversives" were investigated and many were fired for their views from public jobs, even mailmen and railroad workers. Films of the GDR were excluded. Even foreign films with anti-Nazi content like *Casablanca* were banned—or distorted and "de-fanged." Free speech had its angles.

But after the easing of the panic about student revolts in 1968 and the killings in the 1970s by the RAF ("Red Army Fraction," like Weather Underground), the improvement in living standards and the growing glamor of its consumerist culture brought widespread satisfaction—with hardly anyone aware how much it owed to hunger wages in poorer countries. As a result, the FRG, never really threatened in its existence, was able to achieve a freer, relatively easygoing atmosphere, whose media reduced most conflict to a more or less gentle debate between Christian Democrats and Social Democrats. Some political red lines still persist, but they are more subtle, and, for many, invisible. One is a general taboo on praise or even fair treatment of GDR history and achievements.

But back to the Four Freedoms of Franklin D. Roosevelt: "The second is freedom of every person to worship God in his own way—everywhere in the world." The world is still riddled by hatred based on religion—as always against Jews, in a few countries against Christians but now most frighteningly against Muslims, whether in the United States, all over Europe, or even by Buddhists in Myanmar. Religion is crucial in the lives of most world citizens, so this, too, is an important freedom.

Yes, the GDR discriminated too often against people who practiced religion, sometimes in clumsy tit-for-tat conflict with the main established church and, for years, its top (ex-Nazi) bishop in the West. This was closely related to continuing political conflicts, basically defensive in nature. But except for the repression of the small number of Jehovah's Witnesses, whom it considered "U.S. agents," it did not restrict people's freedom to worship in their own way. It subsidized the education of priests and pastors, contributed something toward church rebuilding, helped collect tithes from paychecks, and allowed Mormons to build a temple or two.

I recalled some wonderful concerts: in Bach's Saint Thomas Church in Leipzig, with its famous boys' choir still singing, his gravestone behind the altar and a statue outside—with a pulled-out, empty pocket to chide the old city fathers' miserliness. Or the organ concert in the grand thirteenth-century Gothic church at Doberan and Schubert's Mass in G in a little church in Warnemünde. Also, the concert with music by Heinrich Schütz in the chapel of Hartenfels Castle in Torgau, the first one consecrated by Martin Luther (near the Elbe bridge where U.S. Army scouts and Soviet troops first met in April 1945). Of course, my visits to many wonderful, beautifully kept churches were musically motivated, or simply as a tourist. But my radio series with the music of U.S. folksingers had led to a lasting friendship with another Pete Seeger fan, the pastor of a small town in Thuringia, and his church brethren and sisters. They spoke critically of tensions with officialdom, but not of any *verbot* for church services or activities.

On the question of anti-Semitism, most synagogues had been destroyed by the Nazis, but small congregations, with ten or more practicing Jews, held services in five or six large cities and received financial support from the government. On holidays, I occasionally reveled in the magnificent singing of West Berlin guest cantor Estrongo Nachama (1918–2000) in East Berlin's handsome synagogue on Ryke-Strasse, and my wife and I loved the East German radio broadcasts of Jewish religious music every Saturday, with a fine choir—mostly "goyim"—conducted by Nachama.

72—Freedom from Want

"The third is freedom from want—which, translated into world terms, means economic understandings which will secure to every nation a healthy peacetime life for its inhabitants—everywhere in the world." Roosevelt's words about freedom from want, from poverty, remain all too relevant. Renate and I visited many pleasant places in the United States; most relatives and old friends lived well, even very well, and American supermarket aisles were overwhelming.

But I cannot forget my shock, and that of Renate even more, at the sight of so many homeless men and women sleeping on benches or a fellow human being sleeping in a cardboard box near the UN building. Nor the elderly women with all their belongings in a shopping cart. I tried—and try—to be fair and honest, and I well remember earnest deficiencies in the GDR. I always understood and often joined in the grumbling about the eternal wait for a first new car, or by those still lacking an apartment with modern conveniences or a home telephone, or angry at the scarcity of oranges and bananas, at delays in keeping up with Western fashions or other deficiencies, some more worrisome, like travel restrictions, some less so. It was such deficiencies that caused a constant envy of the West and were at least major contributing factors for those trying to leave the GDR, legally or illegally, sometimes risking their lives.

But since I received constant news from there in my GDR years, also from the Armed Forces Network U.S. Army channel in West Berlin, I was better informed than most of my neighbors about a host of problems few of them ever heard about before 1990. Thanks to the internet, I am still reading about them, and my memory forces me to make comparisons.

Shelter

I read, for example, about a woman called Arleen on a bitter cold day in Milwaukee:

> First, the landlord would summon the sheriff, who would arrive
> with a gun, a team of movers, and a judge's order saying that her

house was no longer hers. Then Arleen would be given two options: "truck" or "curb." Truck meant that her things would be loaded into an 18-footer and checked into bonded storage. She could get everything back after paying $350. Arleen didn't have the money, so she would have opted for curb, which meant that the movers would pile everything onto the sidewalk: mattresses; a floor-model television; her copy of "Don't Be Afraid to Discipline," a nice glass dining table and a lace tablecloth; the meat in the freezer. . . .

These days, evictions are too commonplace to attract attention . . . millions of Americans are evicted every year. In Milwaukee . . . landlords legally evict roughly 16,000 adults and children each year, about 16 eviction cases a day. Low-income women, especially poor black women, are at high risk of eviction. . . . If a tenant in eviction court lives with children, her or his odds of receiving an eviction judgment almost triples. (Matthew Desmond, "Forced Out," *The New Yorker*, February 8, 2016.)

What could follow such an eviction, even in sunny California?

A civil rights attorney described the lives of the homeless in the East Bay Area: "It's an everyday, daily routine. . . . The cops kicking and punching and prodding the homeless, even as they sleep. Beating them awake. . . . Now Mayor Bates and his anti-homeless supporters have succeeded in passing a new batch of draconian laws against the homeless, including one saying that you cannot have belongings that take up more than two square feet on the sidewalk. Can you fit your life's belongings in two square feet?"

A victim describes the situation in Salinas: "In past sweeps I have had my possessions—my tent, bedding, clothes, blankets, food stamps, identification, birth certificate, family photographs, and important legal documents—taken from me and thrown away," said Acosta, a longtime resident of Salinas who is now homeless. . . . "They just start from one end of the street until they make their way all the way around it . . . Whatever we can't take with us they have like a bulldozer thing that just comes in and scoops everything up and puts it straight into the trash . . . into the garbage can. . . . They just tell us, 'We gave you enough time to take your things out.' ' Out? To where?' asks Acosta. ' There is nowhere else to go.' "

Many of these people actually owned homes in Santa Cruz, but during the housing foreclosure crisis folks lost their own places or they were renters that lost their places because their landlords were foreclosed on. (Dennis J. Bernstein, "Driving Out the Mosquitos," *Reader Supported News.org*, January 2, 2016.)

Leafing through Google on the subject of death among the homeless, the numbers were horrifying; in Sacramento, the capital of the richest state in the country, alone in 2016, the bodies of eighty-one homeless people were found.

I HAVE TO think back to the GDR! Even people who ignored warnings and paid no rent for years—an extremely rare event, since rent cost less than 5 or 10 percent of most incomes—could not be thrown out of their homes until a new affordable apartment was found for them. Evictions were prohibited by law. In all thirty-eight years, I saw not one single person sleeping in parks or on sidewalks. And not one beggar!

Ex-Cons

One group is hit especially hard—people leaving correctional facilities. . . . At any given time in Los Angeles and San Francisco, 30 to 50 percent of all people under parole supervision are homeless. In New York City, up to 20 percent of people released from city jails each year are homeless or their housing arrangements are unstable. . . . Federally subsidized housing providers, such as local public housing may—and sometimes must—deny housing to people with a criminal history involving drugs or violence. Still other circumstances make finding a home difficult for people. . . . Ex-offenders who live in a shelter or on the street don't have a fixed address or phone number where potential employers can contact them. They also may be unable to maintain personal hygiene and may not have clean, appropriate clothes to wear to interviews or at work. . . . These factors make it extremely difficult for ex-offenders to find a permanent home and establish stable lives in the community. They may also contribute to an offender's further involvement in the criminal justice system. (Nino Rodriguez and Brenner Brown, "Preventing Homelessness Among People Leaving Prison," *Vera Institute of Justice*, December 2003.)

Sentences in political cases were far too tough in the GDR; too many were arrested for activity ruled politically illegal. Many such prisoners were released to West Germany in exchange for urgently needed West-marks, a dubious procedure to say the least.

But in non-political cases, the judicial system leaned toward leniency and rehabilitation. There was no organized crime scene and therefore, so far as I ever heard (with the whispered exception of one local doctor on morphine and one distressed actress), no drug scene, no drug problem. There was some crime, of course, no hunger thefts but rather fraud or embezzlement and the like out of personal greed. There was occasional violence, but not with firearms, which were limited almost entirely to hunters and sports enthusiasts (and people in uniform), with strict controls on possession and ammunition, indeed on just about every bullet. Some people did go to prison, but after serving their term, ex-convicts were allotted an affordable flat and a job, often a place in a work team charged with helping them integrate into work rhythms and normal life. And in 1987, the amnesty mentioned earlier (not the first one but the biggest) released 32,500 inmates from prison, leaving only 5,300 mostly violent cases behind. All those freed were given homes and jobs.

Pantries

I found this story from Tennessee:

My husband Josh and I have three children. John is seven, Gavin is two and Marietta is one. When we first got married our lives were pretty stable. We had a place to live and both of us worked full time. We could pay the bills; we could buy our children the things they

needed. But then I lost my job and things went downhill from there
. . . Josh lost his job the year after I did. . . . We did everything we
could to find other work but apparently it just wasn't enough. Today,
we are down to our last dime. After the bills are paid, there is no
money left. In fact, there is no money to pay the bills. We constantly
have to make tough choices like choosing between buying diapers
and paying the light bill. If it wasn't for the food bank we would definitely have to choose between paying for utilities and buying food .
. . Each Friday Josh comes home with a bag full of healthy food that
enables me to make quick, easy meals for all my children. Josh and
I may have to skip meals, but we make sure our children never have
to. Without help from the food bank, though, I really don't know
how we'd feed them. ("The Local Faces of Hunger," *Second Harvest
Food Bank of Northeast Tennessee*, Kingsport, Tennessee, October
13, 2016.)

"Feeding America," according to its website, is a

hunger-relief organization and charity, with a nationwide network
of 200 food banks and 61,000 food pantries and meals programs.
The combined network provides more than 3.6 billion meals to
more than 46 million individuals across the country. . . . Food banks,
however, are still reeling from the effects of the 2013 cuts to federal
spending. . . . Research released by the Food Bank for NYC last fall
indicates that over the course of a month, nearly half of all food banks
surveyed ran out of the supplies needed to compile adequate pantry
bags. (Eillie Anzilotti, "More than 520,000 Americans Stand to Lose
SNAP," *City Lab, Atlantic Monthly Group*, March 31, 2016.)

What can I say to such a story and such facts? They arouse sympathy but, more than that, anger. I think back to the GDR. Food pantries
and food banks? What the hell were they? Yes, right after the war, in a
wrecked country with millions searching for refuge, there had to be free
food distribution. But by the time I arrived in 1952, I neither saw nor
heard of such things, not even the word for them; I learned the German

word, *Tafel*, only after 1990. The above article describes severe rural poverty. In the GDR, after those first hard years, the farm population prospered more and more. Wherever I traveled in the countryside, whenever I visited my wife's village, the only times I heard need or hunger even mentioned were in recollections of the Depression era and the first three or four postwar years.

There was indeed a constant undersupply, or absence, of imported fresh fruit, less common vegetables like asparagus, eggplant, or broccoli, prime cuts of meat and those choice kinds of fish that were mostly exported. Except on the coast, there was almost never any beloved eel— or a lack of jokes about its absence. But despite the reduced choice and various hitches and shortages, the causes of the fabled lines at shops, staples were always in supply at the grocer, the bakery, the dairy, or the butcher shop, and until 1990, at the same low prices frozen in 1958 when rationing ended. No one went hungry. And there were some pleasant surprises: big shipments of peaches, grapes, melons, and other fruit from Bulgaria, tasty new fruit jam from Hungary, delicious lobster tails from Cuba or Kamchatka crab meat and tinned fish liver from Soviet Siberia. And even, alas only once, tins of wonderful gefilte fish from Poland.

One group, it is true, was disadvantaged. A decreasing number of older women, housewives before 1945 and often left single by the war, had done low-paid, "unskilled" jobs like laundering and cleaning and were stuck with the lowest retirement sums. All rates increased step by step, but this group, always on the lowest rung, did not have it easy, especially if they had no children to help out and were unable or unwilling to improve pension payments with part-time jobs like punching tickets at a station. But for a very low price, often less than one mark a day, they could get hot lunches at senior clubs, supported by the unions, the state, and the churches. These were not charity, no stigma was attached, and seniors could not only get a simple but full hot lunch but also join in social and cultural activities or take part in projects, aiding their peers with shopping, light home repairs, or just friendly visits. No seniors needed to fear evictions, and, after they turned sixty-five or sixty (for women), they paid no insurance tax of any kind but were guaranteed complete medical and dental coverage, no costs for prescription medicines, glasses, teeth, or hearing aids, support in case of invalidity and, finally, funeral expenses.

Medical Treatment

Long lines for fresh strawberries or cherries or a rare pound of fresh calf's liver, typical in the GDR, might have seemed odd to U.S. customers. But some Americans also encountered lines.

For years, I heard ghastly stories about medical care prices and the short time allowed for in-hospital care. In an encounter of ours, we had no long line, but then it was not typical. When Renate felt ill at Logan Airport in Boston after our late-afternoon arrival from Europe, she was quickly taken to a hospital for a checkup (thus bucking a very, very long line for non-citizens' passport check). Soon found to be okay, she was released the next morning. Later we got the bill: for the ambulance, the brief checkup, a night's rest and breakfast—almost $5,600. We were lucky—the travel insurance I had bought in Berlin covered the bill.

But again and again, I heard or read of others in the United States who were not so lucky. Here is a sample:

As the sun set in the mountains of southwest Virginia, hundreds of hurting souls were camped out or huddled in vehicles, eager for an early place in line when the gates swung open at 5 a.m. for the nation's largest pop-up free clinic . . . The Remote Area Medical Expedition, held at a county fairground in Appalachia over three days ending Sunday, drew more than 2,000 people who endured high heat and long waits for basic health services. It was a dispiriting reminder that as Congress flails around for health plans that could cost millions of people their insurance, many more don't have much or any insurance or access to medical care to lose.

Four years into the rollout of the Affordable Care Act's major provisions, 29 million Americans still lack health insurance. Millions live in states like Virginia that did not expand Medicaid to childless adults among the working poor, as the law allowed. Even for people helped by government programs like basic Medicaid, veterans' care and disability, there are many gaps: Low-income people struggle to afford co-payments, the gas to drive to a doctor and prescription drugs.

"Expect Delays. Heavy Traffic Area," a sign flashed on the normally sleepy country road before the Wise County Fairgrounds. Patients passed the command tent of the charity that runs the clinic, Remote Area Medical, emblazoned with a plea and a promise: "Stop the Suffering." The group, staffed by medical volunteers, has treated more than 700,000 people at free clinics around the country and overseas since 1985. (Trip Gabriel, "When Health Law Isn't Enough, the Desperate Line Up at Tents," *New York Times*, July 23, 2017.)

Have such lines become fewer or shorter in recent years? I don't know. Will they get shorter or longer in coming years? Who knows? I also found an interesting contrast:

UVM Medical Center is Vermont's largest hospital and the only academic one, so it's no surprise that executives there are the most highly paid. . . . John Brumsted, who has been CEO since 2011, made nearly $2.2 million during 2016. His salary was $979,064, but he took home more than twice that, thanks to bonuses and other payments . . . up from nearly $1.7 million the year before. . . . CEOs weren't the only ones making large sums of money. . . . Further down the list were the then-head of human resources, Paul Macuga ($548,356); the head of public relations, Theresa Alberghini DiPalma ($523,892); and five doctors, four of them anesthesiologists, who earned approximately $400,000 each. (Alicia Freese, "Million-Dollar Question: How Much Should Nonprofit Hospital CEOs Earn?," *Seven Days*, August 23, 2017.)

In the GDR, the trade union federation was in charge of social insurance. Every employee paid a monthly 10 percent insurance sum up to a 60-mark maximum, taken automatically from all paychecks and

salaries. The enterprise or institution added on an additional 10 percent. Freelancers like me paid the full 20 percent tax ourselves, taken
out of the fees we earned, but at year's end we usually got back part of
this. As I've mentioned, pensioners no longer paid any tax but were
equally covered.

What did this get you? A full protective umbrella. If you felt ill, you
could go to any doctor you wanted, a private or state-subsidized practice, a hospital, or clinic. If you chose a very popular doctor, this often
meant waiting longer for an appointment. For years I had only lesser
aches and pains (aside from occasional political bellyaches, which were
not covered). When I was thirty-nine, I was found to have hepatitis-B
and immediately tucked into a hospital bed, luckily in a two-patient
room, and luckily with no cost to me. After nine long weeks, the biliru-
bin in my blood had dropped to an acceptable level and I was packed
off to four weeks of convalescence cure (a *Kur* in German) at a beautiful
lakeside sanatorium near Berlin, expropriated from the war-criminal
Siemens family. A year later, to check on any lingering liver damage,
I was sent on a second four-week *Kur* to Karlovy Vary (Karlsbad) in
Czechoslovakia, again with checkups, daily massages, bubble baths,
mud treatments, and the legendary afternoon pavilion concerts where
patients stroll around sipping tepid but healthy mineral waters out
of spouted cups. My wife was sent to three rheumatism cures, four
weeks each, one in the beautiful Harz Mountains, one in the healthy
mountains of southern Poland. In all our *Kurs*, food, lodging, medical
treatment, and travel costs were fully covered; we paid not a pfennig
and got 90 percent of our salaries the whole time (guaranteed for up to
six weeks a year).

The only problems with such *Kurs* were possible amorous relationships of spouses suddenly on their own with much free time and a new
group of people in a pleasant, relaxed environment. Stories of such
new ties, known as "Kur shadows," were an abundant theme of jokes,
good for laughs, and perhaps a few tears as well. But no tears in our
family, at least so far as I know!

I once accompanied a visiting American to a pharmacy in Leipzig
where, while waiting on line, he noted with surprise that people

handed in their prescriptions, received their medicines, and walked out, with not a pfennig changing hands. Whatever was prescribed was free. Everything was covered; not just the ambulance that took Renate to the clinic for our first son but the taxi for our second one, as well as a voluntary course for expectant mothers. The only things not covered, as I recall, were private wishes like deodorants, mouth wash, or, if desired, more stylish eyeglass frames and non-medical sunglasses.

Every GDR borough and county had what was called a polyclinic with a general practitioner, an internist, dentist, gynecologist, and pediatrician, plus lab and X-ray facilities, massage rooms, and ties to a hospital. Smaller towns and villages had "ambulatories," usually with two doctors and up to a dozen nurses or assistants. About a hundred larger industrial plants had their own big clinics.

The present medical system in Germany is more modern than in the GDR and far better supplied with drugs from the world market. Insurance coverage is still obligatory, though with any of a large number of companies with varying prices and offerings. I think the system is certainly far better than U.S. systems, but payments have gone up while services were reduced. Glasses, hearing aids, and the like are only partially covered, prescribed medicines must be paid for in part, there is a daily charge for the first two weeks in a hospital, and convalescent cure treatment, now for two or three weeks, is harder to obtain and often subsidized only partially.

THERE WERE ALSO salary problems in the GDR. Medical students had to study for five or six years, not easy years, even though their schooling was free and included a monthly stipend. Just having to learn the Latin name and location of every human bone and muscle in their first two years seems formidable to me, and this was only a small part of it. Those making the grade enjoyed great prestige but not a very opulent income, perhaps 2–3,000 marks monthly, not much more than double that of a skilled factory worker. Were such limited rewards just and justified? They helped finance total medical coverage care for everyone, and some favored relative equality as opposed to furthering a class of the highly privileged. But no few doctors felt they were decidedly underpaid, especially when they learned that West German colleagues often averaged 10,000 West-marks a month, about seven times what factory workers earned. This made a change of locale very tempting, and almost a quarter of GDR doctors did "go West" before the construction of the Wall made this difficult. In fact, there was a regular Western recruiting program. Since training one specialist could cost up to a million marks (even though East-marks), such losses were true hemorrhages economically and they were also hard blows for abandoned patients. This helps explain the Berlin Wall. Renate, who worked in a hospital, told me how some doctors were recruited to cross to the West even after the Wall, usually using skillfully falsified passports, and there found far better paid jobs ready and waiting for them. ("Der Aderlass," *SpiegelOnline*, September 24, 1958.)

But despite such problems, I never heard of a single GDR citizen having to do without regular free care, from prenatal months until their last breath.

Dental Care

Two hours before sunrise, Dee Matello joined the line outside the Wicomico Civic Center [in Salisbury, Maryland], where hundreds of people in hoodies, heavy coats and wool blankets braced against a bitter wind. Inside, reclining dental chairs were arrayed in neat rows across the arena's vast floor. . . . Dentists arriving from five states were getting ready to fix the teeth of the first 1,000 people in line.

Matello was No. 503. The small-business owner . . . had a cracked molar, no dental insurance and a nagging soreness that had forced her to chew on the right side of her mouth for years. . . . The 46-year-old mother of three had not seen a dentist in nine years. When parts of her tooth broke off, she knew fixing it could cost hundreds of dollars, and other bills were always more urgent.

A little after noon, Matello's number was called. A volunteer took her temperature; she was running a slight fever but not high enough to stop treatment. Two more hours. Finally, she was waved over to an X-ray machine under a basketball hoop. Just as Matello expected to be called for her turn in the dentist's chair, a volunteer announced in a loud voice: "Those up to number 500 will be seen today. The rest will have to come back tomorrow." Matello's eyes filled with tears. She had been waiting 10 hours. . . .

As the distance between rich and poor grows in the United States, few consequences are so overlooked as the humiliating divide in dental care. High-end cosmetic dentistry is soaring, and better-off Americans spend well over $1 billion each year just to make their teeth a few shades whiter. Millions of others rely on charity clinics and hospital emergency rooms to treat painful and neglected teeth. Unable to afford expensive root canals and crowns, many simply have them pulled. Nearly 1 in 5 Americans older than 65 do not have a single real tooth left. (Mary Jordan and Kevin Sullivan, "The Painful Truth About Teeth," *Washington Post*, May 13, 2017.)

In GDR days you made an appointment, went to the dentist, usually spent at most an hour or so in a pleasant waiting room, and then got treatment, maybe not so pleasant but whatever was needed. No money was involved, unless you insisted on gold tooth fillings.

Regular dental care is still covered in Germany today, but anything a little special can be very expensive. My new bridge did not match the Brooklyn Bridge in price but was still painful, at least to my savings account; I have just paid off the twelfth and last installment on it. In the old GDR days, it would have been free.

Abortions

Ever since the *Roe v. Wade* Supreme Court victory for advocates of free choice in 1973 there have been legislative attacks in many or most states, as well as in Congress, to limit women's rights in as many ways as possible. Some were successful, some weren't, and Obama vetoed some attempts by Congress. Between 2011 and 2016, 162 abortion clinics in the United States closed or stopped offering abortions, due largely to legislative regulations by "pro-life" politicians. Eighty-seven percent of all U.S. counties have no clinics where abortions can be

performed, and nasty bullying plus occasional violence is all too frequent. Nearly a dozen doctors, nurses or other clinic personnel have
been murdered. With the current president (and vice president) and
the new Supreme Court all rights are threatened.

I have already mentioned the GDR law of 1972: "Equal rights for
women in education and employment, marriage and the family require
that a woman can decide for herself about her pregnancy and its
course." (With pregnancies of the second or third trimester a medical
opinion was required to avert possible dangers.) Contraception methods and abortions were all fully covered by medical insurance. The
result: in 1971, prior to the law making them legal, thirty-one abortion deaths. Within five years down to three deaths. In the 1980s, there
were no deaths!

Baby Leave

The internet again supplied sad reports, like this one by the journalist
Sharon Lerner:

> According to a 2012 survey, nearly one in four women who took
> leave to care for a new baby took only two weeks or fewer off. . . .
> Natasha Long was back at her factory job within three weeks, get-
> ting up at 4 a.m. to pump breast milk before her 12-hour shifts. She
> developed symptoms of depression. . . .
>
> Erica Hunter begged her doctor for a note to return to her $12/
> hour job after two weeks so that she and her laid-off husband
> wouldn't end up homeless. Seven days after giving birth, Alana
> Adams went directly from the hospital, where she was recovering
> from a C-section . . . to spending 10 hours a day on her feet as an
> emergency med technician. . . .
>
> Indeed, there's a clear class divide between mothers who are forced
> to get back to work early and those who aren't. In the 2012 survey
> [Sharon] Lerner cites, 80 percent of college graduates took at least six
> weeks off, while only 54 percent of those without college degrees did
> so. . . . Low-income workers are also less likely to have other forms of

paid leave, like sick days and vacation time, that they can save up and piece together to create their own de facto paid leave after the arrival of a child. . . . Only about a third of those in the bottom quartile have access to sick days and only half get vacation time.

While the 1993 Family and Medical Leave Act theoretically guarantees all workers up to 12 weeks of unpaid leave to care for a new child or sick family member, it applies only to businesses with more than 50 employees, only covers workers who have been with their employer for at least one year, and doesn't extend to part-time workers. These exemptions are significant. . . . They disproportionately affect low-income workers, who are more likely to work for small businesses, change employers frequently, and piece together multiple part-time jobs. . . . Poor mothers in the U.S. have double the rates of post-partum depression, are half as likely to breastfeed for the recommended six months, and are more than twice as likely to see their babies die within the first year. (Maya Dusenberry, "How America's Lack of Paid Maternity Leave Worsens Inequality," *Pacific Standard*, September 16, 2015.)

It's hard to know where to start here! When my first son was born in 1956, Renate got fourteen weeks of fully-paid leave, about six weeks before and eight weeks after delivery. As the economy strengthened, this went up to twenty-six weeks of maternity leave at full pay plus a second half year, if desired, at reduced pay but with the job guaranteed. In the case of a third child (or more), this was raised to eighteen months. For each baby, a mother received 1,000 marks to cover expenses but, as a health measure, in five installments—two at prenatal checkups, the main sum after delivery, and two sums after postnatal checkups with the baby. A bonus was paid to breast-feeders.

Despite the legalization of abortion, birth rates gradually rose, thanks to family-friendly legislation. Mothers with two or more children were granted longer vacations, nearly a month, and paid leave in case of children's illness. All parents got family allowances, but mothers with three or more children were offered special sanatorium *Kurs*, family-sized vacation possibilities, free summer camps (dirt cheap for all kids), free school milk and lunches. Women working full time and, later, single-household men received one paid "household day" every month. Young newlyweds (unmarried couples were much rarer in those years) received interest-free loans of 7,000 marks to furnish their homes, to be repaid in small monthly installments. 1,000 marks of the debt were waived when a child was born, 1,500 marks after a second child, and 2,500 marks after a third child.

Since nurseries (1–3 years) and kindergartens were free, there was every incentive for women to take and keep employment, and well over 90 percent did. Age-old traditions undeniably burdened most women with household and child-rearing duties, doing far more work with far less leisure than most husbands. This gradually changed, partly due to enlightenment in books, films, and TV; and fewer fathers remained reluctant about fetching offspring to and from kindergarten or doing more in the home than small repairs or taking out the garbage. The fact that, if need be, nearly all women could manage financially without a husband led, for better or worse, to higher divorce rates (without assigning guilt). Since women were no longer forced to stick with a spouse who was abusive, alcoholic, or too old-fashioned and lazy to carry his share they could tell him to go to hell! And often did.

Schooling

I know there are very good U.S. schools, and many youngsters, most of them I hope, may well have happy childhoods. But not nearly all of them. UNICEF reports: "Pre-school education helps all children to achieve more, and the most disadvantaged benefit the most. But the United States ranks near the bottom of the developed world in the percentage of 4-year-olds in early education. . . ."

In 2016, according to the Department of Housing, on any typical night in January 138,000 children were without a home. In 2007 about 12 of every 100 kids were on food stamps; today it's 20 of every 100. Sixteen million kids on food stamps know what it's like to go hungry. (Paul Buchheit, "The Numbers Are Staggering: U.S. Is 'World Leader' in Child Poverty," *AlterNet*, April 13, 2015.)

I read reports about underfunded public schools, where sports, civics, literature, music, and art are shortchanged so as to get test results high enough to keep teachers from being penalized and schools closed down. This coincides with the campaign to privatize education, with "vouchers" aiding a switch to church-run schools or publicly financed, privately run charter schools, which, unlike public schools, can choose their pupils, rejecting those speaking less English or with disabilities or behavior problems. Teachers' unions, one of the last strong sectors of organized labor, are often kept out and are thus weakened while some investors, getting rich with charters, intone piously, "We want to save poor children from failing schools." This switch, supported by giants like Bill Gates and the Walton family, now stands at about 7,000 such schools with 3 million students. Some predict that in ten years there may be cities with no democratically controllable public school education.

In today's Germany, there is also a growing percentage of children hit or threatened by poverty, and the trend to private schools is also picking up steam. Where they are better than the public schools, they are a boon for the children whose parents can afford them, but a loss for the others.

I have written at length about GDR education in an earlier chapter. Suffice it to repeat here that there were no private schools but some special schools for very talented children in music, mathematics, and sports, with higher demands in those fields. Otherwise, all children, urban and rural, received the same equal level of education with all those subjects now under fire in some U.S. schools, and always including sports and swimming for everyone.

College

Even when turning to higher education, I find reports on wonderful colleges and universities in the United States, certainly among the world's best, but also too many depressing statistics:

An increasing number of students tell us that they are struggling in college, sometimes even dropping out, because they can't afford enough of life's basic necessity—food. Beginning in 2008, we began surveying undergraduates attending public two-year and four-year colleges and universities across Wisconsin . . . 27 percent said they did not have enough money to buy food; they ate less than they felt they should; or they cut the size of their meals because of money. . . . When asked if they ever went without eating for an entire day because they lacked enough money for food, 7 percent of students at two-year colleges and 5 percent of students at four-year colleges said yes. (Sara Goldrick-Rab and Katharine Broton, "To Cut Costs, College Students Are Going Hungry," *TheConversation.com*, July 13, 2016.)

I read that tuition fees plus room and board at a private, nonprofit, four-year college in 2014–15 averaged $42,419, up from $30,664 in 2000–2001. At public four-year colleges, costs for the 2014–15 school year, at $18,943, were up sharply from the $11,635 price tag in 2000–2001. As a result, student loan debt stood at more than $1.2 trillion for 40 million borrowers. Almost 71 percent of bachelor's degree recipients will graduate with a student loan, the average graduate of the class of 2015 with a debt of more than $35,000.

I read that college graduates were putting off starting a family. The median age for a first birth had risen to age twenty-six.

A moving story by Matt Taibbi in *Rolling Stone* (November 3, 2017) told of a young teacher, a summa cum laude graduate, whose college debt climbed to $100,000, how the collectors called day and night, at home and in the middle of class while he was teaching, and how, seeing no escape, he came close to committing suicide.

I think back nostalgically to my years at Harvard, 1945–49. Tuition was $200 a semester, my room and meals for a semester were first $65, later about $85 each. An unfortunate B-minus in my seventh semester (thanks to too much politics) meant losing my $250 scholarship for the last semester. I too had to go into debt; I borrowed $250 from a classmate, got my B.A., and paid it back within a year.

And in the GDR?

I paid nothing for my four years at the Karl Marx University in Leipzig nor did my two sons pay, one at the same Journalism Department I attended, the other at the Konrad Wolf Film University. All such education, including post-graduate studies, was free. There was also a monthly stipend, not a lot but enough to cover the extremely low dormitory and daily hot lunch charges and an occasional holiday trip home (this latter for my sons, not for me). It was unknown for anyone to take a job during studies; a few did so during vacations to buy something special. Nobody incurred student debts.

The college departments accepted only as many students as were likely to be needed in that field, conforming to national development. This meant disappointments, often required personal rethinking, and is debatable. In practice it meant that graduates almost always found work right away in the field they had studied and did not have to serve meals or take other unlearned, unskilled jobs to make a living.

There was one stipulation, however; students, though guaranteed employment, were obliged, with due regard for possible family ties, to accept any job allotted to them in their field for the first three years after graduation. I think this was most commonly applied by sending young medical doctors to thinly covered non-urban areas in hopes that they might settle there.

A college degree was not so important in the GDR; only about 20 percent got them. Almost every other young person, after the tenth grade, learned a decent, respectable trade or profession, with its own prestige and livelihood.

In the early postwar years, special schools offered young workers or farmers the courses required for college admission. This was partly to break upper-class German collegiate traditions with their heavy-drinking, dueling, and right-wing activities in nationalist "corps," which are related to the worst U.S. fraternities but with Latin instead of Greek names. The special Workers' and Farmers' Schools were phased out later, but young applicants from working-class or farm backgrounds were always favored, and students who had learned a trade instead of preparing for college could always make up for it and switch, with the help of evening schools or correspondence courses.

Poverty in General

In recent reports on my home country, the world's richest, distressingly often I read about alcoholism, opioid addiction, suicide, and violence, with harmful prescriptions and potentially far more harmful guns easily available. Consider the following gloomy words from the review of a book by MIT professor Peter Temin:

> The economist describes a two-track economy with on the one hand 20 percent of the population that is educated and enjoys good jobs and supportive social networks. On the other hand, the remaining 80 percent, he said, are part of the U.S. low-wage sector . . . where the world of possibility has shrunk and people are burdened with debts and anxious about job security. He found that much of the low-wage sector had little influence over public policy, the high-income sector was keeping wages down to provide cheap labor, social control was used to prevent subsistence workers from challenging existing policies and social mobility was low. Mr. Temin also claims that this dual-economy has a "racist" undertone. The desire to preserve the inferior status of blacks has motivated policies against all members of the low-wage sector. We have a structure that predetermines winners and losers. (Chloe Farand, review of Peter Temin, *The Vanishing Middle Class*, Institute for New Economic Thinking, *The Independent*, April 24, 2017.)

There were times in the United States when a decent job in a factory or other steady enterprise paid enough to comfortably support a family, including money to pay off a mortgage and purchase a car or even two, prerequisites for that sufficient degree of satisfaction that keeps countries stable. It also meant feeling like a member of some more or less hazy "middle class." Then, it became more and more necessary for another family member, typically the wife, to take a job, at least part-time or for a limited period. Now I read that this may no longer suffice; over two million wage-earners, about a third of the total, need food stamps, Medicaid, tax credits for the poor or other public assistance.

As Credit Suisse estimates, "If you have no debts and have $10 in your pocket you have more wealth than 25 percent of Americans." (*SovereignMan.com*, October 20, 2015.)

Bernie Sanders put it this way:

> A vast majority of Americans understand that our current economic model is a dismal failure. Who can honestly defend the current grotesque level of inequality in which the top 1 percent owns more than the bottom 90 percent? Who thinks it's right that, despite a significant increase in worker productivity, millions of Americans need two or three jobs to survive, while 52 percent of all new income goes to the top 1 percent? What person who claims to have a sense of morality can justify the fact that the richest people in our country have a life expectancy about 15 years longer than our poorest citizens? (Sen. Bernard Sanders, "How Democrats Can Stop Losing," *New York Times*, June 14, 2017.)

73—Balancing Freedoms and Opposing Them

I thought again of Roosevelt's Four Freedoms. Without decrying the first one in the least, I tried to imagine a mother in a sub-Saharan hut, barely surviving with a few meager garden rows, hour-long trudges by her daughters for unsafe water, a constant hunt for a few sticks of fuel. What would she think about freedom of the press? "I never learned to read" might be her answer, and that of many others. What about a young seamstress in Bangladesh, overworked, endangered by fire or building collapse? Or a struggling farmer in Punjab, seeing no solution to his usurious debts but suicide? Or those in the favelas of Rio or São Paulo, the slums of Lagos, or in slums and ghettos in countries of the north? What, to them, would take first place?

I recalled a brief, moving experience during the World Youth Festival in East Berlin in 1973. The U.S. group included Native Americans, some of whom had been besieged at Wounded Knee in South Dakota a few months earlier, and of course African Americans. Strolling through the downtown area with a young woman from Harlem, a journalist, we exchanged ideas—despite constant requests for autographs from children who filled the traffic-free streets. She told me that some in the U.S. group, impressed about the job, medical care, and educational situation in the GDR, had wondered about remaining here. I said that in their short stay they had heard only about the good sides and little of young people's problems: stupid restrictions on music groups, dull, one-sided newspapers, lack of travel to the West, an all too ordered course of life, kindergarten, school, apprenticeship or college, a year and a half in uniform for most young men, then a steady job, with few possibilities to break away on their own as in the United States. She looked at me wide-eyed and said: "You don't seem to understand: For us it's a question of survival!"

Freedom of speech and the press can and should be powerful tools in improving people's lives. They must be fought for and, wherever won, courageously defended. But, I reasoned, they are primarily utensils, weapons if possible, in achieving the basic needs: a fair share of food, water, medical care, and schooling for all the people in the world. This question of survival, though at a higher level than simple bare existence, is what made me conclude: "First things first!" Freedom from want is often a survival goal, and the GDR was striving in every way to achieve that goal, not just for itself but for other countries as well. As long as it maintained this goal, and without ignoring failings or misdeeds, I would continue to support it. I found this reflected in another famous speech by Franklin D. Roosevelt, who called for an Economic Bill of Rights, stating: "We have come to a clear realization of the fact that true individual freedom cannot exist without economic security and independence. Necessitous men are not free men." (*State of the Union Address*, January 11, 1944.)

Yes, the fight against want, against hunger and need, was of utmost urgency. But, watching world developments, I found myself forced to think further about the relative importance of each Roosevelt demand:

The fourth is freedom from fear—which, translated into world terms, means a worldwide reduction of armaments to such a point and in such a thorough fashion that no nation will be in a position to commit an act of physical aggression against any neighbor—anywhere in the world. . . . That is no vision of a distant millennium. It is a definite basis for a kind of world attainable in our own time and generation. That kind of world is the very antithesis of the so-called new order of tyranny which the dictators seek to create with the crash of a bomb.

Four months after Roosevelt's death, two bombs did crash, after a decision by his successor, Harry Truman. Within a minute they caused the atomic annihilation of Hiroshima, three days later of Nagasaki, together killing over 200,000, mostly women, children, and the elderly. Some still try to justify those crimes; their motivation is still debated. Later events removed my doubts as to their main purpose in terms of world hegemony.

Just seven months later, in March 1946, Winston Churchill, with Truman at his side, made his speech in Fulton, Missouri, officially kicking off the Cold War. The president made his position even clearer a year later with his Truman Doctrine, arming Turkey at the Soviet border and joining in a civil war in Greece against former partisans, till shortly before our bravest anti-Nazi allies. (Just seven years later, in Bautzen, I made friends with young refugees from that civil war, then studying engineering at a GDR college.)

In 1950, the tense Cold War became a very hot war—in Korea, where in North Korea nearly every house with two stories or more was wrecked by U.S. planes, which then turned to dropping bombs on reservoir dams.

"The physical destruction and loss of life on both sides was almost beyond comprehension, but the North suffered the greater damage, due to American saturation bombing and the scorched-earth policy of the retreating U.N. forces," historian Charles K. Armstrong wrote in an essay for the *Asia-Pacific Journal*:

American planes dropped 635,000 tons of bombs on Korea—that is, essentially on North Korea—including 32,557 tons of napalm, compared to 503,000 tons of bombs dropped in the entire Pacific theatre of World War II.

The number of Korean dead, injured or missing by war's end approached three million, ten percent of the overall population. The majority of those killed were in the North . . . possibly twelve to fifteen percent of the population . . . a figure close to or surpassing the proportion of Soviet citizens killed in World War II.

U.S. officers and soldiers who surveyed the results of the air campaign in Korea were both awestruck and revolted.

"We burned down just about every city in North Korea and South Korea both," recalled Gen. Curtis LeMay. "We killed off over a million civilian Koreans and drove several million more from their homes, with the inevitable additional tragedies bound to ensue." (Darien Kavanaugh, "Why the Korean War Was One of the Deadliest Wars in Modern History," *NationalInterest.org*, May 2, 2017.)

It was because of that war that I was drafted and landed in Bautzen. Thirty miles away, in Dresden, I saw the unforgettable picture of its center: rubble, rubble, rubble; here and there the remains of a church stretching a skeleton arm upward. Renate recalled seeing the lit-up sky as a frightened child.

THERE WAS NO freedom from fear in the world. While I was in training as a soldier in Virginia, instructors did their best to explain why we might soon have to fight and die in Korea and why our country was so deeply involved there, and truly worldwide. An occasional news item told how we were also supporting the people of Iran in their brave fight to safeguard freedom and democracy from communism and implying how grateful the natives should be for U.S. altruism and moral dedication.

Sixty years later, the U.S. National Security Archive at George Washington University published declassified CIA documents revealing facts about Iran: "The military coup that overthrew Mosaddeq and his National Front cabinet was carried out under CIA direction as an act of U.S. foreign policy, conceived and approved at the highest levels of government." The documents detail how the United States, with British help, engineered the coup in August 1953 to overthrow the elected head of government, a man committed to democratic values but insisting that oil should be nationalized, so as to reinstall a monarchy for the next twenty-six years, with a Shah, notorious for bloody repression of all opposition but committed to safeguarding the West's oil interests.

In 1954, it was Guatemala's turn to be rescued. Not until 2011 did the *New York Times* tell the story:

> More than a half-century after Guatemala's elected president Jacobo Arbenz Guzman was overthrown in a coup planned by the CIA and forced into a wandering exile, President Alvaro Colom apologized on Thursday for what he called a "great crime." "That day changed Guatemala and we have not recuperated from it yet," he said. "It was a crime to Guatemalan society and it was an act of aggression to a government starting its democratic spring." . . .
>
> The Eisenhower Administration painted the coup as an uprising that rid the hemisphere of a Communist government backed by Moscow. But Mr. Arbenz's real offense was to confiscate unused land owned by the United Fruit Company to redistribute under a land reform plan and to pay compensation for the vastly understated value the company had claimed for its tax payments. . . .
>
> The CIA organized a paramilitary force to overthrow Arbenz and put Carlos Castillo Armas in his place. This was also considered a great success within U.S. government circles, another way to protect U.S. interests in Latin America. (Elisabeth Malkin, "An Apology for a Guatemala Coup 57 Years Later," *New York Times*, October 20, 2011.)

As a result, Guatemala was ruled for three decades by military men responsible for the murder of at least 200,000 people, mostly Mayan peasant men, women, and children. Arbenz (1913–1971) died mysteriously in a tub with scalding water while exiled in Mexico.

THE CHURCH COMMITTEE of the Senate, investigating the torture and assassination of the first elected prime minister of the Republic of Congo, Patrice Lumumba, found it likely that President Eisenhower's expression of strong concern about Lumumba at a meeting of the National Security Council on 18 August 1960 was taken by [CIA Director] Allen Dulles as authority to go ahead. "Shortly thereafter the CIA's clandestine service formulated a plot to assassinate Lumumba. The plot proceeded to the point that lethal substances and instruments specifically intended for use in an assassination were delivered by the CIA to the Congo Station."

It seems the CIA helped topple Lumumba, who was also a poet, but units from Belgium, until then the colonial rulers, were a bit quicker in capturing, torturing, and killing him. Then Washington stepped in to establish a thirty-two-year dictatorship under army officer Joseph Mobutu, who had aided in the murder. It granted him more than $1 billion in "aid"; many presidents welcomed him to the White House; George H. W. Bush called him "one of our most valued friends." His private fortune, estimated at $4 billion, included grand villas in Europe and many palaces and a yacht at home, while his country, one of the richest in mineral wealth, sank into dire poverty and internal warfare, rape and the death of millions. In the nearly sixty years since, that huge country has never been free of fear.

MOST FAMOUS, THOUGH never successful, were the attempts to assassinate Fidel Castro, planned in collusion with Mafia bosses cut off from lucrative gambling and prostitution by the Cuban revolution. The Church Committee described eight attempts before 1965; Cuba's counterintelligence chief estimated 638 schemes in all, approved of by every president from Eisenhower and Kennedy. The "Operation Mongoose" plans included botulism-poisoned cigars, an exploding cigar, a bacilli-infected scuba-diving suit, and a booby-trapped conch on the sea bottom, a ballpoint pen containing a lethal hypodermic syringe. There was a plan to explode ninety kilograms of explosives under a podium in Panama where Castro was to speak. His ex-lover, Marita Lorenz, agreed to aid the CIA and smuggle a jar of poisoned

cold cream into his room. When Castro learned of the plot, he report-
edly gave her a gun and told her to kill him, but her nerves failed. Castro
once said, "If surviving assassination attempts were an Olympic event,
I would win the gold medal."

I WAS ALREADY living with my family in a pleasant, new East Berlin
neighborhood, replacing a scene of ruin and rubble much like
that in Dresden, when mass-scale bombing and killing exploded
again. In 1945, Vietnam had declared its independence of French
colonial rule, using almost the same words as those proclaimed in
Philadelphia in 1776. By 1954 its determined fighters—I had seen
one of them bounced joyously into the air in Prague—had finally
forced the French occupiers out. But before long, the U.S. Army
marched and flew in to replace them and stayed ten long years, bringing death to two or three million Vietnamese and genetic damage to
a million more. At Documentary Film Week in Leipzig I saw pictures
of the resistance against the mostly drafted GI forces. I also saw films
of action around the globe against the bombing, the poisoned forests,
burned villages, and dead women and children, including scenes of
U.S. veterans dramatically opposing the killing they had recently
taken part in.

I also read Martin Luther King's courageous, stirring speech in The
Riverside Church on April 4,1967—in a way a new, intense proclama-
tion of Roosevelt's call for freedom from fear:

> I knew that I could never again raise my voice against the violence
> of the oppressed in the ghettos without having first spoken clearly to
> the greatest purveyor of violence in the world today: my own govern-
> ment. . . .
>
>   This business of burning human beings with napalm, of filling our
> nation's homes with orphans and widows, of injecting poisonous
> drugs of hate into the veins of peoples normally humane, of sending
> men home from dark and bloody battlefields physically handicapped
> and psychologically deranged, cannot be reconciled with wisdom,
> justice, and love. A nation that continues year after year to spend

more money on military defense than on programs of social uplift is approaching spiritual death. . . .

Increasingly, by choice or by accident, this is the role our nation has taken. . . . It is with such activity that the words of the late John F. Kennedy come back to haunt us. Five years ago he said, "Those who make peaceful revolution impossible will make violent revolution inevitable." Increasingly, by choice or by accident, this is the role our nation has taken, the role of those who make peaceful revolution impossible by refusing to give up the privileges and the pleasures that come from the immense profits of overseas investments. I am convinced that if we are to get on to the right side of the world revolution, we as a nation must undergo a radical revolution of values. We must rapidly begin the shift from a thing-oriented society to a person-oriented society. When machines and computers, profit motives and property rights, are considered more important than people, the giant triplets of racism, extreme materialism, and militarism are incapable of being conquered.

The "extreme materialism" condemned by Dr. King, basically the attack on our planet's climate and welfare, made his warning about the giant triplets as relevant today as it ever was. But after this speech, one year before his murder, he was angrily maligned, in fact virtually ostracized, even by earlier supporters, a matter rarely mentioned in present-day paeans.

That was in 1967. But as the war continued in the early 1970s, and as the freelance reporter Seymour Hersh published pictures and details of the massacre in the village of My Lai, where nearly 500 men, women, and infants were murdered at close range by American troops, when the Viet Cong's Tet offensive in South Vietnam dispelled Pentagon assurances that there was "light at the end of the tunnel," hundreds of thousands of Americans joined with people all over the world to demand an end to the killing, the burning of villages, and bombing of towns, cities, fields, and forests. Americans defied Johnson, Nixon, and Kissinger and demanded peace, in the process moving the country, it seemed then, in a better anti-war direction influenced by the "Vietnam syndrome."

Peace was finally won in Vietnam, where Roosevelt's rejection of "the crash of a bomb" had hardly been heeded; more bombs were dropped in Vietnam than on Germany in the Second World War, often with additives like napalm and Agent Orange. It was rather like a second Korea.

74—Chile and Latin America

The war hawks who lost the Vietnam War could not metamorphose into butterflies or doves of peace and showed it in an episode that took place while that war was just winding down.

I have mentioned the World Youth Festival in East Berlin in 1973, an exciting week with countless cultural attractions and, perhaps most interestingly, discussions between young people from East and West, usually surrounded by swarms listening carefully or trying to get a word in, in streets and squares closed off to all but pedestrians. Most popular foreign participants were surely the Chileans, with their great enthusiasm and great music. They represented the heart of the festival for many, who like me admired their "Milk for Every Child" campaign, their artistic, militant graffiti, and bold nationalization of the copper mines. We felt true affection for mild-mannered Salvador Allende and looked to Chile for tolerant ideas and methods that might be emulated here.

That explains the intense shock and mourning when, a month later, the putsch came, with the death of Allende and, with him, the Chilean experiment—and bringing years of prison, torture, disappearance and exile. I cannot forget the spontaneous surge of many thousands of grieving Berliners onto Unter den Linden Boulevard, the most moving demonstration I have ever seen there.

Some in Santiago were able to escape thanks to quick, tactical emergency aid by the GDR Embassy staff. Several thousand exiles were given refuge in the GDR, where a few became my friends. One Chilean who received asylum in the GDR, where she finished her medical studies, was Michelle Bachelet, who became Chile's president in 2006 and again in 2014.

Perhaps it is not surprising that the putsch and the deaths and violence that followed surely strengthened the determination of GDR leaders not to let the same thing happen to them, or to relax checks and controls.

A major reason why Allende's government was destroyed was because of its nationalization of property owned by the powerful U.S. companies Anaconda and Kennecott, then two of the world's major copper producers, as well as the telephone system largely owned by the U.S. giant, International Telephone & Telegraph (ITT), which also controlled the right-wing newspaper *El Mercurio*. Allende had called this a step against exploitation and poverty and toward socialism. President Nixon and Secretary of State Henry Kissinger called it trespassing, with Chile crossing their self-determined but sacred red lines. In "our Western hemisphere," Kissinger made clear, "I don't see why we need to stand by and watch a country go communist due to the irresponsibility of its people. The issues are much too important for the Chilean voters to be left to decide for themselves." (Peter Kornbluh, "Kissinger and Chile," *National Security Archive*, Washington, D.C.: New Press, September 11, 2013.)

The tragedy in Chile was matched less than a decade later by events far to the north in Nicaragua, where a frightful dictator named Somoza was forced out by a revolutionary movement called the Sandinistas. When the new government set out, as in Cuba thirty years earlier, to educate the largely illiterate population, provide free health care, and overcome miserable poverty, it was now President Reagan's turn to get worried. A force of rough CIA-backed "contra" rebels, partly financed, unofficially, by drug dealing, was soon actively attacking Nicaraguan villages. The Sandinista leader Ortega has changed greatly since those years, but I believe the two conflicting programs remain basically the same.

To train the Contras, a CIA manual called *Psychological Operations in Guerrilla War* was used. Leaked in 1984, it recommended "selective use of violence for propagandistic effects" and to "neutralize" government officials. Nicaraguan Contras were taught to lead "demonstrators into clashes with the authorities, to provoke riots or shootings, which lead to the killing of one or more persons, who will be seen as the martyrs; this situation should be taken advantage of immediately against the Government to create even bigger conflicts." This method, almost to the letter, seems to have guided similar rebels frequently— in Ukraine, Venezuela, and, while I write, once again in Nicaragua. It has usually been accompanied by economic sabotage and a trade embargo. In the 1980s, underwater mines were laid in Nicaragua's port of Corinto, despite condemnation by the International Court of Justice and the United Nations. That didn't bother the Reagan government any more than the almost total unanimity of the world against the U.S. blockade of Cuba has bothered his successors in the White House, with the one hesitant exception of Obama.

75—Wars and Threats of Wars

The decade-long conflagration in Vietnam ended dramatically in 1975 on the roof of the U.S. Embassy in Saigon. Any hopes that peaceful times might follow were soon dashed as new conflicts followed, bitter and bloody, from Cambodia to the Falkland Islands. In the 1980s, Ronald Reagan still found it urgently necessary to "open the gate" in Berlin and to further "close the missile gap" with the "evil empire," his name for the USSR. Such a gap had never existed, but a threatening military policy, "Star Wars," to be based in the stratosphere, impelled the Soviets to try to catch up, ruining themselves in the process. Speaking to evangelists, Reagan warned that "in your discussions of the nuclear freeze proposals" you should "not remove yourself from the struggle between right and wrong and good and evil . . . to write the final pages of the history of the Soviet Union. . . . Let us pray for the salvation of all those who live in that totalitarian darkness—pray they will discover the joy of knowing God."(Ronald Reagan, National Association of Evangelicals, Orlando, Florida, March 8, 1983.)

But even after Reagan's prayers had been answered and "fighting the evil empire" became obsolete, possible worry lines on armament company brows could be relaxed. Even before the Soviet flag was lowered from its Kremlin tower, Iraq had moved into Kuwait, allegedly after assurances by the U.S. ambassador, and the first President Bush moved to the rescue. But too many Americans, recalling Vietnam, were reluctant. For a fee of $10.7 million, a PR firm known for trying to convince people to smoke more cigarettes decided that atrocity stories worked best in winning approval for distant conflicts. A young woman from the diplomatic corps described tearfully on TV how she saw "babies torn out of incubators and thrown onto the cold floor" by Iraqi soldiers in Kuwait. Though fully invented, a total lie, this worked! But when U.S. planes bombed the Amiriya bomb shelter in Baghdad during that first war against Iraq, burning 408 civilians alive, it was hardly noticed.

In 1992–93, Bush and Clinton followed with Black Hawk helicopters in Somalia, bombers against Serbia in 1994, and again in the "Kosovo War" in 1999. And this time, finally, after unification had eliminated the GDR, Germany could once again flex its military biceps, forget any previous moral taboos and send in its air force.

In 1997, with the USSR long gone, a Project for the New American Century (PNAC) was hatched out by the right-wing plotters William Kristol and Robert Kagan and the politicians Dick Cheney, Donald Rumsfeld, and Paul Wolfowitz. Its aim was to maintain "global U.S. preeminence, precluding the rise of a great power rival, and shaping the international security order in line with American principles and interests." In 2001, a new savior arrived, the ex-president's somewhat benighted son, George W. Bush, and he surrounded himself with just those martial men: Cheney as vice president, Rumsfeld as secretary of defense, Wolfowitz as his deputy secretary. Using the emotions aroused by the 9/11 Trade Center attack, they launched the endless "war on terrorism" they had been working toward.

In a TV interview years later, General Wesley Clark spilled some beans:

> About ten days after 9/11 I went through the Pentagon and one of the generals called me in. He said . . . "We've made the decision, we're going to war with Iraq." This was on or about the 20th of September. I said, "We're going to war with Iraq? Why?" He said, "I guess it's like we don't know what to do about terrorists, but we've got a good

military and we can take down governments. . . . I guess if the only tool you have is a hammer, every problem has to look like a nail."

So I came back to see him a few weeks later, and by that time we were bombing in Afghanistan. I said, "Are we still going to war with Iraq?" And he said, "Oh, it's worse than that." He reached over on his desk. He picked up a piece of paper. And he said, "I just got this down from upstairs today"—meaning the Secretary of Defense's office— and he said, "This is a memo that describes how we're going to take out seven countries in five years, starting with Iraq, and then Syria, Lebanon, Libya, Somalia, Sudan and, finishing off, Iran..." (General Wesley Clark, on Amy Goodman, *Democracy Now*, March 2, 2007.)

A lot of water has flowed under the bridges of the Potomac and the Euphrates since then. But aside from a few alterations, this plan seems to have embodied U.S. foreign policy after 9/11. Murderous wars, begun in 2002 in Afghanistan and 2003 in Iraq, were kept going by order of Obama and Trump, then metastasized to Somalia and served as models for the destruction of Libya in 2011. Sudan was split apart. Saudi Arabia was supported with weapons, fueling planes, and radar assistance in its genocidal air war against Yemen. After 2011, fanatic gangs in Syria were able to obtain modern American weapons, and Barack Obama achieved a presidential record, engaging simultaneously in seven wars. His rationale, contained in his parting advice to his successor, had a familiar ring: "American leadership in this world really is indispensable. It's up to us, through action and example, to sustain the international order that's expanded steadily since the end of the Cold War, and upon which our own wealth and safety depend." (*ReaderSupportedNews.org*, September 4, 2017.)

I wonder which action and which example he was thinking of. Afghanistan? Or Libya? Honduras? Iraq? Or the accelerated use of cruise missiles and drones?

His hoped-for successor, Hillary Clinton, used tougher tones in her retaliatory threats when, speaking of Iran, a nation of more than 80 million people, she warned: "In the next 10 years, during which they might foolishly consider launching an attack on Israel, we would be able to totally obliterate them." (ABC, *Good Morning America*, April 22, 2008.)

President Trump, not to be outdone, boasted: "Our military has never been stronger. Each day new equipment is delivered; new and beautiful equipment, the best in the world—the best anywhere in the world, by far." (*Washington Post*, September 8, 2017.)

It was he who once threatened to wreak "fire and fury" on North Korea and its 25 million people, declaring that he was "ready, willing and able" to "totally destroy" that land. Perhaps he was unaware that this mission had already been accomplished, between 1950 and 1953. But then later, amazingly, as with so many of his flip-flops, he met happily with Kim Jong-un. I can only hope that this means peace in that troubled peninsula. And not only there, for he has since followed it with a peaceful meeting with Vladimir Putin. He was immediately bombarded by countless loud voices of people who evidently preferred confrontation to meeting together and cooling off. I only hope that more peaceful views win strength before any new and perhaps final disaster.

76— Who's to Blame?

Without minimizing Roosevelt's other demands, freedom from fear of violent death, whether through attacks, drones, bombs, or, most frightening, atomic war, certainly remains the leading position. Who is really to blame for this, for the world's failure to overcome an unceasing list of oft gigantic human tragedies?

Among the guilty ones, generals hoping for bright new medals and more polished stars can be found in many countries. But they are hardly the basic instigators. In the United States, so madly addicted to hurling death down from the skies—in Korea, Vietnam, Laos, Cambodia, Cuba, Panama, Serbia, Iraq, Afghanistan, Libya, Somalia, Syria—the main culprits, I feel certain, are the same ones a Republican president and top general, Dwight D. Eisenhower, once warned us about: the Military Industrial Complex:

Now this conjunction of an immense military establishment and a large arms industry is new in the American experience. The total influence—economic, political, even spiritual—is felt in every city, every statehouse, every office of the Federal government. . . . In the councils of government, we must guard against the acquisition of unwarranted influence, whether sought or unsought, by the military-industrial complex. The potential for the disastrous rise of misplaced power exists and will persist. We must never let the weight of this combination endanger our liberties or democratic processes. We should take nothing for granted. Only an alert and knowledgeable citizenry can compel the proper meshing of the huge industrial and military machinery of defense with our peaceful methods and goals, so that security and liberty may prosper together. (Dwight D. Eisenhower, TV address, January 12, 1961.)

Despite doubts about "proper meshing," his warning, still so valid, does not only apply in the United States. Among those making tanks, subs, warplanes, carriers, drones, missiles, and Armageddon-aimed nuclear warheads are EADS, which is West European, with strong German participation; BAE Systems, which is British; and in many other countries, there are far more than enough! But most of the biggest are in the United States: Raytheon, Boeing, General Dynamics, Lockheed Martin, Northrop Grumman—all competing for shares of the billions allotted by Congress, with the encouragement and signature of every president, at least since Eisenhower.

Fifty-nine Tomahawk missiles fired in Syria in April 2017 cost taxpayers about $1.5 million each and surely carried the spirits of Raytheon up into the clouds. They hardly worried Raytheon boss Thomas A. Kennedy; his income alone in 2015 had already reached $12,800,000. Figuratively rubbing his hands in expectation, he had predicted "a significant uptick for defense solutions across the board in multiple countries in the Middle East. . . . It's all the turmoil they have going on, whether the turmoil's occurring in Yemen, whether it's with the Houthis, whether it's occurring in Syria or Iraq, with ISIS." (Lee Fang and Zaid Jilani, "Defense Contractors Cite 'Benefits' of Escalating Conflicts in the Middle East," *TheIntercept.com*, December 4, 2015.)

A rival at Lockheed Martin, Marilyn A. Hewson, began her career with the CIA, then switched to hardware. Her firm's sales to the Pentagon include a bloody mix: Trident missiles for submarines, with multi-target thermonuclear warheads, Sikorsky helicopters, and immensely costly F-35 fighters. Hewson has ambitious plans for Southeast Asia and her company cooperates smoothly with her old boss, the CIA. She is handsomely repaid for her efforts, in 2014 with $19 million.

A leading Pentagon official reported proudly that the Air Force regularly tests Minuteman-3 intercontinental ballistic missiles, each with three separate targets; at least fifteen had been tested since January 2011: "And that is a signal . . . that if necessary we are prepared to use nuclear weapons in defense of our country." How much did the executives and stockholders of Boeing take home for each such Minuteman? And who threatens our country enough to make them necessary? (Deputy Pentagon Chief Robert Work, "U.S. Military: "We Are Prepared to Use Nuclear Weapons,' EcoWatch, *CommonDreams. org*, May 8, 2017.)

For the armament folk, each such purchase, each such test, and, best of all, each possible use of such monsters may mean misery, death, and ruined cities for others, but for the bosses it means one or two more oversized mansions, yachts, and jets or more disguised additions to accounts on palm tree islands or with tight-mouthed Alpine bankers. They are never satiated; they must grow or decline. Hangars and launching sites must be emptied to make way for "improved," vastly overpriced new products.

Investing happily in such mass murder enterprises are most of the world's big banks. Leading the pack, as with the Nazis in the 1930s and 1940s, is Deutsche Bank, providing loans to thirteen weapons producers like Northrop Grumman ($468 million), Boeing ($561 million), and BAE Systems ($715 million) and owning bundles of their shares or bonds. Such rewarding ties can make up for errors and losses in more peaceful endeavors.

These folks have accomplices: politicians who do their bidding, vote for budget billions, and are quick to "send messages" to potential foes, ominously warning them that "all options are on the table." And their media collaborators happily and obediently broadcast such messages and such options.

Rewards for the generosity of the willing warriors in Congress are gifts of election funds, often decisive for their campaigns but mere crumbs from the many-tiered wedding cake of profits they help the donors to bake. A tit-for-tat logic is involved; in case they lose elections, the companies they once favored offer them cushy jobs, either as advisers with "good connections" or as lobbyists, who can discreetly deliver well-filled envelopes into the eager, sweaty hands of erstwhile colleagues in key committee positions.

Here's a sample: In an impassioned speech to the House Intelligence Committee, Adam Schiff (CA), its top Democrat, lambasted Russian interference in the 2016 election and tried to explain the threat: "We're in a competition with Russia right now. They are championing autocracy all over the world. We are promoting democracy." (House Intelligence Committee hearing, March 20, 2017.) Schiff did not mention, nor did much of the press, that Raytheon hosted a fundraiser for his election campaign in 2013. In line with promoting democracy, he voted for the Iraq War, in favor of arming Syrian warrior rebels, for arming Ukrainians, for intervention in Afghanistan and in Libya. Raytheon was hardly displeased.

"Promoting democracy" has meant tightening a military noose around Russia, from Norway and Estonia, almost within earshot of Russia's second city, St. Petersburg, down to its only warm water exit to the world along the Black Sea. It has led to big U.S. bases in Kosovo and Iraq, naval bases in Bahrein and Djibouti, five new bases in the Philippines, and a strengthening of older ones around China, from Guam to the bases in Japanese Okinawa and South Korea, both hated by the people there. The Near East is plastered with such bases, almost the entire world is spotted with almost 800 of them, large and small. And each one must be stocked with expensive weaponry. (Russia, by the way, has nine, mostly left over in former states of the USSR.)

Although the United States already spends more on its armed forces than China, Russia, Saudi Arabia, Britain, India, France, and Japan

combined, in February 2018 Congress approved President Trump's
call for an increase, even higher than Obama's Pentagon budget—
$350 billion extra to further modernize American weaponry. Leading
Democrats voted "Aye." Nancy Pelosi emailed them: "In our negotiations, Congressional Democrats have been fighting for increases in
funding for defense." Sen. Charles Schumer's office announced: "We
fully support President Trump's Defense Department's request."

Russia, spending only one-tenth as much on armaments, will again
feel it necessary to expand its atomic sector in response. Today's
nuclear powers, United States, Russia, Britain, China, India, Pakistan,
Israel, and North Korea, possess 16,000 atomic warheads; thousands
of them, sharp-nosed and polished, are in constant, nervous readiness;
a handful could wreck our planet and all life on it. And previous agree-
ments on arms limitations are falling by the wayside.

In Germany, not to be left behind, Bundeswehr troops joined in the
NATO "exercises" near the Russian border, shudderingly recalling the
German invasion in that area in 1941, with the siege of Leningrad costing over a million and a half deaths from starvation. In all, that war cost
Germany 8 million lives and the USSR about 27 million. But some
leaders of Germany love being the No. 1 power again, at least in Europe
and very high up on the world list. Defense Minister Ursula von der
Leyen can't get enough weaponry, not only as part of NATO but for a
new European Union military force.

German armament kings, with a hundred years of experience including two world wars, are discovering an affection for their own drones
and warheads, not just those managed by the United States or made
in Israel. As future banner bearers and principals in a future European
army, they have been rehearsing for it in Afghanistan and Mali, recalling
old traditions on how best to kill people. And make plenty of profits.
Macron in Paris is with them too, as are many, many others!

77—Mergers and Monopolies

While the armament industry, also called the defense industry or "security sector," and the banks are perhaps the strongest and certainly the most dangerous of the giants, there are many other potent players. I can again turn to the words of Franklin Delano Roosevelt, spoken after the worst effects of the Great Depression had been eased somewhat—but had hardly weakened the grip of some powerful dynasties:

> Through new uses of corporations, banks and securities, new machinery of industry and agriculture, of labor and capital—all undreamed of by the fathers—the whole structure of modern life was impressed into this royal service. . . .
>
> It was natural and perhaps human that the privileged princes of these new economic dynasties, thirsting for power, reached out for control over Government itself. They created a new despotism and wrapped it in the robes of legal sanction. In its service new mercenaries sought to regiment the people, their labor, and their property. . . .
>
> For too many of us the political equality we once had won was meaningless in the face of economic inequality. A small group had concentrated into their own hands an almost complete control over other people's property, other people's money, other people's labor—other people's lives. (Franklin Delano Roosevelt, Nomination acceptance speech, Philadelphia, June 27, 1936.)

Four months later, after a rough electoral campaign, he spoke even more vigorously:

> We had to struggle with the old enemies of peace—business and financial monopoly, speculation, reckless banking, class antagonism, sectionalism, war profiteering. . . . They had begun to consider the Government of the United States as a mere appendage to their own affairs. We know now that Government by organized money is just as dangerous as Government by organized mob. Never before in all our history have these forces been so united against one candidate as they stand today. They are unanimous in their hate for me—and I welcome their hatred. (Franklin Delano Roosevelt, Campaign speech, Madison Square Garden, October 31, 1936.)

If Bernie Sanders or anyone like him should run in 2020, such words could become more timely than ever.

Since Roosevelt's day, mergers have cut down the list of "biggies," making the remaining giants more powerful than ever. This process was described a few years ago in the *Washington Post*:

> Like immense amoebas on the prowl, America's already huge corporations are combining like nobody's business. In recent months, Walgreens bought Rite Aid, uniting two of the nation's three largest drugstore chains; in beer land, Molson Coors is buying Miller; mega-health insurers Aetna and Anthem, respectively, bought mega-health insurers Humana and Cigna; Heinz bought Kraft, good news for those who take ketchup with their cheese; and American Airlines completed its absorption of U.S. Airways, reducing the number of major U.S. airlines to four, which now control 70 percent of the air travel market. On Wall Street, the five biggest commercial banks hold nearly half of the nation's bank assets; in 1990, the five biggest held just 10 percent. (Harold Meyerson, "We need a new trust-busting movement in America," *Washington Post*, November 11, 2015.)

The process is not slowing down. With the huge merger, AT&T with Time Warner in 2018, the resulting handshake was worth $85.4 billion and, some experts think, could lead to another big wave of takeovers, leaving in its wake fewer choices for consumers and higher television and internet prices in a sector obviously affecting people's thinking.

MERGERS WITH A resulting increase in monopolization hit in nearly every field. During a visit to my hometown, New York, I was affected very directly. Being diabetic, I must give myself two insulin shots a day, a bothersome ritual that, perforce, I have grown used to. But on this trip, I stupidly left all but one of my insulin pens in my Berlin fridge. That meant a clinic visit, a blood test, and some red tape, but then I got a prescription and marched happily to a pharmacy to buy a boxful of five pens. "That will be $540," the clerk said, almost bowling me over. "What? In Berlin a box costs me 10 euros!" (I did not add that in the GDR there had been no charge at all.) The pharmacist shrugged, admitted that he knew of the problem but couldn't help it. I fetched my wallet from my hotel to pay this idiotic price, hoping for insurance compensation in Germany. On my return, he wanted "only" $450! The price was evidently elastic! Although forty-five times more expensive, the box I received was exactly the same as those I buy in Berlin, made by one of three giants who rule the field, a Lilly field in this case. And my insurance company did not cover the cost! Those three prosperous insulin makers can be sure of many future diabetes customers; two soft drink firms and a few fast-food chains are busy exerting worldwide pressure so kids everywhere can continue to enjoy their tasty products.

Another merger, now evidently certain, and valued at $66 billion, is alarming in a very different way.

One partner is Monsanto. Once a producer of the poisonous Agent Orange, which devastated forests in Vietnam, it is now of interest because of its worldwide activity in spreading genetically modified seeds, so-called "suicide seeds." When crops are harvested from them, the seeds they produce are sterile, so farmers are forced to buy seeds each year anew and, of course, from Monsanto. Some farmers try to resist this domination, which also depletes the wide, important genetic variation of plants. Since Monsanto seeds are patented, whenever they blow onto other fields in the area and Monsanto's many agents discover them, Monsanto can sue for encroaching on patent rights. The control by this one company and the damage it does to small-scale farmers has forced tens of thousands to go out of business, especially in India, where it caused more and more desperate suicides. But Monsanto also spends millions in the United States to pressure or buy lawmakers, even in wealthy California.

Wherever countries try to resist such disastrous expansion and protect their farmers and their environment, also vigorously in Europe, they are subjected to extreme pressure from the U.S. State Department. "Between 2007 and 2009, the State Department sent annual cables to encourage the use of agricultural biotechnology, directing every diplomatic post worldwide to pursue an active biotech agenda that promotes agricultural biotechnology, encourages the export of biotech crops and foods and advocates for pro-biotech policies and laws." (Biotech Ambassadors, *Food & Water Watch*, May 14, 2013)

Monsanto's merger partner, Bayer, also sins against nature and agriculture. But for me, although the men involved are long dead, its history is of greatest interest. During the war, for instance, Bayer wrote the commander of Auschwitz concentration camp to inquire about "purchasing" 150 women for experiments with sleep-inducing drugs. After compromising on the price, the letter from Bayer said: "We received your reply. Select 150 women in the best possible state of health, and as soon as you inform us that you are ready, we will fetch them. . . ." And later: "Despite their emaciated condition they were acceptable. . . . We will keep you informed on the progress of the experiments." And again later: "The experiments were concluded. All persons died. We will soon get in touch with you regarding a new shipment." (Central Commission of Investigation of Nazi Crimes in Poland, *Konzentrationslager Oswiecim-Brzezinka—Auschwitz-Birkenau,* Nuremberg Documents NJ. 7184, Warsaw: Jan Sehn, 1957, 89.)

Bayer certainly plans no such human experiments currently, and Monsanto's Agent Orange is, so far as I know, not now being sprayed from the air on any peasants' fields. But the two hope to become the world's largest private chemical corporation, overtaking Bayer's former wartime partner, BASF. It would control one-third of all commercial seeds, one quarter of all pesticides. Farmers, sharpen your pitchforks for big battles. And bees, beetles, butterflies, frogs, salamanders, and songbirds—beware!

78—Are Social Media Social?

In the summer of 2017, the Federal Trade Commission (FTC) approved the purchase by Amazon of Whole Foods. The merger cost a cool $13.7 billion and chilled the hearts of the entire grocery business; indeed, it threatened the whole retail industry. This trend, which for me is more worrisome than any other except for the armament czars, involves all four giant tech platforms, Amazon, Google, Facebook, Twitter, and how they are gaining more and more power. K. Sabeel Rahman, from Brooklyn Law School, analyzed some reasons for such worries. Here are a few excerpts:

> The danger of the "platform power" accumulated by Amazon, Google, Facebook, and Twitter arises from their ability to control the foundational infrastructure of our economic, informational, and political life. Even if they didn't spend a dime on lobbying or influencing elected officials, this power would still pose a grave threat to democracy and economic opportunity. The fact that these companies provide enormously popular and useful goods and services is indisputable—but also beside the point. The central issue here is not simply the value for the consumer. Instead it is vast, unaccountable private power over the foundations of contemporary society and politics. In a word, the central issue is democracy. . . .
>
> Democracy cannot persist in an information environment that is designed to maximize advertisers' reach without regard for the larger political and social consequences. . . .
>
> This kind of infrastructural power also explains the myriad concerns about how platforms might taint, skew, or undermine our political system itself. . . . The reality is that our economy and politics are already governed and already regulated. They are governed by the opaque judgments of Amazon, Google, Facebook, and Twitter—judgments that are not subject to the mechanisms for representation, participation, or accountability that we would expect of similarly empowered governmental bodies. (K. Sabeel Rahman, "Monopoly Men," *Boston Review*, October 11, 2017.)

The fortune of Amazon boss Jeff Bezos, listed as richest man in the world, just passed the $150 billion mark, $55 billion ahead of Microsoft Corp. co-founder Bill Gates, the world's second-richest. Bezos makes more income in ten seconds than the median Amazon employee makes in a year. Amazon paid no federal income taxes last year, but up to one out of three Amazon workers in some states relies on food stamps to feed their families, food stamps paid for by average taxpayers. Probably due to public attacks by Sen. Bernie Sanders, Amazon announced on October 2, 2018, a pay raise for U.S. employees to $15 per hour, with many devious cuts.

But can we trust any of these big guys at all?

79—Opioids

Have you ever heard of the Sackler family? If you like museums you will certainly have passed Sackler wings in New York's Metropolitan Museum of Art, the Louvre, and the Royal Academy, Sackler museums at Harvard and Peking Universities or a Sackler gallery at the Smithsonian. The Guggenheim in New York has a Sackler Center, the American Museum of Natural History a Sackler Educational Lab. A Sackler Staircase was designed for Berlin's Jewish Museum, a Sackler Escalator for the Tate Modern; a Sackler Courtyard at London's Victoria and Albert Museum glitters with 11,000 white porcelain tiles. A pink rose is named after a Sackler. So is an asteroid.

Are the Sacklers artists, scientists, altruistic philanthropists? No. The original Sackler brothers were psychiatrists and pharmaceutical researchers in New York. They and many of their offspring were also good at business; the family, about twenty in number, is now worth about $13 billion.

But you must have heard of the opioid crisis. More than 200,000 people in the United States have died from overdoses of prescribed painkillers. It is estimated that 100 or more Americans die each day from this same cause, averaging more than weapon or car crash deaths.

It began with a medicine called OxyContin, sold by a company called Purdue, both invented and run by the so very artistically inclined Sacklers, a connection rarely even whispered by the media.

The medicine contained a morphine-like substance, meant for people on their death beds. It greatly eased their pain, enabled them to sleep through the night, and involved no problem with addiction since its patients would not live that long.

But then people began to use it who were very much alive—until they began to lose their health. While its painkilling effectiveness tapered off, many found it almost impossible to break with it.

Drug-dealers discovered that you could "grind up, chew up, snort, dissolve, and inject the pills." OxyContin's sales started out small in 1996 but Purdue doubled its staff to 600 to keep pushing it, targeting especially general practitioners but also dentists, OB/GYNs, physician assistants, and nurses. By 2001, OxyContin sales surged past $1 billion. As one ex-salesman described it, "It was sell, sell, sell. We were directed to lie. Why mince words about it? Greed took hold and over-ruled everything. They saw that potential for billions of dollars and just went after it." Kickbacks, special rebates, generous refunds for pharmacists, thirty-day starter coupons for patients, academics getting grants, medical journals getting millions in advertising, senators and members of Congress on key committees getting donations from Purdue and members of the Sackler family. Doctors were most important and were flown to "seminars," actually just golf trips to Pebble Beach. For "problem doctors" with misgivings, there might be a dinner where "they could make a little fifteen-minute talk and receive $500." By 2001 the number of OxyContin prescriptions soared to nearly six million, often to poor people troubled by pain, illness or existential worries.

Many doctors were finally arrested, and some Purdue executives were fined. But thousands are still dying, the Sacklers are still raking it in, while their names and their rule are still largely secret and sacred. I must visit one of those museums to see if their names and wealthy donations are still honored. (Christopher Glazek, "The Secretive Family Making Billions from the Opioid Crisis," *Esquire*, October 18, 2017.)

80—Ecology

If we view ecological disaster as a result of the materialism castigated by Martin Luther King, then the same evil triplets he warned of—militarism, materialism, and racism—confront us today in our search for freedom from fear. The struggle to save the environment and the planet has become far more urgent than in his day. An important part of Roosevelt's New Deal was the Civilian Conservation Corps (CCC). Between 1933 and 1942 it ran camps for three million jobless, unmarried young men, seventeen to twenty-eight, who set up or improved national parks and planted three billion trees, while receiving a small but desperately needed sum for themselves and their parents. Many today don't consider jobless youth so important, nor trees, either, except as lumber, and I fear that big private companies hardly qualify as ideal social managers, and certainly not as environmentalists. Should foxes guard chicken coops?

The journalist and active ecologist Sarah van Gelder added her warning words:

> Pacific Northwest forests are on fire. Several blazes are out of control, threatening rural towns, jumping rivers and highways, and covering Portland, Seattle, and other cities in smoke and falling ash. Temperatures this summer are an average of 3.6 degrees higher than the last half of the 20th century. . . . Then there is the flooding in India and Bangladesh—less noted in U.S. news media—where 40 million were affected and 1,200 died. The scale and costs of these disasters pale in comparison to the impacts of hurricanes Harvey and Irma: Accuweather is estimating the combined cost of these unprecedented storms at $290 billion. (Sarah van Gelder, "90 Companies Helped Cause the Climate Crisis," *YES!Magazine.org*, September 13, 2017.)

Van Gelder's article quotes the journal *Climatic Change* with the claim that ninety companies are responsible for 42 to 50 percent of the increase in the Earth's surface temperature and 26 to 32 percent of sea level rise. She finds their guilt compounded because the worst climate spoilers knew full well that their carbon emissions and other pollutants are dangerous. Exxon-Mobil knew as early as 1981 of the damage it was doing but instead of trying to improve conditions, it spent millions paying all-too-willing scientists and editors to hoodwink the world:

firstly, there is no climate change, secondly, if there is one then it's not because of human activities, and thirdly, if it is, then our company is completely innocent! Numerous politicians got an incitement to pass this wisdom on and act accordingly. One U.S. senator, Jim Inhofe (R-OK), grinningly displayed a snowball in the summer to disprove climate warming.

The fossil fuel industry was always the nastiest culprit. It was oil that ruined large sections of the giant Niger Delta in West Africa, robbing its inhabitants of clean water, fish, and their livelihoods. The British-led firm BP, because of its greed, smeared the Gulf of Mexico with oil, ruining sea life and the coastal economy possibly beyond real repair.

An earlier event in the Caspian Sea had been hushed up, obviously for political reasons, until WikiLeaks revealed how close BP had come to a major disaster near Baku in Azerbaijan. Edward Chow from the Center for Strategic and International Studies in Washington said: "Unless you were on the inside you didn't know how serious it was."

President Bill Clinton had evidently urged Azerbaijan's President Aliyev to construct a pipeline link with Europe as part of "a very strategic plan" to bypass Russia and Iran. Then one morning in September 2008 a blowout in a gas-injection well forced the evacuation of 212 workers and shut down large parts of offshore production, depriving the Azerbaijan government of revenues of up to $50 million a day until it was repaired. BP concluded that "a bad cement job" caused the leak, just like years later in the Gulf of Mexico. No one really knows how much damage was done to the Caspian and its coast.

Chevron was responsible for more than 18 billion gallons of oil and toxic waste dumped into the Amazonia region of Ecuador; Texaco was actually to blame, but it had been swallowed up by Chevron. Some called this the worst case of oil pollution in history, thirty times worse than the *Valdez* spill in Alaska which, tragically enough, was Exxon-Mobil's doings. And more damage is promised in the Alaskan and Russian Arctic.

Like the oil men, the big automakers have outdone each other in poisoning the atmosphere and cheating on emission checkups. Volkswagen Group admitted in September 2015 that 482,000 of its diesel vehicles in the United States were cheating on emissions. The scandal snowballed; up to 11 million vehicles worldwide had been fitted with "deceptive defeat devices." Some U.S. scientists grew suspicious; checking on nitrogen oxide emissions, everything was clean, legal and nice during testing, but when the car moved on to speed down the Autobahn (or U.S. highway), it could do all the poisoning it wanted. It was crystal clear, unlike the emissions, that dividends and bonuses came first, before public health or even the law.

It has since turned out that not just VW but Daimler-Benz, Porsche, BMW, Audi and many suppliers were all cheating in this together, relying on the tolerance of government agents who were perhaps not averse to a little gift now and then.

Earlier, in October 2013, the environment ministers of the twenty-eight European Union countries had finally reached a compromise on reducing allowable emission values. Though no big step forward, it was a step. That is until, quite unexpectedly, the representative of Angela Merkel's government switched position and voted "No," vetoing even the weak compromise. A few days later, three members of the Quandt family, main owners of the BMW luxury car corporation, donated 690,000 euros to Merkel's party, the Christian Democratic Union (CDU). The Quandt family denied any connection between the two events; the close dates were purely coincidental.

BMW was not alone in such cozy rapport. The Social Democrats (SPD), for years the leading party in the state of Lower Saxony where VW is centered, has always protected its favorite child. And even Winfried Kretschmann, the only state minister-president of the Greens, stays on buddy-buddy terms with two of the biggest companies in his state of Baden-Wurttemberg, Porsche and Daimler, whose newest model he uses as official vehicle.

None of Germany's big carmakers need fear collapse, no matter what fines or other measures prove unavoidable. After all, the German economy relies on them.

There are large-scale sinners in nearly every country. And when I look back at the GDR, a basic element of this book, after all, I can recall that it had a truly model recycling program, kept a tight leash restricting "urban sprawl," and promoted ecologically highly preferable rail traffic over freight and passenger use of trucks and cars—but was a terrible offender with its energy and chemical production. Anyone approaching Bitterfeld or Wolfen (home of Agfa Film) or hoping to admire the little Pleisse River in Leipzig was well advised to keep a clothespin ready near their nose. But the GDR's survival remained dependent on its lignite, even though that earned it stinging criticism from all sides. It is interesting that many of the huge excavators and transport bridges used in the open-pit mines still grind away, twenty-seven years after the GDR departed, though now not out of necessity but for profit. Another difference: in the GDR, whenever a coal deposit ran out and a mine closed, provision had been planned long in advance so that every employee was either offered a job in his trade elsewhere, received training for a new trade at the regular pay level or, if close to pension age (sixty for those in the all too common unhealthy jobs), could retire. No one landed jobless in the street. Although few jobs paid as well as in the fuel sector, it was then healthiest to head for the hills.

81—Globalization

The Wende of 1990 cut the noxious but vital chemical industry to the core. And most others too. Aside from a few luckier areas, it failed to bring East Germany those "blossoming landscapes" promised by Chancellor Helmut Kohl. Eastern Germans earn on average 4,000 euros less than West Germans. Since 1990 their population has fallen by 15 percent down to 12.6 million. The jobless rate is about 8.5 percent, while the national average is now 5.6 percent and would be higher but for the fact that more older workers retire than young ones find jobs. The young men and in greater numbers young women, whose departure left many East German towns seem deserted, were happy if they could find their luck—a job—in more prosperous Western states like Baden-Wurttemberg or Bavaria.

But unified Germany as a whole achieved its old dominant position in Europe. Its great success with exports and a stagnant wage level helped it during the crisis of 2007–2008, which did not hit quite as hard as elsewhere. But it did hit. And with no more GDR comparisons to fear, Germany's giant corporations or its politicians often succeeded in cutting medical care benefits, multiplying the number of short-term, half-time, low-paid jobs with no security, delaying retirement age, and weakening the unions while protecting money-hungry banks. Rents soared and *gentrification* has long ceased to be an unknown foreign word. Hit hardest were single mothers, young people, many of the elderly, and up to a third of the children. Rarely were occasional gains possible, usually before elections.

It was similar to the United States, where unions are far smaller and weaker. At the time of this writing, the summer of 2018, all government sectors are trying to weaken fight-back by working people. There are signs of resistance, luckily, offering some hope, like the teachers in five red states, the nurses, and a growing number of political activists challenging the big business and high-finance interests so powerful in both main parties. It remains to be seen whether they gain in influence and strength, winning advances on the political scene or if they can be distracted by the media into waving the flag and sharpening weapons in opposition to hypothetical menaces of Vladimir Putin. I am forced to recall that Iron Curtain speech in Fulton, Missouri, in 1946 and all that followed. Would people again be fooled and neglect the sharp attacks of the government on their genuine interests?

With ever more regions threatening to sink under floods, mudslides, blizzards, arid sand, or bad politics, with the growing economic rivalry in the trade sector between the United States, China, the European countries, and especially Germany, with the British "Brexit" withdrawal from the European Union, and other signs of its crumbling, even falling apart, the omens of trouble ahead are undeniable. The man in charge of my neighborhood bank warned me: "Mark my words: the 2008 crisis was like a car hitting a haystack while doing 70; the next one will be like a car doing 100 and smashing into a concrete wall!" I hope he's mistaken!

Some economists and op-ed experts claim that globalization, with its easy communications, trade, transportation, and travel between continents, could counteract these dangers and solve some problems. It has indeed brought rapid industrialization to some of the poorest countries of eastern Asia, drawn millions away from primitive villages, and created middle and upper classes interested in homes, cars, travel, Western foods, and the latest fashionable offerings. Maybe those are good sides. But it almost always went hand-in-hand with a suppression of unions or the corruption of their leaders, meaning pitiful wages and horrifying conditions. Where workers defy all pressures and fight back, they do sometimes win improvements, but often enough the companies simply pull up stakes and seek another country with worse—and more profitable—conditions.

In the highly developed United States, globalization, combined with amazing technology and sped-up productivity, plus ever more uncanny robots, has meant fewer and fewer jobs. Big plants making autos and other products moved to non-union "right-to-work" southern states, then further south, turning America's industrial heartland around the Great Lakes into the "Rust Belt." Low-wage textile or furniture towns also emptied out, like similar towns in northern France and the ex-GDR.

Globalization is undoubtedly a boon for those on the top, where fewer and fewer giants own more and more industries and are capturing big swathes of public life, privatizing hospitals, schools, prisons, even water supplies. No matter how high the stormy waves may rise, the razor-thin 1 percent stratum perches high and dry on its luxurious summit. Sometimes one or the other economic baron slips or gets pushed off, but the main rulers of that royal court have rarely been dethroned. Or, recalling Goethe and the Grimm Brothers, these sorcerers are seldom swamped by deluges of water, porridge, or high-piled surplus container loads of useful or useless products. For they, too, possess a magic formula: Profits-Money-Power! Aside from occasional mostly tax-evasive philanthropy, aimed at cleansing their reputations or easing their consciences (if they have any), most of them use this magic formula, not for a better world for humankind but for their own private, gated lives. This thinnest stratum with its malevolent magic is behind the world's gravest problems and is the main threat to future world society.

82—That Old Horror Again

Meanwhile, one in nine people on the planet goes to bed hungry, including many in prosperous Germany and the United States. Even in such areas, people who are pressured, uncertain of their own future, worried about the future of their children or grandchildren, are growing increasingly dissatisfied. Some turn to opioids. Others, as discussed earlier, are getting rebellious.

As always, the Global South gets hit harder than the Global North, benefited in great measure by Southern poverty. It is not only climate change that impoverishes the southern continents, ruining farms and forests, but also the unfair, highly unbalanced trade with underpaid imports from the South like tea, coffee, fruit, cocoa, palm oil, and coltran against a mass of attractive exports to the same regions, the modern, modish MADE IN THE U.S.A. or MADE IN GERMANY appliances, chic jeans, colorful sneakers, and processed foods, from packaged toast and flavored yoghurt to plucked chicken drumsticks produced by wealthy, subsidized Northern companies. That spells bankruptcy for small-scale African farmers and handicraftsmen who can't compete, who give up their few acres or small cobbling and tailor shops and move to the slums of huge central cities. Some find jobs there, others try to survive with illegal activities or outright crime, but many, desperate to feed themselves and their families (or to form families), risk hunger, violence, arrest, and drowning and flee to those richly beckoning Northern lands of hope.

Joining them in taking such risks are refugees from countries torn by warfare, caused mostly by the United States, France, Britain, and their allies, who support warlords and corrupt politicians or engage in massive military bombing, droning, or direct invasion, as in Somalia, Libya, and Mali in Africa and Afghanistan, Iraq, and Yemen in western Asia. Although Germany has not been militarily involved in every one of these conflicts, it has been a source of weapons for all of them. Much the same took place in conflict-ridden Central America.

In Europe it was the arrival of these refugees from hunger, warfare, or both, reaching their highest numbers in 2015–16, which made it easier to divert working-class people in the North from seeing the true causes of their problems. Stories spread that lazy refugees were grabbing jobs, housing, and all kinds of social benefits. This malice was not hard to spread. It was undeniable, after all, that refugees had different languages, religions, clothes, and customs, all so terribly strange and alien to simple souls. Some such bigotry was an almost exact translation of similar prejudices poisoning most of the past 150 years in the United States.

Many companies, always out to slice wage levels and benefits, gladly hire refugees eager or desperate for any jobs, regardless of conditions, to help gain permission to remain in the "haven country" or simply to survive. This can lead to more bigotry on the part of those "Northern" workers, who see only that wage scales are being undercut and are led to blame not the employers but the hard-working immigrants. The mass media, while piously decrying racism and dutifully calling for tolerance, rarely miss a chance to play up any immigrant misdeed. It is obvious that with so many untrained and unwanted young foreign men, often without families and constantly hit by discrimination, a few may indeed do nasty things once in a while (as do local men). The advent of ISIS, although its origins lay clearly in earlier U.S. intentions and blunders, also created the danger of "terrorists," some of them seeking revenge for war atrocities by Western troops, planes, or drones in their countries of origin. The resulting tragedies become an overriding theme, consuming kiloliters of printers' ink and untold hours of broadcast time, augmented by thousands of hate-laden comments in the social media, while self-righteous politicians hold forth on how best to get rid of the refugees without looking openly racist.

The mass media have always tried to turn dissatisfaction and anger among those who speak the native language into hatred against those who don't, or not so well, to blame underdogs instead of top dogs, to keep people apart, pitting older workers against younger ones, those with steady jobs against those with temp jobs, better-paid men against worse-paid women. But always against "those furriners," those "Others." In medieval times witches were to blame—or the Jews, most

tragically in the twentieth century. Sometimes the latter are still utilized for this purpose. In the United States the scapegoats nowadays
are very often the Latinos, always the blacks, and more recently the
Muslims and all immigrants, legal or not, refugees or not. If there is no
active progressive movement to build solidarity, then racism spreads
most easily. Donald Trump's basic core of support is motivated by such
thinking—or lack of thinking. How close are the ties of the alt-right, the
Ku Klux Klan, and a wide assortment of hate groups to people wielding
great power? Recent events have shown that some people, more than
ready to use weapons, have little difficulty in getting them and arming
themselves to the teeth. Add to them the many racists in police uniforms. These alarming arsenals have been made possible by politicians
and their backers.

In recent German politics, what began with weekly marches and
rallies in Dresden by PEGIDA, "Patriotic Europeans against the
Islamization of the Western World," with loose links to older pro-Nazi
groups and gangs, was largely replaced by a new party called Alternative
for Germany (AfD), which grew quickly and won a worrisome number
of seats in city and state legislatures. Most parties lost voters to the
AfD, including the Linke (Left), especially in Eastern Germany. In the
federal elections in September 2017, the AfD made big gains and won
ninety-two seats in the Bundestag, which provided far better media
possibilities than those already granted it for its hateful messages. Its
other positions are hardly known—tax cuts for the wealthy, a military
buildup, resuming the draft of young men, opposing abortion and
same-sex marriage—but all the more its rabid crusade against Muslims,
Turks, Kurds, and Arabs living in Germany, and especially against the
recent refugees.

Current polls show the AfD overtaking the weakening Social
Democrats as the second-largest party. Thus far the established parties have officially rejected any cooperation with the AfD, but many
show signs of moving to the right to win back voters from it, and the
Christian Democratic Union and its Bavarian sister party seem to be
flirting with the idea of possible coalitions with it, like what has happened in neighboring Austria. But Germany is far bigger, weightier,

and better armed than Austria, and some people are already thinking back with a shudder to 1930 or 1931, the years just before Hitler seized total power. When resentful citizens find no other alternatives, no convincing advocates of their rights and needs, they may continue turning to the far right.

Derek Scally, reporting for the *Irish Times* from a middle-sized East German town, gave an indication of this:

> Chancellor Angela Merkel visited Quedlinburg on a federal election campaign stop. Polite applause from supporters was drowned out by hundreds of angry protesters from the far-right Alternative für Deutschland (AfD), furious at her refugee policy that saw 890,000 people granted asylum in Germany in 2015 alone.
>
> "Go to your Moslems," read one sign from a protester from the AfD, which finished second in last year's state election here, with 24 percent.
>
> In the federal elections this district gave the AfD about 19 percent, more than enough to set off the alarm signals. (Derek Scally, "East German Town's Blossoming Landscapes Mask Major Threats," *Irish Times*, July 20, 2017.)

The very institution charged with "protecting constitutional democracy" in Germany was built up by former Nazis, whose experience lay only in fighting leftists, and who maintained murky ties to racist extremists. A ten-year series of murders of men with Turkish or Greek backgrounds, including an explosion in a Turkish area with many casualties, provided a few brief glances at these ties, though much of the evidence was either "mistakenly shredded" or hidden away, some of it for the unprecedented period of 120 years. Protection of prominent names may thus be granted even to their great-grandchildren! In the summer of 2018 the head of the institution was so defensive of neo-fascists that he had to be removed.

When chips are down in critical times, even those who are loudest in praising "Western democracy," if faced with a choice, prefer those on the far right to anyone on the left. The world saw this in Russia in the 1920s, with military support for the tsarist generals, in Spain in 1936–39 for the Franco fascists, in Chile in 1973 for the Pinochet dictatorship, and on many, many other occasions, from Athens and Cairo to Ankara and Caracas.

Racism and hatred toward foreigners within national borders are often paired with preparations for conflict with those outside the borders. As long as Germany was divided, with strong memories of the past war in many minds, German military units never went into action, not the Bundeswehr and not the People's Army, which, in 1968, luckily refrained from joining other Warsaw Pact members sending troops into Czechoslovakia. Indeed, West Germany's Basic Law, its constitution, decreed that the Bundeswehr exists only for defense purposes. But the GDR was hardly down the drain before this changed. First came "peace-keeping" military actions in line with UN mandates in 1991–92 in Cambodia and Somalia, then surveillance and transport planes in a UN-backed mission in Croatia, and then in 1999 the first active participation of German troops abroad since 1945 in NATO's war, without UN approval, against Serbia. The Social Democrats backed all these actions, while the once pacifist Greens, after finally achieving coveted government status in a coalition, enthusiastically joined in.

In 2004, the SPD Defense Minister, Peter Struck, stated that "self-defense is no longer the first priority of the Bundeswehr" and "Germany's security must also be defended in the Hindu Kush mountains" of Afghanistan. Peace advocates, blasting his statement, said it could lead to world chaos and permit Pakistan, India, China or any other country to declare that they must defend themselves along the Rhine. But Christian Democrats, SPD, and most Greens agreed that Germany must not only be defended in Afghanistan but in the sandy Saharan wastelands of Mali and along the seacoast of Lebanon.

"Patriotism" is almost always invoked to create the bellicose atmosphere required for such missions and attacks. But aggressive nationalism, often to divert domestic dissatisfaction, gives rise to the fascists, waiting in the wings, ready to crush all opposition. I have written about the fascist take-over offer to Major General Smedley Butler in 1935. It was luckily not successful in the United States, but it was in Europe and Japan. In his Message to Congress on Curbing Monopolies (April 29, 1938) President Roosevelt warned: "The first truth is that the liberty of a democracy is not safe if the people tolerate the growth of private power to a point where it becomes stronger than their democratic state itself. That, in its essence, is Fascism—ownership of Government by an individual, by a group, or by any other controlling private power."

He had to lead the United States in a war against that awful force, whose power, in Europe and Asia, was not broken until 1945, at the cost of over 50 million lives. Niklas Frank, whose father was Nazi governor of occupied Poland and one of the worst war criminals, came to despise all his father represented. Out of personal experience and emotions he, too, warned of a renewed fascist danger: "As long as our economy is great, and as long as we make money, everything is very democratic. . . . But if we have five to ten years of heavy economic problems the swamp becomes a lake, a sea which will again swallow everything." (Niklas Frank, *BBC HARDtalk, World News,* April 26 2017.)

Where could such a sea emerge the next time, and who would be there this time to block its flooding?

OVER HALF A century ago, on August 17, 1975, Senator Frank Church appeared on NBC's *Meet the Press* and discussed the National Security Agency (NSA), without naming it:

In the need to develop a capacity to know what potential enemies are doing, the United States government has perfected a technological capability that enables us to monitor the messages that go through the air. . . . Now, that is necessary and important to the United States as we look abroad at enemies or potential enemies. We must know, at the same time, that capability at any time could be turned around on the American people, and no American would have any privacy left: such is the capability to monitor everything—telephone conversations, telegrams, it doesn't matter. There would be no place to hide.

If this government ever became a tyranny, if a dictator ever took charge in this country, the technological capacity that the intelligence community has given the government could enable it to impose total tyranny, and there would be no way to fight back because the most careful effort to combine together in resistance to the government, no matter how privately it was done, is within the reach of the government to know. Such is the capability of this technology. (Sen. Frank Church, *Meet the Press*, August 17, 1975.)

83—Solutions

I think back to a personal experience many years ago. Our family was vacationing at beautiful Lake Balaton in Hungary. One day I left them at the beach and took the train to a marsh area farther south, famous for its wonderful bird life. I rejoiced to watch the herons, egrets, spoonbills, a marsh rail. But when it came time to head home I saw not one or two but three thunderstorms moving in from different directions, as if to converge right over my head. (More likely their goal was the big lake nearby.) As it began to patter, I saw a big tree and wondered, with the station fifteen minutes away, if I should take refuge there till the worst was over. But that was dangerous nonsense, so I walked on as fast as I could, getting to the station's safety just as all three storm clouds thundered down. Today, I again perceive three menacing clouds, not arising in the heavens but man-made. Dr. King called them giant triplets: extreme materialism, militarism, racism. Unlike the thunder showers, it is not necessary to escape them but to combat them!

A more drastic simile occurs to me, not so very different in meaning. In Revelations, the last book of the New Testament, we can read of the Four Horsemen of the Apocalypse, with riders on different-colored horses symbolizing conquest, war, famine, and death.

Similar threats, nearly two thousand years later, make it urgent to block such murderous horses by unseating their super-wealthy riders. To achieve this, I am completely convinced, it is necessary to confiscate their factories, banks, and mines, their huge expanses of farm acreage and their hoarded billions, in coins, paper, gold, or long columns of numbers. This wealth derives from sacrifices so many of the

99 percent have endured; it was created by the muscles, brains, skills, and dedication of countless millions of ordinary people. That is what makes confiscation fully justifiable. My thirty-eight GDR years and all the years before and since have fully confirmed my deeply held belief, based on a very different magic formula than theirs: Dethrone the kings of wealth! Get rid of them!

Of course, I don't want their physical destruction. Execution is still practiced in some countries, even by governors in Arkansas and Texas. But for me capital punishment is evil; I reject all forms of it—chopping blocks or scimitars, guillotines, gas chambers, or gurneys. No, it is not their heads but their giant possessions that must be chopped off. As for those who are genuine inventors, engineers, or efficient managers, if they and their work can benefit the majority, not private profit, then they should be rewarded for their efforts and contributions like everyone else. But not their children and children's children, and never in astronomical amounts, financial light years away from what others earn. When a baseball club manager can pocket $20 million a year while the seamstress sewing the baseballs in Haiti or Costa Rica gets, also in a year, less than $800, then that must come to a swift end. After all, I don't believe he invented the game, or its balls. Nor does he play it well enough.

Such a takeover should not affect mom-and-pop shopkeepers, small businesses, artisans, artists, or other independent souls, as long as they do not engage in chiseling on wages or other exploitation. Closing down many such "little fishes" by the GDR in the 1970s under pressure from the Brezhnev patrons in Moscow was hard and harmful and should be avoided.

It has been proven often enough in many countries that private ownership of big enterprises is not more efficient, and all too often it can hurt the economy while robbing all but its top ranks. I saw good, well-planned management in many GDR enterprises, despite a multitude of obstacles and without the kind of giant rewards and bonuses so often awarded capitalist retirees even after the worst of failures.

No, I am not proposing a sudden revolution for, say, 7 a.m. tomorrow. Not even for the day after tomorrow. When I see groups waving red banners on high and demanding a revolution—maybe for Sunday afternoon or sooner, then I may sometimes admire their devotion, perhaps their zeal. But, to express it in German: I am no "*Naivling.*" The timing must be set by the people, very large numbers of people! And when I see black-masked youngsters, sometimes perhaps the ones with those banners, throwing cobblestones, shattering shop windows, and setting dumpsters on fire, all in the name of an almost immediate revolution, I suspect that, consciously or not, they are fulfilling the wishes of the media, providing chances to denounce all opposition as "leftist extremists." I also wonder how many of them are just looking for the same excitement hooligans get at European soccer games, how many are inebriated or otherwise stimulated, and how many, behind the masks, are agents provocateurs throwing the first cobblestone or breaking the first window. Sometimes a few get exposed, like the leading stone-thrower at the G-8 Summit Meeting in Heiligendamm in 2007. When his mask slipped, another man recognized him and cried out: "That's the same guy who arrested me last year in Hannover!"

I am fully convinced that the best, if not the only way to win out is by winning people, not antagonizing them, by explaining one's views and, more important, getting as many as possible involved in organized action—together, on a broad basis, with energy, solidarity, and also group self-discipline.

So, I don't yearn for any bloody revolution! "Ballots not bullets" should be the aim. But not just with biannual visits to a polling booth. Far more important is action in the streets and workshops, in strikes, demonstrations, marches, or wherever people can take part, learn to appreciate their own strength when they stick together, and be convinced about acting for the good of themselves and their related human beings in all corners of our one and only globe. That means seeing through media miasma and seeking not quarrels but coordination with other good souls. And being aware that the wealthy fight back, hard and dirty.

The chances for common people to take over the wealth of this world suffered huge setbacks with the tragic derailments and defeats of the twentieth century. Who deserves how much of the blame is still hotly debated; the minds and political muscles of those hoping for change are still recuperating, far too slowly, from all the blunders and failures. They are too often splintered and weak.

That leads some to believe that a takeover is unrealistic and local workers' or farm cooperatives should rather strive for progress on their own, with constructive people, usually the workers involved, proving what can be accomplished without idle coupon-clippers or super-wealthy bosses in skyscraper offices and handsome mansions. And in fact a few endeavors in Spain and Argentina have indeed organized work in self-run enterprises by people who had been pushed into poverty by mechanized agriculture or robotized industry. Their successes can be dramatic; I see no reason why they couldn't exist in a world of the future.

However, I feel that although this might work well for some farms, factories, or even towns, it offers no basic alternative. Self-sufficiency may be right on a local scale or on some Robinson Crusoe island or in a wonderful Shangri-La valley. But in today's hard world, it is too easily crushed. Since making refrigerators or even flashlights requires parts, materials, and chemicals delivered by road or rail over bridges or waterways and, when produced, must be distributed to retail out-lets, and since such production, either by hand or by robots, requires well-educated experts, some forms of central planning are necessary. Centrality can be overdone, it often was in the GDR, but it was also the key to many of the successes I witnessed and admired. I cannot imag-ine how limited local efforts can really dent the overall control of the few and mighty. And yet I say: more power to them as omens or models for the future! May they flourish!

Some, too, pointing to past defeats, shrink from what they see as "impossibly Utopian" goals or future sharp breaks with the status quo, preferring to stumble along, responding as well as possible to each new threat or crisis. Things have gone fairly well in past years, they maintain, and where rough spots occur or new ones come along, our democratic political system can manage and correct them without toppling the whole apple cart with who knows what results. With the proper leg-islation, they feel, we can tame the might of the Goliaths while saving the planet for our children and grandchildren, who will assuredly have it even better than we did. Such views prevail most strongly, I think, among those feeling current pinches least and not tasting too much of the dissatisfaction.

People who think along such lines, even when they face growing dissatisfaction, tend to stick to established, acceptable parties, like the Democratic Party in the United States, the Social Democratic Party in Germany, or their siblings in other countries. These parties urge improvements for working people, for children, mothers, and the elderly, decry joblessness, and devise plans for combating it, recalling New Deal measures adopted by President Roosevelt during the Depression or calls by the British economist John Maynard Keynes (1883–1946) for governments to take strong measures to help the needy and not rely on "free enterprise." His aim was to rescue the prevailing system from its own self-destruction.

Some such measures may help, and many labor leaders support these parties. But all too often they are part of that old "lesser evil" strategy, which misuses the electoral system to deflect despair or anger. If such politicians win elections, they fill their cabinets with pliant men or women who dilute or drop the promised measures or adopt weak copies of them—or pass bad laws like Clinton's NAFTA treaty and "welfare reform package." Wars are waged at immense cost in blood and expense, and, to pay for them, or buy weapons for the next ones, unfriendly measures are found necessary, though often packed as prettily as those razor-thin, tasteless slices of cheese or sausage in the supermarkets. In Germany it was Gerhard Schroeder, a Social Democrat, whose "Agenda 2010" called for "cutting state assistance, promoting personal responsibility, and demanding more from every individual"—pure gobbledygook to obscure callous blows against those hardest hit. But such language is echoed worldwide.

Meaningful improvements like large-scale job programs cost money, tax money. Although it is working people who pay the most into government treasuries, the 1 percent crowd loathes any and all cuts into its fortunes. Since it is they, with their huge profits and unlimited resources, who have giant political power—those magic words again—their tentacles encircle not only right-wing parties like the

Republicans but the Democratic Party as well, like the plutocratic leader in 1900 graphically described by Frederick Townsend Martin. The U.S. Democrats shared this deceptive "liberal" character with the German Social Democrats, the once radical German Greens, the French Socialists, the British Labour Party (at least until recently), and many others. Their weakness—or ties to the wealthy—explain how welfare-for-the-wealthy tax laws get passed, often with "Aye" votes of Democrats, and shot through with cannily placed loopholes.

Worn-out, eroded compromises can never tame carnivorous octopuses. But there are some truly committed progressives who believe they can change such parties and turn them into genuine pugilists for the good cause. There have been surprising successes in this direction, like the campaign of Bernie Sanders. Although he did not shy away from the long-abhorred word *socialism*, calling himself a "democratic socialist," he received over 13 million votes in the primary campaigns, 43 percent of the total and probably more if rumors about dirty tricks are to be believed. But the rulers of the Democratic Party, with their strongly rooted, Wall Street–backed party apparatus, proved stronger and saw to it that he did not win, despite his popularity. Jeremy Corbyn in Britain, on the other hand, with quite similar views and attacked tooth and nail by the almost hysterical "status quo" forces of Tony Blair's "New Labour," actually succeeded in winning leadership in the British Labour Party

Do left-wing, truly progressive or even socialist-minded elements have any real chances in such parties like the Democrats? One must certainly entertain many doubts. But in view of the dangerous downhill slide of our top-heavy society, I believe it wise to support opposition wherever there are willing participants, outside the Democratic Party but also within it, wherever any gain seems possible. Advances of either group can help the other, until some day they may join forces. I see no contradiction or betrayal in backing good fighters anywhere.

But always with great caution!! The power of wealth still dominates politics, the Democrats and the SPD Social Democrats, in Germany and in the United States. In Middletown or in Munich, one must always ask: Can this leopard change its spots? Rivalry, crookery, bribery, deceit,

cutthroat competition, big ones swallowing smaller ones—aren't they
still the dominant game rules in the economy and in politics? This
system always leads to economic crisis and misery, ecological catastrophe, and military conflict. With Exxon and Daimler, Amazon and
Murdoch, Purdue and Unilever, Bayer and Monsanto, Bank of America
and Deutsche Bank, all enterprises are for profit and power, not for the
people. The buildings and factories can stay; the profiteers must go!

BUT ISN'T A socialist economy owned and ruled by and for the people
now just a hazy, distant dream? True, wild shouts for immediate revolution with no connection to today's realities can do more harm than
good. On the other hand, even if big changes cannot be expected
tomorrow morning, who knows what may occur in the evening, or
maybe next January? The amazing echo of young people to the courageous words of Bernie Sanders and Jeremy Corbyn showed that
while realism is a must, it should never be an excuse for pragmatism,
for expediency, where small gains for today obscure the basic goals for
tomorrow or justify sidelining and gradually abandoning those goals.

Unlike some "pragmatists" I can discern no genteel, mannerly,
smoothly-paved route to a blissful Eden where the wolf lies down
peaceably with the lamb and the lion with the gazelle. In such an Eden,
there would still be too many nasty snakes and too many foul apples.
And lions and wolves would remain hungry and quite possibly desperate. Recalling my simile about the thunderstorms at Lake Balaton, I
see no safe shelter under the boughs of moldering old timber. Political
pledges to improve a law here and a regulation there, grant assistance
to mothers here or seniors there should be taken up. They deserve support—indeed, fresh initiative and fighting leadership! But with major
disasters threatening, they should never eclipse the basic answer. Every
strike, petition, demonstration, or election campaign should be part of
the search for the best and quickest path to that major goal: abolish the
whole 1 percent category!

Not every good person will agree on that goal. Regardless, I would
rejoice at every sign of togetherness and strength for good causes,
whether short-lived or lasting. I am thinking of Occupy Wall Street, of

Black Lives Matter, the fight for 15 dollars an hour at Walmart, Moral Mondays in North Carolina, and the Poor People in Washington, the teachers' strike in Chicago, and, of course, the great Women's March, also the protests of courageous immigrants, legal and "illegal," and the pipeline protests of Native Americans. In Europe I think of the giant demonstrations against the TTIP trade deal, of the short-lived but enthusiastic OXI fight against austerity in Greece, the demonstrations by women, teachers, and democracy defenders in Poland, and the glorious campaign for Jeremy Corbyn.

No one has a crystal ball to warn about an approaching crisis, increasing suffering, and increasing menaces. If a crisis does come, will it move people to open new doors, like after the two world wars, or mislead them to slam doors shut, as with Hitler in the 1930s. Was the man right who predicted a new crisis—like a car doing 100 mph car and hitting a cement wall? If it does arrive, progressives should be getting ready to prevent a total crack-up, by switching drivers and direction.

I still like to chuckle at Woody Guthrie's parable about the strong and the weak: A male and a female rabbit flee for their lives from a passel of hunting dogs. In the nick of time they find refuge in a big hollow tree trunk that the dogs can't get into. "Oh, what can we do now?" the male rabbit sniffled. "We'll just have to wait till we outnumber them!" came the optimistic answer.

That is not exactly the most likely method of resistance, but it hints at the one main asset against the powers that be—that potential of the 99 percent, or a sizable share of it, if only it can be brought together, convinced, and organized.

Woody also indicated the goal: "This land is my land, this land is your land, this land was made for you and me!" Ah, if that bloated little coterie at the top was no longer able, like some modern Dracula, to suck away the wealth produced by so many hardworking people, if it could no longer hoard its loot on lonely islands or in Alpine bank hideouts, and it could be put to good use! How much poverty, how much illiteracy and ignorance, how much misery and fear could be eradicated! Acute hunger threatens 20 million people in sub-Saharan Africa, a result of colonial history, exploitation by Northern owners and exporters and their bribery of local African leaders, plus climate change, for which Africans are least to blame. Just $4.4 billion would quickly alleviate the worst starvation. Many Walmart workers find it hard simply to feed themselves and their children. But Jim Walton's fortune stands at about $35 billion, that of his siblings around $33 billion each. The annual military budget of the United States is set at $587 billion—and President Trump recently demanded an increase of $52 billion—for a country threatened militarily by no one in the world. What a world we might have if these fortunes were returned for proper use to their legitimate owners!

84—Endnotes

Now, reflecting on my full eight decades, I ask myself whether those thirty-eight middle years in the GDR were a lost and mistaken time, wasted on what many see as a "misbegotten corpse." Should I try to erase my memories of them or, like so many in journalism, film, and prose, devote my efforts to what Justice Minister Kinkel called "delegitimizing" the GDR—a shipwreck whose every last spar, now twenty-eight years later, is still being shelled and fired at? Whoever has read this far knows that I cannot join in such endless salvos! But the question remains: Is my nostalgia justified?

I think I have made clear that I was never blind to the limitations, blunders, the bullying, and sometimes cruelty I discovered in those years. How often have I cursed, despaired, even wept at ineptitude and worse, as I watched the little vessel sink, first gradually, then swiftly, under a triumphant tide.

My odd life compelled comparisons. I could not forget the limitations, blunders, bullying, and cruelty I had sometimes witnessed in the land I had fled, McCarthy-era America. But, much as I despised that time, I have never condemned the country of my birth as hopeless or ever given up my U.S. citizenship. I retained my feelings for the good pages of its history, its millions of good people, its potential. Should I have no similar feelings toward my involuntarily adopted home, the GDR?

What was there to sustain such feelings? There was my belief that politics are made by human beings, with strengths and weaknesses based on their personal histories. Most GDR leaders, I knew, spent their younger years struggling against that huge, bloody blot on last century's history, the rule of fascism. That meant rough strikes, police batons, tear gas, prison cells, it meant fighting fascist armies in defense of Madrid or Stalingrad, at back street barricades in Florence or mountain passes in Greece or Slovakia, it meant death camps and guillotines. Tragically, known or unknown to them at the time, it was also shadowed by frightening distortions under the rule of Joseph Stalin. Under his rule it was possible to reshape his giant country amazingly, making its costly victory over the Nazis possible, but also, wrongly and criminally, costing the lives of innumerable good, innocent people.

Could GDR leaders break with their past? Which past? They continued the "good fight" for progress in every way they thought possible and luckily did not copy the man in the Kremlin in all his cruelty, though traces were undeniable. And though I deplored all that was too rigid, too fearful of free, open dialogue with the population, I felt myself in agreement, if not with all their methods, indeed with what I believed to be their main goal.

Nor could I overlook that, from its inception, the GDR was threatened by brutal enemies largely representing the same forces, sometimes the same men, who had oppressed and imprisoned its leaders. They had to fight back. This, too, explains my continued support for the GDR.

IN RECENT YEARS, nearly 70,000 small bronze squares have been cemented into the sidewalks of many cities, first in Germany but now in 24 countries of Europe. Over 8,000 are in Berlin alone. Called "*Stolpersteine*," stumble stones, although they are quite flat and unobtrusive, all are created by one remarkable man, Gunter Demnig, whenever he is called upon. They tell the name, birth year, and, when known, the place and date of death of Jews and anti-fascists who lived here before they were torn away. Four little plaques are across the street from my house. Nathan Schwarzer was born in 1890, Martha, née Pinkus, in 1891, Ruth was born in 1926, and Steffi in 1929. Both children were about my age. What did those young girls, thirteen and sixteen, still hope and dream of? We can only guess: all four, forced on October 26, 1942, from the house that once stood here, they were murdered three days later in the death camp of Riga. Over seventy-five years have passed since then, yet I pause whenever I pass by.

Moving me emotionally in a totally different way is the far lengthier vita of Friedrich Karl Vialon, who died peacefully twenty-eight years ago. He arrived in Riga five months before the Schwarzer family, as finance official in charge of "securing Jewish properties," such as the furniture of Jews who had lived in Riga, or possessions of those sent here. Did Martha Schwarzer have a wedding ring of gold or Steffi perhaps a brooch for Vialon to register?

As witness at a trial after the war, Vialon denied all knowledge of a Holocaust. Asked about the property he registered, he said: "The Jews brought lots of things in their suitcases when they were brought to the ghetto." Despite incriminating evidence provided by GDR authorities, one court rejected charges against Vialon, another annulled an indictment against him. After 1950, Vialon climbed the career ladder with agility and became state secretary (second man) in the Ministry for Economic Cooperation then headed by Walter Scheel, who later became West German president, although he, too, like Vialon, had been a Nazi Party member. I have never favored hatred, not of individuals, anyway. But hatred is not always easy to contain.

The GDR threw out the Vialons and Scheels, the Krupps and Flicks, the Thyssens and Deutsche Bankers, the Globkes and Gehlens—as well as the overwhelming majority of their ardent adherents in schools, courthouses, city halls, colleges, and media offices. Only very few slipped through here and there, but part of the population could not be healed from an awful infection. Polls taken soon after unification found 4 percent of East Germans admittedly anti-Semitic. But in GDR days they had been silenced and kept from influence. As an anti-fascist, indeed a Jewish anti-fascist landing in Germany less than eight years after Hitler, this had always impressed me. (The figure for West Germans, in the same poll, was 16 percent.)

My hatred of those who built and ran Auschwitz and Treblinka led me to resolve "Never again." For me, this included Jews and Palestinian Arabs, Poles and Roma, Congolese and Kurds, Tamils of Sri Lanka, Rohingya of Myanmar, and oppressed people everywhere. Black men or women in the ghettos, gay or transgender victims, or Native Americans on the North Dakota prairie: all are my brothers and sisters!

These thoughts led me to a second reason for supporting the GDR. The world in those years was torn by a giant power struggle. That was hardly conducive to high morality, especially since it was never on level grounds. But I could note with pride that the GDR was a key supporter of the African National Congress, the ANC, symbolized by Nelson Mandela and the men on Robben Island. Their rebellious publication *Sechaba* was printed in the GDR, so was that of the SWAPO Party, for the Namibian freedom fighters. The GDR gave help and training to orphans of the Namibian struggle and helped train young African leaders, always without charge. But in those years, my United States repeatedly vetoed UN attempts to oppose and isolate apartheid. It is believed that the CIA betrayed Mandela to the cops.

The GDR did all it could to help the Allende government break through the boycott of its goods and later, to aid victims of Pinochet brutality. It supplied milk powder for the children of Cuba and helped develop efficient new dairy farms. The GDR supported the long bitter struggle of the Vietnamese led by Ho Chi Minh and aided in rebuilding towns and villages in Vietnam. In Managua, Nicaragua, it set up its Carlos Marx Clinic, free to all the poor folks of the country. A Harvard classmate, an expert in the field, expressed highest praise for this achievement. All this time rulers in Washington and Bonn supported every fascistic dictator from Haiti or Guatemala to Chile!

In earlier pages I have described the efforts and achievements to abolish the age-old curse of poverty. I must think of my own neighborhood, which I watched as it grew up around me, a mix of five-, eight-, and ten-story buildings like my own, all built up in what was a giant field of ruin and rubble, but gradually rejoicing in a wealth of forsythia, laburnum, and lilacs, shadowed by beautifully blossoming chestnut trees and wonderfully aromatic lindens, a real oasis here in the middle of a big city. The kindergarten with its roomy play area was almost under my window. Children still play there today, but I grow nostalgic when I recall the happy animal reliefs outside the entrance, now gone like the onetime name of the kindergarten, Tamara Bunke—after Che Guevara's companera, "Tanya." I recall how the children, also my sons, were taught not only to brush their teeth properly and use a pencil, and perhaps rather too much about their homeland the GDR, but also to care lovingly for small pets, to help children in younger age groups and feel kinship and friendship toward children in all other countries. And I recall too, with a smile, how a few dozen children, after their naps, all happily loud and all happily naked, raced to the nearby wading pool. That custom is no longer with us, nor is the wading pool.

And today, I am afraid, when I see a construction site, I no longer watch its growth with the feeling "That, too, belongs to us!" Now I wonder who will earn money from it.

There were undeniably blots, far too many, which hastened the final failure. I don't want to prettify the past. Avarice, egotism, envy, and other failings could not be eradicated by even the best laws or socially conscious system, especially when burdened by a terrible past and constant pounding from a wealthy, glamorous sibling and neighbor. Humans rarely become angels. But there do seem to have been changes: comparisons shortly after unification showed East Germans on the average less motivated by a craving for more money and laying more value on family life. With little pecuniary rivalry, they tended to be friendlier with one another. Women, despite the burdens of household and family weighing heavier on their shoulders than on men's, were more satisfied at their independent roles on the job with other people, and better able to defy patriarchal pressures.

Yes, far, far too much political control was concentrated in a diminishing number of aging fingers, which were unable to find rapport with those sections of society less able or willing to reject or resist that glistening counter-model across the increasingly transparent border wall.

The system did not eliminate perks and privileges, a constant obstacle to such rapport. And yet these perks had limited perimeters. No big shots had portfolios of stocks and bonds, none dreamed of "making a pile" of millions or billions, with fleets of yachts, jets, Porsches, or mansions and penthouses scattered at the world's best spots. There was plenty to criticize, but always a vivid contrast with those billionaire companies and individuals who decided the fates of many thousands of employees atop their skyscrapers while others, far below, were trying to keep warm while sleeping on a subway floor!

I see the GDR as a noble experiment, important enough to learn from—how to avoid its blunders but profit from its successes, its attempt to create a Germany that did not spread economic and military tentacles from Afghanistan to Mali, debate whether to purchase killer drones from Israel or from the United States, send Leopard tanks to Qatar or Saudi Arabia, build submarines with nuclear capabilities for Indonesia or Israel or both.

I reflect: if Germany and the others would withdraw troops from Asia and Africa, reject destruction in Gaza, Yemen, and elsewhere, send not soldiers or weapons but a few billion euros for schools, hospitals, and industrial training, then surely the "terrorist danger" would subside and eventually disappear, and with it the justification for ever more intrusions into our private lives.

How wonderful things could be with a Germany and a United States rid of the oil, armaments, and media Goliaths! Unlike the needy little GDR, both nations are richly endowed with resources and wealth. Unlike the GDR, neither would be threatened in its existence and therefore justify limitations of the kind that damaged the GDR. The "constitution protectors" in Germany, with their present half-secret ties to the fascist dregs of society, would be as indefensible as the FBI and all its state-of-the-art snooping into the innermost words or even thoughts of its citizens. And while dreaming, why not a United States without any foreign bases?

Can such changes be achieved? I can hardly live to learn the answer. It may well be a stony path, but I am convinced it is a necessary one, an urgent one, to be sought and taken without hysteria, without mutual backbiting or exaggerated inner conflicts, without false haste at the wrong time but without indecision at the right time, with admiration for good leaders but no unquestioning reliance on any individuals. Despite all difficulties it must be possible!

AS FOR MYSELF, do I have regrets? Of course, I missed many good things as an exile. The United States is a remarkably beautiful country wherever it has not been spoiled (which is also true of Germany, East and West, though on a smaller scale). For years I missed some favorite foods, I missed singing the folk and "protest" songs I loved, also square dancing and even such seemingly minor matters as the varied American bird life. I missed my native language with its flexibility and slang, its puns and humor. I was even strangely jealous when hearing of fellow-Americans with the courage to speak up and act against wars, against racism and for equality, in strikes for decent livelihoods, and I felt somewhat guilty at having such a good, happy, largely untroubled life here in East Berlin.

I sought and found compensations, even some unknown foods. German, too, is a fine and varied language, blessed by many great writers and poets, best of all for me the marvelous words of that other rebellious Jewish exile, Heinrich Heine. I even came to enjoy European birds: proud white storks, fresh, arrogant rooks, the throbbing song of the nightingale, the joyful twitter of skylarks high in the sky, even the call of the cuckoo.

During her last visit here, my mother thought a bit, then said, "You know, in the long run perhaps you have had it better here than if you had stayed in the United States." Who knows? Certainly, a major source of my luck was finding a wonderful partner, who lit up my life and whom I have never ceased to miss. We were blessed with two good sons, and three good grandchildren.

And then, both here and there, we are all part of the same world. I believe that what I wrote, said, or did was for a good cause, and despite occasional mistakes I have no real regrets. And I still have great hopes for a happier future for everyone, everywhere! They are expressed in two of my most cherished songs. One is the fighting miners' song "Which Side Are You On?" The other, full of hope for tomorrow's man—and definitely woman: "Imagine no possessions, I wonder if you can, no need for greed or hunger—a brotherhood of man."

INDEX

abortion, 221, 222, 275–76
Abraham, Meghna, 207
Abs, Hermann Josef, 197–98
abstract art, 96
Abstract Expressionism (art), 95, 97
Abu-Jamal, Mumia, 241, 261
Academy of Arts (Berlin), 36; Paul
    Robeson Archive in, 119
Academy of Sciences, 183
Adenauer, Konrad, 16, 18–19, 44, 87;
    Brandt spied on by, 127; on ex-Nazis
    in German government, 49–50; ex-
    Nazis in German military under, 53;
    on Globke, 47, 48; military rebuilt
    under, 52; replaced by Brandt, 101
advertising, 211
Afghanistan, 295, 318
African-Americans, *see* blacks
African National Congress (ANC), 331
agricultural biotechnology, 303–4
Agricultural Production Cooperatives
    (LPG), 69
agriculture, 69–71
Aitmatov, Chingiz, 114, 168
Algeria, 90
Ali, Mohammed, 239
Aliyev, Heydar, 309
Allen, Richard, 150
Allende, Salvador, 215–16, 291, 292,
    331

Alternative for Germany Party (AfD),
    153, 221, 229–31, 316–17
Amazon (firm), 304–6

American Federation of Labor (AFL),
    248, 249
Amnesty International, 207
anti-Semitism: in East Germany, 263;
    in Germany, 113, 114, 331; in
    Soviet Union, 119; in Stalin's poli-
    cies, 144
Anzilotti, Eillie, 268
Apel, Erich, 103
Apitz, Bruno, 144
apparel, 206
apples, 205
apprenticeships, 142–43
Aragon, Louis, 114
Arbenz Guzman, Jacobo, 287
Armstrong, Charles K., 285
art: after Berlin Wall, 104; during
    Cold War, 94–98; Stalin on, 113;
    Ulbricht on, 86
Association of German Officers, 54
Austria, 116–17, 317
automobiles, 73–74, 176; environ-
    mental problems associated with,
    309–10
Avedon, Richard, 258
Axen, Hermann, 51

Azerbaijan, 309

Babel, Isaac, 114
Bach, Johann Sebastian, 263
Bachelet, Michelle, 291
Bahr, Egon, 20, 101–2
Bangladesh, 206
banks, 177–78
Barsky, Edward, 258, 261
BASF (firm), 61, 197
The Bathhouse (play, Mayakovsky), 106–7
Bauer, Franz, 47
Bautzen (Germany), 11–14, 20–21
Bayer (firm), 61, 197, 304
Becher, Johannes R., 36, 88, 125
Beck, C. H., 59–60
Behn, Sosthenes, 257, 259
Benjamin, Hilde, 51
Benjamin, Walter, 51
Berger, Victor, 251
Berkman, Alexander, 248
Berlin: author in, 28–32; blockade of, 17–18; cultural scene in, 32–35; demonstrations in (1953), 20
Berlin Wall, 70, 100–101; impact of, 101–6; opening of, 164; rock concerts by, 133–35
Bernays, Edward L., 212
Bernstein, Carl, 150–51
Bernstein, Dennis J., 266
Bernstein, Leonard, 91, 234
Bertelsmann (firm), 211
Besser, Joachim, 74–75, 223
Bessie, Alvah, 235
Bezos, Jeff, 305
Biberman, Herbert, 235
Biermann, Wolf, 109–10, 139
Bild (newspaper), 173, 211, 214

birds, 195
Bismarck, Otto von, 71
"Bitterfeld Way" campaign, 105–6
Black Panther Party, 238, 240
blacks (African-Americans), 118, 283–84; FBI's COINTELPRO program versus, 239–41; Hoover versus, 236–38
Blair, Tony, 325
Bloch, Ernst, 25
The Blue Angel (novel and film; Mann), 36
Blues Masses, 153
BMW (firm), 310
Boddien, Wilhelm Dietrich Gotthard Hans Oskar von, 189–90
Bowie, David, 134
Boyer, Richard O., 248, 251
BP (firm), 309
Braden, Thomas, 94–95, 97
Brandt, Willy, 34–35, 47, 166; becomes chancellor, 101; censorship under, 262; ex-Nazis in German government under, 50; Hallstein Doctrine dropped by, 76; spied on by Adenauer, 127
Brecht, Bertolt, 33, 83–87, 128, 234
Bredel, Willi, 36
Brezhnev, Leonid, 103, 108, 122, 129, 156
Brockman, Stephen, 35
Broton, Katharine, 280
Brown, Brenner, 267
Brown, Irving, 90–91, 93
Brown, John, 247
Brown, Timothy Scott, 40
Brumsted, John, 271
Buchheit, Paul, 278
Budzislavski, Hermann, 24, 114
Buffalo (New York), 14

Buhle, Paul, 234
Bulgakov, Mikhail, 114
Bulgaria, 161
Bundesnachrichtendienst (BND, the
    Federal Intelligence Service), 45–46
Bundeswehr (West German army),
    156, 318; creation of, 52, 54; names
    for bases used by, 56–57
Bunke, Tamara, 331
Burkhardt, Max, 34
Burnham, James, 93
Burns, Robert, 134
Busch, Ernst, 33
Bush, George H. W., 288, 294
Bush, George W., 294
Bütefish, Heinrich, 61
Butler, Smedley D., 253–54, 319

California, 265–66
capital punishment, 321
Carnegie, Andrew, 248
Casablanca (film, Curtiz), 262
Castillo Armas, Carlos, 287
Castro, Fidel, 288–89
censorship, 214–16, 262; author's
    experiences with, 216–19
Center for International Studies, 97
Central Intelligence Agency (CIA):
    art subsidized by, 94–95; attempts
    against Castro by, 288–89; in Chile,
    215; Cold War cultural work by,
    92–94; under Allen Dulles, 99;
    Eppelmann and, 154–55; exposures
    of, 96–98; family connection with,
    192–93; in Guatemala, 287; in Iran,
    286–87; Lovestone and, 90–91;
    Lumumba assassinated by, 288;
    Mandela and, 331; in Nicaragua,
    292–93

Chamberlain, Neville, 116
Chaplin, Charlie, 234
charter schools, 279
chemical industry, 311
Chemnitz (Germany), 74
Cheney, Dick, 294
Chevron (firm), 309
Chicago (Illinois): Haymarket riot
    in, 248; IWW founded in, 249;
    Memorial Day Massacre in, 253
Chicago Symphony Orchestra, 93
children: child labor, 205; education
    of, 278–79; maternal leave for,
    276–78
Chile, 215–16, 291–92
Chow, Edward, 309
Christian Democratic Union (party,
    Germany): automobile emis-
    sions and, 310; in coalition with
    Alternative for Germany Party,
    316–17; in East Germany, 220, 221;
    in election of 1990, 167
Christ und Welt (German magazine), 40
Church, Frank, 241, 288, 319–20
Churchill, Winston, 10, 112, 285
Citizens' Commission to Investigate
    the FBI, 239
Civilian Conservation Corps (CCC),
    308
Civil War (U.S.), 247
Clark, Wesley, 294–95
Claudius, Eduard, 41
Clayton, Meg Waite, 28
climate change, 308–10
Clinton, Bill, 309, 324
Clinton, Hillary, 295–96
coal, *See* lignite coal
Coca-Cola, 188
Cockcroft, Eva, 95

cocoa, 205
coffee, 205
COINTELPRO (FBI COunter INTELligence PROgram), 239–41
Cold War: art during, 94–96; beginning of, 285; culture during, 88, 92–94; union contacts during, 91
colleges and universities, 279–81
Collins, Phil, 134
Colom, Alvaro, 287
coltan, 207
Coming Out (film), 222
Committee for Cultural Freedom, 93
Communism, end of, in Soviet Union, 121–22
Communist Party (East Germany), See Socialist Unity Party
Communist Party (Germany), 255; founded by Luxemburg and Liebknecht, 138
Communist Party (USA): author as member of, 8, 244; Daily Worker published by, 27; FBI's COINTELPRO program actions against, 239–40; founding of, 252; McCarthyism and HUAC hearings on, 233–36; prosecutions of members of, 258–59
Communist Party (West Germany), 39, 63, 229, 262
Communists: in post-World War II unions, 90; pre-World War II, 117–18; Taft-Hartley Act on, 233
concentration camps, 143, 145
Congo, Republic of, 288
Congress for Cultural Freedom (1950; Berlin), 92–94
Congress for Cultural Freedom (organization), 97

Congress of Industrial Organizations (CIO), 252–53
Congress of Racial Equality (CORE), 240
Contras (Nicaragua), 292–93
Copland, Aaron, 235
Corbyn, Jeremy, 228, 325–27
Corrigan ("wrong-way Corrigan"), 7
countryside, 67–71
The Cranes Are Flying (film), 114
crime, 267
Crossing the River (Grossman), 195
Cuba, 75, 192, 253
currencies: in Berlin, 29, 30; exchange rates for marks, 167; West-marks, after unification, 178
Czechoslovakia, 116–17
Czichon, Eberhard, 60

Daily Worker, 27
Daimler (organization), 310
Dallas (television program), 218–19
Davis, Angela, 145
Davis, Ossie, 235
Davis, University of California at, 242
Debs, Eugene V., 226, 249, 251–52
De Caux, Len, 249
Dee, Ruby, 235
DEFA (East German film company), 35, 108
Demnig, Gunter, 330
democracy, 203–4; in East Germany, 221–22; elections in Western democracies, 224–30; for working people, 223
Democratic German Report, 37–39; on ex-Nazis as judges and prosecutors, 43–45; ex-Nazis exposed by, 40–41
Democratic Party (U.S.), 325–26

dental care, 274–75

Der Spiegel (German magazine): on ex-Nazis as diplomats, 40; on ex-Nazis as police, 44; on Höfer, 58; on Stasi, 127

Desmond, Matthew, 265

Dessau, Paul, 84, 96

Deutsche Bank, 62, 167, 198, 298

Dewey, Thomas, 227

The Diary of Anne Frank, 144

Dickel, Friedrich, 55

Dietl, Eduard, 56

Dietrich, Marlene, 36

DiPalma, Theresa Alberghini, 271

Disney, Walt, 234, 235

dissidents, 150, 155

Die Distel (The Thistle; political cabaret), 82

Dobbert, Andreas, 155

Dodd, William, 254–55

The Dragon (play, Schwarz), 107

Dresden (Germany), 104, 162

DuBois, W. E. B., 92, 236–37

Dulles, Allen, 47, 99, 288

Dulles, John Foster, 17–18

Dusenberry, Maya, 277

Dymschitz, Alexander, 35, 112

East Berlin: commerce between West Berlin and, 29–31; cultural scene in, 32–35; housing in, 158; opening of Berlin Wall in, 164; after unification, 173; *See also* Berlin; Berlin Wall

East Germany, *See* German Democratic Republic

Eastwood, Clint, 186

Eberlein, Hugo, 57

ecology, 307–11

economy: globalization of, 311–13; income inequality in, 282–83; power of giant electronic corporations in, 305; after unification, 175–81

education, 278–79; in East Germany, 141–49; ex-Nazis as teachers, 42–43; higher, 279–81; medical, 273–74; after unification, 184

Edwards, Agustín, 215

Ehrenburg, Ilya, 26

Eichmann, Adolf, 47–48

Eichner, Klaus, 155

Eichsfelde (Germany), 71

Einstein, Albert, 91

Eisenhower, Dwight D., 39, 97–98, 288; on military-industrial complex, 296–97

Eisenhower administration, 287

Eisenhüttenstadt (Germany), 74

Eisler, Hanns, 85, 87, 96, 234

elections: in East Germany, 220–24; in East Germany, of 1989, 160; in East Germany, of 1990, 166–67; in East Germany, of 2017, 316, 317; "lesser evil" strategy in, 324; in United States, 299; in Western democracies, 224–30

El Mercurio (newspaper, Chile), 215

Encounter (magazine), 97

English (language), 111; teaching of, 142

environmentalism, 140, 307–11

Eppelmann, Rainer, 153–55

Equality Party (U.S.), 226

Erhard, Ludwig, 49

European Union, 208, 312

Eurythmics (rock group), 134

ex-convicts, 266–67

Exxon-Mobil (firm), 308–9

Facebook (firm), 305
Fang, Lee, 297
Farand, Chloe, 282
Farrell, James T., 93
Fascism: attempted coup in U.S. tied
    to, 254–55; nationalism leading to,
    318–19; in Spain, 256–57; *See also*
    Nazis and ex-Nazis
Fast, Howard, 259, 261
Faustus, Johann, 85
Federal Bureau of Investigation
    (FBI): author's file in, 245;
    COINTELPRO program of, 238–
    43; under Hoover, 236–38
Federal Republic of Germany (FRG;
    West Germany), 17; Communist
    Party outlawed in, 262; economic
    advantages of, 197; ex-Nazis as
    diplomats for, 40–41; ex-Nazis as
    judges and prosecutors in, 43–45;
    ex-Nazis as teachers in, 42–43;
    ex-Nazis in government of, 48–50;
    former Nazis in, 39–40; Hallstein
    Doctrine in, 74–75; Honecker
    visits, 136–37; impact of Berlin
    Wall on, 101–6; military rebuilt
    in, 52–53, 56–57, 156; in reunited
    Germany, 170–75
Feeding America (organization), 268
Felchow, Christian, 59
Felsenstein, Walter, 34
Fiebig, Konrad, 46
figurative art, 96
films and filmmakers, 35–37, 107–9,
    114; McCarthyism and, 233–35
Flick, Friedrich, 15, 61–62, 65, 66
Flint (Michigan), 252–53

Flynn, Elizabeth Gurley, 250, 259, 261
Foertsch, Friedrich, 53
folk music, 217–18
food, 171–72, 175–76; hunger and,
    267–69; workers producing, 205
food pantries, 267–70
Forrestal, James, 90, 91
Four Horsemen of the Apocalypse,
    320
France: post-World War II unions in,
    90; Vietnam declares independence
    from, 289
Franco, Francisco, 116, 256, 257
Frank, Niklas, 319
Free German Youth (FDJ; organiza-
    tion), 66
Freese, Alicia, 271
Freie Körperkultur (FKK; beach
    nudism), 76–79
French (language), 142
Frick, Henry, 248
fruit and vegetable stands, 171–72,
    204–5
Für Dich (For You; magazine), 185
Furtwangler, Wilhelm, 93

Gabriel, Trip, 271
Gagarin, Yuri, 28
Gage, Beverly, 237–38
garment industry, 206
Gates, Bill, 279, 305
Gehlen, Reinhard, 45–47, 123, 127
General Motors (GM), 252–53
Genesis (rock group), 134
gentrification, 312
German (language), 15–16
German Democratic Republic (GDR;
    East Germany): abortion rights in,
    276; absence of homelessness in,

266; absence of poverty in, 268–69; agriculture and countryside of, 67–71; amnesty in, 136; arts and literature in, 86–88, 96; author flees to, 8, 10; author's life in, 12–14, 328–29, 334; Berlin Wall in, 100–103; censorship in, 214–16; Chilean refugees in, 291; CIA actions in, 99; dental care in, 275; diplomats representing, 41–42; downfall of, 160–67; economy of, after unification, 175–81; education in, 141–49; elections in, 220–24; environmental issues in, 310–11; ex-Nazis as teachers in, 43; filmmakers in, 35–37; freedom of speech in, 261; government officials in, 50–51; higher education in, 280–81; judges and prosecutors in, 44–45; media on, 212–14; military officers in, 53–55; names of army bases in, 57–58; New Course in, 19–20; prisoners in, 267; reasons for downfall of, 155–60; religion in, 263; in reunited Germany, 170–75, 311; social insurance and medical care in, 271–74; Soviet Union and, 110–16; Stasi in, 123–29; steel mill in, 65–66; support for ANC in, 331; uprising of June 17, 1953 in, 25; West Germany's Hallstein Doctrine toward, 74–75

German-Soviet Friendship Society, 14–15

Germany: Alternative for Germany Party in, 316–17; automobile emissions in, 310; Bundeswehr in, 318; dental care in, 275; economy of, since unification, 311–12;

education in, 279; growth of Fascism in, 255–56; health care in, 273; under Hitler, 116–17; intervention in Spain by, 256; media coverage of, 211–14; political parties in, 229–30; proportional representation in, 228–29; reuniting of, 170–75; Soviet proposal to unify (1952), 18–19; See also Federal Republic of Germany; German Democratic Republic

Gilens, Martin, 227–28

Glazek, Christopher, 307

Glezos, Manolis, 145

Glik, Hirsch, 218

globalization, 311–13

Global South, 314

Globke, Hans, 46–48

Goering, Hermann, 49, 56

Goethe, Johann Wolfgang von, 85, 202

Golden, Lily, 119

Goldman, Emma, 248

Goldrick-Rab, Sara, 280

Gomulka, Wladislaw, 26

Gone with the Wind (novel, Mitchell), 214

Goodman, Amy, 295

Google (firm), 305

Gorbachev, Mikhail, 116, 120, 122; in East Germany, 161; perestroika and glasnost policies of, 133, 215

Goulden, Joseph C., 46

Great Railroad Strike (1877), 247

Greece, 90, 285

Green Party (Germany), 229

Greenpeace (organization), 181, 182

Gregory, Dick, 240

Grewe, Wilhelm, 75–76

Grossman, Renate (wife), 111; author

meets, 15–17; family background
of, 68–69; marries author and
becomes parent, 21–22; political
feelings of, 188; retires from work,
186–87; visits U.S., 194, 196
Grossman, Thomas (son), 22–23, 28,
167, 175, 187
Grossman, Timothy (son), 23, 187
Grossman, Victor: in Army, 286;
author assumes as name, 11; cen-
sorship experiences of, 216–19; at
Journalism School, 23–26; marries
Renate and becomes parent, 21–22;
patriotism of, 242; political activi-
ties of, 242–45; *Rawhide* work of,
186; after reunification, 191–93;
Stasi and, 127–28; visits to Soviet
Union and Russia by, 118–21; visits
U.S., 193–97
Grosz, Georg, 24–25
Grotewohl, Otto, 50, 99
Grundig, Hans, 36
Grundig, Leah, 36
Guatemala, 287
Guernica (Spain), 53
Guernica (painting, Picasso), 53, 95
Guinea, 75
Gunkel, Christoph, 182
Guthrie, Woody, 327
Gysi, Gregor, 165–66

Hacks, Peter, 32, 106
Hager, Kurt, 51
Hallstein, Walter, 75
Hallstein Doctrine (West Germany),
74–75
Hammett, Dashiell, 235
Hampton, Fred, 238
Hansen, Julie Hjerl, 205

Harlan County (Kentucky), 253
Harnack, Mildred, 50
Harvard University: author at, 8, 245,
259–60; Communist student group
at, 244; *Harvard Magazine* of, 192;
tuition at, 280
Hawaii, 253
Hawkesley, Humphrey, 205
Hayden, Sterling, 234
Haymarket Martyrs, 248
Haywood, William "Big Bill," 121,
249–51
health care, 270–74; abortion rights
and, 275–76; dental, 274–75;
opioid crisis in, 306–7
`Heartfield, John, 24–25
Hegen, Josef, 41
Heine, Heinrich, 45, 334
Hemingway, Ernest, 258
Hersh, Seymour, 290
Herzfelde, Wieland, 24–25
Hesse, Hermann, 41
Heusinger, Adolf, 52–53, 56
Hewson, Marilyn A., 298
Heym, Stefan, 163
Heymann, Stefan, 41
higher education, 279–81
Hill, Joe, 170, 216, 250
Hindenburg, Paul von, 255
Hiss, Alger, 125
history, teaching of, 143
Hitler, Adolf, 52, 53, 220, 257;
becomes chancellor, 255; Behn and,
257; corporate support for, 62–63;
western European concessions to,
116–17
Hitler-Stalin Pact, 117, 118
Ho Chi Minh, 331
Höfer, Werner, 58–59

Hoffmann, Heinz, 51, 55
Hollywood Ten, 235, 261
Holocaust, 143, 144
homelessness, 196, 264–67
Homestead strike (1892), 248–49
homosexuality, laws on, 222
Honecker, Erich, 51, 140; on culture,
    108; at fall of East Germany, 161;
    housing built under, 157, 158;
    removed from office, 162; replaces
    Ulbricht, 109; visits West Germany,
    136–37
Honecker, Margaret, 147, 148
Hook, Sidney, 93
Hoover, J. Edgar, 90; blackmail used
    by, 240–41; COINTELPRO memo
    by, 239–40; FBI under, 236–38;
    raids on CP by (1920), 252
House Un-American Activities Com-
    mittee (HUAC), 233–34, 236, 259
housing: in East Germany, 157–58;
    homelessness and evictions, 264–
    67; after unification, 174–75
Hungary, 320; invaded by Soviet
    Union, 26
hunger: in current world, 314, 328;
    fight against, 284; food pantries for,
    267–70; during Homestead strike,
    249; refugees suffering from, 315;
    World War II deaths from, 45, 110,
    119, 146, 197

I.G. Farben (firm), 61
immigrants and immigration, 230–32,
    314–15
income inequality, 282–83
India, 303
Industrial Workers of the World
    (IWW), 249–52

Inhofe, Jim, 309
insulin, 302–3
International Organizations Division
    (of CIA; IOD), 92, 97
Iran, 286–87, 295–96
Iraq, 76; Kuwait invaded by, 293–94;
    U.S. war against, 294–95
ISIS (Islamic State), 315
Israel, 39; East Germany and, 144;
    Eichmann tried in, 47–48; in Six
    Days War, 76
Italy, post-World War II unions in, 90
ITT (International Telephone &
    Telegraph), 257, 292

Jakob, 14
Janssen, Kim, 240
Japan, 285
Jehovah's Witnesses, 263
Jews: anti-Semitism against, 113,
    114, 119; compensation paid to,
    39; creation of Israel and, 144;
    in East Germany, 263; Globke's
    rules for, 46–47; killed at Thyssen
    party, 60–61; as scapegoats, 316;
    Stolpersteine commemorating,
    329–30; West German textbooks
    on persecution of, 42; *See also*
    anti-Semitism
Jilani, Zaid, 297
John Paul II (pope), 150, 151
Joint Anti-Fascist Refugee Appeal, 8
Jones, "Mother," 249
Jordan, Mary, 275
journalists, 184–85, 212–14; censor-
    ship and, 214–16

KaDeWe (Kaufhaus des Westens;
    department store; Berlin), 29

Kagan, Robert, 294
Kampfgruppe gegen Unmenschlichkeit
  (KgU; Combat Group Against
  Inhumanity), 123–24
Kant, Hermann, 190
Karajan, Herbert von, 93
Karelia (Russia), 120
Karl Marx University of Leipzig, 8,
  21–26, 281
Kavanaugh, Darien, 286
Kazan, Elia, 30
Kelly, Petra, 57
Kennan, George, 90, 112
Kennedy, John F.: in Berlin, 91, 133;
  on Berlin Wall, 100–101; King
  quoting, 290; military buildup
  under, 99–100; on World War II in
  Soviet Union, 89
Kennedy, Thomas A., 297
Kessler, Heinz, 55
Keynes, John Maynard, 324
Khachaturian, Aram, 113
Khrushchev, Nikita, 122; cultural thaw
  under, 113; meets Kennedy, 99;
  removed from office, 103, 108, 147;
  secret speech on Stalin by, 25, 115
Kiepe, Jan, 44
Kiesinger, Kurt Georg, 50, 101
Kilgore, Harley, 62–63
Kim Jong-un, 296
King, Martin Lulther, Jr., 237–38, 240,
  307, 320; on Vietnam War, 289–90
Kinkel, Klaus, 154, 190–91, 328
Kissinger, Henry, 292
Klarsfeld, Beate, 50
Kneef, Hildegard, 35
Kohl, Helmut, 62, 166, 311; as
  chancellor of unified Germany,
  170; economic policies of, 183;

in election of 1990, 167; meets
  Honecker, 136–37
Köhler, Hennig, 42
Kollwitz, Käthe, 175
Korean War, 285–86
Kornbluh, Peter, 215, 292
Kowalczuk, Ilko-Sascha, 127
Krause, Günter, 179
Krause, Hans, 83
Kreiten, Karlrobert, 58–59
Krenz, Egon, 162–63
Kretschmann, Winfried, 310
Kristol, William, 294
Krupp (firm), 38, 62
Kübler, Ludwig, 56
Kuckhoff, Grete, 50
Kuwait, 293–94

Labour Party (United Kingdom), 228,
  325
La Follette, Robert, 226
Lafontaine, Oskar, 137
Langhoff, Wolfgang, 32
languages, teaching of, 142
Latin America, 291–93
Lawrence (Massachusetts), 250
Lee, Jack, 242
Leipzig (Germany), 22–23, 104, 162,
  164–65
LeMay, Curtis, 286
Lengsfeld, Vera, 152–53, 155
Leningrad (Soviet Union), 118–19
Lent, Helmut, 56
Lerner, Sharon, 276–77
Lessing, Gottfried, 32
Lewis, Sinclair, 24
Liberal Democratic Party (East
  Germany), 220
libraries, 169

Libya, 295

Liebknecht, Karl, 138

lignite coal, 64, 116, 140, 311

Lincoln, Abraham, 226

Linke (Left Party, Germany), 190, 204, 229, 316

Litchfield, David R.L., 61

literature, 149–50; teaching of, 145

Litvinov, Maxim, 116

The Lives of Others (film), 125

Lockheed Martin (firm), 298

Lorenz, Marita, 288–89

Los Angeles Times, 92

Lovestone, Jay, 89–91

Lübke, Heinrich, 61

Luft, Christa, 180

Lumumba, Patrice, 288

Luther, Martin, 263

Lutheran Church, 152–53

Luxemburg, Rosa, 138–39

Macuga, Paul, 271

Mafia, 240, 241, 288

Maizière, Ulrich de, 53

Makarenko, Anton, 112

Malcolm X, 237, 240

Malkin, Elisabeth, 287

Mandela, Nelson, 331

Manifest Destiny policy, 247

Mann, Heinrich, 36

Mann, Thomas, 88, 128

Marriage in the Shadows (film), 35

Marshall, Colin, 233

Marshall Plan, 64, 90, 113; West Germany aided by, 197–98

Martin, Frederick Townsend, 227, 324

Massachusetts, 226

Matello, Dee, 274–75

maternity (baby) leave, 276–78

Mayakovsky, Vladimir, 106–7

May Day, 248

Mayer, Georg, 25

McCarran, Pat, 9

McCarran Act (U.S., 1950), 8

McCarthy, Joseph, 94, 233

McCarthyism, 27, 92, 233–36

McCloy, John J., 52

Mecklenburg (Germany), 71

Media (Pennsylvania), 239

media, 209–11; censorship of, 214–16; coverage of two Germany states in, 211–14; McCarthyism in, 234; *See also* television

medical care, *See* health care

Meer, Fritz ter, 61

Mencken, H. L., 232

mergers among giant corporations, 302–4

Merkel, Angela, 167, 310, 317

Messersmith, George S., 117

Mexico, 247; support for Spain by, 256–57

Meyer, Hans, 25

Meyerson, Harold, 302

Mielke, Erich, 124

Mies van der Rohe, Ludwig, 138

military service, 155

Miller, Arthur, 91, 235

Mitchell, John, 239

Mobutu, Joseph, 288

modern art, 94–96

Modrow, Hans, 165

Mohr, Ernst-Günther, 40

Mölders, Werner, 56

Monsanto (firm), 303, 304

Morais, Herbert M., 248, 251

Mosaddegh, Mohammad, 286–87

Moscow (Russia), 119–21

Mostel, Zero, 235
Mother Courage (Brecht), 33, 84
Müntzer, Thomas, 57
The Murderers Are Amongst Us (film), 35
Murdoch, Rupert, 210
Museum of Modern Art (New York), 95, 97–98
music: CIA-sponsored conference on, 95; East Berlin political music festivals, 104–5; folk music, 217–18; religious, 263; rock music banned, 129–30; rock music by the Berlin Wall, 133–35; Soviet condemnations of, 113
My Lai massacre, 290

Nachama, Estrongo, 263
NAFTA (North American Free Trade Agreement) treaty, 324
Nagel, Otto, 36
Naked Among Wolves (Apitz), 144
Nathan the Wise (play, Lessing), 32
National Committee for a Free Germany, 54
National Democratic Party (East Germany), 220
National Front (East Germany), 220
nationalism, 318–19
National People's Army (NVA; East Germany), 54–56, 156
National Security Agency (NSA), 319–20
National Socialism, 60
National Student Association, 97
Native Americans, 246, 283
NATO (North Atlantic Treaty Organization), 300; ex-Nazis as officers in, 53; in Serbia, 318; West Germany in, 52, 54

Nazis and ex-Nazis: attempted coup in U.S. tied to, 254–55; in German industry, 60–63; as judges and prosecutors, 43–45; as school teachers, 42–43; teaching about, 143; as West German diplomats, 40–41; in West German government, 48–50, 75–76; in West German military, 52, 56–57; in West Germany, 39–40
Neumann, Alfred, 51
New Course, 19–20, 22
New Economic System of Planning and Management, (NÖSPL), 103
New Forum (East Germany), 162, 166
News Corp., 210
New York, 194–95
New York Times: CIA exposed by, 97; FBI Media papers published by, 239
Nicaragua, 135, 292–93, 331
Nixon, Richard, 125, 150, 241, 292
Norden, Albert, 51, 58
North Carolina, 226
North Korea, 285–86
nuclear weapons, 285, 300
nudism (Freie Körperkultur), 76–79

Obama, Barack, 275, 293; Iraq and Afghanistan wars under, 295; military spending under, 300
Oberländer, Theodor, 48
O'Brien, Michael, 100
OCCUPY movement, 242
oil (petroleum), 308–9
opioids, 306–7
Oppenheim, James, 250
Ortega, 292
OxyContin, 306–7

palm oil, 206–7
Parish, James Robert, 234
Parks, Larry, 234
Parry, Simon, 206
Parsons, Lucie, 249
patriotism, 318–19
Paul Robeson Archive, 119
Pause für Wanzka (Wellm), 148–49
Peekskill (N.Y.), 27, 236
Peet, John, 37–38, 40, 81, 107
PEGIDA (organization), 316
Pelosi, Nancy, 300
Peltier, Leonard, 241
pharmaceutical industry, 306–7
Piano, Renzo, 190
Picasso, Pablo, 53, 95, 113
Pickard, Victor, 211
Pieck, Wilhelm, 84, 86; on creation of
 Israel, 144
Poland, 150–51; under Gomulka, 26
police: ex-Nazis as, 45; jokes about,
 132–33
Politburo (East Germany), 51
political cabarets, 82, 83
polytechnical education, 142
Porsche (firm), 310
Potsdam (Germany), 11
poverty, 196, 282–83, 328, 331;
 among children, 278; among ex-
 convicts, 266–67; food pantries
 for, 267–70; in Global South, 314;
 homelessness and, 264–66
pre-schools, 278
prisoners, 267
Professor Mamlock (play, Wolf), 41
Progressive Party (U.S.), 226–27, 242
Project for the New American Century
 (PNAC), 294
Prokofiev, Sergei, 113

proportional representation, 228–29
prostitution, 78–79, 173
Purdue (pharmaceutical firm), 306–7
Putin, Vladimir, 296, 312

Quandt, Herbert, 59
Quandt family, 310

racism, 316; of AFL, 249; in U.S.
 economy, 282; West German text-
 books on, 42–43
radio, 185
Radio Berlin International, 119
Rahman, K. Sabeel, 305
Raines, Bonnie, 239
Rajk, László, 144
Ramparts (magazine), 97
Rand, Ayn, 233
Rau, Heinrich, 51
Rawhide (television program), 186,
 187
Raworth, Kate, 205
Raytheon (firm), 297, 299
Reagan, Ronald, 133, 135, 235;
 Eppelmann and, 155; in HUAC
 hearings, 234; jokes about, 219; on
 Nicaragua, 292; Poland and, 150,
 151; on Soviet Union, 293
Rebling, Eberhard, 36
Red Army Fraction (RAF), 262
Red Channels (report), 234
Reed, Dean, 120
Reed, John, 121
refrigerators, 72, 181–82
refugees, 314–15
religion: Eppelmann's, 153–55; free-
 dom of, 262–63; Lutheran Church,
 152–53; after unification, 170–71
reparations, 64, 67, 144, 198

restaurants, 172
revolutions, 322, 326
RIAS (Radio in the American Sector),
    20, 134, 219
Robeson, Paul, 27; Hoover and, 236;
    during McCarthy period, 235–36,
    261; Paul Robeson Archive, 119
Rockefeller, Nelson, 95
Rodriguez, Nino, 267
Roe v. Wade (U.S., 1973), 275
Rolling Stones, 129
Roosevelt, Franklin D., 116, 260–61;
    attempted coup against, 254–55; on
    corporate power, 301; on Fascism,
    319; four freedoms speech of, 261,
    262, 264, 283–85; New Deal pro-
    grams of, 308, 324
Rositzke, Harry, 46
Rostock (Germany), 67–68
Rostow, Walt, 97
Rottmann, Michael, 180–81
Rumsfeld, Donald, 294
Rupp, Rainer, 127
Rusk, Dean, 100
Russia: author's visits to, 120–21;
    nuclear weapons of, 300; Russian
    Revolution, 89; in U.S. election of
    2016, 299; *See also* Soviet Union
Russian (language), 10–11, 111; teach-
    ing of, 142
Ruthenberg, Charles, 121

Sacco and Vanzetti case, 216
Sackler family, 306, 307
Saefkow, Anton, 57–58
Salt of the Earth (film, Biberman),
    235
Samarkand (Uzbekistan), 119
Samoilova, Tatyana, 114

Sanders, Bernie, 262, 283, 306, 325,
    326
Sanders, Richard, 255
Sandinistas (Nicaragua), 292
Saturday Evening Post, 97
Saunders, Frances Stonor, 94–96, 98
Scally, Derek, 317
Schabowski, Günter, 163, 164
Schäuble, Wolfgang, 179
Scheel, Walter, 62, 330
Schiff, Adam, 299
Schmidt, Paul, 257
Scholz, Ernst, 50
schooling, *See* education
Schroeder, Gerhard, 324
Schroeder, Kurt von, 60
Schulz, Werner, 182
Schumacher, Kurt, 90
Schumer, Charles, 300
Schütz, Heinrich, 263
Schwarz, Yevgeni, 107
Schwarzer, Martha Pinkus, 330
Schwarzer, Nathan, 330
Schwarzer, Ruth, 330
Schwarzer, Steffi, 330
sciences, 183–84
Scientology, 171
Scottsboro boys trial, 118
Second Socialist International, 248
Seebohm, Hans-Christoph, 49
Seeger, Pete, 27, 217–18, 235
Seghers, Anna, 36, 144
senior citizens, 222, 269–70
September 11th terrorist attacks,
    294–95
Serbia, 154, 318
Seven Seas Books (publisher), 37
The Seventh Cross (Seghers), 36
sex shops, 173–74

sexuality, 79
Shays, Daniel, 246
Shays' Rebellion, 246
shelter, 264–66
shipyards, 67–68
Shirer, William L., 81
Shostakovich, Dmitri, 91, 113
Sindermann, Horst, 51
Slánský, Rudolf, 144
Snowden, Edward, 242
social customs, 15
Social Democratic Party (SPD;
  Germany), 255, 310, 326; in elec-
  tion of 1990, 167; military actions
  supported by, 318
socialism: in East Germany, 19; of
  Sanders, 325
socialist enterprises, 198–99
Socialist Party (U.S.), 226, 251–52
Socialist Unity Party (SED; East
  Germany), 51, 154; changes name
  to SED-PDS, 165–66; Communist
  Party merges with, 99; in election of
  1990, 167; in elections, 220; Krenz
  takes control over, 162–63; litera-
  ture and arts appreciated by, 86
social media, 304–6
Solidarity movement (Poland), 150–51
Somalia, 295
Somoza, Anastasio, 292
Sorbs (ethnic group), 67
Southern Christian Leadership
  Conference (SCLC), 239–40
Southern Negro Youth Congress, 8
South Korea, 285–86
Soviet Union: author's visits to, 118–
  21; East Germany and, 110–16;
  end of Communism in, 121–22; in
  Hitler-Stalin Pact, 117; Hungary

invaded by, 26; impact of Berlin
  Wall on, 102; proposal for German
  unification by (1952), 18–19;
  Reagan on, 293; space race between
  U.S. and, 27–28; support for Spain
  by, 256–57; troops stationed in East
  Germany from, 155–56; World War
  II in, 89
Space race, 27–28
Spain, 116
Spanish Civil War, 256–58
Speidel, Hans, 52
sports, 142; media coverage of,
  209–10
Springer, Axel, 211
Sputnik, 27–28
Sri Lanka, 75
Stalin, Joseph, 118, 121, 329; anti-
  Semitism in policies of, 144; on
  art, music, and culture, 113; death
  of, 19; Khrushchev's secret speech
  on, 25, 115; on Mayakovsky, 106;
  proposal for German unification
  by (1952), 18; during World War
  II, 117
Stasi (Staats-Sicherheit; East German
  secret police), 99, 123–29; begin-
  ning of, 54; fall of, 166
State Opera House (Berlin), 34
steel mill, 65–66
Steinbeck, John, 70
Stolpersteine, 329–30
Strauss, Franz-Josef, 47, 49, 62, 137
Struck, Peter, 318
Student Nonviolent Coordinating
  Committee (SNCC), 240
Sullivan, Kevin, 275
Summers, Anthony, 241
Syria, 295, 297

Taft-Hartley Act (U.S., 1947), 233
Taibbi, Matt, 280
Tashkent (Uzbekistan), 119
television, 72–73, 107–9; *Dallas,*
    218–19; *Rawhide,* 186; after unifi-
    cation, 185
Temin, Peter, 282
terrorism, September 11th terrorist
    attacks, 294–95
Thälmann, Ernst, 255
Thompson, Dorothy, 24
Thompson, Robert, 258–59, 261
Thyssen, Margareta, 60–61
Thyssen (firm), 62
toilets, 13
Trabant (automobile), 73–74, 83
Tracy, Spencer, 36
trade, isolation of East Germany in, 98
travel, 159, 173
Trettner, Heinz, 53, 57
Treuhand (Trust Agency), 179–83
Trevor-Roper, Hugh, 93
The Trial of Lucullus (opera, Brecht),
    84
Trotsky, Leon, 168
Truman, Harry: in election of 1948,
    226, 227; on Gehlen, 45; German
    unification rejected by, 18; on
    Hoover, 240; Loyalty Order signed
    by, 233; on modern art, 94; nuclear
    weapons used by, 285
Truman Doctrine, 113, 233, 285
Trumbo, Dalton, 235
Trumbo (film), 235
Trump, Donald, 228, 316; Iraq and
    Afghanistan wars under, 295; mili-
    tary spending under, 300, 328; on
    U.S. military strength, 296
Turkey, 285

Turner, Nat, 247
Twain, Mark, 15
Twitter (firm), 305
two-party system, 225–26

Uhrig, Robert, 57
Ulanova, Galina, 112
Ulbricht, Walter, 34, 83, 108; on arts,
    86; "Bitterfeld Way" campaign of,
    105; Brecht and, 84; Eisler and,
    85; Khrushchev and, 147; replaced
    by Honecker, 109; in resistance to
    Nazis, 51; trade with Soviet Union
    under, 103
Ulysses (Joyce), 262
unions: during Cold War, 91; Congress
    of Industrial Organizations, 252–
    53; in East Germany, 14, 223–24;
    female workers and, 80; historic
    strikes by, 247–49; Industrial
    Workers of the World, 249–51;
    splits in, post–World War II, 90;
    Taft-Hartley Act on, 233
United Kingdom, 228–29
United States: abortion rights in, 275–
    76; author's articles about, 216–17;
    author's visits to, 122, 193–97;
    becomes world power, 253–54;
    censorship and freedom of speech
    in, 261–62; CIA interventions in
    Iraq and Guatemala by, 287; Cold
    War culture of, 92–94; current
    worker activism in, 312; education
    in, 278–79; higher education in,
    279–80; immigrants in, 230–32;
    intervention in Soviet Union by,
    89; in Korean War, 285–86; in
    Latin America, 291–93; maternity
    leave in, 276–78; McCarthyism in,

233–36; military spending by, 299–300, 328; poverty in, 264, 282–83; space race between Soviet Union and, 27–28; two-party system in, 225–26; in Vietnam War, 289–91; violence in history of, 246–54; in wars in Iraq and Afghanistan, 295
Uzbekistan, 119

vacations, 76–77; in Soviet Union, 120–21; travel for, 159, 173
Van Buren, Peter, 199
van Gelder, Sarah, 308
Verner, Walter, 55
Vialon, Friedrich Friedrich, 49, 330
Victims of Nazi Persecution Association (VVN), 43–44
Vietnam, 331
Vietnam War, 289–91, 293
violence, in U.S. history, 246–54
Voegt, Hedwig, 25
Voice of America, 97
Volksbühne (People's Stage), 33
Volkswagen Group (firm), 197, 309–10
von Merkatz, 49

Wagner, Dave, 234
Wagner, Kurt, 55
Wald, Alan M., 258
Walesa, Lech, 151
Wallace, Henry, 18, 226–27
Wallace, Irving, 237
Wallechinsky, David, 237
Walters, Vernon, 151
Walton, James, 328
Wandel, Paul, 35
Wangenheim, Gustav von, 32
Warburg, James, 18

war on terrorism, 294
Warsaw Pact, 54
Washington, George, 246
Washington Post, 239
Wechsler, Stephen, 245; See also Grossman, Victor
Weigel, Helene, 33
Weimar Republic (Germany), 81
Weinert, Erich, 54
Weizsäcker, Richard von, 170
Wellm, Alfred, 148–49
Wells, Orson, 235
Wende (turnaround; unification), 169
Werner, Klaus, 207
Wessel, Horst, 85–86
West Berlin: commerce between East Berlin and, 29–31; opening of Berlin Wall, 164; political cabaret in, 82; See also Berlin; Berlin Wall
West Germany, See Federal Republic of Germany
Westrick, Ludger, 49
White, Josh, 235
Whole Foods (firm), 304
Wiegriefe, Klaus, 127
Wilder, Thornton, 32
Wilhelm (Kaiser, Germany), 191
Wilson, Woodrow, 89, 250
Wismar (Germany), 159
Wisten, Fritz, 33
Wolf, Christa, 109, 163
Wolf, Friedrich, 41
Wolf, Konrad, 36–37, 41
Wolf, Markus, 37, 127, 163
Wolfowitz, Paul, 294
Wollweber, Ernst, 124
women, 79–80; abortion rights for, 222, 275–76; maternity (baby) leave for, 276–78; in space, 28

Woodhull, Victoria, 226
Woodrow Wilson International Center
    for Scholars, 101
Work, Robert, 298
World Federation of Trade Unions, 90
World Festival of Youth and Students:
    1947 (Prague), 260; 1973 (East
    Berlin), 283, 291
World War I, 250–51
World War II: nuclear weapons in,
    285; Russian monuments to, 121;
    Soviet Union in, 89, 110, 117;
    Spanish Civil War leading to, 257;
teaching about, 143–46; United
    States in, 319
Writers' Association (East Germany),
    162

Yemen, 295
Yugoslavia, 75

Zaisser, Wilhelm, 124
Zhdanov, Andrei, 112, 113
Zinn, Howard, 249
Zweig, Arnold, 36
Zyankali (play, Wolf), 41